THE

GUIDE

TO

LONG-PLAYING

RECORDS

Vocal Music

THE
GUIDE
TO
LONG-PLAYING
RECORDS

Orchestral Music
BY
Irving Kolodin

Vocal Music
BY
Philip L. Miller

Chamber and Solo Instrument Music
BY
Harold C. Schonberg

THE

GUIDE

TO

LONG-PLAYING

RECORDS

Vocal Music

BY

Philip L. Miller

1955

ALFRED A KNOPF

NEW YORK

TO *Catharine*

L. C. catalog card number: 55-5609
© Philip L. Miller 1955

THIS IS A BORZOI BOOK,
PUBLISHED BY ALFRED A. KNOPF, INC.

FIRST EDITION

PREFACE

This book aims to be comprehensive, but within limitations. It is to be hoped that no really important vocal music available on LP has been overlooked, yet, as will certainly be noted, not every available recording has been included. Some have been ruled out because of what seems to me limited musical appeal, or because they are so far substandard mechanically that not much can be said in their favor. Some that might have been considered a year or two ago are now definitely superseded by superior performances. In such cases I have often given the older version passing mention. Some recordings I have not succeeded in hearing, despite the usually generous co-operation of the manufacturers and shops.

As for repertoire covered in these pages, it has not always been easy to draw the line between "popular" and concert music, operetta and opera. Such composers as Gershwin, Léhar, and Oscar Straus could not be fully covered for obvious reasons, yet when a performance of their music is issued in the "Masterworks" class, it certainly rates inclusion. The rich and growing field of recorded *zarzuela* (Spanish operetta) is represented by a single disc, for two reasons: a request for review copies produced no more than this, and as the field is such a special one, I have not felt as yet that I could give the necessary time to exploring it. Our one example, however, is a program of samples, and may serve to lead the interested adventurer to the heart of this new continent. Only a bow has been made in the direction of Gilbert and Sullivan, not because their works are unknown or unsympathetic to me (quite the contrary), but largely because I am afraid the real G & S fans are actually more critical of performances from Gilbert's point of view than from Sullivan's. It is indicative that both the Schwann and Goody catalogues list these operas under G, not S. Folk music, needless to say (except where it has been "idealized" by an arranger), is the subject for a book in itself.

But the prime consideration is space. Not so many years ago, when discs came singly, each one containing perhaps a two-part overture, a couple of or three songs, possibly a group of piano pieces, or an operatic selection, it was possible for a reviewer to spread himself, to produce little essays, with his considered opinions of the artist or artists concerned, to pass judgment on the music itself—whether first-rate Ketelbey or inferior Beethoven—to discuss the performer's approach to his selection, and to point out his treatment of this or that phrase. Today a record of the size that used to play eight minutes may run to an hour. Not only that, but all kinds of music, known and forgotten, are pouring onto the market at an alarming rate. No single full-time reviewer has time to hear it all. Even limiting myself to vocal music, I have (as noted above) had to be somewhat selective. Most of the impressions herein set down must, therefore, be general. In the majority of cases only the high spots and the low can be discussed.

Esthetically there are three sides to every record—the music performed, the performance, and the reproduction. It is taken for granted in this book that the reader knows his mind in the first matter, that at least in the case of well-known works he will not come for my opinions. What he wants to know, I assume, is how the music is performed, what this or that interpreter is able to do with it. Reproduction for its own sake is less likely to seem important to the vocal enthusiast than to the connoisseurs of other types of music. Most of the recordings considered herein are at least acceptable in this respect; attention will be called to quality of reproduction only when there is something remarkable about it, whether it is exceptionally good or notably inadequate. Nevertheless, it is often necessary, for descriptive reasons, to speak of "liveness" or "spaciousness" as applied to recorded sound, or to point to reproduction of the "dead studio" type. How these various effects are produced I will leave for more technical authors to explain: suffice it to say that diverse techniques are employed appropriately for different types of music. In too many vocal records the solo voice is allowed to overwhelm chorus and orchestra, often at the same time losing clarity from being too close to the microphone. There is an argument to the effect that the composer might have appreciated the boost modern science can give him in this way; but it is necessary from time to time to point out where such assistance has been overgenerous.

Revivals of "historical" recordings, originally made many years ago by the "acoustical" process, are noted for what they are. In some cases—for instance, the operas of Meyerbeer—the music is not otherwise represented, but the chief interest is in the singer, not the song. It is our good fortune that the voices and vocal styles of most of the great artists singing in the last half-century have been preserved, but in considering early recordings we must accept the inadequacies of outmoded techniques. Perhaps the uninitiated listener should be warned not to expect the composer's orchestrations in the accompaniments.

Certain instruments could not be reproduced by the acoustical method, and it was not until some five years or so after the introduction of electrical recording—around 1930—that the old type of studio ensemble was officially found inadequate for operatic accompaniments.

By far the greater and more important part of this book is the first, the composers' section. In the artists' listing that follows, I have been more selective because of the endless duplication of repertoire. The lack of imagination displayed, particularly in the many available aria recitals, often makes listening no better than a chore. For this kind of thing the advantages of LP are at best questionable, for such "personality" discs are usually of interest only to the fans.

The arrangement of material under the composers' names follows a definite pattern. Choral works are considered first, then operas, finally songs and other works for solo voice. As a general rule, recordings of the same music are listed in order of preference, though occasionally this is rendered impractical by the coupling. The names of choral organizations and orchestras appearing frequently have been reduced to a code, which I hope will not prove too cumbersome. With some regret I find it practical to list only the names of a few principals in opera casts. For this reason the Index of Performers should not be looked upon as a complete discography of any artist listed.

A real problem is presented by the occasional imperfect discs that get by the distributors. It seems neither necessary nor altogether fair to call attention to every badly centered record, for it is always possible that the flaw is an individual case. One can sometimes try copy after copy in a store in a vain effort to find one with a good surface; yet sometimes the second try will produce results. For this reason it seems best to give but little space to complaints of this nature.

It is a temptation to dwell upon "jacket," "liner," or, if you will, "program" notes, which sometimes furnish adequate and helpful information, but only too often serve to becloud the issue. In most cases this temptation has been resisted, though it may be in order to warn the reader not to take these notes for gospel.

Thanks are due to many associates and friends for help and encouragement in preparing this survey. First and foremost is my wife, who has lived through it all, and left her stamp on more than one page of manuscript. I want to express my appreciation to Robert Hughes, who helped convert many reams of rough notes into readable type; to R. D. Darrell, Harold C. Schonberg, James Hinton, Jr., and Thomas B.

Healey for their invaluable interest and advice; to the various producing companies—nearly every one in the field—for their co-operation,
and to the Elaine Music Shop for producing what I could not readily
get otherwise; to the several periodicals in which many of the views
in this book were originally expressed: *The American Record Guide,
The Library Journal, Consumer Reports,* and *The Saturday Review;*
above all to Herbert Weinstock, that most patient of editors.

Philip L. Miller

CODE OF RECORD LABELS

A440	*A440*	IRCC	*International Record Collectors Club*
Alc	*Alco*		
All	*Allegro*	L	*London*
AM	*Audio Masters*	Ly	*Lyrichord*
An	*Angel*	Mer	*Mercury*
Art	*Artist*	MGM	*MGM*
B & B	*B & B*	ML	*Music Library*
BAR	*Bartók*	Mon	*Montilla*
BG	*Bach Guild*	MT	*Magic Tone*
Bos	*Boston*	MW	*Masterworks*
C	*Columbia*	NE	*New Editions*
Cam	*Cambridge*	NR	*New Records*
Cap	*Capitol*	Oc	*Oceanic*
CE	*Classic Editions*	OL	*Oiseau Lyre*
Cet	*Cetra*	Ov	*Overtone*
CH	*Concert Hall*	Pem	*Pembroke*
Col	*Colosseum*	Per	*Period*
Con	*Contemporary*	Pol	*Polymusic*
Cook	*Cook*	REB	*REB*
D	*Decca*	Rem	*Remington*
Den	*Den*	Ren	*Renaissance*
Des	*Desto*	Roy	*Royale*
Dia	*Dial*	RS	*Rachmaninoff Society*
Ele	*Elektra*	Sca	*Scala*
EMS	*EMS*	SPA	*SPA*
Ep	*Epic*	Str	*Stradivari*
Es	*Esoteric*	Tel	*Telefunken*
Et	*Eterna*	Tri	*Triad*
Fes	*Festival*	U	*Urania*
GA	*Golden Age*	V	*RCA Victor*
GAR	*GAR*	Van	*Vanguard*
Hd	*Handel Society*	Vox	*Vox*
HMV	*His Master's Voice*	W	*Westminster*
HS	*Haydn Society*	WCFM	*WCFM*

CODE OF PERFORMING ORGANIZATIONS

ABSO	*Ansbach Bach Society Orchestra*
AC & O	*Angelicum Chorus and Orchestra*
ACS	*Allegro Chamber Society*
AMC	*Amsterdam Motet Choir*
ASO	*Austrian Symphony Orchestra*
BAG	*Bach Aria Group*
BAV	*Bavarian State Orchestra*
BAVOC & O	*Bavarian State Opera Chorus and Orchestra*
BAVRC & O	*Bavarian Radio Chorus and Orchestra*
BAVRO	*Bavarian Radio Orchestra*
BC	*Brasseur Choir*
BCC	*Berlin Chamber Choir*
BCNY	*Bach Cantata Circle of New York*
BCOC	*Berlin Civic Opera Chorus*
BCS	*Berlin Choral Society*
BESO	*Berlin Symphony Orchestra*
BFC & O	*Bayreuth Festival Chorus and Orchestra*
BGC	*Bach Guild Chorus*
BGO	*Bach Guild Orchestra*
BMC	*Berlin Motet Choir*
BO	*Bach Orchestra, Stuttgart*
BPH	*Berlin Philharmonic Orchestra*
BSIC & O	*Bolshoi Theatre Chorus and Orchestra*
BSIO	*Bolshoi Theatre Orchestra*
BSO	*Boston Symphony Orchestra*
BSO STR	*Boston Symphony Orchestra Strings*
BSOC & O	*Berlin State Opera Chorus and Orchestra*
BSOO	*Berlin State Opera Orchestra*
CAS	*Choral Art Society*
CBC	*Copenhagen Boys' Choir*
CBMC	*Copenhagen Boys' and Men's Choir*
CBSC & O	*Columbia Broadcasting Chorus and Orchestra*
CBSO	*Columbia Broadcasting Symphony Orchestra*
CC	*Cetra Chorus*
CC & O	*Cetra Chorus and Orchestra*
CFO	*Cambridge Festival Orchestra*
CHAM	*Chamber Orchestra (Unidentified)*

CHSL	*Choral Society of London*
CIN	*Cincinnati Symphony Orchestra*
CMFO	*Collegium Musicum Orchestra, Frankfurt*
COL	*Columbia Symphony Orchestra*
COLC & O	*Columbia Chorus and Orchestra*
CPA	*Collegium Pro Arte*
CPH	*Czech Philharmonic Orchestra*
CSL	*Cantata Singers, London*
DAC & O	*Detmold Academy Chorus and Orchestra*
DC	*Dessoff Choirs*
DKFC	*Kantorei der Dreikönigskirche, Frankfurt*
DOC & O	*Dresden Opera Chorus and Orchestra*
DRC & O	*Danish State Radio Chorus and Orchestra*
DRO	*Danish Royal Opera Orchestra*
EIARC & O	*EIAR Chorus and Orchestra*
EMC & O	*Early Music Society Chorus and Chamber Orchestra*
EVP	*Ensemble Vocale de Paris*
FM	*Maggio Musicale Fiorentino Orchestra*
FMC & O	*Florence May Festival Chorus and Orchestra*
FOC	*La Fenice Chorus, Venice*
FOC & O	*La Fenice Opera Chorus and Orchestra*
FSC	*Fleet Street Choir*
FSSC	*Frankfurt State School of Music Chorus*
GABT C & O	*GABT Chorus and Orchestra, USSR*
GBO	*Göttingen Bach Festival Orchestra*
GC	*Gouverné Chorus*
GFC	*Glyndebourne Festival Chorus*
GFC & O	*Glyndebourne Festival Chorus and Orchestra*
GFO	*Glyndebourne Festival Orchestra*
GOH	*German Opera House Orchestra*
HBA	*Instrumental Ensemble of the Bach Anniversary, Hamburg*
HCO	*Hewitt Chamber Orchestra*
HMFC	*Musikfreunde Chorus, Hamburg*
HRC	*Harvard and Radcliffe Choirs*
ICO	*Italian Chamber Orchestra*
IOS	*Intimate Opera Society*
JMC	*Jeunnesses Musicales Chorus*
JO	*Jacques Orchestra*
JSO	*Janssen Symphony Orchestra of Los Angeles*
LAM	*Lamoureux Orchestra*

LBE	*London Baroque Ensemble*
LC	*Lamy Chorus*
LGO	*Leipzig Gewandhaus Orchestra*
LIV	*Liverpool Philharmonic Orchestra*
LMS	*Luca Marenzio Ensemble*
LOS	*Little Orchestra Society*
LPC	*London Philharmonic Choir*
LPC & O	*London Philharmonic Choir and Orchestra*
LPO	*London Philharmonic Orchestra*
LSO	*London Symphony Orchestra*
MC & O	*Munich Chamber Choir and Orchestra*
MFC	*Vienna Musikfreunde Chorus*
MFC & O	*Chorus and Orchestra of the Society of Friends of Music, Vienna*
MIC	*Milan Chamber Orchestra*
MIOC & O	*Milan Opera Chorus and Orchestra*
MIPO	*Milan Philharmonic Orchestra*
MISO	*Milan Symphony Orchestra*
MITN	*Milan Teatro Nuovo Orchestra*
MOC & O	*Metropolitan Opera Chorus and Orchestra*
MOO	*Metropolitan Opera Orchestra*
MPH	*Munich Philharmonic Orchestra*
MRC	*Mitteldeutsche Rundfunk Chorus*
MRSC & O	*Munich Radio Symphony Chorus and Orchestra*
MSOC & O	*Munich State Opera Chorus and Orchestra*
NBC	*National Broadcasting Symphony Orchestra*
NETC & O	*Netherlands Philharmonic Chorus and Orchestra*
NEW	*New Symphony Orchestra of London*
NGO	*National Gallery Orchestra*
NHSC & O	*Netherlands Handel Society Chorus and Orchestra*
NHSO	*Netherlands Handel Society Orchestra*
NPSC & O	*New Paris Symphony Association Chorus and Orchestra*
NSSPC & O	*Chorus of New Symphony Society of Paris, and Orchestra*
NWDRC	*Norddeutsche Rundfunk Chorus and Orchestra*
NYPH	*Philharmonic-Symphony Orchestra of New York*
NYPMA	*New York Pro Musica Antiqua*
OCC & O	*Opéra-Comique Chorus and Orchestra*
OCM	*Orchestra de Camera di Milano*
OCO	*Opéra-Comique Orchestra*
OLE	*Oiseau-Lyre Ensemble*
OLO	*Oiseau-Lyre Orchestra*

ONA	*Orchestre National*
OPM	*Orchestra dei Pomeriggi Musicale di Milano*
PAS	*Pasdeloup Orchestra*
PASC	*Pasdeloup Chamber Orchestra*
PC	*Passani Choir*
PCO	*Paris Conservatory Orchestra*
PERP	*Perpignan Festival Orchestra*
PHC	*Philadelphia Chamber Ensemble*
PHI	*Philharmonia Orchestra*
PHO	*Philadelphia Orchestra*
PMA	*Pro Musica Antiqua, Brussels*
PMO	*Pro Musica Orchestra*
POC & O	*Paris Opéra Chorus and Orchestra*
POO	*Paris Opéra Orchestra*
PPC & O	*Paris Philharmonic Chorus and Orchestra*
PPO	*Paris Philharmonic Orchestra*
PRC & O	*Pro Musica Chorus and Orchestra, Stuttgart*
PRCO	*Pro Musica Chamber Orchestra, Vienna Pro Musica Symphony*
PRO	*Pro Musica Orchestra, Stuttgart*
PSC	*Paris Select Choir*
PSO	*Pittsburgh Symphony Orchestra*
RBC & O	*Radio Berlin Chorus and Orchestra*
RBO	*Radio Berlin Symphony Orchestra*
RC & O	*Raugel Chorus and Orchestra*
RCAO	*RCA Victor Orchestra*
RCO	*Ristenpart Chamber Orchestra*
RCZ	*Reinhart Choir of Zürich*
RDFC	*Radiodiffusion Chorus*
RDFO	*Radiodiffusion Orchestra, Paris Radio Symphony*
RIASC & O	*RIAS Chorus and Orchestra*
RIASCC	*RIAS Chamber Choir*
RIASSO	*RIAS Symphony Orchestra*
RIC & O	*Radio Italiana Chorus and Orchestra*
RIO	*Radio Italiana Orchestra*
ROC & O	*Rome Opera Chorus and Orchestra*
ROOC & O	*Royal Opera Chorus and Orchestra, London*
RP	*Radio Paris Symphony Orchestra*
RPO	*Royal Philharmonic Orchestra*
RSPC	*Raymond St. Paul Chorus*

RSQC & O	*Chorus and Orchestra Romana da Camera della Societa del Quartetto*
RSTC	*Radio Stuttgart Chorus*
RWC	*Roger Wagner Chorale*
SACC	*Salzburg Cathedral Choir*
SAL	*Salzburg Mozarteum Orchestra*
SALC & O	*Salzburg Mozarteum Chorus and Orchestra*
SAX	*Saxon (Saxonian) State Orchestra*
SC	*Shaw Chorale*
SCA	*La Scala Orchestra*
SCAC & O	*La Scala Chorus and Orchestra*
SCAO	*Scarlatti Society of Naples*
SCAOC & O	*Scarlatti Chorus and Orchestra, Naples*
SCB	*Schola Cantorum Basiliensis*
SCC & O	*Santa Cecilia Chorus and Orchestra*
SCMC & O	*Chorus and Orchestra of State Conservatory of Music, Stuttgart*
SCNY	*Schola Cantorum of New York*
SCO	*Sta. Cecilia Orchestra*
SCS	*Stuttgart Choral Society*
SDRC & O	*Süddeutscher Rundfunk Chorus and Orchestra*
SEC	*Saint-Eustache Choir*
SFC & O	*Salzburg Festival Chorus and Orchestra*
SFS	*San Francisco Symphony Orchestra*
SPO	*Southern Philharmonic Orchestra, England*
SR	*Suisse Romande Orchestra*
SSAC	*Chamber Choir of State Academy of Music, Stuttgart*
SSO	*Suebian (Swabian) Symphony Orchestra*
STO	*Ton-Studio Orchestra, Stuttgart*
SVC & O	*Scuola Veneziana Chorus and Orchestra*
SVO	*Scuola Veneziana Orchestra*
SWS	*Swabian Choral Society (Singers)*
TC	*Treviso Cathedral Choir*
TCC	*Teatro Communale Chorus*
TMC	*Toronto Mendelssohn Choir*
TORO	*Toronto Symphony Orchestra*
USSRC & O	*Combined Choruses and Orchestra of USSR*
VC	*Wiener Chor*
VCO	*Vienna Chamber Orchestra*
VH	*Vienna Hofmusikkapelle*

VKC	*Vienna Akademie Kammerchor*
	Vienna Chamber Choir
	Vienna Kammerchor
VPH	*Vienna Philharmonic Orchestra*
VSO	*Vienna State Opera Orchestra*
VSOC	*Vienna State Opera Chorus*
VSOC & O	*Vienna State Opera Chorus and Orchestra*
VSY	*Vienna Symphony Orchestra*
VSYC	*Vienna Symphony Chamber Orchestra*
WCC	*Washington Cathedral Choir*
WCHC	*Chamber Choir of Washington*
WIN	*Winterthur Symphony Orchestra*
WINC & O	*Winterthur Mixed Chorus and Orchestra*
WSTC	*Württemberg State Theatre Chorus and Orchestra*
WSTO	*Württemberg State Orchestra*
ZTC & O	*Zürich Tonhalle Chorus and Orchestra*
ZTO	*Zürich Tonhalle Orchestra*

THE

GUIDE

TO

LONG-PLAYING

RECORDS

Vocal Music

INDEXES

After page 381 will be found an Index of Performers, an Index of Composers, and an Alphabetical List of Opera Titles with Composers' Names.

ALBERT, EUGEN D' (1864-1932)

Tiefland. *Kenney, s; Kmentt, t; Equiluz, t; Wiener, bs; Heppe, bs; etc.; VSOC; VPH, Adler, SPA 40-42* [3].

Tiefland, which may be said to typify the German equivalent of Italian *verismo* opera, has held its own only in its native land. It is good to hear this obviously proficient performance; yet one would hesitate to judge the abilities of the cast on this evidence alone: whether all the singing is pretty much on a dead level, or whether the reproduction has been monitored to make it sound so, there is not much relief from high dynamics. The voices are all too prominent. Still, they are healthy and agreeable in quality, especially those of Kmentt and Heppe. Kenney, in the leading feminine role, is strongly temperamental and none too steady. For those interested in hearing some of the music sung by contemporaries of the composer, Eterna has collected a set of "Highlights," including the "Dream" and "Wolf" narratives, Sebastiano's song, and two duets (10" Et ELP 456). Outstanding among the singers are Jacques Urlus and Leopold Demuth. Needless to say, the recording is sketchy; there is some curious quick shifting between early electrical and acoustic reproduction.

ARNE, THOMAS AUGUSTINE (1710-1778)

Thomas and Sally. *IOS, L LLP 292 (*Purcell: Masque in Timon of Athens).*

The Intimate Opera Society, founded in 1930, was the direct result of the discovery by Frederick Woodhouse of the manuscript of Arne's little opera. The company has made a specialty of the work ever since. The singing of the soprano and tenor is sweet and modest, that of Woodhouse himself in the style of a great Victorian. All, as one might say, disarmingly British.

AUBER, DANIEL-FRANÇOIS ESPRIT (1782-1871)

Fra Diavolo. *Beilke, s; Schilp, m-s; Fehenberger, t; Hopf, b; Schellenberg, bs; Frick, bs; etc.; DOC & O, Elmendorff, U URLP 204* [2].

This melodious favorite of our grandfathers was composed to a French text, though here it is sung in German. This fact is bound to have its effect on the melodic lines; yet the spirit of the performance is gay and ebullient. Some of the music's floridity proves embarrassing to the principals, but the voices are attractive and the singing has style.

BACH, CARL PHILIPP EMANUEL (1714-1788)

*Magnificat. Siebert, s; Rössl-Majdan, c; Kmentt, t; Braun, bs; VKC; VSO, Prohaska, BG 516/17 [2] (*Concerto for Orchestra).*

Our one example of the choral works of Bach's most famous son is a finer piece than this recording shows. Soloists, chorus, orchestra, and conductor, are all favorably known in other recordings; yet here their performance seems hectic. I suspect that not enough time went into rehearsals. More could have been made, surely, of the long, elaborate fugue that crowns the composition.

BACH, JOHANN SEBASTIAN (1685-1750)

Cantatas

The numbers associated with the Bach cantatas were not assigned by the composer, and do not represent the chronology of the works. Nor can they be used in connection with the Church calendar, though Bach is reputed to have composed no less than five complete cycles. Actually, these numbers indicate only the order in which the cantatas were published by the Bach Gesellschaft in the nineteenth century. Still, they afford convenient handles for the cantatas, and some of them are now so well known that little purpose would be served by disregarding them.

The names of several conductors and singers reappear frequently on the list below. The most gifted leader, Hermann Scherchen, is not a Bach specialist, but is well known in America (where he has not yet appeared) through his numerous and varied recordings. Never one to be bound by tradition, he sometimes arouses misgivings in the orthodox; but he is never dull, and his interpretations generally are based on strong musicality. Scherchen usually works with an excellent group of soloists, including Magda Laszlo, Hilde Rössl-Majdan, and Alfred Poell. Fritz Lehmann is a reliable conductor, more conventional and less exciting than Scherchen. The admirable lieder singer Fischer-Dieskau and the excellent tenor Helmut Krebs appear in several of Lehmann's performances. The recordings of Felix Prohaska are also on the whole good; Rössl-Majdan and the young soprano Anny Felbermayer sing in several of them. And Hans Grischkat, who rivals Scherchen as a prolific cantata conductor, is a good musician, if sometimes a little stolid. The best of his soloists is Margot Guilleaume, whose singing is sometimes outstanding.

No. 1, Wie schön leuchtet der Morgenstern. Weber, s; Krebs, t; Schey, bs; BMC; BPH, Lehmann, D DL 9671 (*Cantata No. 19).

Because of the beauty of the familiar hymn on which it is founded, and no less because of the seemingly endless ingenuity of Bach's instrumentation, this is one of the most immediately appealing of all the cantatas. It contains, too, an especially lovely soprano aria, *"Erfüllet ihr himmlischen göttlichen Flammen."* The performance is generally well sung, but not perfectly balanced in reproduction. We could do with more of the chorale melody in the first movement. The soloists sing with impressive sincerity and excellent musical intentions, but without full mastery of the difficulties Bach has set them.

No. 4, Christ lag in Todesbanden. Krebs, t; Fischer-Dieskau, b; FSSC; GBO, Lehmann, 10" D DL 7523. BGC; VSO, Prohaska, BG 511 (*Cantata No. 140). SC; RCAO, Shaw, V LM 9035 (*Motet: Jesu, meine Freude).

Preference among these three performances is conclusively decided by Lehmann's soloists (both Prohaska and Shaw assign the solo portions to appropriate sections of the chorus). Fischer-Dieskau, especially, sings eloquently, though he does some transposing where the vocal line approaches the extremes of his range. On the other hand, Decca's reproduction is somewhat lacking in sonority; the Bach Guild recording is mechanically better. Shaw's performance is rather businesslike; some of the singing inclines to be choppy.

No. 6, Bleib bei uns, denn es will Abend werden. Plümacher, c; Hohmann, t; Müller, bs; SCS; BO, Grischkat, Ren X 34 (*Cantata No. 19).

As Schering has noted, this cantata may be considered a "continuation and epitome of the scenes depicted in the *Saint John Passion,"* in a narrative as well as a musical sense. Certainly the opening chorus bears more than a family resemblance to the *"Ruht wohl"* of the greater work. In the recording, some concern is apparent over the matter of balance, for the chorus seems to be placed beyond the orchestra. The effect is generally good, though such an arrangement would account for a certain dullness in the choral tone. The soloists, unfortunately, are too close to the microphone. Plümacher does not manage to make light of the technical difficulties of her first aria; she seems rushed by the conductor, and consequently unable to give the words due weight.

No. 9, Es ist das Heil uns kommen her. Fassbender-Luz, s; Dräger,
c; Stemann, t; Müller, bs; SCS; BO, Grischkat, Ren X 37 (*Cantata No.
137).

The ninth cantata is one of Bach's finest. Spitta says it "gives
us perfect satisfaction by its masterly completeness and fulness
of form." The recording shares the characteristics of that of No.
6, though the solo singing is somewhat less impressive.

No. 11, Lobet Gott in seinen Reichen (Ascension Oratorio). Fass-
bender-Luz, s; Michaelis, c; Hohmann, t; Müller, bs; SWS; BO, Grisch-
kat, Ly LL 34. (In English) Mitchell, s; Ferrier, c; Herbert, t; Par-
sons, bs; CSL; JO, Jacques, 10" L LPS 160.

The chief musical interest here lies in the original contralto aria
later remodeled into the *"Agnus Dei"* of the *B minor Mass*. In
both recordings the best singing is done by the contralto. Although the Stuttgart tenor is ineffectual and the other soloists are
hardly better, the not-too-successful English translation throws
the decision to the German group. Even Ferrier's excellent diction is unable to make the text plain.

No. 19, Es erhub sich ein Streit. Weber, s; Krebs, t; Schey, bs; BMC;
BPH, Lehmann, D DL 9671 (*Cantata No. 1). Giebel, s; Stemann, t;
Müller, bs; SCS; STO, Grischkat, Ren X 34 (*Cantata No. 6).

The gem of this cantata is the tenor aria *"Bleibt, ihr Engel, bleibt*
bei mir," with an obbligato trumpet playing a familiar chorale
melody. Krebs is the more impressive of the two tenors. The
Lehmann performance is the better balanced; while Grischkat's
chorus seems distant, his soloists are too much with us.

No. 21, Ich hatte viel Bekümmernis. Weber, s; Krebs, t; Schey, bs;
BMC; BPH, Lehmann, D DL 9673. Schweiger, s; Cuenod, t; Perners-
torfer, bs; VKC; VSY, Sternberg, BG 501.

Weber sings the famous aria *"Seufzer, Thränen, Kummer, Not"*
effectively under Lehmann, and Krebs shows a good grasp of his
solos. The tenor, however, encounters some formidable competition from Cuenod, whose sensitive singing is the feature among
Sternberg's soloists. The duet in the Decca recording suffers
from the voices being too close to the microphone, but the whole
effect of the cantata is smoother and more penetrating than in the
Bach Guild version.

No. 31, Der Himmel lacht, die Erde jubilieret. Felbermayer, s; Kmentt,
t; Berry, bs; VKC; VCO, Prohaska, BG 512 (*Chorales).

I am not sure the device of reducing the elaborate choruses to solo voices is the best possible solution for the problem of clarity in this work, but this performance has movement. Felbermayer deserves a word of praise for her singing of the aria *"Letzte Stunde, brich herein,"* which brings this festive composition to its sober concluding thought on death and the future life.

No. 32, Liebster Jesu, mein Verlangen. Laszlo, s; Poell, bs; VKC; VSO, Scherchen, WWL 5122 (*Cantata No. 140). Giebel, s; Müller, bs; PRC & O, Reinhardt, Vox PL 7340 (*Cantata No. 57).

If it were the only recording in the field, Reinhardt's would rate as very satisfactory; as it is, the choice falls to Scherchen. Again, were Laszlo's voice less appealingly lyrical and her style less musicianly and beautifully matched with that of Poell, the combination of Giebel and Müller would impress us more. The latter soprano's voice, however, lacks the vibrancy we admire in her rival. After Scherchen, the Reinhardt performance seems just a bit dull.

No. 34, O ewiges Feuer. Sydney, c; Cuenod, t; Pernerstorfer, bs; VKC; VSY, Sternberg, BG 502 (*Cantata No. 56).

Like so many Bach performances, this one is uneven, with Sternberg's youthful spirit and earnestness compensating for some obvious weaknesses, and with a certain nervousness especially noticeable in the first movement. The choral sections are unusually transparent, the vocal soloists generally good, and the instrumentalists excellent, though the trumpeters do not find the going easy.

No. 39, Brich dem Hungrigen dein Brot. Weber, s; Fischer, c; Schey, bs; BMC; BPH, Lehmann, D DL 9672 (*Cantata No. 79).

This cantata, composed for a service of thanksgiving on the arrival in Leipzig of some eighteen hundred war refugees from Salzburg, is particularly touching as we realize the timeliness of its text. The orchestra—two flutes, two oboes, strings, and organ—is strikingly lovely, especially at the opening, and the aria for soprano with flutes in unison and continuo, *"Höchster was ich habe,"* is one of those beautiful flowing melodies of which Bach so well knew the secret. The choral work is clear in texture, but the soloists are uneven. The bass sings with good authority, but the ladies are rather tentative.

No. 46, Schauet doch und sehet. Sydney, c; Cuenod, t; Pernerstorfer, bs; VKC; VSY, Sternberg, BG 503 (*Cantata No. 104).

If the moving opening chorus of this cantata seems strangely familiar, this is because we have met it before in the *B minor Mass*, as *"Qui tollis peccata mundi."* Unlike some of Bach's adaptations, this one retains the same underlying thought in its later guise; but whereas in the Mass text we meditate upon the burden of the whole world's sin, in this cantata it is the sorrow of the Crucified that concerns us. Jonathan Sternberg and the excellent forces he directs succeed in conveying more than a little of the music's power.

No. 51, Jauchzet Gott in allen Landen. Guilleaume, s; BO, Grischkat, Ren X 35 (*Cantata No. 189). Schwarzkopf, s; PHI, Gelhorn, C ML 4792 (*Cantata No. 82; Arias from Cantatas Nos. 208, 68). Danco, s; Stuttgart Cham O, Münchinger, L LL 993 (*Cantata No. 202).

Schwarzkopf's *Jauchzet Gott* is perhaps her most brilliant *tour de force* to date—one wonders if any other soprano could match her for sheer endurance, for accuracy, or for rhythmic precision at breakneck speed. On the other hand, one wonders if this is really all Bach intended. In the more sustained portions the soprano is at her loveliest; only a tendency to sing the words too inwardly is open to any sort of criticism. Neither Danco nor Guilleaume attempts to rival Schwarzkopf's dazzling brilliance. The former, taking the opening movement at a less headlong *tempo*, negotiates the coloratura with notable ease, yet her tone somehow lacks solidity. It remains for Guilleaume to publish Bach's glad tidings without exhausting herself or her listeners. Schwarzkopf's recording has been available for several years as a 78-rpm importation; at 33 it is not seriously hampered by a heavy bass. Danco's version is the most recent of the three and the best mechanically.

No. 53, Schlage doch, gewünschte Stunde. Rössl-Majdan, c; VSO, Scherchen, W WL 5197 (*Cantatas Nos. 54, 170). Hennecke, c; SCB, Wenzinger, D DL 9619 (*Cantatas Nos. 200, 189).

Schlage doch is a contralto's paradise, with long luscious lines to be caressed by a noble voice, and with just the kind of expressiveness only such a voice can give. Strange, then, that more deep-toned ladies have not recorded it; stranger still that neither of the two artists here listed has come nearer to the core of the matter. Rössl-Majdan is a fine singer with a lovely voice, as many discs have shown; perhaps it is Scherchen who keeps the cantata from flowing, for the orchestra part is a little choppy. Hennecke's voice is less rich and less steady: in this case it is definitely the singer who does not thrill us.

No. 54, Widerstehe doch der Sünde. Rössl-Majdan, c; VSO, Scherchen, W WL 5197 (*Cantatas Nos. 53, 170).

The contralto is more successful here than in the better-known No. 53, but in reproduction her voice seems too close upon us.

No. 56, Ich will den Kreuzstab gerne tragen. Fischer-Dieskau, BMC; RCO, Ristenpart, D DL 9595 (*Cantata No. 82). Pernerstorfer, bs; VKC; VSY, Sternberg, BG 502 (*Cantata No. 34).

Fischer-Dieskau's voice is rich, smooth, and appealing in this solo cantata, his style warm, musical, and clean-cut. It is surprising to note that he likes neither high notes nor low, even taking several low G's up an octave. These must be limitations overcome since this recording was made, for later evidence does not show them. His is certainly the better recording of the cantata, despite what sounds like not quite perfect microphone placement. The voice is a little muffled.

No. 57, Selig ist der Mann. Giebel, s; Müller, bs; PRO, Reinhardt, Vox PL 7340 (*Cantata No. 32).

This performance and recording are best summed up in the word "competent."

No. 63, Christen, ätzet diesen Tag. Opawsky, s; Rössl-Majdan, c; Kmentt, t; Hermann, bs; VKC; VSO, Gielen, BG 518.

Despite some good work by the contralto and general adequacy on the part of the other soloists, the performance of this "Christmas Cantata" can hardly be called inspired.

No. 65, Sie werden aus Saba alle kommen. Hilgenberg, s; Sands, t; Isbell, bs; RWC: CHAM, Wagner, Ly LL 50 (*Cantata No. 106).

Cantata 65 has long been familiar in the Anthologie Sonore recording, which, despite some clean singing by Max Meili and the chorus, was never satisfactory. The work was cut down to fit two twelve-inch standard-play sides, and even if we accepted this, the transitions from movement to movement were joltingly hasty. Roger Wagner's restrained tempo in the opening movement —a kind of "March of the Wise Men" to introduce this Epiphany cantata—is definitely good, and the chorus, apparently larger than that on Anthologie Sonore, sings admirably. The bass soloist is outstanding (his part is entirely cut in the Anthologie), the tenor a bit quavering and light.

No. 67, Halt im Gedächtniss Jesum Christ (Hold in affection Jesus Christ). Ferrier, c; Herbert, t; Parsons, bs; CSL; JO, Jacques, 10" L LPS 161 (*Cantata No. 147—Chorale, Jesu, joy of man's desiring).

This cantata, with its special dividend of an attractive and reserved performance of the familiar chorale, is authentic enough in
style, if we accept the translation and the sheer Britishness of
the voices. I am never quite satisfied with the rather stilted effect of the English in the recitatives, and in the arias even
Ferrier's good diction does not make the texts plain enough. It
is, of course, to the contralto's participation that the performance
owes its chief distinction.

*No. 70, Wachet, betet, seid bereit allezeit. Felbermayer, s; Wien, c;
Meyer-Welfing, t; Foster, bs; BGC; VSO, Prohaska, BG 524.*

This fine cantata is done with good spirit, and in the choral parts,
with clarity and finish. The concerted coloratura of the opening
movement comes through as it should, the balance with the orchestra is satisfactory. Among the soloists only Felbermayer is
altogether right, but she is considerably more than that. Foster
produces a rather throaty sound; in the quite astonishing recitative and arioso—in effect almost a *scena drammatica*—his singing wants more bite. Wien produces pleasant tones, but her expression is rather tentative. Meyer-Welfing, after delivering his
recitative directly through the nose, stands up surprisingly well
in his aria, one of the finest moments in the cantata. The reproduction is good, though I found I had to cut the highs in order to
lose some strong sibilants.

*No. 76, Die Himmel erzählen die Ehre Gottes. Laszlo, s; Rössl-
Majdan, c; Munteanu, t; Standen, bs; VKC; VSO, Scherchen, W WL 5201.*

This is a cantata of strong attractions, with a particularly fine
placid chorale closing the first part, and a charming sinfonia for
oboe d'amore, viola da gamba, bass, and continuo opening the
second. Scherchen, who has a way of making such music vital,
is in fine form here, and it would be hard to resist his performance. Laszlo is excellent, and Rössl-Majdan's solos have true
nobility. Munteanu is somewhat tremulous, Standen rather husky,
though both sing intelligently. The splendid final chorale, with
its trumpetings and full trappings, makes a thrilling close.

*No. 78, Jesu, der du meine Seele. Stich-Randall, s; Hermann, c;
Dermota, t; Braun, bs; BGC & O, Prohaska, BG 537 (Cantata No. 106).
Häfliger, t; Schey, bs; WINC & O, Reinhardt, 10" CH 59.*

Clarity in performance and reproduction is chief among the virtues
of the choral portions of Prohaska's recording. In this it is
superior to Reinhardt's. It is blessed, too, with unusually effective soloists, and unlike its rival, it has the delicious duet, *"Wir*

eilen mit schwachen doch emsigen Schritten," sung by solo voices. This movement, however, is quite a new thing here, for the *tempo* is very much faster than is usual, and the continuo played on the organ gives the music a character it does not have with the harpsichord. The speed, I think, is quite in keeping with the text, but the loss in lightness of texture neutralizes some of this gain. The tenor and bass soloists are not only far superior to those in the Concert Hall version; they are exceptionally good by any standards. Over Prohaska's performance I sense a feeling of restlessness which I do not altogether like; still, it is unquestionably the best recording so far available.

No. 79, Gott der Herr ist Sonn' und Schild. Weber, s; Fischer, c; Schey, bs; BMC; BPH, Lehmann, D DL 9672 (*Cantata No. 39).

This cantata for Reformation Day contains, among other things, a charming duet for soprano and bass, moving mostly in parallel motion—*"Gott, ach Gott, verlass die Deinen nimmermehr"*—and an exciting setting of the chorale *"Nun danket Alle Gott,"* punctuated by horn fanfares. The choral singing is clear, though the tone is somewhat breathy. The bass is the best of the soloists.

No. 80, Ein' feste Burg ist unser Gott. Weis-Osborn, s; Rössl-Majdan, c; Equiluz, t; Berry, bs; VKC; VCO, Prohaska, BG 508.

It is perhaps not surprising that Luther's great Reformation hymn should have inspired Bach to one of his most exciting cantatas. From the very first note proclaimed by the tenors, supported by unison violas, cellos, and organ, we are *in medias res:* never once throughout the cantata are we let down. The first chorus and the brilliant and heavily scored unison chorale (*"Und wenn die Welt voll Teufel wär"*) are perhaps the highest spots, though the four-square chorale at the end is thrilling in its own way. The performance is enthusiastic and communicative, if under-rehearsed in places. The opening chorus is clear and the contrapuntal lines are remarkably well brought out; the danger has been averted that so consistently loud a movement might disintegrate into a jumble. Berry sings his solo well, with the obbligato chorale supplied by the sopranos, but this has been too powerfully recorded. The other vocal soloists are good, and there is fine trumpet-playing by Helmut Wobitsch.

No. 82, Ich habe genug. Hotter, bs; PHI, Bernard, C ML 4792 (*Cantata No. 51; Arias from Cantatas Nos. 208, 68). Fischer-Dieskau, b; RCO, Ristenpart, D DL 9595 (*Cantata No. 56).

In their *Record Guide*, Sackville-West and Shawe-Taylor hailed the original standard-play version of the Hotter recording as "the most important contribution to the Bach cantata repertoire which has yet appeared." Certainly the singer has here produced his own masterpiece and done eloquent justice to one of Bach's choicest solo works. The voice, to be sure, is not the most sensuous we have heard in our time, yet it is smooth and expressive in this recording, and the man is a magnificent artist. The aria *"Schlummert ein,"* with its echoes of the final chorus in the *Saint Matthew Passion*, is sung with deep reverence and feeling; the final brilliant number is hardly less successful. The transfer to LP has meant a sacrifice of some feeling of space, but the gain in uninterrupted mood is far more important. Fischer-Dieskau, though at the time of recording he seemed to find the range of the cantata taxing, is only somewhat less convincing.

No. 84, *Ich bin vergnügt.* Laszlo, s; VSO, Scherchen, W WL 5125 (*Cantata No. 106).

Despite some peculiar labeling, this is a solo cantata, sung in Laszlo's bright, appealing tone. The soprano is, however, guilty of some cooing and some scooping. Her diction is hardly a model.

No. 104, *Du Hirte Israel, höre.* Sydney, c; Cuenod, t; Pernerstorfer, bs; VKC; VSY, Sternberg, BG 503 (*Cantata No. 46).

Jonathan Sternberg's forces perform well for him here. Among his chief assets are Cuenod, the seasoned orchestral players, and the choir.

No. 105, *Herr, gehe nicht ins Gericht.* Weber, s; Fischer, c; Krebs, t; Schey, bs; BMC; BPH, Lehmann, D DL 9682 (*Cantata No. 170).

The anxious opening of this cantata, with its almost confused rhythms, is very striking; and the soprano aria *"Wie zittern und wanken,"* with oboe, violins, and viola, is first-rate Bach. The best of the soloists are Weber and Krebs, the latter singing with an easy open tone hardly expected of a German tenor. Fischer is not quite steady in tone, and Schey's singing is curiously measured. The chorus performs well (it seems to be a small one), though its tone is somewhat husky; apparently it has been placed beyond the orchestra, for it is not strong in brilliance. In the tenor aria there is some difficulty with the horns. The final chorale is a wonderful contemplative movement, with shifting accompanying rhythm.

No. 106, *Gottes Zeit ist die allerbeste Zeit.* Stich-Randall, s; Hermann, c; Dermota, t; Braun, bs; BGC & O, Prohaska, BG 537 (*Cantata No. 78). Rössl-Majdan, c; Poell, bs; VKC; VSO, Scherchen, W WL 5125

(*Cantata No. 84). Hilgenberg, s; Sands, t; Isbell, bs; RWC; CHAM, Wagner, Ly LL 50 (*Cantata No. 65).

This is the funeral cantata also known as *Actus Tragicus*; it boasts one of the most sublimely beautiful orchestral preludes to be found in Bach. Scherchen uses gambas and flutes in this with very moving effect, but Prohaska goes him one better in dropping the flutes for recorders. Rössl-Majdan and Poell sing their duet superbly in the Scherchen recording, though the basso finds the *tessitura* high. Prohaska has individual singers for the "choral solos" as well as their extended parts, and they are a superior group—Stich-Randall's voice is especially lovely in the passage that ends the first chorus. Both choruses come through with good definition and satisfactory tone; there is little to choose between the orchestras. Wagner's singers are competent, but they do not reach the standard of their rivals.

No. 112, Der Herr ist mein getreuer Hirt. Fassbender-Luz, s; Plümacher, c; Stemann, t; Werdermann, bs; SWS; BO, Grischkat, Ren X 36 (*Cantata No. 185).

This adaptation of the *Twenty-third Psalm* has a joyous opening chorus with a part for high trumpet, sure in this recording to give trouble if one's turntable is less than perfectly steady. A lovely contralto aria follows, *"Zum reinen Wasser"*—it may be remembered as a part of Marian Anderson's Bach aria program (V LCT 1111). Plümacher performs well, but the rest of the soloists are not very good. Both the bass recitative and the soprano-tenor duet are sub-standard.

No. 122, Das neugebor'ne Kindelein. Opawsky, s; Rössl-Majdan, c; Kmentt, t; Hermann, bs; VKC; VSO, Gielen, BG 523 (*Cantata No. 133).

There is nothing particularly distinctive about this performance. The bass aria sounds like a bit of a chore; the other solos are not notably better. Chorus and orchestra acquit themselves satisfactorily.

No. 131, Aus der Tiefe. Hess, t; Matthen, bs; SC; RCAO, Shaw, V LM 1100 (*Cantata No. 140).

This is one of the best of the Shaw performances. The conductor's usual clean and polished musical lines are once again impressive, as is his general air of proficiency. Indeed, if it has a weakness, this must be that it is *too* proficient. The two soloists are among the best available in this country for this type of music. The reproduction is unusually impressive, combining a sense of presence with a fine effect of space.

No. 133, Ich freue mich in dir. Opawsky, s; Rössl-Majdan, c; Kmentt, t; Hermann, bs; VKC; VSO, Gielen, BG 523 (*Cantata No. 122*).

This Christmas cantata is reasonably well done. Best of the soloists are the contralto and the tenor, both familiar through other recordings.

No. 137, Lobe den Herren, den mächtigen König der Ehren. Fassbender-Luz, s; Dräger, c; Stemann, t; Müller, bs; SCS; BO, Grischkat, Ren X 37 (*Cantata No. 9*).

This cantata is in effect a series of variations on one of the most striking of all the chorales. There is a particularly effective tenor aria with the old melody serving as trumpet obbligato. The performance is a good one.

No. 140, Wachet auf, ruft uns die Stimme. Laszlo, s; Kmentt, t; Poell, bs; VKC; VSO, Scherchen, W WL 5122 (*Cantata No. 32*). Felbermayer, s; Uhl, t; Braun, bs; BGC & O, Prohaska, BG 511 (*Cantata No. 4*). Freil, s; Russell, t; Matthen, bs; SC; RCAO, Shaw, V LM 1100 (*Cantata No. 131*).

To one unfamiliar with the Bach cantatas, there could perhaps be no better introduction than this famous work, of whose remarkable middle movement the familiar chorale prelude *Wachet auf* is a transcription. The Prohaska performance has the advantage of being coupled with another of the acknowledged great cantatas, and its balance is somewhat better than that of the Scherchen version. Still, the exceptional singing of the duets by Laszlo and Poell is enough to make the Westminster record a "must." The Shaw recording is older, and except for Matthen the soloists are lightweight. It is, however, smooth and well prepared.

No. 146, Wir müssen durch viel Trübsal in das Reich Gottes eingehen. Felbermayer, s; Wien, c; Meyer-Welfing, t; Foster, bs; BGC; VSO, Prohaska, BG 525.

The immediately striking thing about this cantata is the predominance of the organ in the long elaborate prelude. In the recording this effect is highlighted to such an extent that the chorus, on its entrance, seems removed from the scene—one wonders where the performance took place. What with such unevennesses, both in reproduction and in performance, this is not one of the happiest of the Bach Guild offerings. Of the soloists, Felbermayer is as usual admirable; Wien is passable; Meyer-Welfing is inclined to put pressure on his voice, with not too happy results. A jubilant duet for tenor and bass is a feature of the work, but its effect is lost because the singers are too close to us.

*No. 152, Tritt auf die Glaubensbahn. Bond, s; Irwin, bs; LBE, Haas, W WL 5067 (*Brandenburg Concerto No. 4).*

After a hearing of this work, the thing most likely to linger in the memory is a soprano aria of a charm similar to that of *"Schafe können sicher weiden."* Though the performance as a whole has a winning lightness of touch, the two soloists are not quite all we might desire. Both are accomplished and conscientious artists of the solid English tradition—hardly ideal credentials for a Bach performance in the original German. Accepting this limitation, however, the performance is creditable and the recording excellent.

*No. 158, Der Friede sei mit dir. Eby, bs; Hess, s; Popeski, s; BCNY, Hauptmann, BS LX 7001 (*Songs).*

The cantata is for bass solo, with the other voices incidental; as Eby sings all the sacred songs on the reverse, the listener must settle down to quite a session with his voice. Unhappily, it is a very deep, thick, almost sepulchral voice, and he does nothing to brighten it or give it tonal variety. The cantata is built around one lovely aria, but one is not likely to remember this very well after such a performance. The voices that join in the chorale at the end are not well blended.

*No. 161, Komm du süsse Todesstunde. Rössl-Majdan, c; Kmentt, t; BGC & O, Prohaska, BG 513 (*Cantata No. 202).*

This cantata, which utilizes the magnificent chorale *Herzlich thut mich Verlangen*, benefits by some good, neat solo singing. The choral work is well balanced; though not too close upon us, the parts stand out distinctly, as do the orchestral instruments.

*No. 170, Vergnügte Ruh', beliebte Seelenlust. Rössl-Majdan, c; VSO, Scherchen, W WL 5197 (*Cantatas Nos. 53, 54). Höngen, c; BAV, Lehmann, D DL 9682 (*Cantata No. 105).*

Spitta calls this cantata "one of the most beautiful of its kind." Of special interest are the happy details of wordsetting, notably the graphic line *"Und will den Nächsten nur mit Füssen treten."* But if this is an outstandingly lovely work, it is also a difficult one. Of the two singers, Rössl-Majdan is the more successful; in fact this is the best of the three cantatas she sings on this one disc. Amusingly, the organ obbligato, fully described in the jacket notes, is played on the harpsichord in this recording. Höngen is bested by some of the problems set her; her tone is tremulous, her pitch uncertain. Her unquestionable understanding of the music is not enough to save her.

No. 185, Barmherziges Herze der ewigen Liebe. Fassbender-Luz, s; Plümacher, c; Hohmann, t; Müller, bs; SWS; BO, Grischkat, Ren X 36 (*Cantata No. 112).

This is an unusually attractive cantata, but the performance does not rise to its material. The opening duet, for soprano and tenor, · is quite awkwardly sung, and the bass recitative and aria are almost metronomical. Plümacher, who sings a recitative designated for tenor, is the best of the soloists. The situation is somewhat relieved when we hear the chorale *Ich ruf' zu dir, Herr Jesu Christ* at the end.

No. 189, Meine Seele rühmt und preist. Ludwig, t; CHAM, Lehmann, D DL 9619 (*Cantatas Nos. 53, 200). Stemann, t; BO, Grischkat, Ren X 35 (*Cantata No. 51). Schiøtz, t; PERP, C ML 4641 (*Beethoven: An die ferne Geliebte).

Ludwig, despite a voice rather operatic-heavy for the ideal in Bach, gives decidedly the best performance we have had of this solo cantata. A feature of his version is the use of the recorder in the ensemble. Stemann sings intelligently enough, but his voice lacks "edge"; too, his singing is inclined to be square-cut, especially in the recitative. The Schiøtz record, made at Perpignan during the 1952 Casals festival, does not show this admirable musician at his best, though the accompanying ensemble is very lovely. Part of the trouble seems to be microphone placement.

No. 198, Trauer-Ode (Lass, Fürstin, lass noch einen Strahl). Laszlo, s; Rössl-Majdan, c; Kmentt, t; Poell, bs; VKC; VSO, Scherchen, W WL 5123.

To my mind, the gem of this funeral cantata is the final chorus, with its almost Gluckian flowing lines and pastoral 6/8 measure. Among the soloists the special heroes are Rössl-Majdan, whose voice rings out with fine fervor and rich tone in her recitative and aria, and Poell, especially noble of tone, despite hints of limitations in his singing range. Laszlo's recitative takes her higher than the best part of her voice, but her aria is well sung, if not clearly enunciated. Kmentt has a very florid piece to sing against a lovely instrumental background, and he does it fairly well,

though his scale is not altogether even; he has a way of opening
up his top tones which does not improve their quality.

No. 200, Bekennen will ich seinen Namen.   Hennecke, c; SCB,
*Wenzinger, D DL 9619 (*Cantatas Nos. 53, 189).*

A good, competent performance by a singer of not exceptional
voice.   The quality is neither strikingly rich nor particularly
steady.

No. 201, Der Streit zwischen Phoebus und Pan.   Schlemm, s; Eustrati,
c; Reinhold, t; Lutze, t; Niese, b; BGC & O, Koch, BG 514.   Nentwig,
s; Michaelis, c; Hohmann, t; Pfeifle, t; Müller, bs; Kelch, bs; SWS;
STO, Grischkat, Ren X 42.

The contrast between these two recordings is saddening, for no
clear-cut preference is possible.   In matters of singing, much is
to be said for the second set, in which the ladies at least have
more charm than their rivals.   As reproduction, however, Renaissance provides no such big, broad sound as that of the Bach
Guild.   And if occasionally we have to take the will for the deed
in the more elaborate arias, Koch's performance has the kind of
mock seriousness Bach wrote into the score.

No. 202, Weichet nur, betrübte Schatten.   Felbermayer, s; BGO, Pro-
*haska, BG 513 (*Cantata No. 161).   Danco, s; Stuttgart Cham O,*
*Münchinger, L LL 993 (*Cantata No. 51).*

This is the "Wedding Cantata" once recorded by Elisabeth
Schumann, whose performance set an abiding standard despite the
effects of a too-close microphone placement.   Felbermayer has a
less positive voice and style, and, as if in reaction, she has been
placed apparently a little too far away, emerging somewhat weakly,
especially in the lower passages.   I could wish, too, for more
crispness in her diction.   The opening of the cantata might have
been smoother, but on the whole the performance is satisfactory.
Danco does her customary musicianly job, and she is better served
by the recording.   But her voice has less warmth and appeal in it
than Felbermayer's.

No. 203, Amore Traditore.   Müller, bs; Elsner, hpschd, Vox PL 8980
*(*Cantata No. 211).*

This little Italian cantata serves as filler for the second side of
the "Coffee Cantata."   It is done in good straight style.   Perhaps
Müller's singing could have been lighter, possibly shaded more,
for there is only the harpsichord accompanying.

No. 205, Der zufriedengestellte Aeolus.   Schlemm, s; Eustrati, c;

Lutze, t; Wolfram, b; BGC & O, Koch, BG 515. Nentwig, s; Michaelis, c; Hohmann, t; Kelch, bs; SWS; STO, Grischkat, Ren X 43.

As in the case of *Cantata No. 201*, the superiority of the Bach Guild reproduction overrules some more appealing singing on the part of the Renaissance soloists. Koch's performers quite rightly present the little drama in all seriousness. The humor, after all, derives largely from Bach's employment of his musical style all in the spirit of fun. Again, some of the singers no more than get by in the more formidable passages they have to sing.

No. 210, Hochzeitskantate. Laszlo, s; VSO, Scherchen, W WL 5138.

Laszlo, for all her intelligence and taste, is not quite comfortable in the high *tessitura* of this *Wedding Cantata*, a fact that affects both her tone and her diction.

No. 211, Schweigt stille, plaudert nicht (Coffee Cantata). Sailer, s; Feyerabend, t; Müller, bs; PRO, Reinhardt, Vox PL 8980 (*Cantata No. 203).

The one previous LP "Coffee Cantata" was a hastily assembled performance that did nobody any particular credit. This new one is not only more "seasoned," but by absolute standards very good. Sailer's voice is bright and limpid, especially appealing in the *"Heute noch"* aria. Müller blusters enough without leaving off solid and legitimate singing, and Feyerabend gives the proper weight to his recitatives. All three realize that the humor of the piece depends on "deadpan." The reproduction is powerful, but it is clean in sound and can be brought down to proper size.

No. 212, Mer hahn en neue Oberkeet (Peasant Cantata). Curtin, s; Matthen, bs; CFO, Pinkham, All 3002.

The one previous recording of the burlesque *Peasant Cantata*, dating back to the thirties, and not available on LP, was abbreviated and sung in French. The new one, despite excellent singing, is annoyingly businesslike in its presentation; one thing passes to another with so little concern that the general result is not impressive. Why this must be so is hardly clear, for the amount of music on each LP side is short by any standard.

Chorales

Easter Chorales: Christ ist erstanden; Christ lag in Todesbanden; Erschienen ist der herrlich Tag; Erstanden ist der heilig Christ; Heut' triumphieret Gottes Sohn; Jesus Christus, unser Heiland; Jesus meine Zuversicht. Heising, s; Kimmel, c; Planyavsky, t; Heppe, bs; Rapf, org, BG 512 (*Cantata No. 31).

These chorales are sung by solo voices with organ; there is little dynamic variety in the delivery, and undoubtedly the music would be more effective given by a somewhat larger group. Musically, there seems little point in stringing them together this way.

Magnificat

Magnificat. Sailer, s; Wolf-Matthaeus, m-s; Plümacher, c; Feyerabend, t; Müller, bs; RSTC; PRO, Reinhardt, Vox PL 8890. Schilling, s; Pitzinger, c; Marten, t; Gröschel, bs; LC; ABSO, Leitner, D DL 9557. Stader, s; Cavelti, c; Häfliger, t; Schey, bs; WINC & O, Reinhart, CH 60.

When Bach composed his *Magnificat* for performance in the Leipzig Thomas-Kirche at Christmas time, between movements of the canticle he interpolated settings of four texts traditionally sung in the church at that season—two in German, and two in Latin. The Vox recording is complete: it includes this special and rarely heard feature. It is also easily the best among the three now listed. The opening chorus always presents a problem, for it was written before Bach had mastered the secret of making polyphonic voices cut through heavy instrumentation. The effect here is as good as we can reasonably hope to hear; the same admirable clarity prevails through most of the choral sections of the work (there is some uncertainty in one of the interpolations). The soloists are a capable lot, and for the most part sing very cleanly. Occasionally one or another of them falls below their established tonal standard, and Plümacher, for one, pokes out the beat in the florid passages she sings. The reproduction is quite brilliant. Neither of the older performances, without the interpolations, does full justice to the work. Leitner's is the better, though the recording balance is poor. Pitzinger is the best of the soloists, though her voice is modest. On the other hand, the lusty tones of Gröschel quite overwhelm the instruments in his aria.

Masses

Mass in B minor. Schwarzkopf, s; Höffgen, c; Gedda, t; Rehfuss, bs; MFC & O, Karajan, An 3500-C [3]. Loose, s; Ceska, s; Burgsthaler-Schuster, c; Dermota, t; Poell, bs; VKC; VSY, Scherchen, W WAL 301 [3]. Weber, s; de Landi, c; Krebs, t; Wolfram, bs; RBC & O, Lehmann, U URLP 236 [2].

It is the glory and the despair of every musical masterpiece that absolute perfection in performance is never quite attainable, that even when the critics cry "definitive," there is something still to be added the next time a vital interpretative mind sets to it. From seven listings of the *B minor Mass* these three are chosen, two because their virtues place them well beyond competition, and one because, on two discs instead of three, it offers astonishing value at a lower price. Karajan and Scherchen both work with forces of the appropriate size, thus avoiding the old temptation to lay on the climaxes and overload the sonorities. Both, however, succeed in making their resources count. In matters of tempo they are at opposite poles: it is as though Karajan, whose performance came later, had studied Scherchen and determined not to do likewise. I well remember my incredulity on hearing Scherchen's first "*Kyrie*": could anyone possibly hold it together at so slow a tempo? It was his great achievement that he did, but Karajan is certainly right in not emulating him. At times, I think, Karajan carries things too far: the second "*Kyrie*," for me, is too fast, especially as it is to be followed by a very rapid "*Gloria.*" Again, I find it difficult to adjust to so agitated a "*Crucifixus*," and I feel this conception takes away from the excitement of "*Et resurrexit.*" But the point at which Karajan takes the lead over the accomplishment of Scherchen is the first solo. The latter seems to consider the solos as necessary relief, something to be gone through in order to make the choruses stand out more magnificently. If an exception must be made in the case of Dermota's beautifully sung "*Benedictus*," the singers have all they can do to keep up with the conductor's beat. Karajan has certainly assembled the finest quartet since the ancient and overweight performance of Albert Coates, with which the work first came complete to discs. Each is an artist, and each is allowed to prove it. The first duet, "*Christe*," is the most reserved and reverent I have ever heard; the two voices match miraculously. In choral precision Scherchen has the edge, and there will be many who find it difficult, as I do, to discard his set while pronouncing Karajan's superior.

Lehmann's offering is thoroughly respectable, sometimes more than that, and though it is not so sharp and clean in sound as either of those discussed above (the effect is that of a slightly echoey church, with some lack of definition in the choral sound), it would be acceptable enough without their standards of comparison. The soprano and the tenor soloists do themselves credit; the others get by. Perhaps because the whole work was to be

pressed on two discs, the passing from one movement to the next
is sometimes almost shockingly rapid.

*Missa brevis No. 1, in F; Sanctus No. 1, in C; Missa brevis No. 2, in
A; Sanctus No. 2, in D; Missa brevis No. 3, in G minor; Sanctus No.
3, in D minor; Missa brevis No. 4, in G; Sanctus No. 4, in G. Giebel,
s; Wolf-Matthaeus, c; Hohmann, t; Kelch, bs; SWS; STO, Grischkat,
Ren X 44, X 45, X 46, X 47* [4].

It was a nice idea to unearth these more modest Masses, and to
call attention to their possibilities for church performance. Also,
here and there is a movement of considerable beauty, if hardly of
the stature of those in the great *B minor*. The best of them, to
my ears, is the fourth, and it is also the most adequately performed. The ending of the *"Kyrie"* rises to real impressiveness,
and there is good singing from the bass soloist in *"Gratias
agimus."* The soprano-alto duet, *"Domine Deus,"* too, is nicely
turned, though it is beyond the power of the singers to make the
words mean much in this setting. I enjoyed the tenor soloist in
the third Mass, but on the whole this, like the first and second,
seems to have been prepared without too great enthusiasm.

Motets

*Jesu, meine Freude; Komm, Jesu, komm; Singet dem Herrn.   VKC,
Grossmann, W WL 5289.*
*Jesu, meine Freude (in English).   SC; RCAO, Shaw, V LM 9035 (*Can-
tata No. 4).*
*Komm, Jesu, komm.   SC; RCAO, Shaw, V LM 1784 (*Schubert: Mass in
G; Brahms: Choruses).*
*Der Geist hilft unsrer Schwachheit auf.   DC, Boepple, CH CAC 44
(*Baroque Choral Music, Dessoff Choirs).*

The motets are never easy to perform; and while it is one thing to
hear them passably sung in an auditorium or church, it is quite
another to repeat the experience by means of records. For this
reason, I am sure, while we can expect the stream of cantata recordings to continue as long as there is equipment to play them,
only occasionally will one of the motets be given release. As it
happens, the most vexing problem of performance has been solved
by the musicologists, those guardians of stylistic rectitude and
most merciless of critics. Scholars now agree that Bach's *a
cappella* music was not performed unaccompanied in his own
church, but that a group of instruments was used to reinforce the

vocal parts. It is therefore no longer necessary to invite fatigue by putting all the burden on the voices, or to take chances on sagging pitch. Robert Shaw, in his recording of *Jesu, meine Freude*, has taken advantage of this knowledge, using a group of instruments; these, however, play so discreetly that a casual listener might not realize they are there. An English text is used, and the diction is reasonably clear; still, one has to be alert to catch it. Grossmann's recording may well be his masterpiece. This conductor uses voices alone; obviously the chorus must have rehearsed long and faithfully, for such clarity of texture and accuracy of intonation are rare. The secret seems to lie in two features of the performance: the well-focused tones of the voices and the calm reserve of their singing. The fugal movement, *"Ihr aber seid nicht fleischlich,"* is beautifully transparent, poised and unhurried. Another striking section is *"Gute Nacht, o Wesen,"* with the chorale melody, in the alto, standing out in bold relief. Perhaps for perfect balance, the basses might be a little stronger. *Komm, Jesu, komm,* and *Singet dem Herrn*, both for double chorus, are performed with similar plasticity. The first of these has had two recordings beside those listed above. The Cantata Singers of London, under Reginald Jacques, present it in none-too-clear English (10" L LS 128), and the Schola Cantorum of New York, under Hugh Ross, sings it in German (10" C ML 2102). Both performances are labored and tiring for the listener. In his recording, Shaw again reinforces the voices with instruments, and his approach to the work is more simple and direct than that of Jacques or Ross. His version seemed satisfactory enough until that of Grossmann arrived. Ross includes in his program another motet, *Lobet den Herrn alle Heiden*, using the harpsichord continuo. *Singet dem Herrn*, considered the most difficult of the eight motets, is done to little purpose under Kurt Thomas's direction (10" Cap L 9077), and more interestingly in Hindemith's Collegium Musicum recording (Ov OVER 4). The performance here, however, is a little square-cut; it is easily outdone by Grossmann's.

The Dessoff recording was made in the Armor Hall of the Metropolitan Museum of Art in New York, which means the effectiveness of the reproduction is all the more remarkable. The performance, as it happens, is one of the best Paul Boepple has given us. A British presentation under Jacques (10" L LS 128) pales by comparison. Though done in English translation, it will mean no more than this one to those who do not understand the German.

Oratorios

Christmas Oratorio. Weber, s; Fischer, c; Marten, t; Gunther, bs; DAC & O; CPA, Thomas, OL 50001/2/3 [3].

Using, we are told, a 220-voice student choir and orchestra, Thomas gives a workmanlike performance of this masterpiece, better reproduced than were Grischkat (Remington R 199–118 [4] and Grossmann (Vox PL 7713 [3]). Interpretatively, Thomas stands somewhere between the leisurely pace of the one and the business-like stride of the other. But his is an uncompromising beat; and the cutting of an occasional *da capo* does not keep the work from seeming long. Lore Fischer gives a nice account of the lovely *"Schlafe, mein Liebster."* The crucial trumpets and horns stand out well in the ensemble, but not without experiencing the usual perils. This, then, is the best of three recordings of *Weihnachts Oratorium,* though not a really satisfactory one.

Easter Oratorio. Dutoit, s; Nussbaumer, c; Gruber, t; Wiener, bs; VKC; PRCO, Grossmann, Vox PL 8620. Weis-Osborn, s; Rössl-Majdan, c; Equiluz, t; Berry, bs; VKC; VCO, Prohaska, BG 507.

The more recent recording here is in all respects an improvement on the first. Whereas the Prohaska performance gives the impression of being more spirited, it is also less carefully rehearsed than Grossmann's. If Prohaska takes almost invariably brisker tempos, the result is a loss of clarity, sometimes an out-and-out scramble. And whereas the Bach Guild reproduction is more powerful, Vox's is equally clean. The soloists, as a group, show better in the newer version. Chief among them is the tenor, for it is his to sing the very beautiful *"Sanfte soll mein Todeskummer,"* with its undulating accompaniment including two recorders. Equiluz has about all he can manage in getting the notes; Gruber is definitely more satisfactory. Dutoit, too, makes more of her big aria than does Weis-Osborn. Between the two contraltos there is less to choose; Nussbaumer is certainly not far behind the always admirable Rössl-Majdan.

Passions

Saint John. Rathauscher, s; Hofstaetter, c; Gruber, t; Kreutzberger, t;

Berry, bs; Heppe, bs; Uhl, bs; Buchsbaum, bs; VKC; VSY, Gross-mann, Vox PL 6550 [3]. (In English) Addison, s; Thebom, m-s; Stern, t; Chabay, t; Harrell, b; Matthen, bs; SC; RCAO, Shaw, V LM 6103 [3]. Weber, s; Plate, c; Hess, t; Gümmer, bs; DKFC; CMFO, Thomas, OL 50023/4/5 [3].

The first recording of the complete *Johannespassion*, directed by Grossmann, set a standard which still holds after the release of the third. The choruses are clean and impressive, the orchestra on the whole satisfactory. Of the soloists, I like especially the rich, smooth, even singing of the contralto, Elfriede Hofstaetter, and I cannot but admire the delivery of the light-voiced Ferry Gruber as the Evangelist. Kreutzberger is admirable in the tenor arias, and all the basses are well above the average, particularly the warm, agile Walter Berry. In fact, the virtues of the performance are so patent that it is difficult to describe them. As for the weaknesses, they are more easily summed up: everything is a little too businesslike. The tempos are on the fast side; the transition from one section to another is always handled with such dispatch that the listener has hardly time to readjust. Consequently, the whole performance does not mean enough. For all that, it means more than the recording conducted by Kurt Thomas. The forces here get off to a leisurely start, the orchestra playing with more precision than Grossmann's, but with less light and shade. The chorus enters almost apologetically with its outcry of "Lord, our Master!" and continues through the first tremendous number without much evidence of enthusiasm. I do not think the soloists should be blamed for catching this spirit too. The individual voices are good, but one feels they could do more with their arias. For the Shaw performance there is a special public, as it is sung to the conductor's own new English adaptation. The timing in this set is generally more leisurely than Grossmann's, and the presentation as a whole is less exciting. The Victor reproduction, too, is less clear than the Vox. Some overloading, possibly caused by too close proximity of the microphones, affects the chorus from time to time, and also one or two of the soloists. Blake Stern does fine work as the Evangelist, and Leslie Chabay well meets the challenge of the not-too-grateful arias. Mack Harrell sings the words of Jesus impressively, and Blanche Thebom is admirable in her big aria. A bargain-price recording conducted by Gottfried Preinfalk presents excerpts (Remington R 199–78) with varying effect. The best thing in the performance is Rössl-Majdan's *"Es ist vollbracht."*

Saint Matthew. Laszlo, s; Rössl-Majdan, c; Munteanu, t; Cuenod, t; Rehfuss, bs; Standen, bs; etc.; VKC; VSO, Scherchen, W WAL 401 [4]. Dutoit, s; Nussbaumer, c; Majkut, t; Equiluz, t; Kreutzberger, t; Buchsbaum, bs; Wiener, bs; etc.; VKC; VCO, Grossmann, Vox PL 8283 [3]. (In English) Marshall, s; Morrison, s; Stilwell, c; Johnson, t; Lamond, t; Milligan, b; etc.; TMC; TORO, MacMillan, V LCB 6101 [3].

The relative merits of the two German performances are such that I do not feel a clear-cut decision between them possible. Grossmann's is certainly the more orthodox, the less erratic, if you will, the less likely to arouse objections. But Scherchen's is the more stimulating, for even where he seems farthest from the musical truth, he is never dull, and one feels he could offer justification. Possibly he takes some of the numbers very fast to avoid consciousness of the work's total length, and in this he is successful. Still, it is not easy to adjust to the opening chorus at quite this clip, and surely the solos *"Buss und Reu"* and *"Blute nur"* (to name but two) are too fast for the singers to make much of the text. The soloists are a more attractive group than Grossmann's, with special honors going to Cuenod as the Evangelist and to Rehfuss singing the words of Jesus. Grossmann's are more modest; again the Evangelist—Majkut—is the best. An earlier recording of Fritz Lehmann (Vox PL 6074 [4]) was not too satisfactory (it was taken from a broadcast), though it too was lent distinction by the tenor in the narrative role, this time Helmut Krebs.

MacMillan's version is intended for a different public, and should not, therefore, be judged by the same standards. This is the way one would hope to hear the work from a local group, sung in English so that all its hearers may understand. The chorus and orchestra are excellent, and the conductor's pacing is generally convincing and practical. Everything is on a large and festival-like scale. Among the soloists, Lois Marshall stands out, with a lovely clear voice, and simple, tasteful style; Edward Johnson (not to be confused with the former General Manager of the Metropolitan Opera) is a satisfactory Evangelist, though his voice is a little thin in the upper reaches; the others are adequate. Margaret Stilwell would be an exceptional contralto were it not that her tone-production interferes with her diction. There are some cuts in the score.

A great disappointment was the performance of Mengelberg, a recording of his last annual Palm Sunday presentation in Amsterdam in 1939. Despite some good singing from the soloists (including the exceptional soprano Jo Vincent and the celebrated veteran Evangelist, Karl Erb) the conductor's tempos are impossibly erratic (C SL 179 [3]). A single disc contains the extended choral sections and the chorales beautifully performed by the Danish State Radio Chorus and Orchestra under Mogens Wöldike (HS HSL 2070). For as much of the music as it offers, this is the best of the records under discussion here.

Arias

Cantata No. 12—Kreuz und Krone sind verbunden; Cantata No. 81— Jesus schläft, was soll ich hoffen; Cantata No. 112—Zum reinen Wasser; Christmas Oratorio—Bereite dich, Zion; Saint Matthew Passion—Erbarme dich, mein Gott. Anderson, c; RCAO, Shaw, V LCT 1111 (*"Great Songs of Faith").

Marian Anderson has chosen some beautiful and little-known arias, and she is in her most expressive voice. The nobility of the music seems to have awakened a special fervor in the singer. The program on the reverse, "Great Songs of Faith," made up of standard oratorio arias, contains a performance in English of *"Es ist vollbracht"* from the *Saint John Passion.*

Cantata No. 68—Mein gläubiges Herze; Cantata No. 159—Es ist vollbracht; Cantata No. 113—Jesus nimmt die Sünder an; Cantata No. 157—Ja ja, ich halte Jesum feste; Cantata No. 185—Sei bemüht in dieser Zeit; Cantata No. 99—Wenn des Kreuzes Bitterkeiten. BAG, Scheide, 10" MGM E 115.

The Bach Aria Group, capable singers and instrumentalists all, worked long and intensively together to achieve a perfect accord and balance. The results are smooth and polished; all that is wanting is a special spark.

Mass in B minor—Agnus Dei; Qui sedes; Magnificat—Et exultavit; Esurientes. Brice, c; CBSO, Saidenberg, C ML 4108 (*Mahler: Lieder eines fahrenden Gesellen).

Carol Brice's opulent tones are a "natural" for her selections, but the recording, made several years back, shows more promise than fulfillment.

Mass in B minor—Qui sedes; Agnus Dei; Saint Matthew Passion— Grief for sin; Saint John Passion—All is fulfilled. Ferrier, c; LPO, Boult, L LL 688 (*Handel: Arias).

In our time the traditional English contralto voice has been represented by the late Kathleen Ferrier, who was gifted at the same time with deep sincerity. Her singing of these Bach arias, therefore, may be taken to represent the best in the British traditions for this music. Yet her very ability to sustain a long phrase may occasionally have led her to overdo; the two arias from the *B minor Mass* are richer in tone quality than in vitality. *"Grief for sin"* (*"Buss und Reu"*) and *"All is fulfilled"* (*"Es ist vollbracht"*) are both a little casual.

Easter Oratorio—Saget, saget mir; Cantata No. 53—O sel'ger Tag!; Cantata No. 133—Getrost es fasst ein heil'ger Leib; Cantata No. 161 —Komm, du süsse Todesstunde; Cantata No. 21—Bäche von gesalznen Zähren; Cantata No. 46—So klage du, zerstörte Gottesstadt; Cantata No. 21—Erfreue dich, Seele; Cantata No. 104—Verbirgt mein Kirte sich zu lange. Rössl-Majdan, c; Cuenod, t; O, Gielen, Prohaska, Sternberg, BG 526.

This program is made up of selections from extended recordings. The singers are among the best engaged in this kind of work. I especially like Rössl-Majdan's *"Komm, du süsse Todesstunde"* and Cuenod's *"Bäche von gesalznen Zähren."*

Songs

Geistliche Lieder. Rössl-Majdan, c; Cuenod, t; Harand, vlc; Holetschek, hpschd, W WAL 402 [4].
Notenbüchlein der Anna Magdalena Bach—Selections. Weis-Osborn, s; Rapf, hpschd, BG 510.

Complete with miniature score reproduced from the *Bach-Gesellschaft,* Westminster offers all seventy-five of Bach's sacred songs —those he composed or arranged for Schemelli's *Gesangbuch,* and the group he included in the *Notenbüchlein,* or musical commonplace book, of his second wife, Anna Magdalena. The two singers who alternate in these miniatures are both known for their musical, clean singing as well as their unimpeachable diction. Many celebrated melodies may be traced to this source—*Komm, süsser Tod, Dir, dir, Jehova, will ich singen, O Jesulein süss*—and others perhaps less familiar but equally sublime—*Brich entzwei, mein armes Herze, Ich halte treulich still, Liebster Herr Jesu.* The order of the songs is alphabetical, which should be warning enough that they are not intended to be taken consecutively in one sitting. One song is duplicated in the Bach Guild recording announced as Vol. 1 of the *Notenbüchlein—O Ewigkeit, du Don-*

nerwort. Mostly given over to harpsichord solos, the disc includes also the favorite *Willst du dein Herz mir schenken*, purportedly the work of one Giovannini though usually included among Bach's songs. The clear-voiced soprano sings it rather deliberately. The aria *"Schlummert ein,"* better known as a part of the bass solo cantata no. 82, is very beautiful as we hear it in this recording. The other songs are *Gedenke dich* and *Bist du bei mir.*

BANCHIERI, ADRIANO (1567?-1634)

Il Festino del Giovedi Grasso avanti Cena. NYPMA, Greenberg, Es ES 516 *(Interspersed with pieces by Dalza, Frescobaldi, Banchieri, and G. Gabrieli, played on the virginals by Winogron).* LMS, Saraceni, HS AS 8 *(*Madrigals).*

The amusement many of us had from the *"Contrapuntus bestiale,"* thrice performed in the International Eisteddfod recording (W WAL 209), leads us on to this madrigal comedy from which that piece was taken. Even though the music is highly imaginative and varied, one must admit that twenty is a large number of madrigals for one sitting. This danger is averted in the first recording by the interpolation of beautifully played pieces for the virginals; in the second only nine of the madrigals are performed. Obviously, a lot of care and study went into the preparation of the New York Pro Musica Antiqua performance, and the vocal blend is unusually good, though the men somewhat overshadow the women. A feature of the ensemble is the presence of a genuine counter-tenor who fills the gap between the sopranos and the tenor. The Italian singers, of course, have the advantage of being born to the language, and they give a performance of such balanced light and shade, of so much jollity and humor, that we can only regret the incompleteness of their version. However, along with the accompanying assortment of madrigals—by Marenzio and Monteverdi, among others—their *Festino* is hard to resist.

BARAB, SEYMOUR (1921-   )

A Child's Garden of Verse. Oberlin, counter-t; Ens, Barab, 10" Es ESJ 5.

This set of twenty-four Stevenson settings was commissioned by Esoteric Records, so presumably what we have here is the world

première. The new music for the well-known texts is of the
sophisticated-naïve type; as this is not overdone, the songs
emerge amusingly enough, though the adult listener may find the
cycle a trifle long. Oberlin's light, high voice is appropriate for
the occasion, though some may feel a tendency to monotony. He
is not gifted with an instrument of many colors, but his singing is
consistently marked by musical intelligence and superb diction,
with only here and there an unmatched tone to break the flow.

BARBER, SAMUEL (1910-   )

*Dover Beach; Chamber Music, opus 10—Rain has fallen; Sleep now; I
hear an army. King, b; Hart House Str Qt; Quincy, pf, CE 1011 (*Symphony No. 1).*

>   *Dover Beach*, a setting of Matthew Arnold, is an early work,
>   dating from Barber's student days at Curtis Institute. At that
>   time the composer himself sang it for a Victor recording, which is
>   today a collectors' item. The music is still effective here, but
>   King's performance is not penetrating. The later Joyce songs
>   with piano show the direction Barber's distinctly lyrical talent
>   has taken; again one wishes for more transfiguring imagination on
>   the part of the musicianly singer. The recording is not en-
>   tirely clear.

*Knoxville, "Summer of 1915." Steber, s; Dumbarton Oaks O, Strick-
land, 10" C ML 2174 (*Four Excursions, Firkusny, pf).*

>   James Agee's autobiographical prose passage may seem a strange
>   text for a song, cantata, or whatever *Knoxville* should rightly be
>   called, but the composer is sensitive to words, and the result is
>   effective. He has, however, taken Steber to the upper reaches of
>   her range, where diction is not her strongest point. The singer
>   performs with her accustomed cool aplomb and her richest tone
>   quality. The orchestra is well balanced and clearly reproduced.

BARTÓK, BÉLA (1881-1945)

*Hungarian Folk Songs (arr. Bartók and Kodály). Chabay, t; Kozma, pf,
Bar BRS 904, 914 [2].*

*Five Songs, opus 16; Fourteen Hungarian Folk Songs. Laszlo, s;
Holetschek, pf, W WL 5283.*

*Five Songs, opus 16; Eight Hungarian Folk Songs. Valery, m-s; Goehr,
pf, 10" All 4020.*

In the early years of the present century, two young musicians spent a good deal of time gathering and arranging the folk music of their native Hungary. Not only did they open up in this way a whole world of lovely and unusual song, but they laid at the same time the very head- and cornerstones of their musical styles. The two selections from the Bartók and Kodály collections performed by Leslie Chabay and Tibor Kozma are unreservedly recommended as sensitive performances. For those who understand the language, of course, the discs are "musts." Magda Laszlo and Nina Valery offer alternative performances of Bartók's opus 16, a set of original songs not too far in style and spirit from the carefully worked-out arrangements. Laszlo is the more vital singer of the two, and her voice has never sounded better. Valery boasts a rich, smooth tone, but her performance is not notably exciting. The same may be said of their singing of the folk songs. To these non-Hungarian ears, Chabay is the most stimulating of the three artists.

BEETHOVEN, LUDWIG VAN (1770-1827)

Choral Works

Cantata on the Death of the Emperor Joseph II, opus 196a. Steingruber, s; Poell, bs; VKC; VSY, Krauss, Vox PL 6820.

This Haydnish cantata, with the inconsistently high opus number, is interesting mainly in that it was composed in Beethoven's twentieth year, and that some of the material later found its way into *Fidelio*. Considering the composer's youth, the work is impressive technically, but, to put it mildly, it hardly ranks among his greatest inspirations. Steingruber and Poell, well known as dependable artists, do their best to make the long-drawn-out arias interesting; vocally they are both in prime form. And under the authoritative guidance of Clemens Krauss, the chorus and orchestra do their considerable bit for the young Beethoven.

*Elegischer Gesang. Randolph Singers; Guilet Str Qt, CH CHS 1084 [2]. (*Haydn: Seven Last Words, Guilet Str Qt).*

This brief piece, used here as a filler for the Haydn, recalls thematically the variation tune from the "Archduke" Trio. It is simple, direct music. While one might wish the performance had a little more "curve," one is grateful for the rare opportunity to hear the work.

Mass in C. Rathauscher, s; Hofstaetter, c; Planyavsky, t; Berry, bs;
VKC; VSY, Moralt, Vox PL 6300.

After the sublime heights of the *Missa solemnis*, the simple
lyricism of this earlier Mass comes as a distinct and pleasurable
surprise. The recorded performance serves to make its qualities
known, though it leaves some of Beethoven's intentions un-
realized. Fortunately, the performers get into their stride as the
work progresses, and the *"Agnus Dei"* comes off better than the
"Kyrie." But no one would call this a highly polished presentation. Of the soloists, the tenor shows up best; his part in the
"Gloria" is one of the finer moments. The others perform with
vocal neatness, though the soprano's higher tones are not steady.
The break between sides comes, unfortunately, between *"Et
sepultus est"* and *"Et resurrexit."* The reproduction is a little
coarse, and there is a persistent hum.

Missa solemnis. Steingruber, s; Schürhoff, c; Majkut, t; Wiener, bs;
VKC; VSY, Klemperer, Vox PL 6990 [2]. Marshall, s; Merriman, m-s;
Conley, t; Hines, bs; SC; NBC, Toscanini, V LM 6013 [2].

Like the Ninth Symphony, the great Mass in D is a masterpiece
in which perfection of performance is hardly to be hoped for. That
one had expected a miracle in the Toscanini recording accounts
for a good deal of disappointment, though that set has other, more
positive factors working against it. One of the weaknesses is the
solo quartet; these singers are no more successful than most in
putting over the message given them to deliver. Nor is the quartet
balance ideal. The four individuals seem to be placed beyond the
chorus, somewhat removed from it. Toscanini's tempos are on the
brisk side, with the resulting impression of tautness and directness of purpose. There are some terrific moments, such as *"Et
resurrexit,"* and some that do not come off, as the lovely *"Benedictus,"* with its distorted violin solo. Klemperer's conception
is, in its way, on an equally lofty plane, and though its high spots
are less brilliant, its weaknesses are less fatal. The soprano
and the bass show up well, but the contralto is hefty and the
tenor thin.

The Mount of Olives (Christus am Ölberge). Opawsky, s; Delorco, t;
Berry, bs; VKC; VSO, Swoboda, CH CHS 1135.

It is interesting to hear this oratorio, source of the celebrated
"Hallelujah Chorus" (Shaw Chorale, V LM 1117), though its value
is historical rather than profoundly musical. Given a performance
by singers not to be embarrassed or dismayed by the Meyerbeerian

floridity, the work could be more effective than it is here. Chorus and orchestra fare better than the soloists. The recording balance is uneven: sometimes the effect is excellent, sometimes no more than fair.

Opera

Fidelio. Mödl, s; Jurinac, s; Windgassen, t; Schock, t; Edelmann, b; Frick, bs; Poell, bs; etc.; VSOC & O, Furtwängler, HMV ALP 1130/1/2 [3]. *H. Konetzni, s; Seefried, s; Ralf, t; Klein, t; Schoeffler, b; etc.; VSOC; VPH, Böhm, Vox PL 7793* [3]. *Bampton, s; Steber, s; Peerce, t; Laderoute, t; Janssen, b; etc.; Ch; NBC, Toscanini, LM 6025* [2].

Combining superior casting, realistic modern recording, and, by no means least, Furtwängler's skillful and penetrating direction, the HMV set is easily the best *Fidelio*. Toscanini's, though released in 1954, was actually taken from his 1944 broadcasts, and is hardly comparable, mechanically. In the Vox set the reproduction is uneven, as is also the cast. Hilde Konetzni, patently an artist and a seasoned one, has only too obviously seen younger days. The supporting cast is good; some of its members are outstanding. An earlier recording (Oc OCSL 301 [3]) might have been acceptable had it not been for the really distressing unsteadiness of the eminent soprano in the title role. Toscanini's singers are by no means ideal, though Bampton performs with impressive sincerity and Peerce gives his long aria with dramatic conviction. Janssen's Pizarro is well routined, but I miss the essential nastiness of the character. Furtwängler's cast, on the other hand, is the pick of present-day singers. Mödl, like Bampton a transposed contralto, is not always comfortable in the upper reaches of her part, but she gains in expressiveness from the extra body her voice retains; there is real drama in her singing. Windgassen is a good Florestan, though his aria wants a little more weight. Jurinac's Marzelline is the best on records, better even than Seefried's because it is more secure. Schock is a presentable Jacquino, though not quite the equal of Peter Klein; and Edelmann, in superb voice as Pizarro, does not match Schoeffler's great characterization. Furtwängler's pacing is always telling and just; the arias have drive and vitality, yet never discommode the singers. The ensembles are beautifully blended, but each voice retains its individuality.

Another recording of Leonora's great aria, *"Abscheulicher,"* by Mödl, may be of interest, for in some respects it is better sung than that in the set (10" Tel TM 68003). Christel Goltz, a fine Strauss singer, is simply not at home in this type of music (10" D DL 4058), and Astrid Varnay can be credited only with a laudable effort against an unsmooth orchestral background (including troublesome horns) (Rem 199–45). A really great performance of Florestan's aria is provided by Julius Patzak (L LLP 427).

Incidental Music

Egmont—Incidental Music.   Laszlo, s; Liewehr, speaker; VSO, Scherchen, W WL 5281.

Scherchen presents all ten pieces of incidental music written for Goethe's drama. Clärchen's two songs are beautifully sung by Magda Laszlo, *"Die Trommel gerühret"* with youthful bravado, and *"Freudvoll und leidvoll"* with simple fervor. Her voice is at its most appealing. Fred Liewehr reads the lines in the melodrama with admirable reserve; the reproduction of his voice is very natural, mercifully not overamplified. Both as a performance and as wonderfully expansive recording, this set is decidedly preferable to the older one directed by Leitner (10" D DL 7540).

Die Ruinen von Athen, opus 113. Woudt, s; Hollestelle, b; NETC & O, Goehr, CH CHS 1158.

The incidental music to Kotzebue's semi-classical drama includes the "Turkish March" and the "Chorus of Dervishes," both well known in transcriptions, but rarely heard in context. That the dramatist's imagination carried him into some strange territory may account for the neglect of the work as a whole, though certainly no one would place Beethoven's contribution among his more significant works. Here it is, in any case, reasonably well done, for the scrutiny of the Beethoven student and the edification of the musically curious.

Songs

*An die ferne Geliebte. Fischer-Dieskau, b; Moore, pf, V LHMV 1046 (*Schubert and Schumann: Songs). Schlusnus, b; Peschko, pf, D DL 9668 (*Brahms: Vier ernste Gesänge, Fischer-Dieskau).*

An die ferne Geliebte; Der Wachtelschlag; Adelaide; In questa tomba oscura; Lied aus der Ferne; Wonne der Wehmut; Ich liebe dich; Mailied; Der Kuss. Poell, bs; Graef, pf, W WL 5124.

Of six recordings of the little cycle *To the Distant Beloved*, the three listed above are easily singled out. Best of the lot is the

collaboration by Fischer-Dieskau and Moore; none of the others
has the warmth and tenderness of this one, the tonal softness, or
the sense of communication. These artists' approach to the music
is freer than is usual, but certainly this is justified. If the singer
has a fault, it is in the strong contrast between his *mezza voce*
and his full voice: one feels that the powerful ending of the cycle
is almost too much. There is, of course, room for differing interpretations in fine lieder-singing, and I still take pleasure in
the more impassioned performance of Schlusnus and Peschko,
coupled, strangely, with Fischer-Dieskau's Brahms. Here the expression is more outspoken, and for that reason less intense.
Poell's version is musically sensitive and admirably intelligent,
yet weighted by the voice itself, and not quite comfortable in
the upper regions. Along with the cycle, the basso sings most of
the best-known Beethoven repertory with a fine grasp of the texts
as well as the music, but all on a rather high dynamic level, and
all apparently in keys just a little above his best range. The two
tenors William Horne (10" Mer MG 15016) and Aksel Schiøtz
(C ML 4641) have the one obvious advantage of singing the songs
in the original keys, and they are partnered by the distinguished
Franz Rupp and Mieczyslaw Horszowski respectively. Yet they
are outclassed. Schiøtz is poorly recorded here, and definitely
not in his best form. Elena Nikolaidi (C ML 4628), combining the
cycle with the *Gellert-Lieder* listed below, is, with her heavy
contralto, definitely miscast.
Since writing the above, I have heard the British edition of
Fischer-Dieskau's recording (HMV ALP 1066), on which the cycle
is coupled with Schubert's five Heine songs, three of which are
included in the program as listed above. Although one gets considerably less for more money in buying British, the tonal qualities of the recording are improved, perhaps because less has been
crowded onto the disc.

*Gellert-Lieder; Adelaide; Mailied; Wonne der Wehmut; Neue Liebe,
neues Leben. Herbert, b; Waldman, pf, 10" All 4022.*
*Gellert-Lieder; An die ferne Geliebte. Nikolaidi, c; Behr, pf, C ML
4628 (*Schubert: Songs).*

The six sacred songs to poems by Gellert may properly be considered a cycle, though the most famous of them, *"Die Ehre
Gottes aus der Natur,"* is frequently sung by itself. Nikolaidi is
more at home here than in the *Ferne Geliebte* songs, though she
is hampered in her diction by a rather mouthy production. A more

satisfactory performance is that of Ralph Herbert; on the reverse
of the disc, the five other songs are sung with exemplary taste,
though the baritone's voice is on the heavy side for such light
pieces as *"Mailied"* and *"Neue Liebe, neues Leben."* The
tessitura of *"Adelaide"* is not altogether comfortable for him, and
some of the higher tones slip out of line. *"Wonne der Wehmut"*
is his best offering.

*Andenken; Ich liebe dich; Mailied; Nur wer die Sehnsucht kennt; Wonne
der Wehmut; Kennst du das Land?; Der Kuss. Glaz, m-s; Mueller, pf,
MGM E 3012 (*Brahms: Zigeunerlieder).*

Glaz gives us the best of the miscellaneous song recitals here
listed. Her approach is gratefully simple, her singing always
cleanly expressive, though occasionally just a suggestion of a
flutter comes into the voice. Hers are certainly the best *"Ich
liebe dich," "Mailied,"* and *"Wonne der Wehmut"* currently
available; also the very fine *"Kennst du das Land?"* and the almost too cute *"Der Kuss"* are excellently done. The recording
has an empty-hall effect.

*Irish and Scottish Songs: Robin Adair; The lovely lass of Inverness;
Sad and luckless was the season; Sally in our alley; The soldier; Oh
harp of Erin; Charley is my darling; Oh might I but my Patrick love;
Faithful Johnny; Auld lang syne. Traubel, s; Bos, pf; Pennington,
vln; Evans, vlc, 10" C ML 2085.*

Among the curiosities of the Beethoven repertoire are the arrangements he made on commission, for voice with piano trio, of Scottish, Irish, and Welsh folk songs. Traubel offers a representative
selection in rather staid concert-platform style. It is amusing,
however, to hear what Beethoven did by way of arranging such
familiar tunes as *"Sally in our alley," "The minstrel boy,"* and
"Auld lang syne."

BELLINI, VINCENZO (1801 - 1835)

*Norma. Callas, s; Stignani, m-s; Filippeschi, t; Rossi-Lemeni, bs;
etc.; SCAC & O, Serafin, An 3517-C [3]. Cigna, s; Stignani, m-s;
Breviario, t; Pasero, bs; etc.; EIARC & O, Gui, Cet 1204 [3].*

Perhaps the most eagerly awaited of recent operatic recordings,
the Callas *Norma* may be set down as a decided success. Once
again the hand of Serafin at the helm is a major asset. The tone
of the orchestra, clean and bright in the overture, sets the standard of recording quality. Throughout the opera, the pacing is

judicious and vital, the phrasing exemplary, the accentuation subtly right. In the first scene, *"Dell' aura tua profetica"* gains new dignity from being just a mite slow by usual standards. The big disappointment in the set is Rossi-Lemeni, whose pitch is, to say the least, uncertain. He affords another demonstration of the fact that "modern" training is not sufficient for the music of Bellini; his voice lacks richness. Filippeschi proves to be one of the better current tenors, perhaps the most satisfactory who could have been engaged for the role of Pollione. Obviously he has worked hard to achieve a vocal line unusual in our day, and he avoids the pitfalls of emotionalism. Stignani's voice is remarkably fresh and vibrant; she ascends the heights for the most part with ease and fluency. As for Callas, I know of no contemporary soprano who could match her achievement. In the first recitative there seems to be something not quite right in the microphone placement, for the voice has a veiled quality, but this is overcome in the *"Casta diva."* The noble cavatina is sung with real insight and with a vocal poise that I find altogether electrifying. She has a subtle way of turning her phrases, of managing her *portamento*, and of employing the *messa di voce* which holds the ear fascinated. She is not, to be sure, perfection. When she touches the high tones lightly, they float with indescribable magic; occasionally when she strikes them more heavily, the tone loses its purity and inclines to flutter. Unfortunately, this happens in the last act, at the very climax of the drama: her pronouncement *"Son io"* just misses its full effect. But hers is a Norma with stature, marked by distinguished singing. Not since the days of Ponselle and Telva (whose *"Mira, o Norma"* is available on V LCT 1004) have I heard the duets so beautifully sung.

The older recording, which still holds its interest for admirers of Gina Cigna, sounds remarkably well, considering that it dates from the thirties. Indeed, this is one of the rare cases in which a recording seemed actually improved by transfer to LP. The popular soprano has the right kind of voice, if not all the art required for the difficult title role (her *"Casta diva"* is poor) and at her best she is impressive. Stignani is again a splendid Adalgisa, and the rich-voiced Pasero is a satisfactory Oroveso. But Breviario is indeterminate as to pitch. Eterna takes us farther back into operatic history with a set of highlights (Et 706). Mario Gilion, one of the lesser-known artists on the roster, reveals a powerful voice, with the ringing high tones requisite to the first-act tenor aria. Boninsegna's is one of the finest of all *"Casta divas,"* and a virtually complete one, comprising two stanzas and *cabaletta.* Russ and Guerrini sing admirably together two duets, but not *"Mira, o Norma."* Luppi's *"Ah! del Tebro,"* piano-accompanied, is the most primitive recording on the list, but the voice is big and beautiful. The tempered tones of the soprano Amerighi-Rutili come as a pleasant novelty for most of us, and Zenatello, for the little he does in the duet *"In mia man,"* is excellent as usual. The rest are at home in their assignments— Mazzoleni, Oldrati, and Righetti—but their singing is less striking. The dubbing from the acoustical originals is satisfactory.

I Puritani. Callas, s; di Stefano, t; Panerai, b; Rossi-Lemeni, bs; etc.; SCAC & O, Serafin, An 3502-C [3].

The versatility of Maria Callas serves to remind us that a century ago there existed no such strong lines of demarcation as we know between "dramatic" and "coloratura" sopranos. In those days every soprano was expected to be both; that today it is remarkable for one young singer to step easily from *Gioconda* to *Puritani,* from *Tosca* to *Lucia,* is merely a commentary on the mutability of the times. Callas's treatment of the florid passages is interesting in itself; her aim is expression rather than brilliance. The voice is always flexible, if not dazzling, in the rapid scales and arpeggios; lyrical parts are sung in tones sometimes as melting as Ponselle's. Best of all, she does not load Bellini's melodies with passionate sobs, but lets the very tone of her voice convey her emotion. She is fortunate in her tenor partner, for di Stefano reveals a dramatic power and ease in the cruel *tessitura* of his part which few contemporary tenors could approach. If once or twice his phrasing falls below his own best standard, we can readily forgive him. Panerai is a serviceable baritone, and Rossi-Lemeni makes up in characterization what his voice lacks in sensuousness. Over all of them one senses the master hand of Serafin, who keeps the performance wonderfully vital and meaningful. The reproduction is very fine indeed, though I noted some variation in the volume level.

To recapture something of the glamour that once surrounded this opera, Eterna has assembled a set of "Highlights" from the so-called "golden age." Outstanding is Selma Kurz in *"Qui la voce"* and *"Vien diletto"*; her vocalization is at once lyrical and brilliant. Fernando de Lucia gives *"A te, o cara"* in the grand old manner, and Mattia Battistini is heard in *"Ah! per sempre"* and *"Bel sogno beato."* Others represented are Amato, Luppi,

Pasini, and Gherlinzoni (Et 486). For some strange reason, there is an encore from *Sonnambula*—Amina's two last-act airs—nicely sung by Finzi-Magrini.

La Sonnambula. Pagliughi, s; Tagliavini, t; Siepi, bs; RIC & O, Capuana, Cet 1240 [3].

The recipe for success with this slight but charmingly melodious opera is just such a cast as this. Pagliughi is one of the few remaining examples of the old-school *soprano leggiero*, a worthy disciple of Tetrazzini. Her voice as here recorded may not have all the brilliance it once possessed, but on the lyrical side she has a melting charm often missing in singers of her category. Tagliavini is just the type for the simple hero of the piece, though one wishes he would depend less on lachrymose expression. Siepi is dignified and rich in voice, but he too might rely more on sheer vocalism for his characterization. The balance in this set is particularly good.

BENEVOLI, ORAZIO (1605-1672)

Festmesse für 53 Stimmen; St. Ruperti Hymnus. Four Solo Quartets; SACC; VSY, Messner, Ep LC 3035.

Since its *première* at the consecration of Salzburg Cathedral on September 25, 1628, this amazing Mass, with its fifty-three vocal parts, has been only an example in the history books, until the performance in 1952, on which occasion this recording was made. "It should be made quite clear," says the annotator, "that in a recording the physical size of numbers cannot produce the same overwhelming effect it does in a live performance." Indeed, it is not surprising that a good deal of perspective has been lost. Still, with all the diffuseness resultant from recording in the Cathedral, and the occasional echo, the effect is decidedly good. The many soloists include such singers as Ilona Steingruber and Otto Wiener. The curiously square-cut hymn that completes the second side is of similar quality.

BERG, ALBAN (1885-1935)

Operas

Lulu. Steingruber, s; Kmentt, t; Wiener, bs; etc.; VSY, Häfner, C SL 121 [3].

The interest aroused by the *Wozzeck* performances in New York, and the recording, is undoubtedly accountable for the follow-up by Columbia with *Lulu,* the opera left unfinished at Berg's death. This is strong meat for most listeners, but there is a flourishing band to whom the Freudian plot of the opera and its Schoenbergian twelve-tone music would seem a nourishing diet. That melody so unsmoothly written for the voice can be made to sound so well is a tribute to the skill of the excellent singers, above all the super-excellent Ilona Steingruber.

Wozzeck.   Farrell, s; Harrell, b; etc.; SCNY; NYPH, Mitropoulos, C SL 118 [2].

Wozzeck—Selections.   Ribla, s; PHO, Ormandy, 10" C ML 2140 (*Schoenberg: Gurrelieder—Waldtaube).   Boerner, s; JSO, Janssen, 10" Art 500.

The complete *Wozzeck* perpetuates a performance that created a considerable stir in New York, demonstrating how the very difficult opera of Schoenberg's outstanding pupil could be effectively sung, and paving the way for the subsequent stage performances at the City Center.   The cast, carefully picked and trained by Mitropoulos, could hardly be bettered, and the recording leaves little to be desired mechanically. The two sets of excerpts cover a good deal of the same ground, presenting a healthy portion of the music allotted to Marie. Boerner won a well-deserved prize when her recording was new; it took courage at that time to record the little-known and not generally attractive music, but that was several years ago. Ribla, also an outstanding interpreter of the moderns, has the advantage of later, more lifelike reproduction.

Songs

Seven Songs of Youth (1905–1907); Two Unedited Songs (1900, 1926); An Leukon (1908). Beardslee, s; Monod, pf. Four Songs, opus 2. Joachim, s; CHAM, Leibowitz. Dia 15. (*Four Pieces for Clarinet and Piano).

Four Songs, opus 2; Seven Early Songs. C. Rowe, s; Tupas, pf, Ly LL 13 (*Sonata for Piano, opus 1; Four Pieces for Clarinet and Piano). Der Wein. Boerner, s; JSO, Janssen, 10" Cap L 8150.

The first disc is a complete edition of Berg's songs, which, it will be noted, are not numerous enough to fill even two sides. The second is sheer duplication, so far as the vocal music is concerned. Outstanding among the performers is Irene Joachim, whose contribution won her a prize when it was released in France. Beardslee, too, is a singer of attractive voice and fine musicianship, specializing in the taxing works of the moderns. Against such competition, Rowe is at a disadvantage. The romantic early songs are essential to a study of Berg's development, and they are pleasing enough to interest the lieder specialist. The two unpublished settings of the same poem, twenty-six years apart, are particularly valuable. *Der Wein*, a concert aria dating from 1929, is a setting of Stefan Georg's translation from Baudelaire. It may be used as an introduction to the Schoenbergian twelve-tone system, especially as the reverse side of the disc is given over to an analytical discussion by Alfred Frankenstein. Boerner, a gifted and experienced singer, is well recorded.

BERLIOZ, HECTOR (1803-1869)

Choral Works

La Damnation de Faust. Danco, s; Poleri, t; Singher, b; Gramm, bs; HRC; BSO, Munch, V LM 6114 [3]. *Laurena, m-s; Jouatte, t; Cabanel, b; Pactat, bs; PC; RP, Fournet, C SL 110* [3].

The Boston recording, made in Symphony Hall on February 21-2, 1954, may very well be Charles Munch's masterpiece. One searches in vain for superlatives to describe the playing of his orchestra, whether in the rousing "Rakoczy March," the delicate "Ballet of the Sylphs," or the blood-curling "Ride to Hell." Again one remembers that sour chord so superbly snarled before the "Song of the Flea," the orchestral detail brought out in the accompaniment to that song, and the recurring bass figure under the "Love Duet." The chorus seems to be having the time of its life. One detail that stands out in memory is the hissing of the name Méphisto in the Infernal Regions. The soloists, though not all ideally fitted by nature for the assignments they carry, surpass themselves in the realization of the score. Poleri, on whom so much of the burden falls, was chosen obviously for the amplitude and good quality of his voice, despite the fact that his French is a little below par. This is not so much a matter of pronunciation, for he shows careful schooling in this as well as in the subtleties of his music; but the text does not come out to meet you as it does whenever Singher begins to sing. The baritone is in unusually good form, though one wishes his gifts of sheer voice had been more generous. He is no more successful than most in sustaining the smooth *legato* Berlioz calls for in *"Voici des roses"* (one remembers the old Plançon record), but he is more than satisfactory in the more flippant moments: the *"Chanson de la Puce"* and the sardonic *"Sérénade."* Danco is another artist of the French school, and she too makes the words count. Vocally she is admirable, though I suspected as I listened that Berlioz knew what he wanted when he called for a real mezzo-soprano. The notes are all there, and they are good, but the singer bears a little heavily on her voice to get them. And in his short role, Donald Gramm stands up to his colleagues. He could give Poleri a lesson in French diction. It would not be quite accurate to call the balance in this set natural, for the effects achieved are the kind of which a conductor (and presumably a composer) dreams, but which are impossible in a concert hall. Poleri, for example, without straining a muscle, can make his voice stand out over the chorus. The older recording is in no sense a rival for the new; mechanically it is killed at the first blow. In its favor are the impeccable French diction of Jouatte (whose vocal material is only a fraction of Poleri's) and of Cabanel (who has several times Singher's resources). Laurena has the right range for Marguerite, and she sings smoothly, but Danco the artist has the stronger appeal.

L'Enfance du Christ. Bouvier, c; Giraudeau, t; Noguéra, b; etc.; RSPC; PCO, Cluytens, Vox PL 7120 [2]. *Davenport, c; Simoneau, t; Singher, b; Gramm, bs; CAS; LOS, Scherman, C SL 199* [2].

The American release of the Vox recording, several years back, may, I think, be fairly credited with arousing belated interest in this tender and reverent work, though the pastoral chorus known as "Farewell of the Shepherds" has long been known in our choir lofts (Shaw Chorale, V LM 1117). Thomas Scherman's annual performance has now become an event of the New York season, which in turn accounts for the Columbia recording. Even when the Vox set was new, its shortcomings were obvious. The reproduction was noted as strangely uneven, with the vocal parts sounding spacious and churchly, while the orchestral sections had the quality associated with studio recording. Some of the soloists seemed too close upon us, and one wished for an occasional *piano,* not to mention a *pianissimo.* In all such respects the more recent Columbia recording is a decided improvement, but for the qualities of performance Vox stands unchallenged.

Scherman's choir and orchestra are good, but the conductor is obviously less in his element than Cluytens. Singher stands out among the soloists, for his authentic style and superb diction, though he is not a real bass and he transposes a couple of low tones. Simoneau is right for the music, too, by virtue of background and schooling, and his voice is brighter than that of Giraudeau in the Vox set. He seems to be somewhat hampered, however, by the staying hand of the conductor. Donald Gramm stands up well in this company, but Mary Davenport is handicapped by the kind of production that strives for vocal richness at the expense of clear diction. Her inadequacy is emphasized by a fresh hearing of Bouvier in the Vox set. In a word, the spirit of Vox is willing, and the flesh of Columbia is all too strong.

Lélio. Charpak, speaker; Kerol, t; Bacquier, b; NPSC & O, Leibowitz, Vox PL 8250.

Lélio, or The Return to Life is labeled by the composer a *"mélo-logue,"* or lyric monodrama; it contains a little of everything in three languages. The thread of the basic thought is spun by the Narrator (here his part is very much cut) and the music parades past in various styles and guises. Opening with a setting of Goethe's ballad *Der Fischer* (in German), we proceed to choruses (one with piano duo), orchestral pieces, and finally a long fantasy on Shakespeare's *Tempest*, for chorus and orchestra. The setting of Goethe is bold and a bit ungainly, so that it is perhaps wrong to blame the tenor for being unable to make it seem natural or easy. He has the high tones needed, but he sings them and all else at a high dynamic level. Such a line as *"Repose, cette tête charmante"* comes strangely from him. The recording is reasonably good, though the choral parts seem overloaded.

Requiem. Jouatte, t; PC; RPO, Fournet, C SL 159 [2].

This wartime recording was considered something of a masterpiece in its day. But the music, with its enormous forces, choirs and orchestras distributed in the galleries around a huge church, is just the kind most difficult to capture even with the latest techniques; a good deal of perspective was bound to be lost in the best efforts of a decade or so ago. Still, the performance as we hear it does not lack a strong sense of the grandeur of Berlioz's conception, and the transfer to LP is far from unsuccessful. Under the auspices of the Berlioz Society a new recording of the *Requiem* will soon be released.

Te Deum. Young, t; Dulwich College Boys C; LPC; RPO, Beecham, C ML 4897.

This huge work is scored for three choirs, organ, and orchestra. For his ideal, Berlioz specified "some hundred strings, the usual winds in proportion, two choruses of one hundred singers each, plus a third of six hundred boys." Sir Thomas Beecham, who has made the *Te Deum* his own, settles for less, but succeeds in making an exceedingly joyful noise. For magnificent clarity in the tremendous mass of sound, there have been few recordings to match this one. To point just one example, the *crescendo* leading up to the cymbal crash at *"Pleni sunt coeli"* is breathtaking in impact. The sound of the organ, too, is wonderfully full and lifelike; for once it is almost perfectly in tune with the orchestra. This is not the kind of music in which it is easy to follow the text (and Berlioz has been free to change the order of its lines); indeed, for the most part the glorious choral tone might as well be totally divorced from words. But this matters little, as we are carried along by music that flows like a great river. One flaw, it seems to me, is in the placement of the excellent tenor soloist; his voice is very close upon us. When he sings, of course, the text comes through clearly enough.

Operas

Les Troyens à Carthage. Mandikian, s; Collard, c; Giraudeau, t; etc.; EVP; PCO, Scherchen, W WAL 304 [3].

That this famous score—the second part of Berlioz's two-day opera *Les Troyens*—is so little known must be due to the difficulties of finding singers with adequate mastery of the classic style quite as much as to the hugeness of the composer's conception. A professed admirer of Gluck and Beethoven, Berlioz expected the same kind of nobility called for by his great predecessors. It was a courageous undertaking to bring the score to life for us, and we cannot but be grateful to Westminster. And in all fairness I ought to add that the performance possesses considerable impressiveness, due to the comprehension and vitality of Scherchen's conducting. The singers, however, achieve the necessary distinction of style only at times. I understand we may expect a recording of *La Prise de Troie* from the same source.

Songs

Nuits d'été. Danco, s; CIN, Johnson, L LL 407.

This is certainly one of the soprano's best discs; the interpretations have been carefully worked out, with considerable vocal variety, and a fine *rapport* with the conductor. Two songs from the cycle were previously known in recordings by Maggie Teyte, who brought to them a warmth and lilt beyond Danco, but her versions have not been issued on LP.

BIZET, GEORGES (1838-1875)

Carmen. Juyol, m-s; Micheau, s; de Luca, t; Giovanetti, b; etc.; OCC & O, Wolff, L LLAP 6 [3]. Michel, m-s; Angelici, s; Jobin, t; Dens, b; etc.; OCC & O, Cluytens, C SL 109 [3]. Stevens, m-s; Albanese, s; Peerce, t; Merrill, b; SC; RCAO, Reiner, V LM 6102 [3].

The importance of a French cast, schooled in the French traditions, for the production of a French opera, is demonstrated by these three complete *Carmens*. The Metropolitan has never made a specialty of Gallic opera, though in the past it did have a "French wing." Today the casts are only too international, as their assorted accents show. If such considerations do not bother you, it is possible you will prefer Victor's American recording to the two more authentic presentations, for certainly it has the mechanical superiority, and it rejoices in a quartet of extremely popular principals. But neither of the rival performances is too far behind in matters of reproduction, and both are excellently sung. Between the Carmens, the choice must rest on personal preference, for where Michel is the better vocalist, Juyol gives the more temperamental interpretation. Libero de Luca is my choice for Don José, Giovanetti for Toreador, though neither his voice nor Dens's has the natural beauty of Merrill's. Angelici's Micaela is easily the most appealing of the three, and she is the most convincing member of the Columbia cast. Columbia's version is given with the original spoken dialogue; Victor's and London's both use the recitatives added by Guiraud after Bizet's death. The palm for conducting must go to the veteran Albert Wolff, though Reiner's is very brilliant.

Although Conchita Supervia died as long ago as 1935, she left many realistic and representative recordings behind her, enough from *Carmen* to make a regular "highlights" set (D DL 9522). The peculiar brassy voice of this singer fascinated multitudes during her brilliant career, and it continues to do so. As Irving Kolodin says in the jacket notes for this disc, Supervia "from her birth ... was destined to sing Carmen." Here is her characterization in all its fullness, perhaps the most Spanish of all Carmens—more Spanish, indeed, than Bizet could make his heroine. The recording is still effective. Jennie Tourel also gives us the principal arias (C ML 4608) with full-blown tone and admirable intelligence. She is well seconded by Morel's orchestra and splendid reproduction; but hers is not a Carmen to "send" you. Other "highlight" sets present Stevens and Jobin (C ML 4013) or Swarthout, Albanese, and Vinay (V LM 1007).

Les Pêcheurs de perles. Dobbs, s; Seri, t; Borthayre, b; etc.; PPC & O, Leibowitz, Ren SX 205 [3].

Bizet's best-known pre-*Carmen* opera is given a fairly good showing here. Mattiwilda Dobbs, an American, has a voice of great promise and some solid achievement. At its best it is lovely and clear, though sometimes in this recording it slips out of line and loses quality. Seri has more than a suggestion of the Italian background his name indicates, though he does not possess the floating tone needed for *"Je crois entendre encore."* He is better in his big duet with Borthayre, whose singing is always effective, if too consistently loud. Perhaps the engineers are to blame for a general lack of shading throughout the performance. The balance is good, however, and the acoustical effect quite spacious.

BLOCH, ERNEST (1880-   )

Sacred Service (Avodath Hakodesh). Rothmüller, b; etc; LPC & O, Bloch, L LLP 123.

Bloch is said to consider this service his masterpiece. In it he has striven to rise above the racialism associated with his musical style, and to speak not simply to his own people, but to all men. It is logical, then, that in making the recording in London he should have chosen to use an English text so that he might be understood by more of his hearers. The performance is altogether admirable. Marko Rothmüller, who as Cantor carries the brunt of the singing, uses his rich and expressive voice with sincere dignity. Here and there a loud tone may lose some of its velvet, but this is only occasional. It would seem that he has been placed rather too near to the microphone, for the balance is not quite perfect, but this does not detract greatly from the fine general effect. Chorus and orchestra are excellent, and the two female soloists are adequate.

BLOW, JOHN (1648/9 - 1708)

Ode on the Death of Mr. Henry Purcell. NYPMA, Greenberg, Es ES 519 (*Purcell: Songs and Instrumental Pieces).

This affecting memorial to Purcell, composed by his teacher to a text by Dryden, is very rarely performed, perhaps because genuine counter-tenors are not plentiful, and this score calls for two of them. Messrs. Oberlin and Bressler are fully equal to the occasion, and the performance is quite delightful. The former makes the most of the long elaborate solo comprising the middle section of the piece. My one reservation is that the whole seems a bit hurried.

Venus and Adonis. Ritchie, s; Field-Hyde, s; Clinton, t; OLE, Lewis, OL 50004.

Incredible as it may seem, here is an English opera older than *Dido and Aeneas* (generally considered to be the first) and one that prefigures not only the music, but the dramatic situations of Purcell's masterpiece. The passage *"Hark! hark! the hunter"* and the argument that follows it are clearly echoed in *Dido*, and the threnody at the very end prepares the way for *"With drooping wings."* The death scene is exceedingly beautiful, worthy to stand beside its great successor. The performance has nice spirit and understanding throughout. One wonders why the harpsichord continuo, usually active, is omitted from the dances, but this is a detail. The voices are mostly modest, with only Margaret Ritchie sounding like a full-blown professional. The reproduction is mostly good, though the higher voices are not altogether clear in some spots.

BOÏTO, ARRIGO (1842 - 1918)

Mefistofele. Neri, bs; Noli, s; dall'Argine, s; Poggi, t; etc.; MIOC & O, Capuana, U URLP 230 [3]. De Angelis, bs; Favero, s; Arangi-Lombardi, s; Melandri, t; etc.; SCAC & O, Molajoli, C EL 9 [3].

Boïto's masterpiece has always been an opera to stand or fall by its protagonist. Neri is one of the best of his type at present active in Italy, an artist with a fine strong voice, though hardly a striking personality like the great Mefistofeles of other days: Chaliapin, Didur, Journet, Plançon, etc. The supporting cast is for the most part good, though Poggi's rather hoarse Faust is just about passable. Fortunately, he has his better moments, one of them being the touching duet *"Lontano, lontano."* Noli is a sweet and appealing Margherita. In the Helen of Troy scene, some good singing by dall'Argine and Ticozzi is marred by too close recording. The boys' choir adds its special touch to the Prologue. The breaks between sides are not always fortunate. A well-known Mefistofele of a generation ago is represented in Columbia's reissued set. Nazareno de Angelis, no longer young at the time of recording, carries the performance on his broad shoulders. Favero is a fine Margherita, but Arangi-Lombardi's Elena and Melandri's Faust help little in lifting the general level of the singing above routine. Naturally the once-impressive recording is no match for Urania's.

Nerone—Highlights. Lombardi, s; Agozzino, m-s; Pertile, t; Pollicino, t; Stabile, b; Journet, bs; Ronchi, bs. Et 704.

Boïto's posthumous opera remained in his workshop for nearly fifty years, becoming a legend and a mystery in the composer's lifetime. After a sumptuous production under Toscanini in 1924, the work quickly became a legend again, with only a few recordings left to dispel the mystery. The collection here assembled includes scenes interpreted by two of the "creators"—Pertile and Journet—and others, including the distinguished Mariano Stabile. The records give us an adequate idea of the vocal style of the score, but one can hardly judge the opera without more of the orchestration than could possibly be caught by the recording equipment of 1924. The transfer to LP is reasonably successful.

BORODIN, ALEXANDER (1833-1887)

Prince Igor. Smolenskaya, s; Lemeshev, t; Ivanov, b; Pirogov, bs; Reizen, bs; etc.; GABT & O, USSR, Melik-Pashayev, Per SPL 552 [3].

When this set arrived, it seemed about the best of the operas to come to us from the USSR; it remains one of the better ones. Outstanding among the singers are the tenor Lemeshev, the smooth baritone Ivanov, and the somewhat Chaliapinesque Pirogov, though the cast also includes the celebrated Mark Reizen. The general level is good—better, as usual, among the men than the women. The reproduction has the common fault of favoring the singers, but is otherwise excellent.

BOWLES, PAUL (1911-   )

*Scènes d'Anabase (1932). Hess, t; Marx, oboe; Masselos, pf, C ML 4845 (*Music for a Farce; Dello Joio: Variations).*

> Set to poems by St.-Jean Perse, the *Scènes d'Anabase* sport a mixed musical ancestry, amusingly accounted for in the composer's explanatory notes. They are not what one would call "grateful" songs for the voice, but Hess delivers them in good direct style.

BRAGA, ERNANI (1898-   )

*Folk Songs of Brazil. Sayão, s; Charnley, pf, C ML 4154 (*Sayão Recital).*

> Braga's arrangements of these simple songs are unobtrusive, yet artful enough to lift them out of the field of folklore. Sayão's singing is likewise decidedly of the concert hall; the best features of her delicate art are shown to advantage. She spins a lovely lyric line, floats her small but telling voice over the high phrases, and then, on occasion, adopts the manner of a *diseuse*. The recording of the piano is on the weak side.

BRAHMS, JOHANNES (1833-1897)

Choral Works

Ein deutsches Requiem. Schwarzkopf, s; Hotter, bs; MFC; VPH, Karajan, C SL 157 [2]. *Steber, s; Pease, b; SC; RCAO, Shaw, V LM 6004* [2].

> The choice here is clean-cut, depending entirely on the relative importance one places on stylistic distinction and technical perfection. Years were spent, we are told, preparing the Shaw Chorale for the ordeal of recording, and no effort was spared to capture their performance with complete faithfulness. Though the recording is no longer new, we still listen to the result with profound admiration. Karajan's forces do not remotely approach the precision of the Chorale; yet for all the ragged attacks, the occasional lack of bite in the orchestral tone, and the sometimes overloaded recording, we snap off the motor at the conclusion of this performance in the full conviction that we have been listening to Brahms, and that his very personal message of comfort and

consolation is a powerful one indeed. A word should be added in praise of Elisabeth Schwarzkopf, the only completely satisfying soloist in either set.

*Der Abend; Nächstens; Zum Schluss. SC; 2 pfs, Shaw, V LM 1784 (*Schubert: Mass in G; Bach: Motet—Komm, Jesu, komm).*

*Gesang der Parzen; Nänie. VKC; VSY, Swoboda, W WL 5081 (*Strauss: Wanderers Sturmlied).*

Marienlieder; Four Songs for Women's Voices with Two Horns and Harp. VKC, Schmid, W WL 5014.

*Nachtwache, I & II; Letztes Glück; Im Herbst. BAVRC & O, Kugler, 10" Mer MG 15011 (*Verdi: Stabat Mater).*

The three choruses offered by Shaw are in that conductor's best manner, especially the first. The singing and the playing of the two pianists have the proper surge and swell; the most is made of the climaxes. *The Song of the Fates* and *Nänie,* opus 82 and opus 98 respectively, are conceded to rank among Brahms's finest; one wishes the recording were better. The listener is too conscious of the conductor's steady beat in the first work, somewhat less so in the second. One or two of the *Marienlieder* occasionally find their way into the American church-choir repertory, but the seven songs that comprise the cycle are little known as a group. The texts are from German folk poetry, just the kind of thing to draw out Brahms at his most Brahmsian. The women's choruses seem, if possible, even more characteristic. The group includes a setting of *"Come away, death"* (in German) and a song from Ossian. The singing on this disc is competent rather than inspired. The effect, especially in the *Marienlieder,* is marred by some too vibrant tones that fail to achieve a perfect blend. Nevertheless, the music itself is enough worth having to minimize these objections. Less satisfactory is the work of the Bavarian Radio Choir, which sounds as though rehearsing such familiar music were no longer considered necessary. I suspect all their attention went into preparing the better presentation of the Verdi on the reverse.

Liebeslieder Walzer, opus 52; Neue Liebeslieder Walzer, opus 65. Hassler, s; Plümacher, c; Weikenmeier, t; Kelch, bs; Michael & Priegnitz, pfs, Oc OCS 28.

Liebeslieder Walzer, opus 52; German Folk Songs (arr. Brahms). RWC, Wagner, Cap P 8176.

The Oceanic recording, made in Stuttgart, is performed in the proper spirit, and with the solo quartet the music calls for. The voices are pleasant and the pianos properly exuberant in this bit of vocal chamber music; there is a nice feeling of intimacy. If the performance does not reach the level of an earlier Viennese one of opus 52, rare in this country, issued at 78 rpm only by English Columbia (with Seefried, Höngen, Meyer-Welfing and Hotter), it is the best released since. The Roger Wagner Chorale follows a custom, prevalent in this country, of turning the quartet into a chorus.

*Rhapsody. Ferrier, c; LPC & O, Krauss, L LL 903 (*Songs). Anderson, c; SC; RCAO, Reiner, V LM 1146 (*Mahler: Kindertotenlieder). Höngen, c; BCS; BPH, Leitner, 10" D DL 4074 (*Zigeunerlieder).*

The completely satisfactory *Alto Rhapsody* recording is still to be made. Ferrier might have done it, had she lived a little longer; a second try was said to have been on her agenda. As it is, we must be grateful to London for transferring her older effort to LP, for it is, taken all around, the best yet made of this music. The noble voice is magnificent throughout, the patent sincerity apparent in every measure. One feels only that time would have mellowed the artist's conception of the work. By all standards, the performance is too slow, and it is to the credit of the singer and the late Clemens Krauss that it does not fall apart. So far, Marian Anderson has had three tries at the *Rhapsody*, and where she has done herself justice in one recording seems always to be the spot that comes off less well in another. The first, prewar, version, with Ormandy and the Philadelphia Orchestra, was naturally the freshest vocally; the second, with Monteux and the San Francisco, the best integrated, though the singer was caught short in some of the longer phrases; the third and at present only available performance is the best recorded, but does the artist least credit. Höngen has not the vocal steadiness and solidity to make a really successful *Rhapsody*, despite her admirable intentions. Perhaps the old recording by Sigrid Onegin would be worth resurrecting in Victor's Treasury series.

Rinaldo. Kerol, t; NPSC; PAS, Leibowitz, Vox PL 8180.

Brahms's excursion into the operatic style is not a sure-fire masterpiece. If it is to prove itself, it needs a better performance than it gets here. The solo tenor, who carries the chief burden, sings in the constricted German manner, and is none too secure in matters of intonation. I found little pleasure in listening to his struggles. Nor does Leibowitz show the ability to suffuse the score with light and to curve the melodic lines, the criterion of the great Brahms conductor. On the whole, the reproduction is satisfactory, though it is not of the most impressive range; the choral tone lacks brilliance.

*Schicksalslied. Stanford U Ch; SFS, Monteux, 10" V LM 149 (*Bach-Respighi: Passacaglia and Fugue). Westminster Ch; NYPH, Walter, C SL 156 [2] (*Beethoven: Symphony No. 9).*

Both performances are sung in English. In the San Francisco version the text is quite unintelligible; in that from New York one is not thankful for what one can catch of so undistinguished a translation. Neither chorus acquits itself with outstanding success. The New York orchestra is superior to the San Francisco, but Monteux gives the more penetrating reading of the work. Columbia's recording is a wartime job; Victor's is better, inevitably, as it is later.

Songs

*Vier ernste Gesänge. Fischer-Dieskau, b; Klust, pf, D DL 9668 (*Beethoven: An die ferne Geliebte, Schlusnus). Symonette, bs; Masiello, pf, Col CLPS 1002 (*Schubert: Songs). Ligeti, bs; Berens, pf, ML MLR 7025 (*Kerpel, Zador, Kodály: Hungarian Songs). Warfield, b; Herz, pf, C ML 4860 (*Schumann: Liederkreis). Ferrier, c; Newmark, pf, L LL 271 (*Schumann: Frauenliebe und Leben); (Brahms only) 10" L LD 9097. Traubel, s; Bos, pf, 10" C ML 2072 (*Sapphische Ode; Die Mainacht; Der Schmied; Wie Melodien zieht es mir).*

Brahms's last four songs are settings of somber texts from the Bible and the Apocrypha. Although the composer's intentions as to performance were made clear enough by his writing of the vocal line in the bass clef, the cycle seems more often than not to be appropriated by contraltos. In this connection, however, it should be remembered that Brahms, according to Coenraad Bos, commended the second singer to present the songs in public, despite the fact that he had deliberately disregarded the composer's dynamic markings. I am sure, therefore, that Brahms would not have disapproved the singing of these songs by so richly endowed, so musicianly, and so deeply sincere an artist as the late Kathleen Ferrier, and I think he would have found something to admire in the performance of Helen Traubel, whose valued collaborator is the same Bos who played the first two public performances, in the presence of Brahms himself. In the latter case, however, we must deplore the poorly balanced recording, in which the important piano part is sadly overshadowed by Traubel's majestic tones. Four recordings are available in the more appropriate male voice. Symonette and Ligeti are both big of tone, solid and musicianly. Both are taxed by a high note or two, but both are satisfactory. The gifted William Warfield somehow misses fire in this cycle. His voice is easily produced, but lacking in intensity, and the recording allows him to overbalance the piano quite unduly. The last song is the best of the four in his performance. All three bass-baritones are overshadowed by Fischer-Dieskau. In this day of so much "good" singing, it takes such an artist to remind us what it means to penetrate to the inner message of a song. This recording is not among his latest, though he is still very young, but it easily outclasses competition. In the other songs that make up Traubel's program, the balance is again too much in the soprano's favor. The tone quality is at its opulent best, showing the unusual richness of her lower register; she sings the songs in their original keys. Stylistically, her *"Sapphische Ode"* is one of the best on records, for she observes the composer's *alla breve* indication, and she does not sentimentalize. Both here and in *"Die Mainacht,"* she is able to meet the demands of the long phrases.

*Wir wandelten; Vorüber; Mein wundes Herz verlangt; Der Tod, das ist die kühle Nacht; Lerchengesang; Immer leiser wird mein Schlummer; An eine Äolsharfe; Wiegenlied. Berger, s; Raucheisen, pf, D DL 9666 (*Strauss: Songs).*

Erna Berger has done nothing finer than this recital; her voice is at its cool and polished best, her art simple, direct, and profoundly musical. At least two of her songs, *"Vorüber"* and *"Mein wundes Herz verlangt,"* seem to be first recordings; *"An eine Äolsharfe"* is new to LP, and surely it has not been done so well before at any speed.

*Die Mainacht; Wiegenlied; Ständchen; Wir wandelten; Meine Liebe is grün. Danco, s; Agosti, pf, 10" L LPS 335 (*Wolf: Songs).*

Danco is one of the few singers of the French school (she is Belgian by birth) whose German lieder are stylistically and linguistically successful; in whatever she does, her musical taste is beyond cavil. She is not a prober of depths; but the songs she offers are distinguished by the cool finish of her crystalline tones. Sometimes her tempos seem overdeliberate.

*Wiegenlied; Die Sonne scheint nicht mehr; Da unten im Thale; Feinsliebchen, du sollst mir nicht barfuss gehn; Schwesterlein; Vergebliches Ständchen; Sandmännchen; Mädchenlied; Dort in den Weiden; In stiller Nacht. Felbermayer, s; Graef, pf, Van VRS 446 (*Dvorák: Zigeunermelodien).*

This recital is entitled "Songs in Folk Style," and it includes the first LP selection of the folk-song arrangements, along with four songs conceived in a more or less similar manner. The soprano's limpid tone, her warm but never aggressive style, are especially well fitted to these miniatures. I liked best *"Die Sonne scheint nicht mehr"* and *"Feinsliebchen, du sollst"*: in the latter the conversation is well brought out. I always feel that something similar should be done with *"Da unten im Thale,"* though most singers treat it as a straight "unhappy love" song. More could be made of *"In stiller Nacht"* (one remembers the broad *legato* of the old Gerhardt recording) and *"Vergebliches Ständchen,"* though in the latter I blame the pianist rather than the singer. But, in this song it is better that the case be under- than overstated.

*Viola Songs; Sapphische Ode; Botschaft. Ferrier, c; Gilbert, vla; Spurr, pf, L LL 903 (*Rhapsody).*

*Viola Songs; Nachtigall; Des Liebsten Schwur. Sydney, m-s; Morawetz, vla; Loibner, pf, Van VRS 411 (*Schumann: Liederkreis).*

The lamented Kathleen Ferrier sings the two songs with viola, *"Gestillte Sehnsucht"* and *"Geistliches Wiegenlied,"* very beautifully, but her well-phrased *"Sapphische Ode"* is too slow for my taste, and her *"Botschaft"* is earthbound. For all that, the final line of the *"Ode"* is hauntingly lovely. Lorna Sydney's good intentions in the viola songs and two encores are marred by her persistent tremolo.

*Zigeunerlieder; Nicht mehr zu dir zu gehen; Wehe, so willst du mich wieder. Glaz, m-s; Mueller, pf, MGM E 3012 (*Beethoven: Songs).*

*Zigeunerlieder. Höngen, c; Raucheisen, pf, 10" D DL 4074 (*Rhapsody).*

Herta Glaz's performances are admirably spirited. The voice is attractive, though moderate in size; her record is among the best Brahms recitals, despite poor balance with the piano. True, there are some loose ends in the singing, and the control is not complete, but Glaz gets life into her interpretation of the *Zigeuner-lieder*, and she shows good understanding of the other songs. The reproduction suggests a large, empty hall. Considerably less successful are the same *Gypsy Songs* as Höngen sings them. The voice is encumbered by overweight production; it is too unsteady to serve as a proper vehicle for these colorful lieder.

Der Gang zum Liebchen; Sonntag; Salamander; Nachtwandler; Bei dir sind meine Gedanken; Alte Liebe; Beim Abschied. Herbert, b; Wald-man, pf. Duets: Die Nonne und der Ritter; Vor der Thür; Es rauschet das Wasser; Der Jäger und sein Liebchen. Liss, c; Herbert, b; Wald-man, pf, 10" All AL 4021.

Ralph Herbert's singing is always intelligent and well in tradi-tion, though he uses a good deal of not too comfortable-sounding *mezza voce*. His partner in the duets suffers from a quick *vibrato*, and the piano part is not well reproduced.

Alte Liebe, Sonntag; Mädchenlied; Von ewiger Liebe; Der Gang zum Liebchen; Nicht mehr zu dir zu gehen; Der Kranz; Immer leiser wird mein Schlummer; Botschaft; Wenn du nur zuweilen lächelst; Auf dem Kirchhofe; Dort in den Weiden; An die Nachtigall; Salamander. How-land, m-s; Ulanowsky, pf, Str STR 610.

Here is a nicely balanced selection of popular and neglected lieder. If the singing is a little clouded in production, it is al-ways musicianly. But the real feature of the disc is the magnifi-cent piano-playing of Paul Ulanowsky. What such an artist can do with the shifting rhythmic patterns of *"Botschaft"* should be a lesson to all who aspire to accompany.

In Waldeseinsamkeit; Der Überläufer; Komm' bald; Bei dir sind meine Gedanken; Auf dem See; Frühlingslied. Marten, t; Theopold, pf, 10" Mer MG 15016 (*Beethoven: An die ferne Geliebte, Horne).

The one tenor on our Brahms list gives us some otherwise un-explored repertory, notably the touching *"Komm' bald,"* but un-fortunately brings no particular vocal distinction to the songs. The voice is of the stiff German school, unyielding, wanting in warmth and tenderness. To emphasize all this, it overbalances the piano.

Auf dem Kirchhofe; O wüsst' ich doch den Weg Zurück; Unbewegte, laue Luft; Feldeinsamkeit; Sapphische Ode; Nachtigall; Dein blaues Auge; Die Mainacht; Der Gang zum Liebchen; Minnelied; Botschaft; Ständchen; O liebliche Wangen; Tambourliedchen; Sonntag. Poell, bs; Graef, pf, W WL 5053.

The excellent Viennese bass-baritone is less happy here than in

others of his recordings. Despite his earnestness, he does not
succeed in communicating much. The tone quality is on the dark
side, the diction not sufficiently forward, and he does not find
all the high tones easy.

*Die Trauernde; Volkslied (Die Schwälble ziehet fort); Feinsliebchen,
du sollst mir nicht barfuss gehn; Schwesterlein; In stiller Nacht;
Vergebliches Ständchen. Seefried, s; Werba, pf, D DL 9743 (*Wolf:
Songs).*

For a pendant to her collection of twenty-two of Wolf's "Italian
Songs," Seefried provides a group of *Volks-* and *Volkstümliche
Lieder*, similar to Felbermayer's selection listed above. Her
first two songs are not otherwise available; all are sung in pure
style and in the soprano's clearest tones.

BRITTEN, BENJAMIN (1913-   )

Choral Works

*A Ceremony of Carols. CBC; Simon, harp; Britten, 10" L LD 9102.
Morriston Boys Ch; Korschinska, harp; Sims, 10" L LPS 57. SC;
Newell, harp; Shaw, V LM 1088 (*Poulenc: Mass).
A Ceremony of Carols; Te Deum in C; Hymn to St. Cecilia. WCC;
WCHC, Callaway, WCFM 11.*

Except for the plain chant *Hodie Christus natus est*, with which
the piece begins and ends in processional and recessional, the
Ceremony consists entirely of Britten's original settings of lovely
old English poetry. The means used are of the simplest: high
voices and a single harp. Among the various performances, the
honors go easily to the Danish boys, who never cease to astonish
by their musical sensitivity and by their mastery of the English
language. The composer has not made it easy for any choir to
put all the words over, but the boys from Copenhagen do it better
than most. One detail from the Morriston boys' performance stands
out in my memory: the almost pagan exultation of their shouts of
"*Deo gratias.*" If the Danes don't match this, they more than
make it up with their lovely "*As dew in Aprille*" and the melting
solo singing of "*That yongë child.*" For those who do not care
for boys' singing, the ladies of the Shaw Chorale provide a
notably smooth and polished performance. I have put off mention
of the Washington presentation, for its value lies chiefly in the
other interesting choral works it carries. In the carols, the American boys must yield to both the English and Danes.

*Rejoice in the Lamb.   Nat Presby Ch, Schaefer, WCFM 4 (*Kodály: Missa brevis).*

   Rejoice in the Lamb is a heart-warming piece, a setting from the *Jubilate agno* of the eccentric poet Christopher Smart (1722–71), whose piety was his undoing.   The composer has ingeniously and unobtrusively seconded the affecting text.   Discounting some little interference in the softer passages, the reproduction is very fine.

Songs

*Les Illuminations.   Pears, t; NEW, Goossens, L LL 994 (*Serenade). Krebs, t; RBO, Rother, U URLP 7104 (*Schillings: Glockenlieder). Mock, s; La Jolla SO, Sokoloff, Alc 1211 (*Martinů: Sinfonietta La Jolla).*

   This British setting of the French poet Rimbaud is masterfully sung by Britten's "official" interpreter.   If the German Helmut Krebs lacks Pears's absolute note of authority, his voice is an unusually fine one, and he too has obviously penetrated the score. His vocal range permits him to take the lower and preferred notes where the composer has allowed an alternative, whereas Pears sticks to the higher.   In the third (and oldest) recording, Alice Mock sings musically and rather confidentially in a sweet, modest voice.   It is necessary to follow the score to get the benefit of her diction, but she negotiates the florid passages effectively. The reproduction is best on the London disc.

*On This Island (Song Cycle); Fish in the unruffled lakes; Mother comfort; Underneath the abject willow.   Troxell, s; Kozma, pf, WCFM 15 (*Hindemith: Songs).*

   The cycle, and the song "*Fish in the unruffled lakes,*" are set to poetry of Auden, for which the composer is said to feel a particular affinity.   The other numbers are duets, here skillfully done, as if by mirrors, with Troxell's voice in both parts.   There will be differences of opinion as to the value of this recital, for the composer (with a genuine interest in the writing of songs) likes to torture the words on occasion, so that it is not always easy to follow them.   The point is emphasized when we turn the record over and remark the masterly treatment by Hindemith of an adopted language.   The soprano finds no terrors in either set of songs, delivering their difficult lines with handsome round tone and impressive assurance.

Serenade.   Pears, t; Brain, hrn; NEW, Goossens, L LL 994 (*Les Illuminations).

Serenade.   Lloyd, t; Stagliano, hrn; BSO STR, Burgin. Folk Songs of the British Isles: The Sally Gardens; Little Sir William; The trees grow so high; The ash grove; Oliver Cromwell; Come you not from Newcastle; Sweet Polly Oliver; O waly, waly. Willauer, s; Lloyd, t; Schanzer, pf. Bos B 205.

The *Serenade* was written for Peter Pears and Dennis Brain; their new recording replaces the pre-LP that did so much to make the work known in this country. If the composer's conducting lent a certain interest to the older version, there is compensation in the superior skill and experience of Eugene Goossens. The singing is well up to the old standard, but something goes wrong in Brain's playing of the Prologue. The high spot of the performance is the "Lyte Wake Dirge," with its cumulative effect so brilliantly realized by Pears. The Boston-made recording offers real competition, for David Lloyd's voice is by nature more beautiful than Pears's, and the performance leaves little to be desired. Nevertheless, one cannot escape the impression that Pears's tone quality is inevitable in this music. Lloyd is happy in his portion of the folk-song program, though Willauer fails to meet his standard in hers. The tenor's diction counts for much. "The trees grow so high" is a real *tour de force*. There is an infectious lilt in "The ash grove" as Lloyd sings it, the very thing one misses in Willauer's hasty performance of "Sweet Polly Oliver." One would hardly know this song tells a story. And "O waly, waly" has been sung more caressingly, notably in Kathleen Ferrier's English Song Recital (10" L LS 538).

BRUCKNER, ANTON (1824 - 1896)

Mass No. 3, in F minor.   Siebert, s; Herrmann, c; Majkut, t; Wiener, bs; VKC; VAO, Grossmann, Vox PL 7940.

Of the lineage of Beethoven's *Missa solemnis*, this elaborate and intense Mass has many passages of imaginative power, as well as monumental movements, such as the big fugue *"In gloria Dei patris,"* which seem almost more than mortal singers could possibly bring off. This performance gives us at least a fair idea of the stature of the work. The chorus is generally proficient, and is recorded with clarity, if not much in the way of atmosphere.

The soloists have been well placed, so that their voices stand out without overwhelming the chorus. The quartet is a good one, though I thought the tenor a bit below his own best standard.

*Psalm 150; Psalm 112. Ceska, s; VKC; VSY, Swoboda, W WL 5055/6 [2] (*Symphony No. 6).*

*Te Deum. Cunitz, s; Pitzinger, c; Fehenberger, t; Hann, bs; MRSC & O, Jochum, D DX 109 [3] (*Symphony No. 8). Holeschowsky, s; Elsta, c; Fehenberger, t; Hann, bs; SFC & O, Messner, 10" Fes FLP 101.*

The two Psalms show Bruckner first full of age and experience, then in his young maturity. The 150th poses difficulties for the singers which have not been fully overcome, but it is a grand conception, and well deserves a hearing. The 112th, with its younger blood, comes off more easily. The reproduction is excellent. The two *Te Deums*, sharing the same tenor and bass soloists, are in striking contrast. That made in Salzburg is an actual-performance recording, complete with coughs and other extraneous noises, and not well balanced. The singing, too, is ragged. It has, however, a certain rough honesty I miss in the more precise and finished Munich performance.

BUXTEHUDE, DIETRICH (1637-1707)

*Alles was ihr tut; Magnificat (five voices). Augenstein, s; Plümacher, c; von Rohr, bs; SCS; SSO, Grischkat, Ren X 30 (*Magnificat noni toni, organ).*

Perhaps the feature of the cantata *Alles was ihr tut*, and of the recording, is the choral aria *"Dir, dir, Höchster, dir alleine,"* one of those wonderful old melodies which will not let you alone, here very beautifully sung. Another recording of the cantata, made in Bavaria, is a stodgy affair, as well forgotten (Mer MG 10086). The balance of the Stuttgart chorus and orchestra is exceptional, but there is an imperfection on the *Magnificat* side.

Erbarm dich mein, O Herre Gott; Führwahr, er trug unsere Krankheit. Guilleaume, s; Luehr, bs; HMFC; HBA, Bechert. Befiehl dem Engel, dass er komm'. HMFC; HBA, Bechert, Vox PL 7430.

Schaffe in mir, Gott, ein rein' Herz; O Clemens, O Mitis, O Coelestis Pater; Herr, wenn ich nur dich hab'; Ich sprach in meinem Herzen; Also hat Gott die Welt geliebt. Guilleaume, s; HBA, Bechert, Vox PL 7330.

Ich bin die Auferstehung und das Leben; Ich bin eine Blume zu Saron;

Mein Herz ist bereit. Müller, bs; Stuttgart O, Grischkat. O Lux beata Trinitas. Guilleaume, s; Groth, s; HBA, Bechert, Vox PL 7620.

Guilleaume is the bright particular star of this section: her voice is very lovely, her style a delight, not only in her five solo cantatas, but in her contributions to the other works. Though really a high soprano, she seems surprisingly comfortable in her part of *Erbarm dich mein*, where the composer has kept her lingering in the lower regions. Her bass partner, Luehr, is a good singer, if hardly an exciting one. *Führwahr* is less successful, but for this I blame the conductor; the performance is on the heavy side. Again, the strictly choral *Befiehl dem Engel* is rather tamely done. Müller sings his three cantatas (the composer's entire output for the bass voice) in good solid style. *Ich bin eine Blume zu Saron* is the finest of them. The singer seems too close to the microphone. But the feature of this disc, after all, is the duet for two sopranos, who, incidentally, are better placed; with them we have a sense of space, as though they are singing in a church.

Herr, auf dich traue ich; Singet dem Herrn. Boatwright, s. Lauda Sion salvatorem; Jesu, meine Freude. St Thomas Ch, New Haven, Boatwright, Ov Over 6.

O Gottes Stadt; O fröhliche Stunden; Singet dem Herrn; Also hat Gott die Welt geliebt. Neway, s; Ens, All 3085.

The first record is certainly the most satisfying of all the Buxtehude offerings. Helen Boatwright's voice is a strikingly pure, clear high soprano, just the kind of voice, indeed, for her two solo cantatas. She is happily placed at enough distance from the microphone to give some of the atmosphere of the church in which the recording was made. The two choruses on the second side, under the direction of Howard Boatwright, are major experiences; they are performed with electrifying effect by healthy and enthusiastic young voices. *Jesu, meine Freude*, a magnificent motet in itself, and especially interesting when compared with the famous Bach work on the same chorale, was formerly available in an acceptable organ-accompanied performance in English by the choir of the National Presbyterian Church (Den DR 2). Needless to say, that recording is now more than replaced. Patricia Neway is at a considerable disadvantage after the Boatwright performance of *Singet dem Herrn*. One applauds her enterprise rather than her achievement. The balance in her recording is strange, to say the least; the orchestra is apparently very much with us, but the soprano seems to be singing in a large empty room next door.

Missa brevis; In Te, Domine, speravi; Aperite mihi portas justitiae; Jesu dulcis memoria. Hastings Ch, Bath, All ALG 3035.

These performances are disappointing. Both the *Missa* and *Aperite* have been better recorded, though not on LP.

BYRD, WILLIAM (1542/3-1623)

The Great Service. WCHC, Callaway, Van VRS 453.

William Byrd, a Roman Catholic, wrote music for the Anglican Church as well as the Masses listed below. The "Great" service consists of seven numbers: *Venite, Te Deum, Benedictus, Kyrie, Creed, Magnificat* and *Nunc dimittis*. The settings are elaborate, with plenty of word repetition, drawing on Byrd's seemingly infinite contrapuntal resources. The choir sings with admirable clarity and excellent intonation, bringing out such salient points as the voice-leading at the end of the *Te Deum*—"Let me never be confounded"—the passage for two altos in the *Creed*—"came down from heaven"—the involved contrapuntal web in the *Magnificat* at "He hath scattered the proud," and many more. The voices, to be sure, are just a little vibrant: an English group, with the characteristic "flat" tone-production, would blend more perfectly, and at certain spots the singing seems a little tentative. But this is wonderful music well done.

Mass for Three Voices; Mass for Four Voices. CHSL, Bath, All 3005.
Mass for Four Voices; Mass for Five Voices. PMA, Cape, EMS 234.
FSC, Lawrence, L LL 888.

Here are three contrasting approaches to the performance of Byrd's Masses. The older tradition is represented by the late T. B. Lawrence's Fleet Street Choir, with its stronger contrasts, its subtler, more artful shading, its long-sustained moods. Safford Cape, conductor of the Pro Musica Antiqua, in his full and informative notes (the back of the jacket is supplemented by a leaflet) explains his "conviction...that no variation of tempo between the different movements of the Masses was intended by Byrd.... Slowness or quickness was obtained by using slow or quick notes, and not by slowing or quickening the basic tempi...."
He tells us, too, that as the Masses were written by the devout composer at a time when the Roman Catholic Church in England had to function modestly underground, the use of one voice to a part is probably closest to Byrd's own practice. What he does not

clarify is the distribution of parts: the four-voice Mass is sung by alto, two tenors, and bass. Fellowes, in his edition of the works of Byrd, transposes the Mass down a tone; Cape takes it down another minor third. Favoring a middle course between Lawrence and Cape are John Bath and his Choral Society of London. His is a small group, though larger than Cape's, and he is neither so rich in contrasts as the one nor so strict as the other. Each performance is proficient according to its aims; the student will find comparisons extremely instructive. One peculiarity of the Fleet Street group is the use of academic Latin pronunciation rather than that generally favored in church. Lawrence, it seems, felt that the effect was thus made more forceful. Originally issued on ten-inch discs, the four-voice Mass suffered from a rearrangement in the order of its movements, while the five-voice work was broken in mid-Credo. Happily these flaws have been eliminated.

CAMBINI, GIOVANNI GIUSEPPE (1746-1825)

Andromaque (Cantata).   *Tyler, s; ICO, Jenkins, HS 76 (*Pergolesi: Orfeo; Galuppi: Overture No. 2).*

This performance is better described as expressive than as tonally satisfying. The soprano's voice is not sensuous, and it is marred by a persistent flutter. A good deal of the French text is obscured by this defect.

CANTELOUBE, JOSEPH (1879-)

Chants d'Auvergne. Grey, s; O, Cohen, C ML 4459 (*Weill and Emanuel: Songs at School). Reed, s; Ens, C ML 4368 (*Folk Songs). Swarthout, m-s; RCAO, Morel, V LM 1156 (*French Operatic Arias).

To collectors in the thirties, the name of Madeleine Grey and the *Songs of the Auvergne* were practically synonymous. Her recording of a selection of Canteloube's elaborate folk-song arrangements was one of those rare cases where the right artist had found the right music. Word got around slowly, and the three 78-rpm discs, dropped from the Columbia catalogue, had to be restored by popular demand. They have survived the LP revolution, and indeed they carry their years remarkably well. The performance is unquestionably definitive. Susan Reed, a folk singer, has studied the Grey recordings, has learned the dialect and absorbed some of the proper style. The orchestra has been cleverly reduced to a chamber ensemble, not without some loss in local color. Swarthout brings more vocal richness to the songs, but she is less simple and straight than Reed, and certainly less penetrating than Grey. From her disc, however, we can hear the full orchestra in up-to-date recording. The selection of songs is largely the same with all three, though Grey sings eleven and Reed eight (including one not duplicated) while Swarthout gives us only six.

CAREY, HENRY (ca. 1687-1743)

*True Blue, or The Press Gang. IOS, 10" L LPS 293 (*Anon.: The Dustcart Cantata; Hook: The Musical Courtship).*

The humor and the tunes of this tiny nautical skit (by the composer of *"Sally in our alley"* and possibly *"God save the King"*) are as British as Gilbert and Sullivan or *The Beggar's Opera*. The Intimate Opera Society is notable for style and wit rather than for voices, which is as right as can be for this type of music. The playfulness of the anonymous *Dustcart Cantata* is even less subtle than that of its companion pieces.

CARISSIMI, GIACOMO (1605-1674)

*Jepthe. Vivante, s; Penno, t; E. Arie, bs; etc.; AC & O, Gerelli, Vox PL 6100 (*Marcello: Beato l'Uomo).*
*Jonas. Vivante, s; Malipiero, t; Ferrein, bs; etc.; AC & O, Gerelli, Vox PL 7180 (*Vivaldi: Stabat Mater).*

It is good to have the "father of oratorio" represented by two interesting scores. The more beautiful of them is *Jepthe*, a work that will stand in any company. *Jonas*, too, has its points, one outstanding moment being that in which the whale disgorges its passenger. The performances, by competent opera singers, are Italianate, but reasonably restrained. The orchestra sounds right enough, though it may have been somewhat augmented (no full score has been available for checking). The atmosphere suggests that the recordings may have been made in a church.

CAVALLI, FRANCESCO (1602-1676)

Il Giudizio Universale. Rossi, s; Salvi, m-s; Besma, t; Gaggi, bs; etc.; RSQC & O, Nucci, Col CLPS 1032.

A long-forgotten and notably attractive oratorio comes to us by way of the Vatican Radio. If we accept the piano playing the continuo part and a little raggedness here and there, the performance is satisfactory.

CHABRIER, EMMANUEL (1841-1894)

*Ode à la musique; Le Roi malgré lui—Sextuor des serves; Chanson tzigane. Micheau, s; BC; PCO, Fournier, L LL 639 (*Debussy: La Damoiselle élue).*

These brief pieces are not of great moment musically, but they have a certain charm as well as novelty. They are handsomely performed.

*Les Cigales; Ballade des gros dindons; Villanelle des petits canards; L'île heureuse. Jansen, b; Bonneau, pf, L LL 644 (*Debussy, Ravel: Songs).*

At the least, this recording presents the four most celebrated songs of Chabrier in one package, along with two cycles by Debussy and one by Ravel. No other recording singer has done as much for Chabrier. Jansen's singing is clean and true, a little over-careful, which is hardly the ideal approach to the drollery of the *"Ballade des gros dindons."* Singher has included this little masterpiece and the *"Villanelle des petits canards"* in his French song recital (C ML 4258), and Bernac, with Poulenc at the piano, offers *"L'île heureuse"* and the *"Villanelle"* (C ML 4484). None of the three baritones, when these recordings were made, had much to offer by way of sheer vocal charm.

CHARPENTIER, GUSTAVE (1860-   )

Louise. Vallin, s; Thill, t; Pernet, bs; etc.; RC & O, Bigot, C EL 7 [2].

The reissue of this old-timer is justified by the fact that no other *Louise* is available (even here we do not have more than a sampling of the score) and that it was made under the composer's supervision. It is important, too, in that it presents three of the finest recent French singers in their heydays. Surely it is not necessary to add details in praising the well-known principals. Unfortunately, the loss in transfer to LP has been considerable, not only in brilliance and liveness, but even in the singers' intonation. Something is gone from the tone, and in its place we have a certain tubbiness. Anyone owning the old set will think at least twice before exchanging it for this one.

CHARPENTIER, MARC-ANTOINE (1634-1704)

Choral Works

Magnificat in D; Offertory; Sub tuum praesidium; Plorans, ploravit; Regina Coeli; Salve Regina. Collart, s; Melchior, c; Archimbaud, male-s; Gianotti, t; Noguéra, bs; JMC; PASC, Martini, HS HSL 102.

This *Magnificat*, a grand work, rolls over us like a tidal wave. The effect of the chorus is finely spacious, and the soloists are happily placed in relation to the microphone. The instrumental *Offertory* is full of striking contrasts, and the pieces for solo voices are beautifully sung. Outstanding, to my mind, is *Plorans, ploravit* (first Tenebrae Lesson for Wednesday in Holy Week) in the rich contralto of Yvonne Melchior. But the crown of the program is the *Salve Regina*, with its three choirs building up climax after climax. The impact of this is indescribable. We are informed in the program notes that some transcription has been necessary to accommodate Charpentier's music to modern instruments.

Mass and Symphony, Assumpta est Maria. Angelici, s; Michel, c; Giraudeau, t; Noguéra, b; etc.; JMC; O, Martini, Vox PL 8440.

Charpentier, pupil of Carissimi, may have owed to the "father of the oratorio" the never irreverent dramatic sense that makes this music so poignant: for example, the contrast of the *"Crucifixus"* sung by the low voices and *"Et resurrexit"* by the high. The singing is excellent on all counts, with special honors to Angelici for her long solo at the Elevation. The organist, too, deserves a word. The churchly atmosphere is very effective, even to the reverberating echo, not sufficient to cause a serious blur.

*Midnight Mass. EVP; O, Jouvé, W WL 5287 (*Vivaldi: Gloria).*

This is, as its title suggests, a Mass for Christmas, and it is based on several old carol tunes. The organist throws in a few extra carols by way of interludes in this performance. Certainly I have never heard so gay and festive a Mass as this. The performance is appropriately jocund and most decidedly extrovert. There is not much relief from a high dynamic level, and there is some high *tessitura* to tax the soprano soloists, especially in the duet *"Quoniam."* But here is an amazing work, a fascinating one that throws a new light on the neglected genius of Charpentier.

Te Deum; Troisième Lecon de Ténèbres du Vendredi Saint; Oculi omnium in Te sperant. Collart, s; Archimbaud, male-s; Gianotti, t;

Noguéra, b; JMC; PAS, Martini, HS HSL 2065 (*Air de trompette No. 2; Marche de triomphe).

The performance of the elaborate and exalted *Te Deum* is a little disappointing. On the credit side are the singing of Collart and Noguéra, and, if one readily accepts the sound of a male soprano, M. Archimbaud. The others sing rather tentatively. Chorus and orchestra are satisfactory. One realizes in the lovely *Tenebrae* service (which recalls the briefer works of Couperin) that the problems of style and proper embellishments have not been completely solved. Nor do the soloists blend together as a fully satisfying quartet. The best work all around is in the closing Psalm. The reproduction is rather brassy, and there is a prominent echo. But after all this criticism, I commend the disc for as much as it offers of fine and little-known music.

Opera

Médée—Excerpts. Sautereau, s; Kolassi, m-s; Derenne, t; Conrad, bs; Ch & O, Boulanger, D DL 9678.

The first cause of *Médée's* non-success, we are told, is a bad case of libretto trouble. Another difficulty becomes apparent as we listen to this recording: the fact is that in performing music of the grand classic school, good intentions and a sure sense of style are not enough. The work cries out for voices of heroic caliber. Nadia Boulanger is noted for her ability to make any singer give of his best, and one feels a real authority in her conducting here. But the singers are not impressive, however earnest. Still, it should be remarked that Derenne, with the lightest voice of all, makes the most creditable impression. The score has been trimmed down to a fraction of its true size, so that while one gets an impression of the music and its style, the recording gives no idea of the work as a unit.

CHAUSSON, ERNEST (1855-1899)

Poème de l'amour et de la mer. Swarthout, m-s; RCAO, Monteux, V LM 1793 (*Song Recital). Osborne, s; Vetlesen, pf, ML MLR 7009.

This is the extended work (a symphonic song cycle, if you will) ending with the well-known *"Le Temps des lilas."* Of the two recordings, the first is easily preferable, because it uses the full orchestration. Like some of the songs of Duparc (to whom the work is dedicated), the *Poème* is too big for the piano; it needs the varied colors of the orchestra to sustain its length. Furthermore, the conductor is Monteux, and no one living is better able to reveal everything there is in such a score. In his hands the music swells and surges like the sea itself. For her part, Gladys Swarthout has been in better voice in other years, but she takes fire from the conductor's inspiration. It is possible that a little too much music has been crowded into the grooves of this record-side, for the reproduction is not quite Grade A. The rival recording is different in every respect. Of course one misses the orchestra, and this is all but fatal to the total effect. The singer, however, uses her pure, limpid voice to achieve an expressiveness subtler than Swarthout's, and she gives every evidence of long familiarity with the score and affection for it. There is no crowding here, for the cycle consumes both sides of the disc. And Music Library has given us the complete French texts of the songs, along with translation and notes, while Victor is content with an English paraphrase.

CHERUBINI, LUIGI (1760-1842)

Requiem. SCC & O, Giulini, An 35042.

This *Requiem*, the subject of impressive tributes from such notables as Beethoven, Berlioz, and Cardinal Newman, is known to us chiefly through the memory of Toscanini broadcasts; it seems odd that one of those performances was not preserved by Victor. By some freak, the first recording issued in this country was the victim of confusion with a Mass performed, apparently, at the same place: the *Requiem* was issued with labels and annotations descriptive of the Mass, while the Mass itself appeared in proper order about the same time, under a different company label. Both recordings, as it happens, are as well forgotten now. This newer disc is something else. From the brooding introduction, one feels a great reverence and the kind of atmosphere that goes with the better kind of church acoustics—though I suspect the recording actually was made in a hall. With the *"Dies irae"* come a number of thrills, especially at the terrific climax on the words *"Inter oves locum praesta."* The performing forces (there are no soloists) are so placed that the orchestra can occasionally overwhelm the chorus, which is right enough where it happens. Another out-standing moment comes with the fugue, *"Quam olim Abrahae,"* and the brief but beautiful *"Sanctus"* is masterful. The crown of it all is the *"Agnus Dei,"* with its feeling of intense yearning. On the whole this performance is very well reproduced, though some of the softer passages lose in clarity.

CHOPIN, FRÉDÉRIC (1810-1849)

Seventeen Polish Songs. Kurenko, s; Hufstader, pf, Ly LL 23. Con-rad, bs; Jackson, pf, Vox PL 8310.

Only one or two of these songs (Chopin's entire output in the field) are likely to sound familiar to most Americans, yet Mme Kurenko tells us that "...most of the elements of the composer's greatness are embodied in these works." The moods range from little mazurkas to the final intensely patriotic outburst, and, as the soprano sings them, they have plenty of variety. Hers is a penetrating artistry, and she retains a remarkably smooth and even tone. The capable pianist is somewhat overshadowed in the re-production. After the lightness of Kurenko's touch, the burly voice of Doda Conrad comes as something of a shock, especially as the program opens with *"The Maiden's Wish."* Some of the group, to be sure, suit his voice and style better than this; still the general impression is heavy, with everything in very low keys.

CILÈA, FRANCESCO (1866-1950)

Adriana Lecouvreur. Gavazzi, s; Truccato Pace, m-s; Prandelli, t; Meletti, b; etc.; RIC & O, Simonetto, Cet 1218 [3]. Favero, s; Nicolai, m-s; Filacuridi, t; Borogonovo, b; etc.; SCAC & O, del Cupolo, Col CLPS 1018/19/20 [3].

Despite the presence of Mafalda Favero as the star of Colosseum's performance, and the superiority of Elena Nicolai—to whose lot falls the big and effective aria *"O vagabonda stella"*—the Cetra version will be found the more satisfactory. Mechanically, the Colosseum is constricted in range and tubby in quality, with enough fading in and out of the voices to suggest a public performance. Gavazzi's voice is not so steady or so nicely in line as Favero's, but the latter's tone sounds shrill and thin. Truccato Pace's tone is light for the big aria, though she sings it with conviction. Prandelli and Meletti are easily superior to their counterparts. Though the volume level of the Cetra set is somewhat variable, the reproduction is on the whole satisfactory.

L'Arlesiana. Tegani, s; Oncina, t; Protti, b; Ulivi, bs; SCAC & O, del Cupolo, Col CLPS 1016/17 [2].

No score of this opera has been available to me; therefore I cannot vouch for the accuracy or completeness of the performance. The music is pervaded with that pastoral quality we know in the famous tenor "Lament," though in moments of passion it is pure *verismo*. The singing is on the whole pleasing enough, but the competent soprano inclines to shrillness. The tenor's quality recalls Tagliavini's, and this suits the character admirably. The recording is on the one hand constricted, and on the other brilliant, so that the highs have to be cut down. The second side has a pronounced hum, nowhere else disturbing.

CIMAROSA, DOMENICO (1749-1801)

Il Matrimonio Segreto. Noni, s; Simionato, m-s; Valletti, t; Bruscantini, bs; etc.; FM, M. Wolf-Ferrari, Cet 1214 [3].
Il Matrimonio Segreto—Overture and Excerpts. Ribetti, s; Blaffard, t; OCM, Gerelli. Il Maestro di Capella. Maugeri, bs; OCM, Gerelli, Vox PL 8450.
Il Maestro di Capella. Corena, bs; OPM, Amaducci, 10" L LD 9118.

The complete recording of *The Secret Marriage* was released by Cetra with some misgivings, caused by insurmountable mechanical difficulties. Admittedly, then, it is not first-rate. As a performance, it is rather competent than inspired, though the cast is an able one. There is a place for the abridged version, in any case, as most listeners will find six sides rather too much of this graceful music. The two singers are acceptable, and they blend charmingly in their duet. The companion piece, translated as *The Conductor*, pokes some rather broad fun at the music of its day. Though Maugeri sings it perceptively enough, he is outdone by Corena, probably the finest buffo of the day. The breaking of the latter performance into two ten-inch sides is the only possible cause for complaint.

COPLAND, AARON (1900-)

In the Beginning. Surian, s; San José St Col Ch, Erlendson, ML MLR 7007 (*Motets, San José).

The chorus performing this setting of the opening of *Genesis* is excellent; the soprano soloist, a student apparently, shows promise, though in a performance preserved by recording she must stand out as the weak point: much more can be made of her part. The recording is of the studio type, very clean and precise, without any suggestion of hall resonance.

Old American Songs. Warfield, b; Copland, pf, 10" C ML 2206 (*Dougherty: Sea Chanties). Symonette, bs; Harnley, pf, Col CLPS 1008 (*Symonette Recital).

Copland has set his own hall-mark on these old songs without sacrificing their essential homely character. They are a well-contrasted group; one or two of them are haunting. Curiously, though Warfield and Symonette both sing them pleasantly enough, neither brings sufficient intensity to the quieter moods. *"Long time ago,"* the smoothest and most ingratiating of the melodies, is memorable in the Warfield recording chiefly because of Copland's piano-playing. Both singers are more at home in the spirited *"Simple gifts"* and the droll *"I bought me a cat."*

CORNELIUS, PETER (1824-1874)

Weihnachtslieder. Seefried, s; Werba, pf, 10" D DL 7545 (*Seefried Recital).

Seefried is entitled to some sort of minor prize for reviving this tender, simple, lyrical Christmas cycle, and for presenting it in tones so limpid and style so right. Each of the little songs is a model of unpretentious perfection, and each is sung with that feeling of direct faith which has become so rare in our time. The pastoral *"Die Hirten"* and the reverent *"Simeon,"* with its introduction of the *Nunc dimittis*, are especially appealing in Seefried's interpretation.

COUPERIN, FRANÇOIS (1668–1733)

Leçons de Ténèbres. Cuenod, t; Sinimberghi, t; Holetschek, hpschd and org; Harand, vlc, W WL 5387.

Première Leçon de Ténèbres; Air sérieux; La Pastorelle; Les Solitaires; Audite omnes. Cuenod, t; Ens, Pinkham, All ALG 91.

Cuenod took part in the celebrated prewar recording of the third *Tenebrae* service. He is one of the very few contemporary singers with sufficient understanding of the essential style for such singing, and he has assimilated it to a point where the ornaments and the intense expression seem to be second nature to him. This performance of the third "Lesson," for two voices, is a very different matter from that referred to above, for which the work had been edited to include chorus and orchestra. Sinimberghi matches his Italian name with a style less direct than Cuenod's, but his voice is good, and the two work together excellently. The first and last "Lessons" are accompanied on the harpsichord, the second on the organ. There is a slight edge on the voice in the Westminster recording. The earlier Allegro disc is valuable for the three secular songs and the motet, though the first side, of course, is a duplication.

DARGOMIZHSKY, ALEXANDER SERGEIVITCH (1813–1869)

Russalka—Mad Scene, Act III. Reizen, bs; Nelepp, t; BSIC & O, Nebolsin, CH CHS 1302 (*Glazunov: Symphony No. 5).

This performance will bring back memories of Chaliapin and a recording he made of the scene. Reizen, indeed, has a good deal of the quality of his great predecessor, and he seems to belong to the line of outstanding Russian singing actors. The voices may be too prominent here; otherwise the excellent singing is well recorded.

DEBUSSY, CLAUDE (1862–1918)

Choral Works

La Damoiselle élue. Micheau, s; Collard, c; BC; PCO, Fournet, L LS 639 (*Chabrier: Ode à la musique; Le Roi malgré lui). Sayão, s; Nadell, c; *U of Penn Women's Ch; PHO, Ormandy, C ML 4075 (*Ravel: Concerto for Left Hand).*

Sayão, who made her American debut under Toscanini in Debussy's youthful setting of Rossetti, sings the music with sweet, expressive, pure tone and clean musical style. The choral work is notable for diction, if Nadell, as Narrator, is not—her tone is pleasant but not forward enough for the French language. More recently recorded, and more impressively reproduced, is the French performance. Micheau's touching delivery of the lines of the Damoiselle and Fournet's masterly molding of the musical phrases combine to suggest the word "definitive."

Le Martyre de St. Sébastien. Yeend, s; Kaskas, c; Stewart, s; Oklahoma Ch & O, Alessandro, All ALG 3004.

This collaboration of Debussy and the poet D'Annunzio was designed for the use of the famous dancer Ida Rubinstein. Its manner of expressing religious mysticism brought down abuse on poet and composer, and may account for the neglect the work has suffered since. Aside from a suite of "symphonic fragments," it has remained virtually unknown. The recording was one of the surprises of the year 1951. The work of chorus and orchestra was hailed as an impressive debut, and the soloists won deserved praise. The recording is among the best issued by the Allegro company before reorganization.

Opera

Pelléas et Mélisande. Joachim, s; Ben Sedira, s; Cernay, m-s; Jansen, b; Etcheverry, b; Cabanel, bs; etc.; GC; O, Désormière, V LCT 6103 [3]. Danco, s; Wend, s; Bouvier, c; Mollet, t; Rehfuss, b; Vessières, bs; etc.; SR, Ansermet, L LLA 11 [4]. (Abridged) Nespoulous, s; Croiza, m-s; Maguenat, t; Dufranne, b; Narcon, bs; O, Truc, C RL 3092.

When the Désormière recording was given American release, it was already some years old, and therefore placed in the "historical" classification. Historical indeed it is, for it represents a labor of love and patriotism produced in Paris during the occupation. But it is more than a "dedicated" performance, for the singers were all thoroughly at home in their parts, and the conductor had a special affinity for the score. The very fact that the reproduction was not an example of "High Fidelity" as we have sometimes known it to our cost seemed in its favor, for the intangible characters in this drama, and the misty atmosphere, do not take well to brilliant sunlight. After a decent interval, the second complete *Pelléas* was offered by London, with a cast in every way comparable to Victor's, in some respects even finer, and recording so clear and clean that every nuance of Ansermet's masterly reading was brought out. There is no question that Danco is gifted with more voice than Joachim, or that Ansermet's pulsating orchestra brings a thrill of a kind unknown in the older recording. Still, the Victor *Pelléas* has not lost its power to move, and there are some who still prefer its orchestral half-tints. In re-listing one of the two abridged performances that graced the prewar catalogues, Columbia has preserved at least two great characterizations: the Golaud of Dufranne, who created the role, and the Geneviève of Croiza, who read the letter as no one else I have heard. For these we must accept the outmoded recording and the rest of the sometimes no more than honorable cast.

Songs

Ariettes oubliées (C'est l'extase; Il pleure dans mon coeur; L'Ombre des arbres; Chevaux de bois; Green; Spleen); L'Échelonnement des haies; Mandoline. Cuenod, t; Blancard, pf, Van VRS 414 (*Fauré: Songs).

Cuenod devotes both sides of his disc to settings of Verlaine. The contrast between France's two leading modern song writers is the more striking because in several instances the artist has chosen both composers' settings of the same poem. The program throws a new light on Cuenod, so generally associated with music of the older schools, and a curious light it is. Surely, no one will deny the virtues of this splendidly musical and musicianly singer, nor fail to admire the ease and purity with which he enunciates the texts, at the top as well as the lower portions of his range. But the line of his singing is stiff, lacking in tenderness. Admirable as it is, it is not moving, not quite right. He is recorded with great clarity, but at rather a high level.

Trois Chansons de Bilitis (La Flûte de Pan; La Chevelure; Le Tombeau des Naïades); Fêtes galantes (En sourdine; Fantoches; Clair de lune; Les Ingénus; Le Faune; Colloque sentimental); Le Promenoir des deux amants (Auprès de cette grotte sombre; Crois mon conseil, chère Climène; Je tremble en voyant ton visage); Proses lyriques No.

2, De grève; Ballade de Villon No. 3, Ballade des femmes de Paris.
Teyte, s; Cortot, pf, V LCT 1133 (*French Songs).
Trois Chansons de Bilitis; Le Promenoir des deux amants; Ariettes
oubliées. Danco, s; Agosti, pf, 10" L LPS 336. Trois Chansons de
Bilitis. Tourel, m-s; Reeves, pf, 10" C ML 2184.

Danco, an admirable musician, has the sensitivity we miss in
Cuenod, and it is hard to think of anything wanting in her singing
unless it be an element of excitement, the impact of a vital personality. In recordings of this type, the piano often offers problems not completely solved here. Tourel also gives practically
flawless renditions of the Bilitis songs, and she is recorded with
fine clarity and good balance. Still, though Maggie Teyte's recordings are now quite old, hers remains the classic performance,
not only of this Pierre Louÿs cycle, but even more especially of
Le Promenoir des deux amants. The haunting power of her chest
voice in the final line of the third song, where she sings "la
neige," is not to be passed over lightly, even for vastly superior
recording. She has, too, a very special partner in Cortot.

Trois Ballades de François Villon. Singher, b; CBSO, Abravanel, C
ML 4152 (*Ravel: Don Quichotte à Dulcinée; Operatic Arias).
Trois Ballades de François Villon; Le Promenoir des deux amants;
Fantoches. Jansen, b; Bonneau, pf, L LL 644 (*Chabrier, Ravel: Songs).
Ballade de Villon No. 2; La Grotte; Mandoline. Souzay, b; PCO,
Lindenberg, 10" L LD 9091 (*Ravel: Don Quichotte à Dulcinée).

Neither Singher, who sings to Debussy's own orchestration, nor
Jansen, piano-accompanied, brings to these ballades much vocal
charm or the twinkle of warm humor they need. The gem of the
set, of course, is the second song, the prayer written at the request of Villon's mother, but this calls for tenderness, of which
neither baritone provides much. Souzay sings only this second
ballade, along with two separate songs that would have been better
done to the original piano accompaniment. In reproduction the
voice is a little heavy, and, especially in the quiet places, it
overbalances the orchestra. Still, this is artistic singing.

Cinq Poèmes de Charles Baudelaire (Le Balcon; Harmonie du soir; Le
Jet d'eau; Recueillement; La Mort des amants). Tourel, m-s; Kahn, pf,
C ML 4158 (*French Songs).
Romance; La Grotte; Le Faune; Colloque sentimental. C. Panzéra, b;
M. Panzéra, pf, Mer MG 10097 (*Piano Pieces; Fauré: Songs and Piano
Pieces).

Clair de lune; Fantoches; Romance; Nuit d'étoiles; Mandoline; Il pleure dans mon coeur; Green; Voici que le printemps; Rondel chinois; Pierrot; Apparition. Pons, s; La Forge, pf, 10" C ML 2135.

The Baudelaire songs date from 1890, just as Debussy was finding his mature style. The poems are a bit overloaded to be ideal subjects for musical setting, but the composer makes them always interesting, if not altogether convincing. Performances of the cycle are rare. Tourel meets the composer on his own ground, singing with taste, musicianship, and intelligence. The balance with Kahn's excellent piano part is very good.

Panzéra, a prolific recording artist in the twenties and thirties, and a singer with more than a few masterpieces to his credit, demonstrates in this program what can be done by sheer force of musicianship, penetration, and personality, even when the voice is pretty well gone. As a vital projection of these poems-in-music, his performance stands out among the Debussy song records. Pons is sincere and earnest in her effort, and she deserves thanks for the unusual repertoire. However, since this record was issued, the three virtually unknown early songs with which she closes the program have been given with greater vocal security by Erna Berger (U URLP 7060).

DELIBES, LÉO (1836-1891)

Lakmé. Robin, s; Collart, s; de Luca, t; Borthayre, b; Jansen, b; etc.; OCC & O, Sebastian, L LLA 12 [3].

Lakmé is a *prima donna* opera. That is to say, in this recording, it must stand or fall by Mado Robin. Well, it stands, but not without occasional uncertainty. The soprano owns a fine electrifying top voice, especially effective in the "Bell Song," and a haunting lyric quality that wants maturity and some further study. The men of the cast are good, particularly Jansen and Borthayre. Libero de Luca seems less happily cast than in the London *Carmen* set, but he is acceptable. With this recording is furnished one of the most inept of libretto translations. An interesting souvenir is provided in a disc containing Lakmé's three principal arias: *"Pourquoi dans les grands bois?,"* the "Bell Song," and *"Dans la forêt, près de nous"* sung by Lily Pons even before she made her American debut (10" D DL 4024). The vocal quality (Robin's voice bears a kind of resemblance to it) is fresh and alive; the old recording has been well transferred to LP.

DELIUS, FREDERICK (1862-1934)

Eine Messe des Lebens. Raisbeck, s; Sinclair, c; Craig, t; Boyce, b; LPC; RPO, Beecham, C SL 197 [2].

Though Delians consider it the supreme achievement of their composer, *A Mass of Life* has rarely been performed, largely because of the Beethovian difficulties it offers the singers. Inevitably, Beecham was the man to bring it to us, and as usual he has gotten the best out of everyone concerned. Certain passages linger in the memory—the peaceful intermezzo titled *"Auf den Bergen,"* the wonderful outburst at *"Herauf! nun herauf, du grosser Mittag!"* the introduction to Part 4, and the almost Mahlerish ending, *"O Mensch, gib acht!"*—these are things to come back to many times. Chorus and orchestra are splendid; in the recording the massed singers seem to have been placed beyond the orchestra, which makes for a certain diffusion in the choral tone, but by no means a lack of clarity. The important baritone solo part is carried by Bruce Boyce, a singer of fine intelligence, whose voice is apparently a little frayed by use. Monica Sinclair is a real find, a contralto of lovely rich tone. For the rest, the singing is good, the diction as clean as we could ask.

DELLO JOIO, NORMAN (1913-   )

Psalm of David. Crane Ch & O, Hosmer, 10" CH CHS 1118.

Here is a significant American work, composed on commission for the choir that has recorded it. The text is the Fiftieth Psalm, the music based on a *cantus firmus* borrowed from Josquin des Pres's setting of the same words (recorded in the Anthologie Sonore, HS AS 5). A slight hum in the recording is not too noticeable.

DONIZETTI, GAETANO (1797-1848)

Operas

Betly. Tuccari, s; Gentile, t; Catalani, b; RSQC & O, Morelli, Per SPL 585.

To many of us *Betly* has been known simply as the source of the *coloratura* air *"In questo semplice,"* recorded some years ago by Margherita Carosio. The score proves to be quite charming, with other attractive tunes, and a good bit of clowning and ribbing of operatic conventions. The Rossinian overture emerges in this recording almost sanitary in sound, and the reproduction throughout is as clean and spacious as one might wish. Tuccari's voice is bright and agile, if not especially warm, and she sings with a respectable degree of neatness. Gentile, a tenor of the light Italian type, has something of the lachrymose style not uncommon in his school. Catalani, to whose lot falls an aria amusingly reminiscent of Bellini's *"Vi ravviso,"* is less impressive. There is an entertaining moment when the tenor falls asleep. The score has been telescoped to bring it down to twelve-inch size, but I doubt that much of value has been lost.

Il Campanello. Scarangella, s; Truccato Pace, m-s; Mercuriale, t; Capecchi, b; Bruscantini, bs; RIC & O, Simonetto, Cet 50027.

Here is another example of Donizetti's broad humor, long forgotten, presumably for lack of a *"Quel guardo il cavaliere,"* an *"Una furtiva lagrima,"* or an *"Udite, o rustici."* The performance is an unctious one, all in the best Italian tradition, with Bruscantini responsible for most of the fun. The shrill-voiced soprano is also typical. The recording balance is excellent, with none of that feeling that the singers are right beside our ears.

Don Pasquale. La Gatta, s; Lazzari, t; Poli, b; Corena, bs; etc.; SCAC & O, Parodi, U URLP 228 [2]. *Aimaro, s; Oncina, t; Colombo, b; Luise, bs; VKC; VSO, Quadri, W WAL 206* [2].

In so farcical a comedy as *Don Pasquale* it is the men who count for most. Urania, it seems to me, has a slight edge in the difficult choice before us, because the male members of its cast (especially Corena) are capital, where Westminster's are merely excellent. On the other hand, I prefer Westminster's Aimaro as Norina, though she hardly approaches the ideal. Whereas Aimaro inclines to sing back in her throat, La Gatta is more uneven in quality and tends towards shrillness. But either of these sets is acceptable.

L'Elisir d'Amore. Carosio, s; Monti, t; Gobbi, b; Luise, bs; etc.; ROC & O, Santini, HMV ALP 1067/8 [2]. *Noni, s; Valletti, t; Poli, b; Bruscantini, bs; etc.; RIC & O, Gavazzeni, Cet 1235* [3]. *(Highlights) Tellini, s; Solari, t; Conati, b; Faticanti, bs; etc.; SCAC & O, Molajoli, C ML 4408.*

Superficially, the greatest difference between the two "complete" performances is in bulk and price. Cetra's, to be sure, is the more conveniently packaged, and includes an elaborate libretto with introductory notes. In over-all sound, Cetra's is more powerful, with instruments as well as voices closer upon us; HMV has more atmosphere, a more natural theater sound. There is surprisingly little to choose between the two casts, which is not to say they are very similar. Carosio has been known for some years by her pre-LP recordings; hers are a clear, high voice and an unusual sense of style. She is no longer in her first prime, as the new recording attests: the tone is a little dry, not always free of shrillness, and not invariably accurate in intonation. Noni's is a fresher instrument, very nearly as appealing as Carosio's best, but she does not quite match the stylistic distinction of her rival. The acid test of this is the last-act aria, *"Prendi, per me sei libero,"* in which Carosio is superb. Monti's voice is thinner in quality than Valletti's, but he is guilty of fewer emotional excesses. This shows most plainly in the first act aria, *"Quanto è bella."* Both sing *"Una furtiva lagrima"* creditably enough, though in Monti's performance the fundamental rhythm is rather free, the dynamic contrasts a little strong. Neither tenor, it seems safe to assume, has reached full artistic maturity as of these recordings. Gobbi has a vocal robustiousness not inappropriate to the character of Sergeant Balcore, but he is not a notably fluent or accurate vocalist. Poli sings with less bluster, but he too is content to approximate some of his notes. Luise impersonates Doctor Dulcamara with magnificent unction, resorting to *parlando* effects more frequently than the also convincing Bruscantini. The best Dulcamara on recent records, however, is represented only by the entrance scene, *"Udite, o rustici."* He is Fernando Corena, of the magnificent voice and the incomparable *buffo* humor (10" L LS 701). Columbia's Highlights date back well into the thirties, so that to enjoy the recording we have to accept orchestral sound without "bite" and a general lack of brilliance. The singers are very good and well cast, if hardly an improvement on those in the "complete" sets. The performance has spirit, and the recording on LP is not bad.

La Favorita—Highlights. Brohly, m-s; Parsi-Pettinella, m-s; Beyle, t; Bonci, t; Battistini, b; Sammarco, b; Luppi, bs; etc.; Et 489.

The best justification for this set of revivals is the fact that we have had no complete *Favorita*, and hardly dare hope for a stylistically distinguished one. On the whole, I feel, some of

Eterna's other "Highlights" have proved more interesting. Bonci
is at his best in the two tenor arias—*"Una vergine"* and *"Spirto
gentil"*—but his voice sounds thin in a duet with the impressive
bass of Luppi. Battistini's *"Vien, Leonora"* also is excellent,
but the best singing on the disc, to my mind, is in the final duet
by Brohly and Beyle. Their singing in French is not out of keeping, for the original libretto was in that language. Strangely, the
selection does not include *"O mio Fernando,"* probably the most
famous aria in the opera. Anyone interested in Bonci's two arias
will find them again included in a program devoted to this tenor
(GAR 101); and Battistini's *"Vien, Leonora"* is duplicated in one
of his "recitals" (Et O-462). Good modern versions of a couple of
the arias are to be had, *"Spirto gentil"* by Nicolai Gedda (An
35096), and *"Vien, Leonora"* by Ivan Petroff (Rem 199-93).

*La Figlia del Reggimento. Pagliughi, s; Valletti, t; Bruscantini, bs;
etc.; RIC & O, Rossi, Cet 1213* [2].

I found Pagliughi less satisfying here than in the more serious
Donizetti and Bellini operas. I suspect that she is too straight a
singer to shine in so light a character role, where personality
counts for much. Her coloratura is still among the best to be
heard nowadays, but whether this recording caught her past her
prime, or whether there is a less obvious reason, she is not at her
very fine best, and does not always quite make the grade with the
pitch. As for vocal color, she does not go into that to any great
extent, nor does she make her points with diction. The rest of
the cast acquits itself well, though I could wish for a little more
body in Valletti's tones (I have liked him better in other roles).
Bruscantini is, as ever, dependable.

*Lucia di Lammermoor. Pagliughi, s; Malipiero, t; Menaccini, b; Neroni,
bs; etc.; EIARC & O, Tansini, Cet 1205* [3]; *Callas, s; di Stefano, t;
Gobbi, b; Arie, bs; etc.; FMC & O, Serafin, An 3503-B* [2]. *Wilson, s;
Poggi, t; Colzani, b; Maionica, bs; etc.; MIOC & O, Capuana, U URLP
232* [3].

In *Lucia* success depends primarily on the *prima donna*, though
the ensemble of the Sextet and the lyrical abilities of the tenor
count for a lot, too. In the three complete sets, we have room for
personal preference, as the three Lucias are in the strongest possible contrast. Young Dolores Wilson is best described as promising, for though the quality of her voice is attractive, she has
some work ahead to eliminate a flutter in the more lyrical passages. Her "Mad Scene" is reasonably brilliant, and she does

hold the interest throughout. Callas, as everyone must know by now, is a dramatic-coloratura singer, ranging in recordings from Gioconda and Tosca to Elvira in *Puritani*. Somehow her Lucia is not quite so breath-taking as the last-named achievement; the whole performance seems a little studied and careful; the microphone placement may be to blame for not altogether satisfactory reproduction of her darkly colored tones. The Cetra recording with Pagliughi is some years older than either of its rivals, and in itself the sound is not as impressive, but the soprano is nearer the time-honored ideal for the title role, dazzling in execution, somehow dramatic in her roulades and trills, beautifully in line in her *cantabile* passages. For the rest, Urania's Poggi is a dry-voiced Edgardo, Angel's di Stefano a melifluous and authentic one; Cetra's Malipiero is only less impressive than di Stefano. The oldest recording gives us the best-balanced Sextet; in it we can actually follow the lines of Alicia and Arturo. In the Angel performance, Gino Sarri, the hero of complete *Otello* and *Andrea Chénier* sets, takes the small part of Normanno.

Victor has a set of Highlights enlisting a cast of present and past Metropolitan luminaries, including Munsel, Peerce, Merrill, and Pinza (V LM 1710). Munsel does a creditable job on the "Mad Scene." Cellini is the conductor. Another "Mad Scene" is offered by Mado Robin (10" L LS 676), who seems to be creating a sensation these days. I find little for which to commend her here beyond the ability to sing higher than any currently practicing soprano.

Arias

L'Elisir d'Amore—Una furtiva lagrima; Quanto è bella; La Figlia del Reggimento—Qual destino; Eccomi finalmente; Don Pasquale— Sogno soave è casto; Povero Ernesto; Com'è gentil; Tornami a dir. Valletti, t; etc.; RIC & O, Cet A 50154.

These are all excerpts from Cetra's complete operas. The singer has a light and flexible voice of the Schipa order, perhaps a little pale in quality, but well adapted to this type of music. He has a sense of style, and his vocal control is unusual. I particularly enjoyed his duet with Alda Noni, from *Don Pasquale*. For the most part, the reproduction is excellent, though the sound develops some fuzz toward the center of the disc.

DOWLAND, JOHN (1562-1626)

If floods of tears; Fine knacks for ladies; Sweet, stay awhile; Say, love, if ever thou didst find; Toss not my soul; Weep you no more, sad fountains; When Phoebus first did Daphne love; Woeful heart; I saw my lady weep. Langstaff, b; Chessid, hpschd, Ren X 27 (*Purcell: Songs).

In this generous sampling of the songs of the great Elizabethan lutenist, the lute parts are played on the harpsichord in a manner intended to suggest the original instrument. The best-known masterpieces are here: the somber *"If floods of tears,"* the lightsome *"Fine knacks for ladies,"* the caressing *"Weep you no more, sad fountains,"* and the inexpressibly lovely *"I saw my lady weep,"* among others, and they are done with infallible taste and fine intelligence, if not too much tonal variety. The disc also holds a fine selection of Purcell songs. *"I saw my lady weep"* and the equally fine *' Flow, my tears"* may be had in more authentic guise in a recital of English songs by that excellent artist, Hugues Cuenod, with lute played by Hermann Leeb (W WL 5085).

DUFAY, GUILLAUME (ca. 1400-1474)

Resvelons-nous, amoureux; Pouray-je avoir vostre mercy; He! compaignons; La Belle se sied au pie de la tour; Adieu, m'amour; Ce moys de may; Je donne a tous les amoureux; Bon jour, bon mois; Par droit je puis bien complaindre et gémir; Ce jour de l'an; Mon cuer me fait tousdis penser; Je languis en piteux martire; J'atendray tant qu'il vous playra. PMA, Cape, EMS 206.

The history books acknowledge Dufay the greatest musician of his day, yet only recently has it been possible to form an opinion based on extensive performance. Pro Musica Antiqua has no superiors in its field, and the finely reproduced program is nicely varied. The scholarship that has gone into the venture should not be allowed to scare away anyone with an appreciation for lighthearted conceits and not too weighty sentiments. This generous sampling should serve as a fine introduction to fifteenth-century secular polyphony.

DUPARC, HENRI (1848-1933)

La Vie antérieure; Le Manoir de Rosamonde; Élégie; Phidylé; Soupir; Chanson triste; Lamento; La Vague et la cloche; Sérénade Florentine;

Testament; Extase; L'Invitation au voyage. Souzay, b; Bonneau, pf,
L LL 813.

This program includes all but one of the thirteen songs left by
Duparc as the major portion of his musical legacy. Souzay is in
his best voice, and there is imagination in his singing. Still, one
misses the quality of intensity which would have transformed his
thoughtful conceptions into a really vital experience. Several
times the bottom all but falls out of a song, as toward the end of
"La Vie antérieure," the *"Sérénade Florentine,"* and *"L'Invita-*
tion au voyage." Most successful of the lot is *"Chanson triste,"*
which is done with real affection. One regrets that some of the
jacket space was not used for translations.

DVOŘÁK, ANTONIN (1841-1904)

Choral Work

Stabat Mater. Soloists; Czech Singers Ch; CPH, Talich, U URLP 234
[2].

This performance of Dvořák's rather different setting of the time-
less text has all the marks of authenticity; there can be no question the performers put themselves into it heart and soul. If the
results are not as tidy as we might wish, we must perforce admire
and be moved by the spirit that has gone into the work. The soloists are variable, with the rich-voiced contralto, Krásová, outstanding. She makes much of her big aria, *"Inflammatus,"* and
she stands out in the quartet as the best vocalist. The soprano is
not too steady; one does not have the feeling she has her voice
well under control. The bass does creditably in his *"Fac ut*
ardeat cor meum," but the tenor's tone is constricted. Recording-wise, the set again is uneven: the chorus comes through with
clarity, but the soloists are all too close. When they join together,
they do not achieve a blend; each seems to wander in his own way.

Opera

Rusalka. Trötschel, s; Schindler, t; Zimmermann, t; Frick, bs; etc.;
DOC; SAX, Keilberth, U URLP 219 [3].

This strongly nationalistic opera contains some fine music, though
its stageworthiness remains an open question. The most striking
thing about its story (to English-speaking listeners) is a certain

relationship to Sullivan's *Iolanthe*. It would be hard to take all
these water sprites seriously in our day and generation. Cast and
recording are well above the average. Trötschel has a sweet,
floating voice, as well as poise and charm; Frick makes a sympathetic Water Sprite; Schindler, the hero, is a little stiff tonally,
but not without his good points. The score has been heavily cut
in this recording.

Songs and Duets

Biblische Lieder; Zigeunermelodien; Liebeslieder. Rössl-Majdan, c;
Holetschek, pf, W WL 5324.
Biblical Songs. Duarte, c; Murphy, pf, ML MLR 7024.
    Properly, of course, Dvořák's songs should be sung in Czech;
neither the German version of the *Biblical Songs* nor the published
English one is by any means a perfect fit to the music. Rössl-
Majdan's approach is simple and direct. Her tones are admirably
full and solid, though she cuts some of the phrases into short
lengths, and in the more sustained movements her conception is
not always as broad as it might be. More of the drama could be
brought out of *"By the waters of Babylon"* without loss of dignity.
Hers is the most satisfactory recording yet of the *Gypsy Songs*,
though I miss the elemental quality I have admired in the three of
them once recorded by Povla Frijsh. The *Love Songs* call forth
the best singing on the disc. Esther Lucretia Duarte, who sings
the *Biblical Songs* in English, is said to have been only seventeen
when her recording was made, and she may be set down as a young
artist of promise, apparently free from obvious faults that might
endanger her future. She follows the shifting moods of the psalm
settings with only occasionally a not quite perfectly pronounced
word to interfere with the feeling.
*Zigeunermelodien. Felbermayer, s; Graef, pf, Van VRS 446 (*Brahms:*
Songs).
Gypsy Songs; Love Songs, Nos. 1, 2, 3, 6. Warenskjold, s; Concert
*Arts O, Greeley, Cap P 8247 (*Grieg: Songs).*
    These two sopranos have a number of things in common. Both
have voices of unusual lyric appeal; both are musical and stylish
singers. Yet neither is right for the *Zigeunermelodien*. After all,
Dvořák's gypsies are not ladies. Felbermayer sings in German to
the proper piano accompaniment (in another sense, it is altogether
too proper), while Warenskjold favors the English translation (the

original, after all, was Czech) and a too elaborate orchestration.
We can, however, be grateful to both sopranos for not sentimen-
talizing the very familiar *"Songs my mother taught me."* Warenskjold is better in the *Love Songs*, but the orchestration does not
belong here.

*Mährische Klänge. Fuchs, s; Klose, s; Raucheisen, pf, 10" U URLP
5002.*

The duet record shows Fuchs and Klose blending their superb
voices with vitality and the intimacy essential to chamber music.
For some reason, only twelve of the thirteen pieces in this opus
are given, and the singing is in German. Texts and translations
are provided with the disc, and the label even gives the timing.

FALLA, MANUEL DE (1876-1946)

Operas

*El Retablo de Maese Pedro. Rodrigues Aragon, s; Renom, t; Ausensi,
b; Gouarne, hpschd; RDFO, Toldra. El Amor Brujo. Iriarte, m-s;
PCO, Argenta, An 35089. Seoane, s; Navarro, t; Gonzalo, bs; Champs-
Élysées Th O, Halffter. El Amor Brujo. Rivadeneira, c; Madrid SO,
Freitas-Branco, W WL 5238.*

*El Retablo de Maese Pedro. Steingruber, s; Kmentt, t; Wiener, bs;
VPH, Adler, SPA 43.*

A choice between the Angel and the Westminster recordings of
the delightful marionette opera is not made easily. Before the
arrival of the Angel, the Westminster seemed quite definitive.
But if Seoane, the "boy" of Halffter's cast, was particularly winning, Aragon seems just that much more nearly perfect, with her
contrasting tone qualities, now almost stridently boyish, now
sweetly lyrical. Gonzalo, Westminster's Don Quixote, is effective
in a Chaliapinesque sort of way, but there is a noble dignity in
Ausensi's singing which sets it far above its rival. His treatment
of the Dulcinea passage is very moving. As for the Viennese
Retablo, its first disadvantage is that it runs to two sides, which
is uneconomical. The second is that, for all the earnestness and
musicality of the performers, I find no evidence of a flair for the
Spanish idiom, such as is eloquently disclosed by its competitors.
Simply as voices, Adler's singers are superior, but they are altogether less convincing. Both Angel and Westminster have coupled
with this work the ballet with songs *El Amor Brujo*, and again both

performances are remarkably fine. But once more the palm goes to Angel, not only for the beauty of the orchestral playing, but because of the superbly brassy Spanish mezzo-soprano who sings the songs.

La Vida Breve. De los Angeles, s; Gomez, m-s; Civil, t; Payá, b; etc.; Capilla Classica Polifónica; Barcelona Op O, Halffter, V LM 6017 [2] (*Songs, de los Angeles).

La Vida Breve was produced at the Metropolitan in the season of 1925-6, but, despite the presence of Lucrezia Bori in the leading role, it did not last into a second year. Listening to the delicate scoring in this refined and sensitive performance, one can only account for its non-success in New York by the size of the auditorium. No such problem confronts us here. The cast has been chosen with unerring taste; each of the singers is vocally pleasing and dramatically in the picture. The orchestra plays eloquently—excitingly in the famous dance—always smoothly and in superb balance. The choral effects in which the score abounds are realized with a sense of the stage. It is hard to believe that Bori, for all her personal appeal, could have sung the role of Salud more expressively or with more exquisite art than does de los Angeles. In this music she is completely at home; the quality of her voice has a melting sweetness that stays with us after the final curtain. She had recorded two of the scenes before, beautifully, if not quite with the perfect poise of the new performance; and for comparison there exists a standard-play disc of the principal aria, *"Vivan los que rien,"* charmingly sung by Bori.

Songs

Siete Canciones Populares Españolas. Ibarrondo, m-s; Sandoval, pf, 10" C ML 2189 (*Sandoval: Songs). De los Angeles, s; Moore, pf, 10" V LM 131 (*Songs). Supervia, m-s; Marshall, pf, 10" D DL 7510 (*Granados: Songs).

For the historical-minded, and for those who find themselves fascinated by the peculiar *timbre* of the late Supervia's voice, hers is the most interesting of the three performances listed above. But the recording is old. At the opposite pole is the tonally lovely, beautifully recorded, almost ladylike singing of de los Angeles. Somewhere in the middle we must place the rich, if less distinctive, voice and style of Ibarrondo. Spanish though these two artists be, they have their temperaments well under control. Yet another performance is available by Souzay, but he is out of his element, as any man would be, in these colorful songs (10" L LS 536).

FARNABY, GILES (ca. 1565 - ca. 1640)

Among the daffadillies; My lady's colored cheeks; Lady, the silly flea; The curtain drawn; Sometime she would; Construe my meaning; Ay me, poor heart; Simkin said that Sis was fair. Oriana Singers, Hobbs, EMS 5 (*Six Pieces for the Virginals).

It would seem that Farnaby's canzonets should rather have been called madrigals, so impressive are they in size and elaborate in workmanship. When sung by so large a choir as this, they gain in sonority, but lose intimacy. Still, the beauties of such pieces as *"Construe my meaning"* and *"Ay me, poor heart"* are richly apparent.

FAURÉ, GABRIEL URBAIN (1845-1924)

Choral Work

Requiem. Angelici, s; Noguéra, b; SEC & O, Cluytens, An 35019. Beems, s; Uppman, b; RWC; Concert Arts O, Wagner, Cap P 8241. Alarie, s; Maurane, b; BC; LAM, Fournet, Ep LC 3044. Sautereau, s; Demigny, b; PPC & O, Leibowitz, Oc OCS 26. Dupont, s; Didier, b; Chanteurs de Lyon & Trigentuor, Bourmauck, C ML 4529.

The choice here is not easy, for every one of these sets has something to commend it. Perhaps the most quickly disposed of is the old Columbia transfer from 78 rpm, an admired recording in its day but never a model of choral neatness. On all counts, it is superseded by any one of the four newer takes. For the choral portions of the work (which is to say, most of it), the Angel disc has the most atmosphere, with the Oceanic running second. The Epic is perhaps a little too solid, not so elevated and meditative as the others. The baritone soloist in the Capitol set, however, is good enough, almost, to throw the balance of favor that way. No soloists in this work, to be sure, have ever matched those of the first, long-since-withdrawn recording (Victor 11154-8), but Uppman is in their class. Beems, his partner, however, is far below them; for a pair of good singers, Epic has the edge, as Maurane sings with notable dignity and reserve, and Alarie wants only a little more intensity to be first-rate. Her *"Pie Jesu"* is curious acoustically, however, for her position seems to change in mid-aria. Angelici, in the Angel recording, clips her phrases, but her vocal quality is characteristically good. Both soloists in the Oceanic cersion are above average. To sum up: Cluytens's performance has the most churchly atmosphere, inclines to slower tempos, and gives the impression of the deepest thought on the part of the conductor; Fournet's is the most powerful, effectively contrasted in the opening supplication, but disappointing in the otherworldly *"Sanctus"*; Leibowitz makes the most of the music's restlessness and supplication; Wagner's has an outstanding soloist.

Songs

*La Bonne Chanson. Danco, s; Agosti, pf, 10" L LS 589. Cuenod, t; Holetschek, pf, W WL 5278 (*Gounod: Biondina).*

This cycle of nine Verlaine settings comes best from a male singer, but Cuenod is disappointingly out of his element in music of this kind. Perhaps some of the effect should be blamed on Holetschek's playing, but whosever the fault, the performance is square-cut, almost metronomic. It would not be right to call the artists insensitive, but they are certainly not at home in this cycle. Unfortunately, Danco, reliable artist though she is, does not quite bring the songs off either. Somehow her singing is all on the surface; there is not much to criticize—it simply doesn't carry conviction. Unfortunately again, a fresh, charmingly lyrical performance by the young American soprano Joan Brainerd (10" CH CHC 49) has been dropped from the market. And the near-definitive interpretation by Charles and Madeleine Panzéra has not found its way, as yet, to Victor's LP Treasury series.

*La Chanson d'Ève. Kolassi, m-s; Collard, pf, L LL 919 (*Milhaud: Poèmes juifs).*

This late cycle is rarely performed and was never before recorded; it is therefore an important addition to the repertoire. Happily, Kolassi seems just right for this kind of music. Her voice is limited, but of appealing quality, and is always used with the greatest discretion. The songs are allowed to speak their own pure and classical language. Many passages are hauntingly lovely.

Les Mélodies de Venise (Mandoline; En sourdine; Green; A Clymène;

C'est l'extase); Spleen; Clair de lune.   Cuenod, t; Blancard, pf, Van VRS 414 (*Debussy: Songs).

Lydia; Chanson du pêcheur; Adieu; L'Horizon chimérique.   C. Panzéra, b; M. Panzéra, pf, Mer MG 10097 (*Piano Pieces; Debussy: Songs and Piano Pieces).

Tristesse; Au bord de l'eau; Après un rêve; Clair de lune; Arpège; En sourdine; L'Horizon chimérique.   Souzay, b; Blancard, pf, L LLP 245 (*Schubert: Songs).

Le Secret; Soir; Aurore; En sourdine; Le Parfum impérissable; Nell; Au cimitière; Les Roses d'Ispahan.   Vallin, s; Faure, pf, 10" Vox PTL 1730.

Cuenod has devoted his disc to settings of Verlaine by Fauré and Debussy. As was inevitable, this musicianly singer presents them all with unfailing intelligence and taste, but unfortunately he does not reveal any particular affinity for this type of music. The high, clear, true voice is rather stiff. One misses the needed warmth. Warmth there certainly is in the Panzéra program, and a searching art to overcome the limitations placed by advancing age on his once-beautiful voice. Old-time collectors will recognize every one of the titles as having been recorded by the same artist in his prime, but such older discs are no longer easy to come by. At any rate, here is lofty art. Souzay's program benefits by a lovely *legato*, appealing tone, and musical poise. *"Au bord de l'eau"* and *"Arpège"* are reason enough for buying the record. And the cool perfection of *"Clair de lune"* is very striking. The Vallin disc is a dubbing of several of the best of her prewar recordings. They have come through the transfer with only a little of their brilliance lost. The superb *"Soir," "Aurore,"* and *"En sourdine"* add several cubits to the artist's stature. There are some odd statements in the accompanying notes: for example, that Fauré's last work was the opera *Pénélope*. Original texts with translations are provided.

FICKENSCHER, ARTHUR (1871-1954)

Willowwood. Porter, m-s; Ens, ML MLR 7020.

Whether or not one agrees with the annotator that Fickenscher is the most neglected of American composers, it is at the very least interesting to have these Rossetti settings as a sample of his style. Obviously, the singer understands and loves the songs; indeed she seems more greatly interested in Fickenscher than in Rossetti. One complaint concerns the length of the music on these two twelve-inch sides. Considering how short the cycle is, the break in the middle seems as unnecessary as it is unfortunate.

FIORAVANTI, VALENTINO (1764-1837)

Le Cantatrice Villane. Noni, s; Orell, s; Lazzari, t; Bruscantini, bs; etc.; SCAO, Rossi, Cet 50102.

This little post-Mozart comedy comes as a complete novelty. The cast is mostly familiar from various other operas of like period released by Cetra. They are all perfectly at home in the rather modest music, and they are well recorded.

FLOTOW, FRIEDRICH VON (1812-1883)

Alessandro Stradella—Arias. Jokl, s; Slezak, t; Jadlowker, t. 10" *Et ELP 461 (*Slezak Operatic Recital).*

The first of these selections, Stradella's prayer, will have a familiar ring to all who remember the overture. It is sung by Slezak, in magnificent voice, probably about the time he appeared in the opera in New York (1909-10). Fritzi Jokl's contribution, *"Seid meiner Wonne stille Zeugen,"* is an early electrical recording; it is very brilliantly sung, in tones at once unusually sweet and admirably firm. Jadlowker's aria is *"Tief in den Abruzzen,"* a good vehicle for his impressive coloratura, but he is less well recorded than the other singers.

Martha. Berger, s; Tegetthoff, c; Anders, t; Greindl, bs; etc.; BCOC; RBO, Rother, U URLP 217 [3].

It is good to hear this charming, if lightweight comedy—*"Last Rose of Summer"* and all—in the original German; for many years it has been an occasional part of the Italian repertoire. The stronger Teutonic accents take away some of the extra sentiment induced by the soft Italian. The cast is expert, with special credit to Erna Berger in the title role. Peter Anders, the Lionel, has, like Berger, a long and honorable career behind him, and his voice shows it in a way the soprano's does not. But if the tenor is not too steady or too mellifluous in his solos, he fits well into the sprightly ensembles, of which there are so many in this score.

Tegetthoff and Greindl, as Nancy and Plunkett, do their last act duet, *'Ja, was nun?''* with unction. Although the balance in the set is fairly good, the reproduced sound is not consistently clean. On the last side, at the beginning of the finale, something happens to both quality of sound and pitch.

FOSS, LUKAS (1922-)

A Parable of Death. Zorina, speaker; Stevens, t; Southern Baptist Theological Seminary Ch; Louisville O, Whitney, C ML 4859 (*Martinů: Intermezzo; Milhaud: Kentuckiana).

The composer informs us that he has sought to write a melodrama avoiding the pitfalls that beset this medium. The text is a translation from Rilke; the narrator tells the story, with intermittent commentary by chorus and tenor soloist. The inspiration for this, Foss tells us, was found in the Bach Passions, where the flow of the story is broken by meditations. All of which would have been more effective had we been given the text to follow, for the words do not come through in the choral singing. Zorina certainly needs no such help, for her delivery is very beautiful in itself, and it is as clear and understandable as it could be. Aside from this obscurity in the work of the other participants, the recording seems not to lack much.

The Jumping Frog of Calaveras County. Biller, s; Brock, t; Cavalucci, b; Ukena, bs; etc.; Kurzweil, Ly LL 11.

This operatic treatment of the famous Mark Twain story was first produced in New York as an informal piano-accompanied entertainment. It is the same group in the same spirit singing it here. The music is functional rather than memorable, and there are few opportunities for the singers to use their *legato* style. Not all the diction is easy to follow, for things happen fast, and the demands on the listener's attention are considerable. In short, here is modern American opera serving comedy, as Weill's *Down in the Valley* served tragedy.

FRANZ, ROBERT (1815- 1892)

Sonntag; Schlummerlied; Nebel; Die Liebe hat gelogen. Schloss, s; Brice, pf, IRCC L-7000 (*Wolf, Schumann, Strauss: Songs).

Aus meinen grossen Schmerzen; Vöglein, wohin?; Stille Sicherheit; Bitte; Liebchen ist da; Mutter, o sing' mich zur Ruh'; Gute Nacht; Widmung. Schumann, s; Schick, pf, Roy 1404 (*Mendelssohn: Songs; Purcell: Songs—Brownlee).

For all their polished perfection, most of the well-known songs of Franz are so slight, so lacking in "effectiveness" for the singer, that we rarely have a chance to hear them. It is significant, however, that Lotte Lehmann included five of them on her farewell recital program, presumably made up of personal favorites (Pembroke 1, one 12" disc, one 10"). Aside from an occasional individual song, those listed above and those sung by Lehmann are the sum total of Franz on LP. Marjorie Schloss, pupil and assistant of the late Edyth Walker, puts us in her debt especially for the lovely *"Schlummerlied"* (with the same text as Brahms's *"Ruhe, Süssliebchen"*). The voice is ample in size and of eminently satisfying quality; more important is the absorption of the singer in the songs she sings. Schumann, great artist though she remained to the end of her life, was in poor vocal estate when her recital was made; what is worse, she was not well recorded: apparently the singer was right inside the microphone.

GABRIELI, ANDREA (ca.1520-1586)

Motet and Missa "Pater peccavi"; Christmas Motet "Angelus ad pastores." TC, d'Alessi, Vox PL 8370.

The chesty quality of the boys' voices in these performances, and the lusty, extrovert approach, are by no means inappropriate to the full, expansive musical style of the elder Gabrieli. The idea of presenting first the motet *Pater peccavi*, then following it with the "parody" mass, which the composer based upon its thematic material, is excellent, and adds special interest to the longer work. Perhaps the record is for a particular kind of specialist, but for those who approve the style (not quite like anything in any country but Italy) the performances are splendid. Listeners who like a lot of shading in *a cappella* music will not find much comfort here.

GABRIELI, GIOVANNI (1557-1612)

Magnificat; Benedixisti Domine; O quam suavis; Beata es Virgo Maria; Exaudi Deus; Cantate Domino; Ego dixi Domine; Inclina Domine; Mise-

rere mei Deus; O magnum mysterium; Sancta Maria; Domine exaudi orationem meam. TC, d'Alessi, Vox PL 8830.

Gabrieli's music is in its nature both brilliant and magnificently sonorous. Certainly it was never meant for the kind of ethereal, otherworldly singing done in English cathedral choirs. Msgr. d'Alessi's group really gives it "the works," which may possibly be not too far from the practice of the composer himself. With some rather obvious exceptions, most of the singing is solid and true, and the recording admirably clear, so that the antiphonal choruses stand out in bold relief. But the dynamics rarely drop below a stentorian *forte*, with the boys of the choir entering into the spirit of the thing as though their little chests would burst. Twelve motets (accepting the *Magnificat* as one) done in this manner make a long program.

GERMAN, SIR EDWARD (1862-1936)

*Merry England—Vocal Selections. Baird, s; Thomas, c; Young, t; Cameron, b; NEW, Olof, L LL 772 (*Nell Gwynn—Dances; Henry VIII —Three Dances).*

A revival of at least the outstanding portions of German's light score was an inevitable feature of the Coronation Year. The performance here recorded is given with devotion and a lack of affectation. The nimble voice of Patricia Baird illuminates the Sullivan-like waltz song, and Marjorie Thomas is properly dignified in the most famous air, *"O peaceful England."* To crown all, there is a stirring rendition of *"God save Elizabeth"* at the end.

GERSHWIN, GEORGE (1898-1937)

Porgy and Bess. Williams, s; Matthews, s; Winters, b; Long, t; Matthews, b; etc.; Ch & O, Engel, C SL 162 [3].

This recording is of the "authentic" school, making every effort to recapture the spirit of the first production. Those who wish to compare may still be able to pick up Decca's original-cast recording of some years back. But anyone who never saw Todd Duncan and Anne Brown in the title roles will find enough to enjoy and admire in the present protagonists. The one jarring note is the embarrassingly overdrawn Sporting Life of Avon Long.

GESUALDO, CARLO, PRINCE OF VENOSA
(ca.1560 - 1613)

Io pur respiro; Felice primavera; Danzan le ninfe; Moro lasso; Mera-viglia d'amore; Et ardo e vivo; Io tacerò; Mercè! grido piangendo. Randolph Singers, W WL 5171 (*Monteverdi: Madrigals).

Because of its fiendish difficulties for the performers, Gesualdo's music is less well known than the fact that he was also a murderer. Perfection is hardly to be hoped for, but the Randolph Singers, with one voice to a part, have at least approached it. If they don't quite toss the madrigals off with carefree unconcern, they do manage to get a good deal of spirit into them. Complete texts, translations, and full analytical notes are furnished. One of these same madrigals—*"Io pur respiro"*—and another very striking one —*"Dolcissima mia vita"*—are included in the Hindemith Collegium Musicum recording (Ov OVER 4). Though the group is a larger one, the performance is a revelation, because of Hindemith's insight into the music and his ability to communicate this to his singers.

GIORDANO, UMBERTO (1867 - 1948)

Andrea Chénier. Caniglia, s; Gigli, t; Bechi, b; etc.; SCAC & O, Fabritiis, V LCT 6014 [2]. Sacchi, s; Sarri, t; Manca Serra, b; etc.; ROC & O, Paoletti, U URLP 218 [3]. Tebaldi, s; Soler, t; Saverese, b; etc.; RIC & O, Basile, Cet 1244 [3]. (Highlights) Roselle, s; Seine-meyer, s; Lauri-Volpi, t; Zenatello, t; Piccaver, t; Pattiera, t; Cor-radetti, b; Formichi, b; Et 484.

If one wants an exciting performance, unusually well controlled but tellingly intense and sung by first-rate voices, there is little question that the listener will accept Victor's older and less brilliant reproduction. As a matter of fact, the sound is unusually good for a transfer to LP, and the balance of voices and orchestra is far preferable to much that has been done more recently. The three principals are all in fine form. Caniglia's voice is sure and generally steady; it shows a lyric quality not always notable in her recordings. Both she and Gigli curb their natural tendency to emotionalize; their singing of the big duet in Act 2 is eloquent, though, like many others, they disregard the *p*'s Giordano has placed at the end of the scene. The tenor has rarely sounded better: only the high tones betray that his very best days were past when the recording was made. There is no possible doubt that his *"Improvviso"* would bring down any house. And by all odds, this is the best singing I have ever heard from Bechi. His first-act aria, in particular, is splendidly delivered. Later on I feel a lack of "bite" in his diction, but the tone is always handsome. Among the lesser singers are Simionato and Taddei, both of whom have achieved stardom since the time of recording. The more modern recordings are both of the better grade of Italian production. Cetra's Tebaldi sings (save for a few high tones) with incomparable tonal beauty, but with less temperament than Urania's Sacchi. She gives the great aria *"La mamma morta"* with the most thoughtful declamation, so that every word counts; except for the climax, the voice is at its creamiest. (An earlier Tebaldi performance of this aria, part of an operatic recital—10″ D DL 4005—is more consistently steady.) Soler, Cetra's Chénier, reveals a hard tone, not too certain of its bearings in much of the opera, but capable of fine, ringing high B-flats. Urania's more lyrical Sarri is decidedly preferable. Cetra's Savarese makes a good start in his opening aria, and he meets the general standards of modern Italian productions. Manca Serra is more dramatic, perhaps too much so, and he makes a stronger characterization. The balance is better in the Urania set; the Cetra recording is uneven. The Highlights set brings us well-known interpreters of the past. Far and away the most impressive of them is Cesare Formichi, once of the Chicago Opera, whose voice, electrically recorded, is strong and telling in the monologue *"Nemico della patria."* Unfortunately, the orchestra is sketchy. From an earlier generation is Ferruccio Corradetti, a prolific recording baritone, whose account of Gerard's first-act aria, *"Son sessant' anni,"* is almost equally impressive. The strong-winded Lauri-Volpi is heard as a young man in the *"Improvviso"*; it is interesting to hear how he handles the dramatic text. Following immediately, Giovanni Zenatello's tone sounds thin in Chénier's *"Credo"* from the second act; the fine artist is at a disadvantage in something less than the best recording. Anne Roselle, electrically reproduced, does not seem to be at her ease in *"La mamma morta"*; the tone is a little rigid, and she does not let herself go. The admired Alfred Piccaver wants intensity in his delivery of *"Come un bel dì di maggio."* The final duet is sung in German (not too clear on the part of the tenor) by Meta Seinemeyer and Tino Pattiera. The soprano's voice is straight as a die, and thrilling in its purity. The orchestra (electrically recorded) is primitive.

Fedora. Caniglia, s; Prandelli, t; Colombo, b; etc.; RIC & O, Rossi, Cet 1222 [2]. *Calma, s; Pellizzoni, t; Gilardoni, b; etc.; SCAC & O, Quadri, Col CLPD 1021/2* [2].

Neither of these sets is really satisfactory. Cetra's cast is competent rather than brilliant, headed by a well-known soprano past her prime and an excellent tenor not quite arrived at his. The reproduction is good enough. In the Colosseum performance, recording difficulties militate against whatever effect the high-strung, characteristically Italian production might give. The singers seem to have good voices, and to project them for all the drama Sardou and Giordano could have had in mind, but the sound is over-brilliant, even shrill, not properly balanced with the somewhat tubby-sounding orchestra.

Mese Mariano. Calma, s; Villani, s; Palombini, m-s; Rovetta, b; etc.; SCAC & O, Rivoli, Col CLPS 1023.

This little-known opera might be called Giordano's *Suor Angelica*, for it treats of a conflict of religious atmosphere and very human passion in a manner not unlike that of Puccini's one-acter. As no score or libretto has been available to me, I can only speak generally of the sound of the performance in an opera not likely to make its way in the United States. The voices are more or less typical of contemporary Italian productions, and the singing has more fire than finesse. The recording is good if we compensate for a heavy bass and some rather piercing highs. It is all loud, but loudness is really not out of place in this type of music.

GLINKA, MICHAEL IVANOVITCH (1803-1857)

A Life for the Czar. Shpieler, s; Nelepp, t; Mikhailov, bs; etc.; BSIC & O, Melik-Pashayev, Van VRS 6010/11/12 [3].

A Life for the Czar is one of the great landmarks in the history of Russian opera, but from the way it is done here, the unprejudiced hearer will have a hard time convincing himself that it is a masterpiece. Perhaps those who understand Russian will get more out of it. In any event, the recording seems well enough made, though it is not always consistent. There is some echo in the big, expansive sound of the overture—the rests are not always silence. Two of the most famous scenes are available on a single side (Col CRLP 117), the performance being also from the Bolshoi Theater, the conductor this time Samosud. The same Mikhailov sings Sussanin's long monologue from Act 4, and the soprano Barsova offers Antonida's aria from the same act. The latter I found preferable to Shpieler; the voice is richer and more pleasing. However, the reproduction is on the dull side, quite definitely inferior to Vanguard's.

GLUCK, CHRISTOPH WILLIBALD VON (1714-1787)

*Frühlingsfeier. Berlin Mozart Boys' Ch; German Op House Cham O, Steffin, U URLP 7018 (*Ballet Suite).*

This is a twentieth-century adaptation of the composer's re-working of parts of his opera *Il Re Pastore*, fitted to a text by Klopstock. It is not important, however you take it, but its pleasant melodies emerge charmingly from the mouths of the boys. There is one soloist with a particularly melting voice. The accompanying orchestra is hardly a model of precision.

Alceste. Semser, s; Seri, t; Demigny, b; etc.; Ch; PPO, Leibowitz, Oc OCS 304 [3].

If such a masterpiece as *Alceste* is ever to hold its own in the repertoire, it must be performed by artists with exceptional voices and the grand manner. This recording was apparently timed to capitalize on the interest aroused by Flagstad's Metropolitan farewell in the title role; this may account for evidences of hasty preparation. Semser as Alceste, on whom so much depends, shows a voice of splendid possibilities, but not the schooling and the poise that are the essence of Gluck singing.

Iphigénie en Tauride. Neway, s; Mollet, b; Simoneau, t; etc.; Ch; PCO, Giulini, Vox PL 7822 [2].

It would be pleasant to hail *Iphigénie en Tauride* as a recorded masterpiece, but such are the inadequacies of this performance that one begins to wonder about the strength of the opera itself, despite so much first-rate music. Once again it seems that a cast has been hastily assembled and not sufficiently rehearsed. Only Simoneau shows any feeling for the heroic Gluck style. Neway, whose considerable reputation was built in the music of Menotti, was a strange choice for the title role.

L'Ivrogne corrigé. Lindenfelder, s; Collart, s; Betti, s; Benoit, t; Demigny, t; etc.; PPO, Leibowitz, Ren X 38.

This youthful comedy, with its premonitions of the greater Gluck, is performed all in the spirit of good clean fun. It comes through the ordeal of recording with colors flying higher than those of the composer's more significant works. These singers have a sense of style, and their voices sound well; everything seems thoroughly under control from the podium. Especially delightful is the trio near the end. One wonders, on being told the score has been revised by conductor Leibowitz, how much editing has actually been done, and how much of the music has been cut. The spoken dialogue running through the work seems less likely to pall than that in many such pieces.

Orfeo ed Euridice. Klose, c; Berger, s; Streich, s; Fleig, s; BCOC & O, Rother, U URLP 223 [3]. *(Abridged) Ferrier, c; Ayars, s; Vlachopoulos, s; GFC; SPO, Stiedry, L LL 924.*

Orphée et Euridice (abridged). Raveau, c; Feraldy, s; Delille, s; Vlassoff Ch; O, Tomasi, Vox PTL 6780.

For purposes of comparison, it is interesting to have both the Italian and the later French version (both authentic) of this masterpiece. The Tomasi performance has long been a phonographic classic, partly because of its substantial merits, but partly, too, because for many years it was the only recording available. Raveau enjoyed a big reputation in the title role, and it is good to have her singing of it preserved. The rest of the cast is adequate. For those who find the Italian language better suited to Gluck's classic lines, we now have the presentation of a distinguished German cast. Klose has certainly one of the noblest of latter-day contralto voices, and she has a sense of style, though her voice seems less rich here than when she sings in her own language. There are weak moments: in the duet with Euridice, the contralto's delivery is heavy and labored, nor is her conception of *"Che farò"* sufficiently simple and direct. At this crucial point, Raveau too falls down, for her tempo is incredibly slow—so slow, indeed, that to suit the exigencies of the twelve-inch 78-rpm disc for which she sang, she had to call it a day in mid-aria—which some may find ironically amusing in this day of LP! The Urania recording is uneven, but on the whole satisfactory; the Vox shows undeniable signs of its age. Mention has been left to this point of the London recording, distinguished only by its incomplete realization of Ferrier's noble Orpheus. At the time of this performance the contralto had not yet found her definitive interpretation, and apparently no one was greatly inspired by the conductor. The score was mercilessly cut, and the pruning has been carried still further in the transfer to LP. And unhappily the once-respectable reproduction has noticeably suffered with the change of speed. A vocally handsome and highly intelligent performance of *"Che farò"* (in German) by Martha Mödl is worth investigation (10" Tel TM 68009).

GOETZ, HERMANN (1840-1876)

Der Widerspenstigen Zähmung. Teschemacher, s; Trötschel, s; Nilssen, b; Ahlersmeyer, b; Frick, bs; etc.; DOC & O, Elmendorff, U URLP 221 [3].

Goetz's *Taming of the Shrew*, the masterpiece of a pitifully short career, waited many years for a hearing at the Metropolitan, and then, after a brief sojourn, returned to oblivion so far as the United States is concerned. This performance is presented by some of the most dependable of recent German singers, who give us a pretty good idea of the interesting, though not very Shakespearean score. Teschemacher, perhaps, does the most impressive job in the title role, for though her lovely voice does not always sound its best, she manages much in the way of characterization. One might wish for more lyricism in the singing of Ahlersmeyer, though he is fully equal to the vocal demands of his role. The rest are competent, but variable. Urania apologizes for the recording, which should have been better; it was felt that the work was worth attention, even in an imperfect presentation.

GOLDMARK, KARL (1830-1915)

Die Königin von Saba—Highlights. Elizza, s; Kurz, s; Bland, s; Slezak, t; Wiedemann, b; Hesch, bs; Et O-473.

The Queen of Sheba, once a sensational opera, retained its popularity in Vienna many years after the rest of the world had forgotten it. The singers of these Highlights were all stars of the great opera house in the Austrian capital in the first decade of the present century. Slezak enjoyed the greatest reputation internationally, and though his early recordings do not show all that I am sure he had, these examples are among his best. The voice obviously was huge, which fact must have made recording a problem for him. His singing of the aria *"Magische Töne"* has long been a collector's item, and is certainly beautifully controlled vocalism, though his ideas of melodic articulation were rather free. Wilhelm

Hesch, a magnificent basso who died in 1908, shows a fine breadth
of style in the aria *"Tritt ohne Zagen ein,"* though the recording
is weak. Elise Elizza is very lovely in Sulamith's first-act aria,
assisted by a sketchy women's chorus, and Selma Kurz is beyond
praise in the love-call from the second act. Kurz was celebrated
for the most nearly perfect trill in memory, and we have a breath-
taking example of it here. Elsa Bland and Friedrich Wiedemann
strike me as estimable, but less arresting, singers in their contributions to various duets.

GOUNOD, CHARLES FRANÇOIS (1818-1893)

Operas

*Faust. De los Angeles, s; Angelici, s; Michel, m-s; Gedda, t; Borthayre,
b; Christoff, bs; etc.; POC & O, Cluytens, V LM 6400 [3]. Geori-
Boué, s; Noré, t; Bourdin, b; Rico, bs; etc.; Ch; RPO, Beecham, V
LCT 6100 [3]. Steber, s; Conley, t; Guarrera, b; Siepi, bs; etc.; MOC
& O, Cleva, C SL 112 [3].*

Surely most listeners will find the latest "complete" *Faust* the
most satisfactory all around. For one thing, it is the most comprehensive, including, as it does, the "Walpurgis Night" scene,
with the ballet; for another, it benefits by the experienced guiding
hand of André Cluytens. But *Faust* is a singers' opera, and in
this as well as the other two sets the singing is variable. On the
right-hand side of the ledger, we have the Marguerite of Victoria
de los Angeles, even though she does little to suggest the character of the simple heroine; she simply sings ravishingly—perfectly, except for a high tone or two. Just a touch of the kind of
direct appeal Angelici brings to the role of Siébel would put her
out of this world. Michel is an unusually strong Martha. Best of
the men is the authentically French Borthayre; Gedda is a promising, not quite developed Faust, Christoff an unbearably mannered and un-French Mephistopheles. This is one opera in which
he should not have played on his strong resemblance to the late
Chaliapin. The advantages of a really French cast are demonstrated, by contrast, in the other two sets. Beecham's recording
was sensational when it was new, less because of the singing
than because for the first time a new side of Gounod's score was
revealed: the orchestration. Naturally, as the performance ante-
dates LP, it no longer scores for top-flight reproduction, and in-

deed there was always room for criticism of the placement of the
voices in relation to the microphones. But Sir Thomas had imported his cast from Paris, and with all their tendency to shrillness, they knew how to sing *Faust*. The original version of the
score was used, which means that the baritone aria composed for
the first London production—to Chorley's words, *"Even bravest
heart"*—is omitted. There are other cuts, more or less standard.
Cleva's reading of the score has none of the distinction of Beecham's, and the singers are an international group. Steber's voice
voice may be finer by nature than Geori-Boué's, but she has less
lyrical appeal; Conley's Faust has plenty of power and an Italianate
style; Guarrera seems to tire as he sings, and Siepi, potentially a
fine Devil, remains incorrigibly an Italian.
A set of Highlights by the New York City Center Opera Company
(MGM E 553, 10", or E 3023, coupled with *Aïda* Highlights) allots
an aria apiece and part of the Love Duet to Yeend, Bible, Petrak,
Cassel, and Scott, under the direction of Laszlo Halasz. It is all
reasonably well done in rather thick French. From Victor's historical archives another set has been assembled, featuring Farrar,
Mme Gilibert, Caruso, Scotti, and Journet (V LCT 1103). Most of
the recordings date from 1910, when the artists were at their peak.
An unfortunate exception is Farrar's "Jewel Song"—the superior
1908 version was passed up for that of 1913. The dubbing is good,
as such things go. Journet, it will be recalled, took part near the
end of his life in the first "complete" electrical recording of
Faust, a performance that might well be revived for his magnificent Mephistopheles. Assorted luminaries of the past are brought
together in Eterna's set of Highlights, the recordings ranging from
1905 to the early thirties (Et 487). Campagnola and Cerdan, excellent and authentically French singers, are able to triumph over
a completely inadequate orchestral background in the first act duo
for Faust and Mephistopheles. The only other "natives" in the
set are Talexis and Rigaux, whose Church Scene is inevitably
pale because of the inability of the early recording to catch the
atmosphere this music needs. The Italians are represented by de
Luca in Valentine's aria (with piano accompaniment), Bonci in
"Salve dimora," Arimondi in a wonderfully sonorous Serenade,
and Pasini-Vitale, Grassi, and Luppi in the final trio. Michael
Bohnen may be remembered by old-timers for the ructions he caused
with his Mephistopheles in New York, and it is not hard to sympa-

thize with the critics on hearing his erratic Germanic performances of *"Le Veau d'or"* and the *"Invocation"*—I doubt that any other recording contains as many or such prominent rolled r's as the latter. The limpid tones of Berta Kiurna triumph over the awkward German words in her electrically recorded "Jewel Song," but Bettendorf and Piccaver are less at home in the Garden Scene duet; the soprano allows her lovely voice to slide around, and the tenor seems not greatly interested in the whole thing. The dubbing throughout is successful.

Roméo et Juliette. Micheau, s; Collart, s; Jobin, t; Rehfuss, b; Cambon, bs; etc.; POC & O, Erede, L LLA 18 [3].

Such a recording can do much to reverse the positions of *Faust* and *Roméo* as Gounod's masterpiece and his second-best, for this was one of those rare occasions in the studios when everything seems to have gone just right, a circumstance that has never yet befallen *Faust* on records. Most important component of this success, of course, is the conductor, and I do not recall anything Erede has done on records or in the opera house to compare with this vital and masterful performance. Micheau makes a somewhat tentative beginning as Juliet, but by the time she reaches the famous waltz she is in her stride. A lovelier, more appealing heroine would be hard to find today. Jobin, too, does the best work we have had from him; in the love duets these artists blend with touching sympathy. Such a line as Romeo's *"Va, repose en paix"* sheds a new light on the capacities of the Canadian tenor. Pierre Mollet does a splendid job in the Queen Mab bit, and Collart is excellent in Stephano's aria. Rehfuss, as Frère Laurent, is likewise outstanding, and Cambon's treatment of the *couplets* in the first act might be taken as a model. For those who would like the fourth-act love duet only, there is a reasonably good (but quite American) performance, interestingly coupled with Tchaikovski's *Romeo and Juliet* duet, by Jean Fenn and Raymond Manton (Cap P 8189).

Songs

*Biondina. Cuenod, t; Holetschek, pf, W WL 5278 (*Fauré: La Bonne Chanson).*

Cuenod has usually been associated with the older schools of music, and his excursions into more modern repertoire have not

been unqualified successes. This simple little cycle of Gounod
fares better. Perhaps the very directness of the music was a
challenge; at any rate the twelve songs are given for all the charm
there is in them. One of them, *"Ho messo nuove corde,"* may be
familiar on its own right, but as a cycle, *Biondina* is new, at least
to me.

*Chanson de printemps; Ce que je suis sans toi; Ma Belle Amie est
morte; Venise; O ma Belle Rebelle; Viens! les gazons sont verts!;
Les Deux Pigeons. Souzay, b; Bonneau, pf, 10" L LD 9110.*

My first reaction on seeing this recorded recital was to scan the
list of titles in search of *"O ma Belle Rebelle,"* gratefully remembered from one of the first Souzay discs given American release, before LP. I am happy to report that it is here and thriving,
along with the rustling *"Chanson de printemps"* (not to be confused with the better known *"Au printemps"*) and *"Venise,"* for
which some of the best modern French musicians have expressed
admiration. The disc, indeed, is a good advocate for Gounod the
song-composer, though I suspect it might have won more friends
had some of the strophic *mélodies* been cut down to one time
through. I think the sympathetic annotator goes a little too far in
talking down the piano parts of the songs, for in the hands of
Jacqueline Bonneau several of them are quite beautiful—*viz.*, the
aforementioned *"Venise."* Souzay has given us nothing more
persuasive than this recital.

GRIEG, EDVARD HAGERUP (1843-1907)

*Peer Gynt—Incidental Music (original stage version). Maurstad,
speaker; Prytz, s; etc.; Oslo Phil O, Grüner-Hegge, Mer MG 10148.*

The comprehensiveness of this performance shrinks on examina-
tion: according to the jacket note, the disc contains thirteen of
the twenty-four pieces in the score, the remaining eleven being
mostly functional to the drama and not independently interesting as
music. Some of the numbers we hear, however, have vocal parts
not here included: for example, the familiar *"In the Hall of the
Mountain King"* should properly have a chorus. Most interesting
of the vocal numbers included is the little-known *"Chorus of the
Saeter Girls,"* with Peer Gynt's spoken lines. *"Solvejg's Song,"*
reduced to a single stanza, is nicely given by Eva Prytz, but the

singer surpasses this effort in the moving *"Cradle Song"* with which the work ends.

Gutten; Fra Monte Pincio; Ved Rondarne; Vaaren; Eros; En Svane.
Flagstad, s; PHI, Braithwaite, Süsskind, 10" V LM 99.
En Svane; Modersorg; Med en Vandlilje; Tak for dit raad. Niemela, s;
*Koskimies, pf, WCFM 5 (*Sibelius, Kilpinen: Songs).*
Solvejg's Song; On St. John's Eve; Tides of Spring; I love thee; A
Dream; Thanks for thy advice; A Swan. Warenskjold, s; Concert Arts
*O, Greeley, Cap P 8247 (*Dvořák: Songs).*

Grieg's measure as a song-writer is apparent only when we hear his music sung in the original language. It is a major tragedy that so many of his works in this field, first published in Germany, have become internationally known in none-too-happy translations. It is greatly to Flagstad's credit that her recitals did so much to make this clear; she never sang so eloquently as in her own tongue. Her program of Grieg therefore is one of the most valuable souvenirs she has left, including as it does several of the masterpieces. The fact that the group has been orchestrated is by no means fatal (though unfortunate, at least in the case of *"A Swan"*) for they are mostly big songs. Perhaps a passing sigh is in order over the memory of this singer's prewar recording of the *Haugtussa* cycle, surely one of the finest things she did for the phonograph (V M 714). A re-make in the days of LP was far less satisfactory, and has been for some time on the retired list (LM 1094).

Niemela's group is part of a program called "Songs of Scandinavia." Hers is a sweet, expressive voice and a good degree of interpretative talent. Her *"En Svane"* is more intimate than Flagstad's, and her *"Modersorg"* is outstanding. One curious shortcoming in the singer is a lack of support in some of the softer and lower passages. With the Warenskjold disc we go back to orchestrations and hear the songs in English. One or two survive the first ordeal well enough—*"Tides of spring"* (*"Vaaren"*), for example—but most are too delicate for such treatment. And it is the same *"Tides of spring"* that suffers most in translation. I must confess to so much pleasure derived from the limpid voice of the singer and her unfailing good taste in performance that I cannot condemn the record.

GRUEN, JOHN (1927-   )

Vier Studentenbuch Lieder; Die Sirenen; Hälfte des Lebens; Four Songs (e.e.cummings); Chansons de Geishas. Bannister, s; Gruen, pf, Ele 1.

Pomes Penyeach; Thirteen ways of looking at a blackbird. Neway, s; Gruen, pf, Con AP 121 (*Donovan, Kraehenbuehl: Woodwind Quartets).

Born in Paris, educated in Berlin and Milan, Gruen is a man of many languages, which accounts for the breadth of his selection in poetry. So far, he has devoted himself almost exclusively to the writing of songs, though a sample of his choral compositions may be found in the Concert Choir's "Contemporary Christmas Carols" program (Con AP 122). Of the two song recordings, Bannister's is the more ingratiating, largely because of the soprano's lovely voice and clean style. The most likely to achieve popularity are the haunting Cummings settings and the delicate French *Geisha Songs*. Neway's approach is more aggressive; she shows power rather than intimacy, and her voice lacks Bannister's appeal.

HAHN, REYNALDO (1875-1947)

Chansons grises; Quand je fus pris au pavillon; L'Incrédule; Paysage; Phyllis; Si mes vers avaient des ailes; Mai. Jansen, b; Bonneau, pf, 10" L LS 645.

Chansons grises; D'une prison; Si mes vers avaient des ailes; Offrande. Chelsi, b· pf, MT MLO 1008.

This composer's representation on LP is disappointing. Any singer making up a program is likely to include "*Si mes vers avaient des ailes*"—Dobbs (An 35094), Sayão (10" C ML 2152), Singher (C ML 4258), Swarthout (V LM 1793), Teyte (V LCT 1133), Tourel (C ML 4158)—but few seem to realize that he wrote other and better songs. Neither program listed above is really satisfactory, though the repertoire is attractive. *Chansons grises* is a cycle of seven songs, including "*L'Heure exquise*" and "*En sourdine.*" Jansen omits two of them. Unfortunately, his singing lacks the element of grace without which these songs simply do

not come off. The voice as we hear it in this recording is stiff
and unresilient; the songs, in consequence, sound a little dull.
If Chelsi, who sings the cycle complete, had been as well recorded as Jansen, his would be the preferred disc. But alas! his
lyric voice and tasteful style are at a hopeless disadvantage. The
anonymous pianist, no master at best, is cruelly treated. The best
sampling of Hahn, then, remains the three songs included in the
oldish Maggie Teyte recital: *"Offrande," "L'Heure exquise,"* and
"Si mes vers."

HALÉVY, JACQUES-FRANCOIS (1799-1862)

*La Juive—Highlights. David, s; Scampini, t; Mann, t; Slezak, t; Mar-
dones, bs; Didur, bs; Hesch, bs, Et 0-475 (*Kol Nidre, Schwarz, b).*

Very little of Halévy's still vital opera has found its way to discs:
only the tenor aria *"Rachel, quand du Seigneur"* and the bass
cavatina *"Si la rigeur"* seem to keep their popularity outside the
opera house. The former (so intimately associated with the voice
of Enrico Caruso) is represented in these Highlights by the good
performance in German of Josef Mann. The voice is unusually
meaty, the style excellent. José Mardones, once of the Metropolitan, sings the cavatina with all the glory of his uniquely rich
organ and stately style, using the Italian text. Another late Metropolitan basso, Adamo Didur, gives a good account of the "Malediction" from Act 3. There is also a duet by Leo Slezak and Wilhelm Hesch. And by way of an encore, Josef Schwarz sings *Kol
Nidre.* The recordings, all acoustic, have the inevitable inequalities of such selections.

HANDEL, GEORGE FRIDERIC (1685-1759)

Choral Works

*Alexander's Feast. Scheunemann, s; Chabay, t; Falkner, bs; Cornell
U Ch; Handel Soc O, Hull. Hd HDL 13 [2].*

A good deal of thought, scholarship, and plain hard work have
gone into the preparation of this recording. Robert Hull, the conductor, and John Beaven, who plays the continuo, have applied
their considerable knowledge to the problems of realization and
ornamentation; where liberties have been taken with the score (including negligible cuts and some trimming at the end of the work),

Hull explains the reasons in his jacket notes. Chorus and orchestra have been thoroughly trained. The soloists are an admirable trio. Chief honors are due Chabay: both he and Scheunemann furnish some examples of phrasing and breath control well worthy of study by aspiring oratorio singers, though the soprano has some apparent difficulties too. Mechanically the set is acceptable, if not quite grade A.

Belshazzar. Sailer, s; Muench, c; Metz, c; Fehringer, t; Titze, bs; SCMC & O, Grischkat, Per SPL 594 [2].

This recording appeared almost simultaneously with another from Berlin, directed by Helmut Koch (BG 534/5 [2]). If one worked hard to find something in favor of the latter, one could say that the Bach Guild reproduction is more brilliant and powerful than Period's; but at the same time it is consistently coarser and less clear in definition. In performance, too, Grischkat's offering is far more satisfactory than Koch's. The Stuttgart soloists are definitely superior. I do not recall hearing Sailer sing so well in any of her various other recordings; the dramatic recitative with which she opens the work is electrifying in its effect, and the succeeding aria has style as well as vocal appeal. Muench, too, proves an exceptionally able artist, with one of the richest, most impressive voices yet heard in a Stuttgart recording. Fehringer's tone is admirably solid, though some of his passage work is rough. The voice has the size and quality, however, to give his singing the necessary weight. Titze delivers his solos well. The performance possesses the spirit so obviously lacking in that of Koch. One is aware of the beauties of the chorus *"By slow degrees the wrath of God,"* and the opening solo parts of *"Tell it out among the heathen,"* details that pass by us in the other set. Both are sung in German, of course, and both are extensively cut.

Chandos Anthems, No. 6, As pants the hart for cooling streams; No. 11, Let God arise. Van Doorn, s; Woudt, c; Larsen, t; Hollestelle, bs; NHSC & O, Loorij, Hd HDL 17.

These performances are full-blooded and honest, adequate to bring to us the majesty and power of the music, but not free from faults that should have been prevented. First, the soloists might have been coached in the English language—taken in the average, they are neither correct nor consistent. Sometimes they say "the hart" in the accepted manner; sometimes they make it "thee hart." The soprano is the best in this, as in other respects, the tenor perhaps the worst, what with a thin, nasal tone and unclear diction. The chorus sings with considerable enthusiasm, its principal weakness being in the tone of the tenors. The altos are covered up a good deal of the time, but the over-all tone is solid and sonorous. Sonorous, too, is the competent orchestra. The acoustics of the recording are rather peculiar; there is little attempt to capture any room atmosphere, and the placement of the components is not consistent.

Dettingen Te Deum. Hansel, s; Koerner, c; Barritt, t; Ronk, b; Nat'l Presby Church Ch; NGO, Schaefer, WCFM LP 6.

This *Te Deum* includes the famous "Prayer," or *"Vouchsafe, O Lord,"* otherwise, *"Dignare, Domine,"* known in Flesch's violin transcription and as a staple of Marian Anderson's repertoire. The work as a whole is festive in character, curiously reminiscent of *Messiah.* The chorus is the feature of this effective performance. The tone is incisive and clean. The soloists are the very type of modest church singer, capable but not too impressive. One wishes for a weightier voice in the bass parts, such as *"Thou art the King of Glory"* and the aforementioned *"Vouchsafe, O Lord."* The virtuoso trumpeter, Lloyd Geisler, deserves a word of praise.

Israel in Egypt. Morrison, s; Kalmus, s; Thomas, c; Lewis, t; Lea, bs; Riley, bs; Handel Soc Ch & O, Goehr, Hd HDL 1. (In German) Welting, s; Bialas, s; Münzig, c; Horst, t; Räker, bs; Rungenhagen, bs; BCC; BESO, Koch, BG 521/2 [2].

Neither of these recordings is a masterpiece; the Handel Society version is preferred largely because it uses the original English text. The choruses, which carry most of the weight, are not the last word in clarity, despite the fact that the group numbers no more than fifty singers. Even so, the grooves of the record seem overloaded. The soloists are well seasoned in the oratorio style, especially Richard Lewis, who gives an impressive performance of the florid aria *"The enemy said."* In the German presentation, the positions are reversed. Of the soloists, only the tenor is passable; at times one of the sopranos is almost painful to hear. But the chorus makes more of its descriptive opportunities than does its English rival. Here we can recapture the famous excitement of the "Hailstone Chorus" and admire the graphic representation of lice and flies. I was struck anew by the pastoral beauty of *"But as for His people,"* and I found *"But the waters overwhelmed their enemies"* terrific. But these points do not add up to a performance of *Israel in Egypt.*

Judas Maccabaeus. Soloists; U of Utah Ch; Utah SO, Abravanel, Hd HDL 12 [3].

This is a performance in the festival tradition, the result of long and patient preparation. Chorus and orchestra have, however, been kept to reasonable size, so that the score is heard cleanly, free of old-fashioned Handelian overloading. The soloists appear to be a group of young people, promising enough, but hardly ready to give a definitive performance. Indeed, the set having been issued under so official-sounding a sponsorship, some explanation should have been provided for the various cuts and of the solutions arrived at for the textual problems.

Messiah. Vyvyan, s; Procter, c; Maran, t; Brannigan, bs; LPC & O, Boult, L LLA 19 [4]. Ritchie, s; Shacklock, c; Herbert, t; Standen, bs; LPC & O, Scherchen, W WAL 308 [3]. Suddaby, s; Thomas, c; Nash, t; Anthony, bs; Luton Ch Soc; RPO, Beecham, V LCT 6401 [4]. Marshall, s; Palmateer, c; Vickers, t; Milligan, bs; TMC; TORO, Mac-Millan, V LBC 6100 [3]. Baillie, s; Ripley, c; Johnston, t; Walker, bs; Huddersfield Ch; LIV, Sargent, C SL 151 [3].

The score of *Messiah*s now stands at one decidedly up, four down, and two to go: Sargent's second version has already been released in England, and Beecham is rumored to be preparing his third. Whether or not Sir Thomas will match the two latest additions to the American lists in striving for stylistic correctness, he is rightfully entitled to the credit for starting the trend in this direction. His first *Messiah*, released more than twenty years ago, was hard for the traditionalists to accept: he had re-studied the work from the ground up, and made an attempt to get away from the British "choral festival" approach to which the score was usually subjected. The subsequent publication of J. M. Coopersmith's edition of the score, shorn of all excrescences, complete to the inclusion of all authentic variants of the many numbers, has opened the way for "pure" Handel performances. Such the two latest recordings claim to be, Scherchen's restoring the "original Dublin version, 1742," Boult's adhering to the "original manuscript" and "original orchestration." While Scherchen's is certainly a very interesting venture, it suffers from a couple of fallacies. This may well be *Messiah* as Handel originally conceived it, but, as the Coopersmith edition shows, the composer changed his mind about a number of things, and why should his uncorrected score be considered *the* authentic one? The performance itself, while returning to the fountainhead, has had no divine guidance to keep it from straying too far from the traditional. There are times when Scherchen's tempos and details of his reading can be described only as erratic. On the credit side are the clean and finely balanced choruses, especially the florid ones, and the general, if not altogether consistent, level of the solo singing. Boult has all the advantages of a similarly reduced choir (we are not told how large it is), excellent orchestral support, and soloists easily as satisfactory, taken as a group, as those who sing for Scherchen. And Boult, while also leaving the paths of tradition, and favoring splendidly brisk tempos that would have shocked our grandfathers, never strays beyond the bounds of good taste and solid, defensible musicianship. The over-all impression of the recording is of a great healthiness, admirably in keeping with the spirit of the work, and a masterly finish in every detail. Best of the eight soloists is Boult's contralto, Norma Procter, whose tones are of a richness once not unusual in England, but associated in recent years chiefly with the late Kathleen Ferrier. Her opposite number wants tonal solidity; hers are a less imposing instrument and a less searching art. Ritchie may be said to typify the British oratorio soprano, and a right good one she is. She has the facility for *"Rejoice greatly,"* the lyrical line for *"He shall feed His flock"* (of which she sings the entire aria, not just the second part), and the breadth for *"I know that my Redeemer liveth."* The last aria emerges with an effective violin obbligato, but Scherchen does not probe the depths as did Beecham for Elsie Suddaby in the Victor recording. Jennifer Vyvyan sings almost entirely without vibrato, which induces a boyish, sometimes rather hooty quality. She is at her best in the floridity of *"Rejoice greatly"*: in the more sustained numbers one cannot forget her Britishness. Both tenors make notable soft effects in *"Comfort ye"* and *"Ev'ry valley."* Herbert surprises us later with his effective *forte* in *"Thou shalt break them";* Maran gets more contrast into his earlier numbers. Neither bass is notable for sensuous tone; Standen's is the better controlled, the less gruff, the more stylishly employed. It might be added that in the Boult performance it is not uncommon for the soloists to break their long-drawn phrases, though they do it neatly enough. Of course, Beecham's Victor recording is mechanically outmoded, and transfer to LP has not bettered its faded colors. But it remains, as a performance, in some ways the finest of the five listed. Never a deliberate pur-

ist, Sir Thomas is incorrigibly musical; he can often convince us
that his least orthodox effects are right. In the interests of clarity
he has reduced his chorus for the more florid numbers, but he is
not afraid to make a joyful noise when sonorities seem called for.
The soloists are not the best imaginable (hardly comparable to
those in the original Columbia Beecham set), but they are adequate.
The MacMillan offering is in the accepted festival spirit, solid
and impressive. The choral tone is big and pleasing, with an unusually strong alto section, and the group manages the patches of
coloratura with good success. Marshall is outstanding among the
soloists, though she suggests a fine artist on the threshold of her
career rather than a set, mature vocalist. The others start rather
tentatively and improve as the work progresses, though Palmateer
never seems to have her fine vocal material really in hand. This
is not an uncut *Messiah*. Mechanically, it is not far behind the
Scherchen and the Boult. As for Sargent's, it is better reproduced
than Beecham's, with which it was more or less contemporary,
but it is more the orthodox conception, and by no means so exciting. As a quartet, the soloists are better than Beecham's, though
none of them rises to comparable heights. What the conductor
does in his new version will be of considerable interest.

Since the above was written, the new Sargent recording has arrived (An 3510-C [3]). Apparently reacting against the trend of the
times, the conductor tells us: "The Liverpool Philharmonic play
the original Handel string, trumpet and drum parts, plus orchestration which I have arranged, unhesitatingly adopting any good ideas
from earlier experienced editors." The performance is not uncut.
Strangely, the customary *appoggiaturas* are eliminated. But what
one is likely to quarrel with is not the "unscholarly" approach,
which could be quite refreshing, so much as the fact that Sargent
has not struck a spark as have Beecham, Boult, and Scherchen.
There is needless fussiness in some of the choruses, and the soloists—Morison, Thomas, Lewis, and Walker—do not seem very
strongly convinced of the sheer beauty in the music. The recording is spacious and clear.

*Ode for St Cecilia's Day. Hoffmann, s; Ludwig, t; LC; RBO, Rother,
U URLP 7023.*

If one accepts the anomaly of hearing the Dryden text sung in German (both languages are given on the jacket), there is much to admire in the authoritative vocalism of the veteran Walther Ludwig

and the less dazzling but appealing lyrical work of Lore Hoffmann. The recording setup for once has not favored the singers, who seem to be placed beyond the orchestra. The resulting effect is not one of especially sharp outlines, but of unusually natural balance. The tone is not, however, altogether free from distortion.

Passion According to St. John. Harvey, s; Pfenninger, c; Häfliger, t; Olsen, bs; Zurich Bach Ch; WIN, Henking, Hd HDL 16 [2].

This performance has vitality; it is technically and musically proficient, though it does not remain consistently at its own highest level. The choral parts are sung with assurance and good clarity. Of the soloists, the men show up better than the women. The soprano shoots rather widely in some passages; the contralto, called upon to impersonate Pilate, drives her voice, perhaps for purposes of characterization. The tenor delivers his lines in a nicely round and solid tone, and the bass acquits himself with credit in a cruelly difficult assignment. The recording has clarity and solidity, if not much atmosphere. The soloists are all rather close upon us.

Saul. Craner, c; Moonan, t; Griffeth, bs; etc.; Crane Ch & O, McElheran, Hd HDL 15 [2].

The Handel Society seems to divide its attention between recordings of professional singing made abroad and the preservation of college performances in this country. Although these latter are certainly creditable enough for what they are, too often they do not represent any special effort to present the works in full authenticity. The score of *Saul* is cut considerably, for one thing. For another, the soloists are obviously drawn from the student body, except for one or two who stand out—doubtless faculty members. All this would be acceptable enough, even admirable, if one were attending the performance on the campus; but for recording it leaves much to be desired. However, the orchestra is good, and cleanly reproduced; the chorus meets the standards, though it is somewhat muffled in reproduction, especially the soprano section. Best of the soloists is a pleasing contralto, Jane Craner, who has a sense of style. For the rest, too many of the recitatives are metronomic, too many of the arias just too much for the singers.

Te Deum for the Peace of Utrecht; Let Thy hand be strengthened (Coronation Anthem). Soloists; DRC & O, Wöldike, HS HSL 2046.

Three things, above others, strike the listener in this recording: the fresh, unencumbered approach of the performers to the music, the mastery of our language by this group of invading Danes, and the fine clarity of the reproduction. The music, cut in Handel's familiar pattern of brief alternating choruses and solos, thus comes to us in all its eloquence, and though, because of the setting, the text is not always easy to follow by ear alone, one feels that there is little in the work that has not been realized. The numerous soloists acquit themselves admirably.

Operas

Acis and Galatea. Ritchie, s; Lewis, t; Herbert, t; Anthony, bs; Handel Soc Ch & O, Goehr, Hd HDL 2 [3].

If not a complete realization of Handel's admired pastoral (with a libretto by John Gay of *Beggar's Opera* fame), this is good enough to bring out many of its happy inspirations of melody and descriptive instrumentation. And if the work seems to run a bit to length, with a certain monotony resulting from the succession of solos by alternate tenors, there is much in it with which we would not willingly part. Soloists and chorus have the British virtues of steadiness and accuracy, and all sing with style. Ritchie is especially good, but she seems too close to the microphone. The reproduction of the chorus could be clearer.

Giulio Cesare. Gaehwiller, s; Brueckner-Rueggeberg, t; Sandoz, bs; etc.; Handel Soc Ch & O, Goehr, Hd HDL 18 [2]. Roon, s; Handt, t; Wiener, bs; VKC; PRCO, Swarowsky, Vox PL 8012 [2].

It is depressing to report that neither of these two presentations of Handel's opera does it anything approaching justice. Both performances are heavily cut, the Handel Society version eliminating the repeats in many *da capo* arias, the Vox dispensing with the *secco* recitatives and reducing the cast from eight to five. Both are sung in the Germanic tradition, rather heavily and without much vocal charm. Of course, complete authenticity in a Handel opera is hardly possible today: the role of Caesar, for example, was composed for a *castrato*. The solution in both sets is the only possible one: he has become a baritone. Of the two Caesars, Sandoz has the lighter, more supple voice; Gaehwiller is a more satisfying Cleopatra than Roon; as Sextus, the promising Herbert Handt has more to offer than Brueckner-Rueggeberg. In neither case is the recording balance ideal, though perhaps here the preference should go to the Handel Society.

Il Pastor Fido. Warner, s; Hunt, s; Rowe, s; Rogier, b; etc.; CHAM, Engel, C ML 4685.

Although the writer of the jacket notes goes to some lengths to tell us of the improvements made by Handel when this little opera was revived in 1734, turning a failure into a resounding success, a comparison of the first and second versions in the Handel Gesellschaft edition reveals that Engel has prepared an abridged version of the first. A certain proficiency is in evidence throughout the performance, strongly controlled by the conductor, as is a general sense of the proper style, if not a complete achievement of what this implies. One wonders why a piano was used rather than a harpsichord for the continuo. The singers are on the whole good, with chief honors going to Genevieve Warner. Hers is a nice, easy delivery, and she shows admirable neatness in the execution of the florid passages. The reproduction is clear and solid.

Rodelinda. Sailer, s; Lipp, c; Fehringer, t; Hagner, bs; etc.; SDRC & O, Müller-Kray, Per SPL 589.

The first strike against this recording is the ruthless cutting the score has undergone: the opera simply cannot be done justice on one disc. Even the lovely aria *"Dove sei"* (well known in the English adaptation, *"Art thou troubled?"*) appears minus its middle section and repeat. Fortunately, the more important of the two essentials for an adequate performance of Handel—style and voice—is the former, for the singers in the set are all by nature quite modestly endowed. They do have intelligence and good intentions. Sailer's voice is neat and compact, quite obviously small; Fehringer's well matches hers; others are even smaller. The recitatives are tossed off rather casually—a triumph, it may be, for a cast of Germans who do not always succeed in pronouncing such words as *"questo,"* but not quite fair to the music.

Cantatas

Apollo e Dafne. Ritchie, s; Boyce, b; Ch & O, Lewis, OL LD 14.

Handel's treatment of the Daphne story takes the form of a cantata, the major portion of which is here the lot of the admirably robust Bruce Boyce. Margaret Ritchie's ethereal tones are less well served by the microphone.

No. 6, Cecilia, volgi un sguardo. Van Doorn, s; Larsen, t; NHSO, Loorij. No. 8, Dalla guerra amorosa. Hollestelle, bs; NHSO, Loorij. Hd HDL 19.

No. 8, Dalla guerra amorosa. Hudemann, bs; Wenzinger, vlc; Neumeyer, hpschd; 10" D DL 7542 (*Telemann: Cantata No. 1).

No. 13, *Armida abbandonata; No. 14, Agrippina condotta a morire; No.
17, Pensieri notturni di Filli (Nel dolce dell' oblio).* Giebel, s; STO,
Lamy, Oc OCS 30.
No. 15, *Dolce pur d'amor l'affano.* Woudt, c; NHSO, Loorij. No. 17,
Pensieri notturni. Van Doorn, s; NHSO, Loorij. No. 20, *Spande ancor
a mio dispetto.* Hollestelle, bs; NHSO, Loorij. *Salve Regina.* Van
Doorn, s; NHSO, Loorij. Hd HDL 20.
No. 17, *Pensieri notturni.* Lamoree, s; NYPMA, ES 515 (*Sonata; Trio
Sonata).

The first of these cantatas takes up a little more than one side.
Van Doorn sings well, on the whole, in a modest, sweet little
voice. Larsen may not be quite up to some of the florid passages,
but his tone is mellifluous, his taste excellent. The final duet
has been pointed out as first-rate Handel; it is also the best-sung
portion of the work. Hollestelle, in the second cantata, shows
himself a capable basso, a little soggy in tone, but flexible and
musical. His *Dalla guerra amorosa* is well recorded, though perhaps there is a little too much of his voice for the good of the balance. Hudemann gives an entirely different view of this cantata,
treating it with more enthusiasm and a streak of humor. His concern is in putting over the text, while Hollestelle aims (with some
success) at virtuosity. The balance in the Decca record is better,
with the harpsichord quite prominent. *Nel dolce dell' oblio* turns
up three times, and the versions offer a marked contrast. For vocal attractiveness, a choice would favor Lamoree, who has a beautifully realized recorder obbligato played by Bernard Krainis. The
pace of the performance, however, is a little fast and nervous.
The sustained parts are better sung than the recitative, in which
the soprano slights the words. Agnes Giebel is even less impressive in the recitatives, and hers is not a particularly attractive
voice. Still, the tempos of the arias seem about right, and she too
has a superior obbligato, played by Alfred Mann. Dora Van Doorn
is better where her rivals are weak, but she falls behind them in
the arias. These she sings quite slowly, without much vitality.
The recorder is here displaced by a flute. To cap all, the reproduction is unclear. The other cantatas on the disc with hers are
better, and she redeems herself in the *Salve Regina.* Woudt's voice
is rich and creamy. The Oceanic and Esoteric recordings are excellent; that of the Handel Society is variable. To complete the
list, mention should be made of a superficial performance in Ger-

man of the cantata *In Praise of Harmony* by Valerie Bak (Mer MG
10085).

Arias

*Samson—Return, O God of Hosts; Judas Maccabaeus—Father of
Heaven; Messiah—O Thou that tellest; He was despised. Ferrier, c;
LPO, Boult, L LL 688 (*Bach: Arias).*

> Outstanding among these selections is the noble air *"Return, O
> God of Hosts,"* sung with stylistic breadth and gorgeous tonal
> quality. *"He was despised"* also is done in a manner all too rare
> in our time.

*Acis and Galatea—O ruddier than the cherry. Bispham, b. Joshua—
O hätt' ich Jubals Harf. Lilli Lehmann, s. Serse—Vo godendo vez-
zoso e bello. Anselmi, t. Rodelinda—Eitler Glanz, wo weilst du?
(Dove sei). Leisner, c. Il Pensieroso—Sweet bird (in French).
Ritter-Ciampi, s. Cantata con stromenti—Dank sei dir, Herr. Leisner,
c. Judas Maccabaeus—Sound an alarm. Kingston, t. Giulio Cesare
—Es blaut die Nacht (V'adoro, pupille). Liebenberg, c. Et 488.*

> The "golden age" herein represented stretches from the early
> acoustic Lehmann and Anselmi selections to the electrical re-
> cordings of Ritter-Ciampi, Leisner, and Liebenberg, a span of
> twenty years or so. Vocally, the singers all had plenty to offer;
> stylistically, they were uneven, as any such assembly is bound to
> be. Lehmann's *"Oh, had I Jubal's lyre"* is a masterpiece of
> steady rhythmic flow, all but incredible for a woman around sixty.
> Bispham's piece of bravado is delightful, and Kingston proves
> himself a tenor of robust voice and heroic style. Ritter-Ciampi's
> aria is a fine piece of expressive singing (obscured by a strong
> hum retained from the original recording); but Anselmi's *métier*
> was obviously not Handel; and Leisner's *Rodelinda* and Lieben-
> berg's *Caesar* are weighted down by the translations. Leisner's
> *"Dank sei dir"* (a noble aria, whose authenticity the Handel au-
> thorities question) has impressive breadth and sweep.

HANSON, HOWARD (1896-   )

Songs from Drum Taps. Eastman Ch & O, Hanson, Mer MG 40000.

> Hanson and the Mercury engineers have here surpassed them-
> selves in a magnificent presentation of this Whitman setting. Not
> the least of its virtues is the choral diction, thanks to which every
> word stands out with perfect clarity. A powerful effect is achieved
> by the use of persistent drum beats.

HAUER, JOSEF MATHIAS (1883-   )

Hölderlin Lieder.   Batic, c; Leukauf, pf, NR NRLP 405 (*Křenek, Kodály: Songs).

Although little known in America, Hauer was in his time a leader among the radical modernists of his native Vienna. He claims, indeed, to have worked out a twelve-tone system before Schoenberg began thinking along these lines. The lieder on this record sound curiously angular and do not seem altogether certain of their direction. This impression may be the responsibility of the quavery singer. The total effect is interesting rather than attractive.

HAYDN, JOSEF (1732-1809)

Masses

No. 1, Missa brevis in F. Heusser, s; A. Berger, s; VKC; VSYC, Gillesberger.   No. 5, Missa brevis St. Joannis de Deo.   Heusser, s; VKC; VSYC, Gillesberger, Ly LL 30.
No. 5, Missa Brevis St. Joannis de Deo.   Frederiksen, s; CBMC; Palace Chapel O, Wöldike.   Aus dem Dankliede zu Gott; Der Augenblick; Die Harmonie in der Ehe; Die Beredsamkeit; Der Greis; Abendlied zu Gott.   Danish St Rad Cham Ch; Linderud, pf, Wöldike, HS HSL 2064.

Haydn is reported to have harbored an affection in later life for his first effort with the Mass text, a product of his eighteenth year. He even revised the instrumentation with a view to publication, but in this recording his original intentions are respected. The *St. Joannis de Deo* Mass, often referred to as the "Little Organ Mass," dates from about fifteen years later. Its most memorable movement is the soprano solo *"Benedictus,"* with organ obbligato. The contrasting performances offered are both good, the Viennese version being the larger in conception, but on the whole the less satisfactory. Heusser's voice is on the thin side and a little hooty, and the reproduction of the organ (a seventeenth-century *portativ* is used) is not altogether clean. To me there is something much more appealing in the boy soloist used by Wöldike. His recording was made in the palace chapel at Christiansborg, where the organ dates from 1854. Aside from a rather heavy bass, the reproduction is excellent. The part-songs range from religious to humorous subjects; all are done with the almost superfluous piano. Most memorable of the set is *"Der Greis,"* which in Haydn's later years became something of a theme-song for him.

No. 2, Grosse Orgelmesse, in E flat. Roon, s; Rössl-Majdan, c; Kmentt, t; Berry, bs; VKC; VSY, Grossmann, Vox PL 7020.

Mendelssohn thought this Mass "scandalously gay," and indeed it is not a strikingly devotional work; but, considering Haydn's nature, the setting is certainly not inappropriate. Again the organ is prominent, especially in the *"Benedictus,"* and in this performance the sound of the instrument used is a particular delight. The work of the chorus is generally good, though we must count their enthusiasm to some extent as balancing some not quite unanimous attacks. Occasionally, as in *"Et vitam venturi,"* the conductor allows them to rush. The soloists are capable, but not always perfectly matched: the soprano and alto duet is better than that for alto and tenor. The fine restrained singing of Rössl-Majdan is outstanding. On the whole, the balance is happy, with just enough acoustical "blending" to give atmosphere.

No. 3, Missa Sanctae Caeciliae. Schweiger, s; Wagner, c; Handt, t; Berry, bs; VKC; VSY, Gillesberger, HS HSLP 2028 [2].

In contrast to those listed above, this Mass is a long one, appropriate rather to a festival than to a church service. There are plenty of elaborate sections, much florid writing, and many word repetitions. Allowing for some emotionalism on the part of the tenor soloist, the performance is up to the best Haydn Society standards. The recording balance is admirable in the choral sections, but the quartet is a bit too close.

No. 6, Missa cellensis in C ("Mariazellermesse"). Rathauscher, s; Janacek, c; Equiluz, t; Berry, bs; VKC; VSY, Gillesberger, HS HSLP 2011.

This Mass is said to be especially popular in central Europe. It is a brief work, unusually bright and festive with its trumpets and timpani. The performance has spirit and life, with excellent choral and orchestral work, but some tentative singing on the part of the soloists. A musicological feature is the special treatment of grace notes, a subject on which misunderstanding has been universal for lo! these many years. The recording, outstanding when it was new, remains effective, though it is not one of the finest from the Haydn Society.

No. 7, Paukenmesse (Missa in tempore belli) in C. Topitz-Feiler, s; Milinkovic, c; Handt, t; Braun, bs; VKC; VSO, Gillesberger, HS HSLP 2021.

Not only is the composer in his best form here, but performance and recording are outstanding in several ways. Chorus and orchestra acquit themselves nobly, and the recording engineer (H. Vose Greenough, Jr.) has caught with especially fine effect the full mass of sound. The vocal soloists, perhaps, are a little close, just enough to emphasize their less admirable aspects. The voice of the soprano emerges as somewhat thin, and one is conscious of the fact that the bass is not absolutely comfortable in the *tessitura* of *"Qui tollis."* But this is a major Mass and a major recording. Those who teach with records should be pleased with the number of spirals dividing the movements. To split one hair: I wish we could have had the *"Et resurrexit"* follow directly after the magnificent *"Crucifixus"* without the interruption between sides.

No. 8, Missa Sancti Bernardi de Offida ("Heiligmesse"). CBMC; DRO, Wöldike, HS HSLP 2048.

This fine, clean recording might serve as a model in performance and reproduction. There may be more of musical interest in some of the other Masses, but none is more satisfactorily presented.

No. 9, Missa solemnis in D minor ("Lord Nelson Mass"). Della Casa, s; Höngen, c; Taubmann, t; London, bs; VKC; VSY, Sternberg, HS HSLP 2004.

The outstanding feature of this performance is the lovely singing of Lisa Della Casa; the rest of the soloists are adequate, though not in her class. The Mass itself is one of the most exciting, and Sternberg, with a well-trained chorus and a good orchestra, does himself considerable credit. The sound of the chorus is particularly good in reproduction.

No. 10, Missa solemnis in B flat ("Theresienmesse"). Felbermayer, s; Hermann, c; Patzak, t; Poell, bs; VSOC; VSY, Krauss, Vox PL 6740.

This is perhaps the most sheerly beautiful of all the Haydn Masses, and the names of the participating artists make the most impressive display of all the listings in this section. I suspect, however, that the late Clemens Krauss and his cohorts did not have enough time to prepare the work. Nevertheless, for my part, I accept the recording with gratitude, so lovely is the music. The two distinguished male soloists outshine their companions, though Felbermayer's voice is beautiful, as usual. The chorus seems a bit removed from us.

No. 12, Missa solemnis in B flat ("Harmoniemesse"). Katschinka, s; Kenney, c; Löffler, t; Engen, bs; Orch Soc of Vienna C & O, Larsen, Per SPLP 541.

This is one of the less good Haydn Mass recordings. The reproduction is coarse and lacking in depth. The soloists are not out-standing, and they were a little close to the microphone.

Oratorios

Die Jahreszeiten.   Eipperle, s; Patzak, t; Hann, bs; VSOC; VPH, Krauss, HS HSLP 2027 [3].   Trötschel, s; Ludwig, t; Greindl, bs; RIASCC; St Hedwig's Cath Ch; RIASSO, Fricsay, D DX 123 [3].

Dismissing as operatic and unidiomatic the oldest recording of *The Seasons* (Cetra 1202), sung in Italian under Vittorio Gui, we are left with something of a Hobson's choice.   The Haydn Soci-ety's performance seems over-recorded: it was made in the Grosser Musikvereinsaal (where there is considerable reverberation), with the soloists close and the chorus remote, yet all consistently loud and brilliant.   Nevertheless, it has an atmosphere that I missed in the later Decca recording.   In both cases the choral and orchestral work is good, and in both the best of the soloists is the tenor. Patzak, though quite obviously past his best days, gives a nota-ble account of his aria *"Hier steht der Wanderer nun."*   Ludwig, also a veteran, is first-class, too, from the dramatic recitatives to the quiet passages and the brilliantly florid arias.   Greindl does fine work; his voice is less powerful and unyielding than Hann's. To him falls one of the priceless moments of the score, the *"Hus-bandman"* aria, with its quotation from the *"Surprise"* Symphony. Trötschel is tasteful, but tonally stiff, hardly equal to the hea-vier technical demands of the music or able to sustain the aria *"Welche Labung für die Sinne"* as it must be sustained.   Eipperle is a superior artist, though plainly no longer in her prime.   If the Haydn Society recording offers some problems in reproduction, this is also true of the Decca.

Die Schöpfung.   Eipperle, s; Patzak, t; Hann, bs; etc.; VSOC; VPH, Krauss, HS HSLP 2005 [3].   Korch, s; Unger, t; Adam, bs; RBC & O, Koch, U URLP 235 [2].

Neither of these *Creation*s is all one could wish.   It seems a lit-tle strange that, with the recent interest in Haydn, nothing nearer justice has been done his most popular choral work.   The Clemens Krauss performance was one of the earliest offerings of the Haydn Society, and though the hand of a major conductor is in evidence throughout, the results are uneven.   Chorus and orchestra perform creditably, but are not always reproduced with full clarity.   The veteran soloists sing with style, if with waning resources; the big bass voice is too close to the microphone. Another soprano and a lighter bass take over the Adam and Eve portions. Some doubling of the time in *"The heavens are telling"* is said to be historically defensible, but without the explanation it sounds like imperfect splicing of the tapes. One cannot complain that the soloists in the Urania performance sound old—on the contrary I suspect that their experiences have been limited. Unger is remembered as the David in two complete *Meistersinger* recordings, but in Haydn his good taste does not make his thinnish tone very ingratiating. Korch's voice is almost boyish in quality, lacking in vibrato, a little stiff, and not too secure in intonation. There is no thrill in her singing in such passages as the ascending scales of *"With verdure clad."* Adam's voice is heavy and rather thick. He gets little contrast into *"Rolling in foaming billows."* Over all the performance hangs a cloud of lethargy, a lack of inspiration. There is more in *The Creation* than meets the ears in either set.

Die sieben Worte des Erlösers am Kreuze. Gueden, s; Oschlager, c; Patzak, t; Braun, bs; SACC; SAL, Messner, Rem R 199-66 [2].

The choral version of *The Seven Last Words* is too important to be overlooked: it is more than surprising, therefore, that aside from a very old recording made in Japan, this Salzburg performance has been the only attempt to reproduce it. As a listing, this one is, of course, tempting enough, and it has its share of virtues. The soloists are very good, especially Gueden and Patzak; the chorus, while not a model of precision, is acceptable. But no amount of playing with the dials can make this a good, undistorted recording.

Stabat Mater. Felbermayer, s; Wagner, c; Kmentt, t; Wiener, bs; VKC; VSYC; Gillesberger, Vox PL 7410.

This oratorio, which amounts in effect to a long series of arias and choruses, is certainly in good hands with the forces listed above. Just why the work does not come off, it would be hard to say, yet the total impression left with me after several hearings is one of dullness.

Operas

Der Apotheker (in English). Wolf, s; Chelsi, t; Myers, b; Davis, b; O, Kramer, MT MLP 1007.

To hear the Vienna Choir Boys in this little comic opera is an amusing experience, and one does not complain if one has to accept some musical things on faith. However, for a group of adults making a record there are greater obligations than seem to have been realized here. The performance is done in English (a version made especially for the troupe), and a very smart and snappy translation it is. I doubt that many people will want to hear it often.

Il Mondo della Luna (in German). Schneider, s; Muench, m-s; Gassner, t; Schwert, b; Hagner, bs; etc.; Munich Cham Op O, Weissenbach, Per SPL 703.

This little comedy, with its many Mozartean and near-familiar tunes, requires a lighter touch than is brought to bear upon it in this recording. The voices in themselves are adequate, but there is not much sparkle in the singing, and in some cases the vocalism is downright amateurish. All this is coarsely reproduced.

Orfeo ed Euridice. Hellwig, s; Heusser, s; Handt, t; Wadleigh, b; Poell, bs; Berry, bs; VSOC & O, Swarowsky, HS HSLP 2029.

With Mozart's *Idomeneo* and *Don Giovanni* this must rank among the most ambitious offerings of the Haydn Society, and in several ways it makes a strong bid for the top place. Because of circumstances beyond his control, Haydn never got to produce his opera on the most popular of musico-dramatic subjects, and the work remained forgotten and dismembered until the Society set about locating the parts and putting them together again. The recording is therefore a world *première*. Stylistically the hurdles for the singers are not quite so formidable as those in the first of the Mozart operas, but the score had to be studied from the ground up. All in all, an impressive and invaluable job has been done.

Philemon und Baucis. Roon, s; Naidic, s; Kmentt, t; Majkut, t; VSOC; VSY, Zallinger, Vox PL 7660.

This Haydn work is a *singspiel*, which is to say that much valuable time is consumed by mildly interesting dialogue, not conducive to many repeats. The music is slight but charming, and is nicely sung.

Songs, Arias, etc.

Arianna a Naxos; The Mermaid's Song; She never told her love; The Spirit's Song; Fidelity; My mother bids me bind my hair; The Sailor's Song. Tourel, m-s; Kirkpatrick, pf, HS HSL 2051.
Ein' Magd, ein' Dienerin (Aria pro Adventu); Son pietosa, son bonina

(Aria di Lindora); Chi vive amante so che delira (Aria di Errisena);
Berenice, che fai? (Scena di Berenice); Solo e pensoso i più deserti
campi (The Russian Aria). Hopf, s; VSY, Zallinger, HS HSLP 2045.
Das Leben ist ein Traum; The Mermaid's Song; She never told her love;
My mother bids me bind my hair; The Spirit's Song. Niemela, s; Kos-
kimies, pf, WCFM 10 (*Schubert: Songs).
Das Leben ist ein Traum; Heller Blick; She never told her love; The
Sailor's Song (Ger.). Rogers, t; Mitrani, pf, 10" All AL 13 (*Mozart:
Songs).

Arianna is a long cantata, taking a full disc side, sung in the
grand manner, and accompanied on a reproduction of an eighteenth-
century piano. Tourel's English songs are several shades less
happy, though she and Kirkpatrick are incapable of an unmusi-
cianly performance. It is just a quality of brightness that is not
there. Hopf's collection of attractively operatic concert arias
brings us into little-explored territory. Though the singer is more
effective in the dramatic moments than in those calling for sustained lines, her sense of style is always good. Style, combined
with a lovely lyric voice, distinguishes the singing of the Finnish
Tii Niemela. Hers is certainly the most attractive of the song programs considered here. After such singing, the rather thin voice
of Earl Rogers is especially unexciting. On his program the rousing "*Sailor's Song*" somehow turns up in German.

Scottish Songs: O Philly, happy was the day (duet); Saw ye Johnie
come, quo' she; O Logan, sweetly didst thou glide; Behold the hour,
the boat arrive (duet); The moon had climbed the highest hill; When
trees did bud and fields were green (duet); When o'er the hill the east-
ern star; Wha wadna be in love; Thou ling'ring star with less'ning ray;
Sleep'st thou or wak'st thou, fairest creature. Bleiberg, s; Charney,
m-s; pf; vln; vlc, MT MLO 1014.

Haydn was one of the succession of eminent composers (which also
included Beethoven) engaged by George Thomson for his publication of Scottish, Irish, and Welsh folk music. Like the Beethoven
songs, Haydn's have trio accompaniments and a good deal of
chamber-music atmosphere. These songs are little known; the selection is as welcome as it is musically charming. The singing
is vocally appealing, especially on the part of the mezzo, the approach to the songs gratefully simple. The ensemble is reasonably successful, and the recording considerably better than has
sometimes been the case with Magic Tone.

HINDEMITH, PAUL (1895-   )

Apparebit repentina dies. Singakademie Ch; VSY, Hindemith, Cap P 8134 (*Philharmonic Concerto).
A Requiem "For Those We Love." Höngen, c; Braun, b; VSOC; VSY, Hindemith, 10" Vox PL 1760 [2].

Both recordings give evidence of being taken from broadcasts; in the *Requiem* there was only too obviously a large audience present. *Apparebit*, composed in 1947, is a setting of a medieval Latin text concerned with the Day of Judgment. It is a beautiful work, and one wishes the authoritative performance had been better recorded. The *Requiem* comes rather strangely in the German language, for the text is Walt Whitman's *When lilacs last in the dooryard bloomed*. One regrets that the *premi̇ère* under Robert Shaw was not preserved, for it was in every way superior. It is said that the composer has strongly objected to this one being offered for sale. At best, then, it is an important work inadequately presented. The soloists are good.

Das Marienleben (1948 Edition). Tourel, m-s; Kahn, pf, SL 196 [2].

Hindemith tells us he considers this Rilke cycle not only one of his most important works, but a milestone in modern German song. Originally composed in 1923, the work was found so difficult, so unvocal, indeed, that virtually no one could sing it. The composer came back to it, therefore, in the late forties, and brought the vocal part into line. Jennie Tourel and Erich Itor Kahn introduced the new version to New York as long ago as 1949, but their recording did not appear until some five years later. Meanwhile the gap was filled by Frances James and George Brough (Lyrachord LL 6), a recording now outclassed. Indeed, without discounting for a moment the tremendous achievement of the present artists in their penetrating performance, it becomes clear on repetition that even they have not given us the last word. In the first place, Tourel, being a mezzo, finds the *tessitura* uncomfortable. This means not only that we miss the feeling of freedom in the higher reaches, but that her dynamic and tonal palette is somewhat limited. With this she has an unfortunate habit of sliding up to some of the tones, especially the more sustained ones. Kahn's playing is magnificent.

Nine English Songs. Troxell, s; Kozma, pf, WCFM 15 (*Britten: Songs).

The English songs were composed during Hindemith's sojourn at Yale. One is struck not only by the expressiveness of the close-knit music, but also by the composer's understanding of our language. There is much variety in the set, from the clever canonic setting of Moore's *"Echo"* to the retrospective *"On hearing the last rose of summer"* by Charles Wolfe. Miss Troxell sings them superbly, and is acceptably if not evenly recorded.

HONEGGER, ARTHUR (1892-   )

Jeanne d'Arc au Bûcher. Zorina, speaker; Yeend, s; Lipton, c; Lloyd, t; K. Smith, bs; etc.; Temple U & St Peter's Boys' Chs; PHO, Ormandy, C SL 178 [2].

Though classed as an oratorio, this work has been mounted as an opera. It might, perhaps, be called a modern miracle play. But however you choose to class it, *Joan of Arc at the Stake* is a composition of crushing impact. Vera Zorina reads Claudel's lines with tremendous eloquence, and the almost Handelian choruses are sung with magnificent impressiveness. Any way you consider it, this recording is a major achievement.

Le Roi David. Micheau, s; Collard, c; Mullet, b; Hervé, speaker; BC; French Radio O, Honegger, W WAL 204 [2].

For all its mixture of styles, the early *King David* remains a masterpiece, a work with sincerity and spontaneity all too rare in our century. The performance under the composer's direction is big, vital, magnificently contrasted, and wonderfully thrilling. I liked the simple singing of the Twenty-third Psalm at the beginning by the boy's voice (I have always heard it sung by a contralto); I was roused by the fine *crescendo* in the *"Cortège,"* and above all by the final movement, "David's death," with its Bachian chorale melody. On the other hand, I am not sure using a baritone for the tenor part was completely happy, though Mullet is a good artist. Nor do I find the balance ideal, especially in the soprano solo passages. Jean Hervé reads the connecting narrative well, though I felt a bit too much of classical French tragedy in the "Lamentation" section. In this role any speaker will be at a disadvantage with those who remember Léon Rothier in Bodanzky's performances some years ago with the Friends of Music in New York.

HOOK, JAMES (1746-1827)

The Musical Courtship (arr. Woodhouse). IOS, 10" L LPS 293 (*Carey: True Blue; Anon.: The Dustcart Cantata).

The Musical Courtship is a satire in dialogue once a staple in the repertoire of the composer's popular contemporaries Mr. Incledon and Miss Iliff. This quaint and typical bit of old-time English humor is properly realized with mock seriousness, and less of voice than of style. The singers' diction might serve as a model.

HOWE, MARY (1882-   )

Mein Herz; Ma Douleur; Fragment; O Proserpina; When I died in Bern-
ers Street. Hansel, s; Schaefer, pf. Lullaby for a forester's child;
The rag-picker; Innisfree; To an unknown soldier. Ronk, b; Schaefer,
pf. Williamsburg Sunday; The horseman; Music when soft voices die;
Chain Gang Song; Cavaliers; Song of Ruth. Howard U Ch; Kindland,
pf, Lawson, WCFM LP 13.

This disc provides a cross-section of the vocal works of Mary Howe, with one side devoted to solo songs, the other to short choruses. There are poems in French and German, as well as the English of Shakespeare, Elinor Wylie, Frances Frost, and others. Mrs. Howe has a fine sense of climax, and her songs are consistently interesting. The singers perform them sympathetically; the baritone is notable for fine diction.

HUMPERDINCK, ENGELBERT (1854-1921)

Hänsel und Gretel. Schwarzkopf, s; Grümmer, m-s; Felbermayer, s;
Schürhoff, m-s; Metternich, b; etc.; Chs of Loughton High Sch for Girls
& Bancrofts Sch; PHI, Karajan, An 3506 B [2]. Berger, s; Schilp, s;
Arndt-Ober, c; Nissen, b; etc.; Berlin Boys' Ch; RBO, Rother, U URLP
212 [2]. (In English) Conner, s; Stevens, m-s; Votipka, m-s; Brownlee,
b; etc.; MOC & O, Rudolf, C SL 102 [2].

The first question here is, are you for opera in English? If so, the Metropolitan performance has the familiar virtues of the most recent cast at the New York institution. The singers obviously enjoyed this work, and the casting was fortunate. Mechanically, though not of the newest, the Columbia set outranks the Urania, but hardly approaches the Angel. Between the two German productions there is room for question only among those who favor certain singers, for Berger is a natural as Gretel, and the veteran Margarete Arndt-Ober, of the Metropolitan before World War I, shows what a really great singer can do as the Witch. The rest of the cast is excellent too, but the recording is sub-standard. As for the Angel set, its reproduction is extraordinary. If it has a fault, it is that of the over-confident virtuoso who wants you to know he can play more slowly and more softly than anyone else. Perhaps it is all stretched just a little too far. The cast could not easily be bettered. Schwarzkopf adopts a girlish tone hardly recognizable as her own, and she is matched by the lovely un-clouded voice of Grümmer. Schürhoff as the Witch scratches and screeches without, perhaps, raising any gooseflesh among her hearers (for one doesn't take this performance seriously as drama), and Metternich is a bluff, hearty Father. The orchestra has a bright, roomy sound.

ISAAK, HEINRICH (ca. 1450 - 1517)

Missa Carmina. VKC, Grossmann, W WL 5215.

Isaak being remembered nowadays chiefly as the composer of his touching little farewell to Innsbruck (see Anthologie Sonore, HS AS 5, or History of Music in Sound, V LM 6016), this Mass has especial interest. For lo! here is the Innsbruck song woven into the polyphonic texture, and emerging clearly in the *"Christe elei-son."* The performance given the work is full-blooded and pol-ished, perhaps over-shaded. The recording is strong and a little close.

IVES, CHARLES E. (1874 - 1954)

When stars are in the quiet skies; Tolerance; A night thought; At the river; At sea; A Christmas Carol; Walt Whitman; I'll not complain; In summer fields; At parting. Greissle, s; Wolman, pf, SPA 9 (*Revuel-tas: Songs).

A program of Ives songs was needed; it is unfortunate that this one cannot be greeted with great enthusiasm. The selection is representative, showing the composer in various stages, from the 1891 setting of Bulwer's *"When stars are in the quiet skies"* to the 1921 *"Walt Whitman"* and *"At sea."* Some of the composer's strange experiments with translations from the German (the ori-ginal texts being thrice familiar in settings of Brahms and Schu-mann) make curious listening, as does his *"At the river,"* simply the old gospel hymn of that ilk with a new chordal background. Unfortunately, the singer on this record is modest (which an Ives interpreter can hardly afford to be) and rather shaky. Nor are matters improved by the reticent pianist. A better sample is the single song *"Charlie Rutledge"* in Randolph Symonette's Americana program (Col CLPS 1008).

JANÁČEK, LEOŠ (1854-1928)

Slavonic Mass. Moravian Mixed Ch; Brno Radio SO, Bakala, U URLP 7072.

The *Slavonic* or *Glagolithic Mass* was Janáček's crowning work. Set in the old Czechish language, it is more an expression of faith than a liturgical composition, an affirmation of striking, even barbaric drive. The cruelly difficult solo parts are handled with assurance in this earnest, sometimes overwhelming performance.

JONES, SIDNEY (1869-1946)

The Geisha (in German) (abridged). Seegers, s; Falvay, t; etc.; RBC & O, Dobrindt, U URLP 7059.

The old-fashioned charm of this 1896 English smash hit apparently still holds not only British, but also German audiences. To American ears it may sound a little strange in so thoroughly Teutonic a performance, but a very respectable performance it is, and not without power to bring back memories. An even shorter selection from the score (one 10" side) has been made also in Berlin under Hansgeorg Otto's direction (10" L LD 9068), but that one is a little *too* slick. The lush performing style is better suited to the purely orchestral selection from Benatzky's *Im Weissen Rössl* (*White Horse Inn*) on the reverse of the disc.

JOSQUIN DES PRES (ca. 1450-1521)

*De profundis clamavi a te; Ave Maria. DC, Boepple, CH CHC 47 (*Lassus: Lamentations).*

These sublimely beautiful works are somewhat weighted down by the size of the performing chorus. Essentially music of supple lines and clear texture, it here emerges rather squarely. The recording, made in Carnegie Hall, New York, is good.

N'esse pas un grand déplaisir; Parfonds regretz; Bergerette savoyenne; Fortuna d'un gran tempo; Douleur me bat; Pour souhaitter; Faulte d'argent; Petite Camousette; Incessament mon povre coeur lamente; Je me complains de mon amy; La plus de plus; Allégez moy; La Déploration de Johannes Ockeghem; Battez-moy. PMA, Cape, EMS 213.

This is one of the most valuable and delightful recordings yet made. Fittingly devoted to vocal and instrumental chansons of the greatest fifteenth-century master, it is Volume 13 (though the first installment issued) of an extended anthology of Medieval and Renaissance music. No need to praise the music, whose votaries know it for an unmitigated delight; the Belgian performers are noted for their work with the Anthologie Sonore and for their infrequent and too brief American appearances. Among interpreters of this kind of music they have few rivals, for they balance scholarship with musical vitality, correctness with enthusiasm. Such singing and playing, superbly recorded, cannot fail to spread understanding of this music.

JOSTEN, WERNER (1888-   )

Sumer is icumen in; Der verschwiegene Nachtigall; Die heiligen drei Könige; Roundelay; Gefunden; Hingabe; Lied; The Indian Serenade; La Partenza delle Dondinelle; Guarda, che bianca luna; Frühlingsnetz; Im Herbst; Weihnachten; Waldeinsamkeit. Endich, s; McGrath, t; Josten, pf, SPA 34.

Werner Josten is a German-born conservative in the romantic tradition of the lied. Most of the poems here represented are well known in other settings, some of them very famous. Josten's versions are well-made and effective, though they cannot be said to efface memories of their predecessors. The better of the singers is Endich, who performs most of the German songs with nice line, lyric quality, and penetration. Most effective is *"Weihnachten,"* with its familiar echoes in the piano part. McGrath sings mostly in English, doing even one of the German songs in translation. His voice is open, his style outgoing, and his diction notably good. The accompaniments supplied by the composer are admirably solid. The last of the songs is a duet.

KILPINEN, YRIÖ (1892-   )

Tunturilauluja; Lieder der Liebe. Niemela, s; Koskimies, pf, WCFM LP 5 (*Sibelius, Grieg: Songs).

In some informed opinions, Kilpinen is the greatest of contemporary song-writers; certainly he is the finest artist in Finland specializing in this field. Before the war a society was formed to record some of his songs, and the great baritone Gerhard Hüsch made a magnificent set of six discs with the composer's wife at the piano. Beyond the importation of these recordings, little has been done in this country by way of propaganda for Kilpinen. Niemela's disc contains a cycle of six *Laponian Mountain Songs*, with poems by Veikko Tormanen, sung in Finnish, and five *Lieder der Liebe* with German texts by Christian Morgenstern. The singer's voice is an appealing lyric soprano used with admirable taste and fine musicianship.

KODÁLY, ZOLTÁN (1882-   )

*Missa brevis in tempore belli.   Nat Presby Ch, Schaefer, WCFM 4 (*Britten: Rejoice in the Lamb).*

This Mass, a memento of World War II, was introduced to America in 1947 by the excellent choir that sings it here, and since then has been a kind of specialty in the National Presbyterian Church in Washington, D. C. With its sonorities and tone colors, its Gregorian thematic flavoring, it is one of the most important Masses produced in recent years. The playing of the imposing organ part and the balance of that instrument with the choir are features of the recording.

*Psalmus Hungaricus.   Krebs, t; RBC & O, Rother, U URLP 7014 (*Dances from Galanta).*

This is one of the masterpieces of modern choral literature, composed in 1923 for the fiftieth anniversary of the union of the cities of Buda and Pest. The text is the sixteenth-century poet Michael Veg's translation of *Psalm 55*, interspersed with his own comments and lamentations over the Turkish domination of his country. Kodály's setting calls for an adult choir, a children's choir, and a tenor soloist. It is exciting music from start to finish, and shows the composer as a master of choral composition. Previously recorded in the original Hungarian in Texas under Antal Dorati (V WDM 1331, 45 rpm), it here receives a fuller-sounding and more searching performance in German.

*Te Deum.   Jurinac, s; Wagner, c; Christ, t; Poell, bs; VC; VSY, Swoboda, W WL 5001 (*Theater Overture).*

Here is a strikingly different setting of the familiar Latin text, musically very big and impressive, with the composer's characteristic Hungarian coloring. The performance is a very powerful one, with good work from chorus and orchestra and the unusually strong solo quartet.

*Folk Songs of Hungary. Chabay, t; Kozma, pf, Bar BRS 904, 914 [2] (*Bartók: Folk Songs of Hungary).*

*Sappho's Love Song; At night; The forest. Batic, c; Leukauf, pf, NR NRLP 405 (*Hauer: Hölderlin Lieder; Křenek: Fiedellieder).*

With his friend Béla Bartók, Kodály spent years collecting, studying, and editing the folk songs of their native Hungary, and, like Bartók, he was influenced very strongly in his own musical style by what he found among his people. Chabay's two discs of the Bartók and Kodály arrangements are thoroughly authentic, for the tenor and his pianist, Kozma, are both Hungarians and have been friends of the composers. Actually these pieces are subtly modeled into art songs by the two masters, though they retain their original flavor. The contralto Polly Batic sings three original songs from opus 9, which make an interesting comparison with their ancestors on the Chabay disc. One wishes the contralto's voice were steadier.

KORNGOLD, ERICH (1897-   )

*Die tote Stadt—Glück, das mir verblieb. Zadek, s; Dermota, t; ASO, Korngold, MW 46 (*Instrumental Compositions).*

The selection generally known as *"Marietta's Song to the Lute"* is most frequently sung as a soprano solo; here we have it as it occurs in the score of Korngold's most successful opera. It is well sung, better by Dermota than by the unsteady Zadek; the composer's baton gives a special interest to the interpretation.

KŘENEK, ERNST (1900-   )

*Fiedellieder, Opus 64. Batic, c; Leukauf, pf, NR NRLP 405 (*Hauer: Hölderlin Lieder; Kodály: Songs).*

Křenek, of *Johnny spielt auf* fame, has produced some surprisingly melodious songs. The singer here has a rich and ample voice, unfortunately marred by a quaver and a certain lackadaisical quality. One wishes for a lighter touch.

LAMBERT, CONSTANT (1905-1951)

*The Rio Grande. Ripley, c; Ch; PHI, Lambert, 10" C ML 2145 (*Britten: Peter Grimes—Interludes).*

Old-timers remember the sensation created by the 1929 recording, made on the occasion of the world *première* of this effervescent work. Mechanically, it was outstanding in its day. This replacement is at least equally impressive, with a particularly fine display of percussion and some clean, spirited choral singing. The entire Sacheverell Sitwell text is happily printed on the container: to catch all the words in so elaborate a setting would otherwise be impossible.

LASSUS, ROLAND DE (1532-1594)

*Lamentations of Jeremiah, I & II. DC, Boepple, CH CHC 47 (*Josquin des Pres: Choral Works).*

Considering that this is a semi-amateur public-performance recording, the results are amazingly good. What is more remarkable, the concert was given in the Armor Hall of the Metropolitan Museum of Art in New York, where the echo is a thing of wonder. The effect on the recording seems to have been good, for the sound of the chorus has a liveness not matched in the companion pieces of Josquin, taken in Carnegie Hall. The choir is at its best in the Lassus; its inordinate size does not seem amiss in the impressive sonorities of this music.

*Psaumes de la pénitence 'a cinq voix. AMC, de Nobel, CH CHS 1196 (*Monteverdi: Messa a Quatre Voci da Cappella).*

Despite its inclusive label, this disc-side contains only the first of the *Penitential Psalms*. It is noble and affecting music, done energetically and solidly, but not in a cut-and-dried manner. The churchly atmosphere is enhanced by a reverberating echo.

LECOCQ, CHARLES (1832-1918)

La Fille de Madame Angot. Dachary, s; Michel, m-s; Peyron, b; Dens, b; etc.; RSPC; LAM, Gressier, Vox PL 20000.

Lecocq's once-famous little work is delightful when so idiomatically performed. Its irresistible tunes are better known to balletomanes today than to opera-goers. The score is abridged in this recording, but there is a running commentary for the benefit of listeners who understand French.

LÉHAR, FRANZ (1870-1948)

Das Land des Lächelns. Schwarzkopf, s; Loose, s; Gedda, t; Kunz, b; etc.; Ch- PHI, Ackermann, An 3507-B [2].

To most of us *Das Land des Lächelns* means little more (until we have listened to this recording) than the setting of one of the great Tauber hits, *"Dein ist mein ganzes Herz."* Actually, there are several other more or less familiar songs in the Viennese operetta tradition, and the work is the composer's most successful production after *The Merry Widow.* Schwarzkopf is in top form, and she shows a strong affinity for this type of music. At moments her voice recalls the young Lotte Lehmann; always she sings with great intensity. Gedda is a good match for her; the music holds no terrors for him, and he brings something of the Tauber style to play without ever seeming to be a "second Tauber." *"Immer nur lächeln."* his first air, and one of the gems of the score, lies low for him in spots, but this does not hinder his effectiveness. Kunz shows what can be done by a genuine artist singing a smooth vocal line directly on the text, one of the great secrets of fine singing. He is superb throughout, notably in his first-act duet with Schwarzkopf. Loose, too, is first-rate. The way the speaking parts are handled might serve as a model for producers of this kind of thing: they are kept very low and suggestive, never out of balance with the musical portions of the recording.

Die lustige Witwe. Schwarzkopf, s; Loose, s; Gedda, t; Kunz, b; etc.; Ch; PHI, Ackermann, An 3501-B [2]. *(In English) Kirsten, s; Warner, s; Rounseville, t; Harvuot, b; etc.; Ch & O, Engel, C ML 4666.*

The Angel *Merry Widow* is one of those very special things calculated to reach a much greater audience than either the admirers of Léhar or the fans of the various stars concerned in the performance; the combination adds up to something very near perfection. Schwarzkopf and Kunz sing their parts for all the character there is in them, and their voices are in fine fettle. The genuinely lyrical vocalism of Emmy Loose and the appealingly youthful Nicolai Gedda provide the perfect foil. The teamwork bespeaks endless rehearsing. There is a long overture based on the principal themes, composed for a revival in 1940, and there are notes by no less than Ernest Newman. Columbia's offering is said to follow the original 1907 score. After so fine and authentic a production as Angel's, I confess I find this gilt-edged Broadway-style performance more than a little tame, but I doubt that the Kirsten and Rounseville fans will enjoy it any the less.

Der Zarewitsch.   Della Casa, s; Funk, s; Roswaenge, t; Hendrik, t; ZTO, Reinhagen, L LLP 219.

Among other things, this tune-laden score is the source of the *"Wolgalied,"* once a favorite with Richard Tauber's audiences. Failing Tauber, we still have Helge Roswaenge, who knows what to do with melodies like these. We also have Lisa Della Casa, to me the bright particular star of this production. The songs simply melt in her mouth.

Zigeunerliebe.   Seegers, s; Groh, t; Karell, b; RBC & O, Dobrindt, U URLP 205 [2].

Though hardly of a perfection to rival Angel's *Merry Widow*, this has an excellent cast presenting a popular success in the authentic Viennese manner. Perhaps just as a change from the more familiar work, this operetta might be preferred.

LEONCAVALLO, RUGGIERO (1858-1919)

*I Pagliacci.   De los Angeles, s; Bjoerling, t; Warren, b; Merrill, b; SC; RCAO, Cellini, V LM 6106 [3] (*Mascagni: Cavalleria Rusticana). Amara, s; Tucker, t; Valdengo, b; Harvuot, b; MOC & O, Cleva, C SL 113 [2] (or C SL 124 [3], with Mascagni: Cavalleria Rusticana). Petrella, s; Del Monaco, t; Poli, b; Protti, b; SCC & O, Erede, L LL 880/1 [2]. (*Del Monaco Operatic Recital). Pacetti, s; Gigli, t; Basiola, b; Paci, b; SCAC & O, Ghione, V LCT 6010 [2]. (*Gigli Operatic Recital). Gavazzi, s; Bergonzi, t; Tagliabue, b; Rossi, b; RIC & O, Simonetto, Cet 1227 [2]. La Pollo, s; Donati, t; Sarri, b; Petroff, b; TCC; FM, Ghiglia, Rem RLP 199-40.*

If what one wants is a *Cav*-and-*Pag* combination, unquestionably the best value is LM 6106. There may be some better vocalism here and there in the rival sets, but Victor has assembled probably the best voice-and-temperament combination to be heard at the Metropolitan today. The performance gets off to a good start with Warren's solid *Prologue*, and this artist is consistently admirable throughout the opera. Bjoerling sings ardently but not without strain. De los Angeles is a case of sheer vocal attractiveness and—save for one high tone—masterly singing, yet she does not succeed in portraying the peasant girl deceiving her husband. Victor has been lavish in giving the role of Silvio to another premier baritone, and Merrill brings to it his finest, sturdiest tones.

Beppe, too, is in exceptionally capable hands, for Franke is a Metropolitan *comprimario* who may be ready to graduate to more imposing things. I was a little disappointed in the ending of the opera, which did not seem to me to have sufficient tension. It could be that the singers in this recording were a little too close to the microphone. The "official" Metropolitan cast was somehow issued with a novice as Nedda, a promising novice, to be sure, but the recording was Amara's first essay of the role. Tucker, however, is at the least a worthy rival for Bjoerling, and Valdengo's Tonio is one of his best roles. Harvuot is no more than passable as Silvio, but Hayward is another unusually mellifluous Beppe. The reproduction is very good. If Petrella in the London set shows the temperament De los Angeles lacks, she will displease the fanatics for intonation. Her style is authentic, and her voice has more than ordinary beauty, though sometimes it spreads. Poli is a good and serviceable baritone, Protti rather less impressive. Del Monaco is, of course, the star, and he is in his best voice, which is to say he sings with great power, rides over most of the high passages without batting an eye, and gives plenty in the emotional scenes. If occasionally he does some wild shooting at the pitch, what does it matter? The recording of the choral parts has lots of space; it even seems a little diffused, but the soloists seem to come too close. In his recital, which serves as a filler, Del Monaco includes the *Prologue*, perhaps on the theory that what was good for Tauber is good for him too. The effect of this baritone music on his voice is most curious; although the tone takes on a deeper hue, he does not seem comfortable, and rushes through the piece.

The Gigli set is, of course, famous, and bears its years lightly, if not well enough to cancel the superiority of the recordings already mentioned. The tenor is at his best, with his voice eloquent and ringing, his emotions under unusual control. Pacetti's instrument is a lovely *spinto*, just a little heavy for the higher flights. Through her fault or the conductor's the *"Ballatella"* seems earthbound. Basiola is pleasant-voiced but not exciting; the others are good.

The Cetra set is a competent, run-of-the-mill job, with a rather heavy-handed Nedda. Only the Silvio, Rossi, compares favorably with the singers considered above. More cannot be said for the bargain-priced abridgment from Remington, vocally acceptable if rather insensitive. From older recordings Victor has pieced together another Highlights set, featuring Albanese, Peerce, Warren, and Merrill (LM 1160). This is coupled with *Cavalleria* Highlights.

Arias

Bohème—Testa adorata. Piccaver, t. Zaza—Buona Zaza. Sammarco, b. Zaza—Mai più, Zaza. Bonci, t. Zaza—Zaza, piccola zingara. Schwarz, b. Et ELP 490 (*Mascagni: Arias).

This disc is really not so much a show of the less familiar Leoncavallo as a collection of famous singers. Piccaver sings an aria usually associated with Caruso (V LCT 1034), but without Caruso's intensity. Sammarco and Bonci, both well known to collectors, are represented by good examples; the baritone is recorded well forward. Josef Schwarz shows his fine rich voice to advantage, though his singing is on the placid side.

LISZT, FRANZ (1811-1886)

Missa choralis. PSC, Leibowitz, Oc OCS 37.

This impressive work typifies in a peculiarly fitting way the mixture of the mystic and the earthly, the sacred and the secular, which was Franz Liszt. It is simply scored for chorus and organ, though one hardly follows the program annotator's description of the setting as "short and to the point"—the *"Kyrie"* has all the extension its passionate mood calls for, and the *"Benedictus"* is an elaborate and imposing movement. On the other hand, the *"Sanctus"* is brief and understated. The performance is full of spirit and expression, good in sound and for the most part able, though the choral pitch is sometimes at variance with that of the organ. The tone is clear enough, but there is the kind of echo one might expect in a church recording.

LOEWE, CARL (1796-1869)

Edward; Der Nöck. Greindl, bs; Klust, pf. Odins Meeresritt; Meeresleuchten. Hann, bs; Leitner, pf. D DL 9610. (*Schumann: Frauenliebe und Leben, Höngen, c).
Prinz Eugen, der edle Ritter; Die Uhr; Odins Meeresritt; Edward; Der Nöck; Der selt'ner Beter; Tom der Reimer. Strienz, bs; Haeusslein, pf, L LLP 310.

*Kleiner Haushalt; Glockentürmers Töchterlein; Hochzeitslied; Süsses
Begräbnis; Odins Meeresritt.   Warfield, b; Herz, pf, C ML 4545 (*Warfield Recital).*

It is ironical and typical of the misunderstanding surrounding the
name of Loewe that when one company issued a collection of his
songs, sung in English by Emile Renan under the title *Scottish
Border Ballads* (10" All Al 108, withdrawn), a name and classification was thereby found to fit anything of his that might be released thereafter. To justify the makers of that first disc, *"Edward"* and *"Tom der Reimer"* are based on Scottish lore, though
of course Loewe set the poems in Herder's German translations.
But *"Archibald Douglas"* is an original German poem by Theodor
Fontane, for all its ancestry in Caledonian folk poetry. In any
case, the singing on that record was not inspired; unless one particularly wanted the songs in English, there would be no point in
trying to find it. Hardly better is the more generous offering of
Wilhelm Strienz, though it includes the delightfully simple *"Die
Uhr"* and the extremely florid *"Der Nöck."* One can admire the
singer's diction and phrasing as well as the fine work of the pianist, all of which are excellently recorded, but the spirit is not
in the singing. A side of Loewe is shared by Josef Greindl and
Georg Hann; the star in this case is Greindl, who sings *"Edward"*
for all the grim power there is in the song, and proves in *"Der
Nöck"* that he can sing both high and low. Hann does *"Odins
Meeresritt"* nearly as well, but sadly overweights the folksy
"Meeresleuchten." The best buy in Loewe on LP is William Warfield's recital, combined with some early German sacred songs.
The American bass-baritone has developed a magnificent forward
diction that enables him to sing the breath-taking (in more senses
than one) *"Hochzeitslied"* and the delightfully naïve *"Kleines
Haushalt"* with the ease of a Gilbert and Sullivan virtuoso. At
the same time he has the tonal beauty required to bring out the
best of the Schubertian *"Süsses Begräbnis."* The searcher for
single songs will find a good *"Erkennen"* and *"Der Nöck"* in a
Schlusnus recital (D DL 9624), and he might want to compare
Strienz's orchestrally accompanied *"Der Nöck"* (U URLP 7026)
with the piano version mentioned above. Somehow the voice benefits by the richer background.

LORTZING, ALBERT (1801-1851)

Zar und Zimmerman. Junker-Giesen, s; Ludwig, t; Günther, bs; Neid-linger, bs; WSTC & O, Leitner, D DX 129 [2].

There was a time when *Zar und Zimmermann* enjoyed some currency at least in German communities of America, but in general the Lortzing operas do not export well. One regrets, for this reason especially, that the recording does not sport one of those super-casts occasionally assembled nowadays for the lighter operas. The present assemblage falls a little below the spectacular, though the individual singers are obviously competent and well routined. Best of the lot is Gustav Neidlinger, to whom falls the unctious comedy role. His *"O sancta justitia,"* a summing-up of the character he portrays, is capitally done. Horst Günther, in the title role, does the most famous number—*"Sonst spielt' ich mit Zepter"*—with dignity, but the excellent Walther Ludwig is not in his best form in this recording. Junker-Giesen, as Marie, is of operetta caliber, though she executes some of the rapid passages neatly enough. The reproduction is very "live," and has the aura provided by a slight echo. The spoken dialogue is omitted in this version, and there are some cuts in the score.

LÜBECK, VINCENT (1654-1740)

Hilf deinem Volk; Gott, wie dein Name. Augenstein, s; Plümacher, c; Hohmann, t; Rohr, bs; SCS; SSO, Grischkat, Ren X 32 (*Preludes and Fugues, Hölderlin, organ).

These examples of the few surviving works of Vincent Lübeck will make him many friends, for his choral writing is worthy to stand with that of his contemporary, Buxtehude. The cantatas are well done, with especially fine work by the chorus, modest but effective singing by the soloists. An exception must be made to this in the case of Rohr, outstanding in a formidable assignment. Another hero of the occasion is the player of the all but impossible trumpet in C. The reproduction is exceptional.

LULLY, JEAN-BAPTISTE (1632-1687)

Te Deum. Collart, s; Cahn, c; Friedmann, t; Abdoun, bs; EVP; Orch de la Sainte de Musique de Chambre (Paris), Capdevielle, W WL 5326.

This music is even more festive than the works we have come to know of Lully's contemporary, Charpentier. The score calls for two choirs, many incidental solos, and an orchestra with trumpets and tympani added to the strings and organ. The singing through-out is very energetic and enthusiastic, perhaps a little wearing in so long a piece, but this we may surely charge to the composer's account. The soloists are not remarkable, except for Claudine Collart, who has the least to do. Mme M. T. Cahn, the alto, seems to be afflicted with a lisp. The reproduction is broad and bright, altogether in keeping with the nature of the music.

Cadmus et Hermione—Amants, aimez vos chaines; Belle Hermione, hélas, hélas; Vous êtes le charme; Thésée—Trop heureux qui mois-sonne; La Naissance de Vénus—Rochers, vous êtes sourds; Atys— Espoir si chère; Atys est trop heureux; Psyché—Admirons le jus de la treille; Que vos âmes s'émeuvent à mes larmes; Phaéton—Dieu, qui vous déclarez mon père; Amadis—Amour! que veux-tu de moi?; Persée—Hymen, ô doux Hymen! Rowe, s; Linville, bs; Duvernoy, hpschd; Ly LL 16.

One can only regret that so promising a program should prove so disappointing. The music is first-rate, and we may at least thank the artists for their tasteful choice. Still, the two singers do not have the equipment for this type of music, and it seems unfortu-nate that they have gone to so much trouble. Such music must be well sung if it is to commend itself to more than a very special audience.

MACHAUT, GUILLAUME DE (ca. 1300 – ca. 1377)

Notre Dame Mass. DC; NY Brass Ens, Boepple, CH CHS 1107.

Machaut's Mass is the oldest surviving polyphonic setting of the text written by a single hand. What the listener should know (and what the producers do not tell him) is that this effective perform-ance involves much larger forces than were ever available to the composer, that the work in consequence gains an imposing sonor-ity. No information is given as to the source of the edition used. The Anthologie Sonore contains a partial performance by the Para-phonistes de St.-Jeans des Matines, under Guillaume de Van, which will certainly be preferred by the history professors (HS AS 3). In this case we are told that the score used was reconstructed by Van; it is more modest than that favored by Boepple. After the impressiveness of the Dessoff performance, there is a fascination about the very sparseness of this one. A still simpler conception of the music may be sampled in the History of Music in Sound, Vol. 3 (V LM 6016). Here the *"Benedictus"* is well sung by the Brompton Oratory Choir, with instruments, under Henry Washington.

MAHLER, GUSTAV (1860-1911)

Choral Work

Das klagende Lied. Steingruber, s; Wagner, c; Majkut, t; VKC; VSO, Fekete, Mer MG 10102.

This choral ballad, which might have become an opera, was a product of the composer's twentieth year, but twice later underwent revisions. It has Mahler's folk-song melodic style and shows his great skill at orchestration. The performance is capable; if we accept a less than perfect balance and a background rumble, the recording is satisfactory.

Songs

Des Knaben Wunderhorn. Sydney, m-s; Poell, b; VSO, Prohaska, Van VRS 412/13 [2].

Here are thirteen of Mahler's best songs, all set to words from the famous early-nineteenth-century collection of folk poetry compiled by Arnim and Brentano. No miniaturist, Mahler orchestrated several of the songs himself, and they sound best with all the instrumental color of which he was master. This set is so arranged that the two singers more or less alternate in the songs best suited to their respective voices; the result is a satisfying program. Poell is here at his best; Sydney's fine voice is not perfectly supported in some of the high sustained singing, but she is an intelligent artist. The orchestral background is excellent, the recording uncommonly lifelike.

Early Songs from Des Knaben Wunderhorn; Rückert Songs. Felbermayer, s; Poell, b; VSO, Prohaska, Van VRS 421.

Lieder aus der Jugendzeit. Felbermayer, s; Poell, b; Graef, pf, Van VRS 424.

Fourteen Youth Songs. Steingruber, s; Haefner, pf, SPA 20/1/2 [3] (*Mahler: Symphony No. 3).

Erinnerung; Scheiden und Meiden; Nicht wiedersehen; Ich ging mit Lust durch einen grünen Wald; Ablösung im Sommer; Hans und Gretel;

Frühlingsmorgen; Starke Einbildungskraft. Halban, s; Walter, pf, C SL 171 [2] *(*Mahler: Symphony No. 5)*

The "early songs" here variously designated are forerunners of the later and better-known *Des Knaben Wunderhorn Lieder*. The idea of combining some of these fresh and charming lieder into one cycle with the five Rückert songs is not ineffective, though the reasons behind it are not obvious. Poell is less happy here than in the *Wunderhorn* set; such pieces as *"Ich bin der Welt abhanden gekommen"* and, above all, *"Liebst du um Schönheit"* call quite definitely for a contralto voice, and they take this admirable artist beyond his best range. The star of the disc, as it turns out, is Felbermayer, a soprano of a freshly lyrical voice, intelligence, and style. As in the *Wunderhorn* recording, Prohaska shows affection for the music; the orchestral playing, is, if anything, even better this time. In the second disc listed, the same two artists complete the early collection, even repeating some of the songs, this time with the original piano accompaniments, as opposed to orchestrations not by Mahler himself.

As a filler for Adler's splendid recording of the Third Symphony, Steingruber gives us a group of the early songs, sung with bright tone and admirable reserve. One might complain of looseness in some of the songs, both as regards rhythmic pulse and diction. But such a performance as she gives of *"Ich ging mit Lust durch einen grünen Wald"* is as lovely as one could ask. The well-played piano parts are satisfactorily reproduced. Halban's set was released originally in 1949, and mechanically it is inferior to the other recordings considered in this group. Special interest attaches to the singer, as the daughter of Selma Kurz, once a protégée of Mahler. While hardly in her mother's class, the singer has an expressive voice; she is musical too, and has the feeling these songs require. There is, however, a certain "diffuseness" in her tones, emphasized by the poor balance of the recording. Walter, fine musician though he is, is rather a modest pianist; even so, the reproduction lets him down. After the original release at 78 rpm, these songs seemed improved in their LP version.

Kindertotenlieder. Ferrier, c; VPH, Walter, 10" C ML 2187. Schey, b; Hague PO, Otterloo, Ep SC 6001 (*Bruckner: Symphony No. 4). Lail, m-s; RBO, Kleinert, U URLP 7016 (*Lieder eines fahrenden Gesellen, Metternich). Anderson, c; SFS, Monteux, V LM 1146 (*Brahms: Rhapsody). Rosza, c; VSO, Fekete, Mer MG 10103 (*Rückert Songs).

Ironically, although the *Kindertotenlieder* is best heard in the baritone register, most of the recordings are made by contraltos; the one baritone on the present list offers little competition to the best of the ladies. Indeed, the first recording ever made of the cycle (by Heinrich Rehkemper), now long a collector's item, remains for me the only completely satisfying performance. These songs contain some of the most self-revelatory music ever written, and as much for this reason as because of the way in which the vocal part is composed, the sentiment easily becomes overripe in the deeply sympathetic tones of a contralto. Neither Ferrier, Anderson, nor yet Lail really merits this rebuke, yet none is quite satisfying after Rehkemper. Ferrier had the fullest and most vibrant voice, and she sang with the deepest understanding. Lail, for her part, could certainly not be said to overdo expressiveness. Ferrier had the advantage of Walter's conducting, with every note in the orchestral part clearly brought out. Anderson, unfortunately, is not at her best, and Schey, though a long-admired artist, does not strike below the surface. Like most of the others, he misses the bitterness of the final song. The Rosza performance is to be considered only as a filler for the Rückert songs.

Das Lied von der Erde. Cavelti, c; Dermota, t; VSY, Klemperer, Vox PL 7000.

Das Lied von der Erde; Three Contralto Songs. Ferrier, c; Patzak, t; VPH, Walter, L LL 625/6 [2].

Klemperer and Walter are Mahlerites from way back, and both plead the composer's cause eloquently in these recordings. Walter is the stronger advocate. Cavelti produces a rather mouthy tone for Klemperer in the gorgeous contralto part; Dermota outshines her with really first-rate singing. Ferrier showed a particular affinity for this music, and her voice is here at its noblest. The veteran Patzak is almost as powerful as his companion, and Walter's orchestra outdoes itself to realize a penetrating interpretation. On the final side of the set Ferrier sings three of the Rückert songs, *"Ich atmet einen Lindenduft," "Ich bin der Welt abhanden gekommen,"* and *"Um Mitternacht."*

*Lieder eines fahrenden Gesellen. Brice, c; PSO, Reiner, C ML 4108 (*Bach: Arias). Thebom, m-s; O, Boult, V LM 1203 (*Wolf: Songs). Metternich, b; RBO, Ludwig, U URLP 7016 (*Kindertotenlieder, Lail).*

Between the two ladies the choice is Brice's gorgeous vocal richness or Thebom's more subtle expression. Reiner's collaboration is a distinct asset to the former, but the reproduction of the latter is more impressive. There has been a turning of tables in the Urania recording, for Metternich's light baritone would have been more appropriate to the *Kindertotenlieder*, just as Lail might have lent the requisite richness to the *Songs of a Wayfarer*.

*Five Songs from Rückert. Steingruber, s; VSO, Fekete, Mer MG 10103 (*Kindertotenlieder, Rosza).*
Ich bin der Welt abhanden gekommen; Urlicht. Cahier, c; BSOO, Meyrowitz. Rheinlegendchen; Tambourgesell. Schlusnus, b; BSOO, Weigert. 10" Et LP 471.

Though here one associates with the songs the rich and expressive tones of a contralto, the intelligent and musical Steingruber sings them well. The Cahier-Schlusnus program has special interest, coupling the contents of two outstanding prewar discs. Mme Cahier, a friend and protégée of Mahler, devoted a large portion of her distinguished career to his music, so that her two songs come from close to the source. She did little recording; this, her most valuable legacy, was made late in her career and early in that of electrical reproduction. Nevertheless, discounting a few blemishes, this is very beautiful singing, obviously by the type of rich voice the composer had in mind. The Schlusnus songs, from the *Des Knaben Wunderhorn* collection, show his magnificent instrument at its best, and the colorful orchestral background is reproduced remarkably well for a dubbing.

MARCELLO, BENEDETTO (1686-1739)

*Beato l'Uomo (Psalm 1). Colasanti, m-s; Modesti, bs; AC & O, Gerelli, Vox PL 6100 (*Carissimi: Jepthe).*

This interesting example of the work of an all-but-forgotten composer seems to have undergone some arranging. The original score calls for two voices, and one wonders how it would sound done that way. The performance is adequate, though less remarkable than that of the Carissimi accompanying it.

MASCAGNI, PIETRO (1863-1945)

L'Amico Fritz. Tassinari, s; Tagliavini, t; Meletti, bs; EIRAC & O, Mascagni, Cet 1203 [2].

Probably destined to stand as the definitive performance of Mascagni's one successful comic opera, this recording is fortunate in having Tassinari and Tagliavini as its leading lights and the composer as conductor. The music is tuneful and light, but with some echoes of *Cavalleria Rusticana* and some foreshadowings of Puccini. The recording, as we hear it on LP, is somewhat uneven, which is not surprising considering its age. The balance favors the singers more than it should, and there is some blasting and distortion.

Cavalleria Rusticana. Callas, s; di Stefano t; Panerai, b; etc.; SCAC & O, Serafin, An 3509-B [2, *last side blank*]. Milanov, s; Bjoerling, t; Merrill, b; etc.; SC; RCAO, Cellini, V LM 6106 [3] *(*Leoncavallo: Pagliacci).* Nicolai, m-s; del Monaco, t; Protti, b; etc.; MIOC & O, Ghione, L LL 990/1 [2] *(*Del Monaco Recital).* Simionato, m-s; Braschi, t; Tagliabue, b; etc.; CC & O, Basile, Cet 1233 [2]. Harshaw, s; Tucker, t; Guarrera, b; etc.; MOC & O, Cleva, C SL 123 [2] *(*Verdi: Overtures)* or C SL 124 [3] *(*Leoncavallo: Pagliacci).* Bruna Rasa, s; Gigli, t; Bechi, b; etc.; SCAC & O, Mascagni, V LCT 6000 [2]. *(Highlights)* Milanov, s; Bjoerling, t; Merrill, b; V LM 1160 *(*Leoncavallo: Pagliacci—Highlights).*

Serafin's performance gives every evidence of being the most carefully prepared of any on records. In the opening chorus he seems almost too careful, for the lighthearted peasant spirit of the scene could be more apparent. But as the drama unfolds and the passions of the characters are expressed, this, I am convinced, is Mascagni's masterpiece as it has rarely been heard—never, certainly, on records. The amazing Callas adds another character to her gallery, singing with fervor, if with less temperament than Milanov in Victor's set. Her voice ascends the heights of the *"Easter Hymn"* with ease and expressiveness, if with rather too much presence, and she realizes the drama of the later scenes. She has a wonderful match in Di Stefano, whose high tones ring out magnificently, and who achieves a lyricism hardly hinted at by Victor's Bjoerling. The *"Siciliano"* really sounds for once as though it were behind the curtain. The *"Drinking Song"* is wonderfully free and exciting. Panerai may not make a great thing of Alfio's song, but he is the best of the baritones in this competition. The orchestral tone is grand and rich in the climaxes, perhaps a little thick in the soft passages. The later Victor set and the Columbia are practically twins, for both draw on the Metropolitan roster, and both date from 1953. Columbia points with pride to the fact of its all-American cast, which means something in vocal neatness if nothing else. Harshaw, more generally identified with Wagnerian roles, is tonally admirable, but not very color-

ful; Tucker shows her up, singing as one to the manor born; he is
in excellent voice. Guarrera's Alfio does not carry much weight,
and in his song both he and the chorus have pitch trouble. Victor's Milanov may be less even vocally than Harshaw, but she has
the invaluable temperament her rival lacks. Bjoerling would have
sung an easier Turiddu a decade or so earlier; he sounds strained
in the *"Siciliana,"* though he rises to the later dramatics in fine
style. I wish more thought had been given to the backstage effect in this part of the Prelude, for Bjoerling is too much with us
(whereas Tucker might be singing in a neighboring bathroom). If
Merrill lacks the bravado of the Amatos and Ruffos of yesteryear,
he turns in a good job. The Victor Highlights enlists members of
the identical cast in older recordings, originally released as
singles. The more recent London set has the best *pianissimi* of
any of these recordings, and the opening chorus is wonderfully
clear and sonorous. There is more excitement here than in Serafin's performance. The *"Siciliano,"* sung by Del Monaco at a
proper distance, gives promise of good stage-distance effects,
which materialize. But throughout the action, the popular tenor
"gives" with his ample voice, and makes no attempt to modulate
it. I am afraid he outsings Nicolai rather unfairly in their big
duet. The mezzo-soprano has the disadvantage of all lower-
voiced Santuzzas; she has the range, and she rides up to the high
tones successfully enough in the dramatic moments, but she does
not float over the top of the *"Easter Chorus,"* nor does she produce much of a tone in the *cantabile* of her duet with Protti. Another mezzo, Simionato—the Lola of the older Victor set—shares
Nicolai's difficulties. The impression that her voice is carried
above its best registers is not so much a matter of range-strain as
of vibrato. She does not succeed in bringing the character to life
for us. Braschi sings acceptably in a thinnish voice; Tagliabue's
Alfio is indefinite as to the tonal center, but he is obviously well
seasoned. Unfortunately the authorized performance led by the
composer was made too late in Mascagni's life, too late, alas! in
Bruna Rasa's and Gigli's too. Bechi is the most satisfying member of the cast.

Arias

Guglielmo Ratcliff—Ombra esecrata. Taccani, t. Sylvano—S'e spento
il sol. Taccani, t. Iris—Io piano. Cannetti, s. Il piccolo Marat—Si
l'ammante più bella. Granforte, b. La mamma ritrovo la bimba.

Baldassare-Tedeschi, s. Finale, Act 2. Zamboni, s; Bergamaschi, t.
Et ET 490. (*Leoncavallo: Arias).

Interest here centers on the singers, for the reproduction is mostly
acoustic and highly variable. Taccani, however, is electrically
recorded, and his voice had both power and brilliance, as well as
the gift of strong utterance. Cannetti is the typical Italian soprano, but Granforte ranked among the best baritones his country
has produced. His singing is in the grand manner. The rest,
again, are typical.

MASSENET, JULES (1842-1912)

Manon. Micheau, s; de Luca, t; Bourdin, b; etc.; OCC & O, Wolff, L
LLPA 7 [3]. Feraldy, s; Rogatchewsky, t; Villier, b; OCC & O, Co-
hen, C EL 6 [3].

The first recording listed features a narrator to fill in between the
acts and to make possible some smooth cuttings. As he speaks in
French, he will not be of much help to the listeners most likely to
want his help. The performance as such is excellent. Micheau
has a nice lyric line and only a mild streak of that shrillness so
often associated with French sopranos. Bourdin is outstanding;
he is one Lescaut who can make something interesting of *"A quoi*
bon économie." Libero de Luca combines an Italianate quality
with a French method, which fits him well for such an opera.
Some of his mixed tones are rather open, but he does the "Dream"
aria well, and *"Ah, fuyez"* is mercifully unforced. The Columbia
recording is a revival; it was highly considered when it was new.
Feraldy has not the brilliance to dazzle in *"Je marche sur tous les*
chemins," but she is lovely in the lyrical passages. She, too,
sometimes tends to shrillness. Rogatchewsky is in fine voice,
and rises especially well to the St. Sulpice scene. The reproduction is naturally uneven, with some fading, and one big ensemble
has no bottom to it.

Thaïs. Geori-Boué, s; Giraudeau, t; Bourdin, b; etc.; POC & O, Se-
bastian, U URLP 227 [3].

Geori-Boué, as demonstrated in the Beecham complete *Faust*, is
an excellent artist whose voice sometimes takes on acidity. If
one accepts this, her singing is very good. In the theater she
must be a striking Thaïs, for she is a handsome woman and an excellent actress. Bourdin's Athanaël has a world-weary quality al-

together in character, and Giraudeau is good as Nicias. The reproduced sound is not altogether even throughout the set.

Werther. Juyol, m-s; Leger, s; Richard, t; Bourdin, b; OCC & O, Se-
bastian, U URLP 233 [3]. Tassinari, s; Neviani, s; Tagliavini, t;
Cortis, b; RIC & O, Pradelli, Cet 1245 [3].

The choice here is between French style and voluptuous Italian
voices. The Paris performance has spirit and temperament. Richard has a good free production in the Georges Thill tradition, with
fine ringing high tones; Bourdin, of course, is an old and accomplished hand, perhaps by now a little dry tonally, but always the
fine artist. Juyol is not the evenest singer ever to sing the role
of Charlotte—one wishes for a smoother line—but she has a real
dramatic ring in her voice, especially in the passionate outbursts
of the *"Letter Scene."* Leger is competent, but on the shrill side
and not too steady. The sound of the orchestra seemed rather
shallow at first, but not seriously; the voices, as so often in recorded opera, are too forward, which does not help in the stretches
of small talk in the first act. The children's voices lend a touch
of charm.

Like most Italians singing French, Tagliavini strikes out into a
language of his own; he produces a good deal of pretty *mezza voce*
and some solid *forte*, without bringing the two together. Tassinari, a more distinguished artist, is too patently Italian in tone to
be right in this music, though the quality of her voice remains appealing. Cortis does the best work of the three; one would accept
him in any cast. The sketchiest French comes from Neviani.
After all, it is not so much a matter of pronunciation as of making
the words count. The reproduction is on the whole very good,
though some of the voices are decidedly too close. There are a
few slight cuts in the performance.

MENDELSSOHN, FELIX (1809-1847)
Choral Works

Elijah. Baillie, s; Ripley, c; Johnston, t; Williams, bs; Huddersfield
Ch; LIV, Sargent, C SL 155 [3].

This is an English oratorio performance in the grand old tradition,
with well-schooled soloists and a large, splendidly prepared
chorus. As the set was issued some time before the advent of LP,

it naturally does not stand up to the best modern standards of reproduction, though it is acceptable enough. There is a tendency
to tubbiness in the bass, and the texture of the mass sound is not
transparent. Nevertheless, this is not only the sole *Elijah* on the
market, but fundamentally a good one.

*Die erste Walpurgisnacht, opus 60. Woudt, c; Larsen, t; Hollestelle,
b; NETC & O, Ackermann, CH CHS 1159 (*Songs, Graf).*

A good, lusty performance puts this Goethe ballad over in grand
style, though the choral tone is a little weak in the soprano section. The music is at once charming and exciting: one wonders
why it has been neglected by our choral societies.

*Paulus.   Dutoit, s; Nussbaumer, c; Loeffler, t; Wiener, bs; VKC;
PRCO, Grossmann, Vox PL 8362 [2].*

The overture to *St. Paul*, a fantasy on the chorale *Wachet auf*,
makes a stirring opener. The playing here is capable rather than
masterly, and this situation holds pretty much throughout the set.
One suspects the work was not sufficiently rehearsed. Easily the
best of the soloists is Wiener, who sings the title part with dignity and tonal beauty. Dutoit, with excellent intentions, cannot
keep her voice from spreading in the upper reaches, but her delivery of the text is good. Loeffler does well with the part of
Stephen. Nussbaumer wants more poise for her famous solo—
known in this country as *"But the Lord is mindful of His own."*

Songs and Duets

*Die Liebende schreibt; Neue Liebe; Der Mond; Schilflied; Auf Flü-
geln des Gesanges. Graf, s; Pommers, pf, CH CH 1159 (*Erste
Walpurgisnacht).*

*Das erste Veilchen; Die Liebende schreibt; Bei der Wiege; Der Mond;
Frühlingslied. Schumann, s; Schick, pf, Roy 1404 (*Franz, Purcell:
Songs, Brownlee).*

*Auf Flügeln des Gesanges; Schilflied; Venezianisches Gondellied;
Der Mond; Neue Liebe; Frühlingslied. Lichtegg, t; Haeusslin, pf, 10"
L LS 799 (*Tchaikovsky: Songs).*

For a sampling of the best Mendelssohn lieder, the Graf recital
can be recommended: *"Die Liebende schreibt"* is a great song,
"Auf Flügeln des Gesanges" a deservedly famous one. The soprano sings appealingly, with an uncommonly pure and expressive
voice. Schumann's program is a reissue of a never-too-successful
recording originally put out by Allegro. Though the songs are pre-

sented with the insight of a great artist, the recording was made in the soprano's last years. Vocally, she had done many finer things in the past, and many times she had been better recorded. *"Der Mond"* and *"Die Liebende schreibt"* will give pleasure if one can hear them over a formidable surface swish. The recital as a whole is only for those who cherish everything the artist left. Lichtegg sings his attractive program like the operetta tenor he is. There is little subtlety in his delivery, and not much grace. To round out the picture, two Mendelssohn songs are included in a Schlusnus recital (D DL 9624): *"Venezianisches Gondellied"* and *"Auf Flügeln des Gesanges,"* and *"Der Mond"* and the *"Gondellied"* are a part of Lotte Lehmann's Farewell (Pem 1).

Duets, opus 63; opus 77; Drei Volkslieder. Carlton, s; Tobias, c; Ulanowsky, pf, 10" MGM E 118.

There may be a scent of lavender about these duets, but my own reaction to the recording is regret that nowadays we do not do this sort of thing more often. The two ladies work uncommonly well together.

MENOTTI, GIAN-CARLO (1911-   )

Amahl and the Night Visitors. Allen, boy-s; Kuhlman, m-s; etc.; Ch & O, Schippers, V LM 1701.

Because of the opera's subsequent stage successes, this recording of the original television cast is something of a document. One is thankful that the performance was captured before Chet Allen's voice changed, for it is hard to believe the title role will ever be done fuller justice. The supporting cast is just what Menotti ordered, and of course Schippers's direction is very sensitive and sympathetic.

Amelia al Ballo, Carosio, s; Prandelli, t; Panerai, b; etc.; SCAC & O, Veneziani, An 35140.

Amelia Goes to the Ball has a kind of historical interest, as the first of Menotti's series of successful operas. In the days of its composition the young composer had not become Americanized; it is appropriate, therefore, that it should be sung in his native language by a group of the best-known contemporary Italian singers. Carosio is an attractive and accomplished soprano, if sometimes rather acidulous in tone; she makes the most of her opportunities for characterization and humor. Prandelli sings openly, which is just what is needed, and Panerai is a seasoned artist, though his tones have a way of spreading. The solo singers are too strong for the orchestra, but they do not cover up its details. The chorus, when it arrives, is pleasantly confused in sound, which is altogether in keeping with the dramatic situation.

The Consul. Neway, s; Lane, c; Powers, c; McNeil, t; McKinley, t; Lishner, bs; etc.; O, Engel, D DX 101 [2].

There is little to say of the performance of this most nightmarish of operas, beyond that it preserves for us the original cast of the successful Broadway run. It is safe to say it represents the composer's choice of interpreters and is recorded with his blessing. Patricia Neway made her reputation in the leading feminine role, and Marie Powers was provided with a part cut skillfully to her measure. A feature of the recording, to my ears, is the fine voice of Gloria Lane, who has become better known since this engagement. The reproduction is full, strong, and very brilliant.

The Medium. Keller, s; Powers, c; etc.; O, Balaban. The Telephone. Cotlow, s; Rogier, b; O, Balaban. C SL 154 [2].

The Medium. Alberghetti, s; Powers, c; etc.; RIO, Schippers, Mer MGL 7 [2].

The first of these two recordings represents the Ballet Theatre production with the original Broadway cast; it also includes the curtain-raiser *The Telephone*, in itself good light comedy, and since successfully produced on its own. The second recording is taken directly from the sound-track of the Italian-made film. Of course *The Medium* was Marie Powers's show, and she is present in both casts. The film production has special interest as the debut of a sensationally gifted young soprano, Anna Maria Alberghetti, and it includes about a half-hour of music not heard in the stage version. In other respects, the Columbia recording seems to me the better of the two; the reproduction is cleaner and more even, though even here I noted some fading of Powers's big voice in the final monologue.

MESSAGER, ANDRÉ (1853- 1929)

Monsieur Beaucaire. Angelici, s; Dens, b; etc.; RSPC; LAM, Gressier, Vox PL 20300.

This adaptation of Booth Tarkington's novel by the French composer was written for London, and so originally had an English libretto. Still, Messager could not translate his style, so the present production is in the proper tradition. In the voices of Angelici and Dens, the melodies could hardly go wrong.

Véronique. Angelici, s; Renaux, s; Roux, bs; etc.; RSPC; LAM, Gressier, Vox PL 21100.

This is the operetta with the "Swing Song," the "Trotting Duet," and the "Letter Song." The production is typical of its series, the cast including some lovely voices and some singing-actors pure and simple. Again the chief vocal ornament is Angelici.

MEYERBEER, GIACOMO (1791 - 1864)

L'Africaine—Selections. Litvinne, s; Talexis, s; Dubois, t; Lazaro, t; Badini, b; Stracciari, b; Blanchart, b. Dinorah—Selections. Kurz, s; de Luca, b. Et 485.

The case of Meyerbeer is often cited as an indictment of our present-day singers: given adequate performances, we are told, the works of this once-famous master could not fail of success. But adequate performances of his music must be great performances, down to the smallest role, and so we do not hear any Meyerbeer. A few arias survive as vehicles for popular singers, but the only recorded "performances" are these Eterna Highlights, consistent in neither language or style. Meyerbeer's operas are French operas, but only Litvinne's "Slumber Song" and the duet *"Combien tu m'es chère,"* by Talexis and Dubois, represent the French school. Badini was a fine Italian baritone, but not fine enough to lift *"Figlia dei re'"* out of dullness. Blanchart does well enough with *"Averla tanto amato,"* and Stracciari is splendidly virile in the *"Adamastor"* ballad. Lazaro is at his best in *"O paradiso,"* but his best was more a matter of natural endowment than of subtle art. From *Dinorah*, Kurz gives a dazzling "Shadow Song," and De Luca, in *"Sei vendicata assai,"* demonstrates the difference between adequate baritones and a great one.

Les Huguenots—Selections. Kurz, s; Hempel, s; Kemp, s; Bland, s; Slezak, t; Jadlowker, t; Mardones, bs; Knüpfer, bs; Delmas, bs; Mayr, bs; etc; Et ELP 458.

This is truly an assemblage of top-flight talent, singing often impressively, each in his own tongue, and recorded generally well by the old acoustic process. The Hempel performance of *"Marguerite's Aria,"* very beautifully sung, was unfortunately recorded at the wrong speed, so that the voice emerges higher and more brilliant than was possible even for this gifted singer. The *"Page Song,"* usually the province of a contralto, is here back in its original range, delightfully interpreted by Selma Kurz. The giant Slezak gives the "Entrance of Raoul" as well as the celebrated "Romance," takes part in the Sextet, and joins with Elsa Bland in the "Love Duet." Hempel and Jadlowker are splendid in the Marguerite-Raoul duet, and Kemp and Knüpfer offer that for Valentine and Marcel. José Mardones sings the sardonic *"Piff, paff, puff!,"* and our one Frenchman, Jean-François Delmas, displays his magnificent voice in the *"Benediction of the Swords."*

Le Proph'ete—Selections. Branzell, c; Manceau, c; Slezak, t; Berger, t; Et ELP 0-476.

The inequalities noted above in other Meyerbeer selections are even more remarkable here. Karin Branzell, always an admirable artist, sings *"Ach, mein Sohn"* and *"Donnez, donnez"* in two languages, obviously at different places and stages of her career. Slezak is in his element in German recordings of the *"Pastorale,"* *"John's Dream,"* and the *"Triumphal Hymn,"* and Rudolf Berger supplies the *"Drinking Song."* The Cavatine from the Prison Scene enlists the voice of Jeanne Manceau, and for good measure an orchestra plays the *"Coronation March."* One wishes for representation of two of the most famous exponents of the role of Fid̈es, Schumann-Heink and Matzenauer.

MILHAUD, DARIUS (1892-   )

*Les Amours de Ronsard. Bollinger, s; Glaz, c; Chabay, t; Harrell, b; 10" Con AP 102 (*Concertino d'Été).*

This performance, we may take it, owes its existence to the Aspen Festival in Colorado, where the four singers have been associates of the composer. They are unusual in that, though each is an outstanding soloist, they are not troubled with *prima donna* complexes. As a quartet they are a blended unit.

*Cantate de l'Enfant et de la M'ere. M. Milhaud, speaker; Juilliard Str Qt; Hambro, pf; Milhaud, C ML 4305 (*La Muse m'enagi'ere, Milhaud, pf).*

The *Cantate* belies its name: it is a recitation with music. Unlike most works of its kind, it is a close fusion of its two elements, the speaking voice actually serving as a member of the musical group. This performance, featuring the composer's wife, must be the most authentic possible.

Poèmes juifs. Kolassi, m-s; Collard, pf, L LL 919 (*Fauré: La Chanson d'Ève).

This set of songs dating from 1916 is based upon poems translated from the Hebrew; each is dedicated to a Jewish friend or relative of the composer, or to the memory of one. They are deeply felt works, and call for the kind of selfless interpretation Kolassi gives them. Some, to be sure, seem more appropriate to a male voice, but it is hard to imagine them more sympathetically sung.

MONTEMEZZI, ITALO (1875-1952)

L'Amore dei Tre Re. Petrella, s; Berdini, t; Capecchi, b; Bruscantini, bs; etc.; RIC & O, Basile, Cet 1212 [2].

One of the few continuingly successful twentieth-century operas, this setting of a Sem Benelli play is good drama in memorable, if not easily remembered, music. The capable cast is headed by the gifted Clara Petrella, a Fiora of youthful charm if not complete vocal finish. Of the three kings, it is the Archibaldo of Bruscantini who stands out as a characterization. The balance is good by usual operatic standards, though the singers are really a little too far forward. The orchestra plays well.

MONTEVERDI, CLAUDIO (1567-1643)
Choral Works

Beatus vir (Psalm 111—Six Voices); Laudate Dominum (Psalm 116— Five Voices); Ut queant laxis (Lauda—Two Voices). Giancola, s; Piovesan, s; Amadini, c; Cristinelli, t; Cortis, b; Ferrein, bs; SVCO, Ephrikian, Per SPLP 536.
Salve Regina. Moss, c; Sefton, t; Steinhoff, bs; Woodside, bs; Magnificat Secondo. PHC, Fleetwood, All ALG 3019 (*Verdi: Choruses).
Messa a Quatro Voci da Cappella. AMC; de Klerk, org; de Nobel; CH CHS 1196 (*Lassus: Psalm).

What goes wrong in the three psalms is hardly Ephrikian's fault, for the solo groups under his direction acquit themselves with honors. But the tape editors or others along the line seem to have decided to give an encore; we come to the end of our Psalms, and there is space left over. The encore, unannounced, turns out to be sections of the Vivaldi *Dixit* made under the same auspices. The *Salve Regina* and *Magnificat* offer magnificent music only partially digested by the performers. The Mass is a short setting in which the text is sensitively treated but not lingered over. There is wonderful vitality and excitement in the *"Sanctus,"* a movement far removed from the otherworldliness of Palestrina. As the score of this Mass has a continuo part, it is accompanied here by the organ, which fact rather strengthens the impression that the performance is taking place in a church. The sound has a definite atmosphere, and there is the appropriate kind of echo, which, however, sometimes obscures the attacks. The singing is of the healthy school, good, straight, and full-blooded, with fine climaxes and no self-conscious polishing. The individual parts stand out clearly, and the balance is very good.

Io mi son giovinetta; Non più guerra, pietate; O rossignol; Si, ch'io vorrei morire; Sorra tenere herbette; A un giro sol; Ohimè! Randolph Singers, W WL 5171 (*Gesualdo: Madrigals).

Madrigals for Five Voices—Book I (1587). Wagner Madrigal Singers, Ly LL 43.

Randolph has gone about the task of preparing his fine program with great earnestness, evidenced by the full, informative program notes he has provided. His group is small (one voice to a part) and its singing is generally clean and transparent. The Wagner disc was to have been the first of a series embracing all the Monteverdi madrigals, but so far as I know, Book I was the only one of the nine volumes actually brought out this way. This too is a solo group, and a well-matched one. Perhaps the lovely pieces are best not taken too many at a time, but they will bear many a repetition. There are occasional bands separating the madrigals, but not enough to set each one apart. And the transition from one piece to the next is often too swift. The jacket notes give complete Italian texts, but no translations.

Lamento d'Arianna; Lagrime d'amante al sepolcro dell'amata. Ens Marcel Couraud, Vox PL 6670.

This set is of an older vintage, transferred to LP acceptably enough, but without some of the brightness of the original 78-rpm version. Couraud's is a larger group than Boulanger's—too large, perhaps, for the best interests of some of the madrigals. But in the cycle *Tears of a Lover at the Tomb of the Beloved*, this is all to the good, for it is a long and taxing work. It is also an extremely beautiful one. The singing is not the smoothest possible; perhaps the accentuation is overdone. A decidedly superior performance is a part of the Hindemith Collegium Musicum program (Over 4). Here the music speaks to us in all its eloquence.

O mirtillo; Era l'anima mia; Damigella tutta bella; O come vaghi; Sfo-
gaya con le stelle; Dolcissimo uscignuolo; Interrotte speranze; A un
giro sol de bell' occhi lucenti; Quel sguardo sdegnosetto; Su su pasto-
relli vezzosi; Qui rise Tirsi. Voc & Inst Ens, Boulanger, D DL 9627.

Nadia Boulanger is one of the great musicians of our time, but one
with little reverence for the name of tradition. She is a conductor
for whom a musician can hardly help giving his best, and though
she may arrive at stylistic results in spite of the textbooks, she
is usually persuasive. Before the war she made with her group of
singers a Monteverdi set now remembered as a classic despite the
fact that she used a piano for accompaniment. She does not do
that here, but adopts the more proper harpsichord. If I were to
single out one or two of the most striking things in this set, they
would be *O mirtillo* and *Dolcissimo uscignuolo*. The recording of
the voices seems a little close.

Vespers of 1610 (Vespro della Beata Vergine; Magnificat) (ed. Schrade).
Ritchie, s; Morrison, s; Herbert, t; Lewis, t; Boyce, b; London Sgrs;
OLO, Lewis, OL 50021/2 [2].

The third recording to appear of this magnificent work is by all
odds the best. Hearing the brief selection from it which was offered first in a performance made under Ephrikian (Period 558),
one could enjoy it and wish for more of the score. The second attempt was made in Stuttgart, using the Hans Redlich edition, which
omits two of the most beautiful Psalms (Vox PL 7902). There
was some lovely solo singing by Margot Guilleaume, and the whole
effect was striking, but that was before this Oiseau Lyre appeared.
Leo Schrade, whose edition is used by Anthony Lewis, has taken
issue with Redlich on the proper interpretation and correct editing of the music. But, scholarship and authenticity aside, neither
of the earlier performances could give you the thrills this one can.
A festive atmosphere is evident at the very outset, and it is sustained to the end. The chorus sings with respect for unanimity;
the soloists are excellent. The recording setup is also very good,
for no one seems to be right on top of us; there is a nice, churchly
kind of atmosphere.

Operas

Il Ballo delle Ingrate. Tegani, s; Carbi, s; Sgarro, b; OCM, Gerelli,
Vox PL 8090.

A portion of this work was included in the prewar Nadia Boulanger set of Monteverdi madrigals and other works for voices. Here the edition and revision of Roberto Lupi are used, and the modernization of the orchestra is considerable. Following the score in the Malipiero collected edition of Monteverdi, I cannot account for some of the dances or a good deal of the embroidery of those I can find. There are also a couple of minor cuts. Otherwise the performance merits praise; the singers are more notable for their devotion and their sense of style than for any outstanding vocal gifts, but their voices are serviceable. Most of the problems have been ironed out, though we are left in the dark as to the proper performance of the *trillo*. There is real nobility in the recitative which makes up so much of the score, and it is allowed its effect. A lovely moment is the touching duet *"Ecco, ecco ver noi,"* another is the eloquent *pianissimo* choral ending. And the passage for the Ungrateful Soul, *"Aer sereno e puro, addio per sempre,"* will linger long in the memory.

Il Combattimento di Tancredi e Clorinda. Carbi, m-s; Tegani, s; Nobile, t; Monteverdi O, Soresino. Ballo in Onore dell' Imperatore Fernando III della Casa d'Austria; Amor che deggio fa? Madrigalisti Milanesi, Fait, Vox PL 8560.

Il Combattimento. Ribacchi, m-s; Rapisardi, s; Carlin, t; SCA, Sanzogno, Col CLPS 1014 (*Albinoni: Concerto No. 2).

Il Combattimento. Amadini, c; Giancola, s; Ferrein, bs; SVC & O, Ephrikian. Ballo delle Ninfe d'Istro; Mentre Vaga Angioletta. Giancola, s; Piovesan, s; Truccato Pace, c; Cristinelli, t; Ferrein, bs; Per SPLP 551.

In a prefatory note to his edition of the score, used in the Vox recording, Virgilio Mortari tells us: "Such a performance, carried out by the customary string orchestra, provides a sonority which, to our ears, is in effect equivalent to that which the choir of *viole da braccia* and *viole da gamba* must have represented to the liseners three or more centuries ago." It should be added that the conductor works from the harpsichord. Of the three performances listed, this is not only the nearest to authenticity in these respects, but decidedly the most satisfactorily sung. Claudia Carbi, the Narrator, has the richest, surest, most intense voice, and she seems most thoroughly at home in the music. The two title roles are so much smaller that it is of less interest to say that they are well done too. It used to be said of Elena Gerhardt that she conveyed the feeling of modulations and shifting harmonies in the

tone of her voice; Carbi has this kind of sensitivity. The reproduction leaves little to be desired, though a few details, such as
a strange cut-off effect at the pause just before the final line of
the opera, might be noted. Of the rival presentations, I prefer the
Colosseum, because of the supple singing of Ribacchi, an excellent artist. Amadini's voice is on the ponderous side. Sanzogno
may allow too much good old Italian passion in his performance,
but it is more telling than Ephrikian's. It should be remembered,
incidentally, that the Anthologie Sonore has an excellent performance of the *Combattimento*, with a tenor Narrator, Max Meili. The
Haydn Society might do well to make this available on LP.

The *Ballo* on the reverse of the Vox disc is a captivating piece,
with a long tenor solo leading into the chorus. The unidentified
singer is competent enough, though his voice is somewhat tremulous and lugubrious in quality. The canzonetta *Amor che deggio
fa?* is well done, if we accept some vestiges of romantic *portamento* in the singing. The madrigals that accompany the Period
performance are worth buying for their own sake. The tenor Cristinelli especially distinguishes himself.

*L'Incoronazione di Poppea. Gaehwiller, s; Helbing, c; Witte-Waldbauer,
c; Brueckner-Rueggeberg, t; Kelch, bs; etc.; ZTC & O, Goehr, CH CHS
1184 [3].*

This performance follows a reconstruction of Monteverdi's score
by conductor Goehr; it is somewhat abridged, but in generally excellent taste. The best singing is done by Margarete Witte-
Waldbauer, whose lovely voice is seconded by her sense of style.
Helbing shows promise of similar distinction, but her work here is
not quite mature. Gaehwiller, in the name part, is the weak link in
the chain, though the Nero of Brueckner-Rueggeberg is also casual.
With all this, the performance gives the sense of classic nobility
which is the essence of the work.

*Orfeo. Trötschel, s; Meili, t; Krebs, t; etc.; RBC & O, Koch, Vox PL
6440 [3].*

*Tirsi e Clori; Il Ritorno d'Ulisse in Patria—Iro's Air; Concerto for
Tenor and Strings. Scherz-Meister, s; Meili, t; SCB, Wenzinger, CH
CHS 1085.*

Orfeo is Meili's show; he sings with the musicianly style for
which he is known, though he does not have all the vocal resources that were his in the days of his prewar recordings. The
rest of the cast is passable. Despite the advantages of LP, then,

this performance does not replace the HMV set made in the thirties, possibly a rarity by now. The general level of singing was higher in that performance, and every attempt was made to recapture the authentic style (even to the use of all but obsolete old instruments). Meili is again the star of the Concert Hall disc, offering some even less familiar music of the first great opera-composer. The ensemble here leaves something to be desired.

MORLEY, THOMAS (1557-1603)

Sing we and chant it; Cease, mine eyes; Now is the month of Maying; Miraculous love's wounding; Now is the gentle season; I go before, my darling; Lady, those cherries plenty; Phyllis, I fain would die now; My bonnie lass she smileth; Lo, she flies when I woo her; Leave this tormenting and strange anguish; Clorinda false, adieu; Fire! fire! my heart! NYPMA, Greenberg, Es ES 520 (*Interludes for Virginals).

This is by all odds the richest vein of Morley so far struck by the recording angels, a program of abundant variety. Along with the most familiar of all English madrigals are others too little known; and lest the program become monotonous, it is punctuated by Blanche Winogron's interludes on the virginals. While admiring the arrangement of this concert, and the proficiency of the singing, one wonders how much time went into rehearsing. I noted a tendency to drive the music rather than let it take its own shape. This is less disturbing in the familiar ballets, *Now is the month of Maying, My bonny lass she smileth*, etc., than in such sustained pieces as the three-voice *Cease, mine eyes* and the five-voice *Leave this tormenting*. I suspect that with longer familiarity the group would have made more of these great part-songs.

MOZART, WOLFGANG AMADEUS (1756-1791)

Choral Works

Masonic Music. Cuenod, t; Giraudeau, t; Souzay, b; Mulhouse Oratorio Soc; PMO; Hewitt Cham O, Meyer, Vox PL 6540 [2]. *(Selections)* Christ, t; Majkut, t; Berry, bs; VKC; VSY, Paumgartner, Ep LC 3062.

This is a collection of various Köchel numbers, music for solo voice, for vocal duet, for orchestra, and for chorus, all centered around Mozart's membership in the Freemasons. Not all of it is important, except for the light it throws on *Die Zauberflöte*. The

Funeral Ode, or *Masonic Funeral Music*, is worthy of the composer at his best, and is, of course, not altogether unfamiliar. With this, the cantata K. 471 is the best music in the set. In the Vox recording Cuenod bears the brunt of the solos, and as usual acquits himself impressively. His colleagues are satisfactory, though some of the choral work is ragged. The Epic disc contains three cantatas and the *Ode*, all conceived on a grander scale, and more powerfully, if somewhat diffusely recorded. The chief soloist, Rudolf Christ, falls considerably short of Cuenod's standard; indeed one wishes the second tenor, Majkut, could have changed places with him.

Mass in F (Missa brevis), K. 192; Dixit and Magnificat. Leitner, s; Franz, c; Grabner, t; Lassner, b; SALC & O, Schneider, Ly LL 18.

This recording will do more to satisfy the curiosity and interest of established Mozarteans than to win converts (if anybody still needs converting) to this composer's way of musical life. There is something a bit superficial, precious perhaps, in the singing, especially in the first movement. The tempo seems fast, and it has a kind of nervous twitch. By the time the *"Agnus Dei"* has been reached, this has worn off, and the music has begun to flow as it should. The soloists produce some wobbly sounds, especially the alto and the bass. Nor is the reproduction altogether satisfactory: it has a rather shallow brilliance, hardly enhanced by its considerable power. Perhaps the Salzburg Cathedral is not an ideal place for recording.

Mass, K. 194, in D (Missa brevis); Mass, K. 220, in C (Missa brevis) ("Spatzenmesse"). Rathauscher, s; Hofstädter, c; Heppe, b; Berry, bs; VKC; VSY, Grossmann, Vox PL 7060.

These two *Missae breves* show Mozart at his less inspired. Both seem to have been written to order to fit specifications hardly conducive to lively inspiration. Einstein even senses in K. 220 a certain defiance of Archbishop Colloredo, who could call the tune but not the spirit. Neither Mass is performed in a manner to make it seem better than it is.

Mass, K. 317, in C ("Coronation"). Schweiger, s; Burgstaller-Schuster, c; Handt, t; Pernerstorfer, bs; VKC; Mozart Fest O, Gillesberger, 10" HS HSLP 2007. Zadek, s; Gifford, c; Patzak, t; Braun, bs; SFC & O, Messner, Fes FLP 100.

Unhappily, neither recording of this lovely Mass is all we might wish for. Messner's was made at a public festival performance in the summer of 1949. Something of the cathedral atmosphere has been caught in the reproduction, but the dynamic level is uneven. Uneven, too, is the performance: the soloists are four individualists, and there is little evidence of *rapport* among them. Nor is the chorus a model of precision. Some of the tempos seem wrong. The work of Gillesberger's forces is more acceptable, and the soloists do some fine singing, but the recording is not happy. The choral parts are much overloaded, the solos not so bad. The best moments in the recording are in the *"Benedictus."* All in all, the Haydn Society disc is the better of a none-too-tempting choice.

Mass, K. 427, in C minor. Schweiger, s; Toepper, s; Meyer-Welfing, t; London, bs; VKC; VSY, Zallinger, HS HSLP 2006 [2].

This is an important work and a valuable recording, though I suspect the performance was hastily prepared; it is hardly notable for precision. The soloists, speaking generally, are adequate, the most striking voice being that of the first soprano, who has a good trill, íf not complete security of intonation. In the choral sections the recording balance favors the orchestra, with some loss of clarity in the voices. Especially in the quartet setting of the *"Benedictus"* the reproduction is inclined to be loud and coarse.

Motets: Offertorium de Tempore Misericordias Domini, K. 222; Graduale ad Festum B. Mariae Virginis: Sancta Maria, Mater Dei, K. 273; Lacrymosa, K. Anh. 21; Jubilate, K. 117; Benedicite Angeli, K. 342; Offertorium de B. V. Maria: Alma Dei Creatoris, K. 277; Regina Coeli Laetare, K. 276. Soloists; Anthologie Sonore Ch & O, Duruflé, org; Raugel, HS AS 34.

The most remarkable thing in this collection of minor Mozart is the statement in the first motet of Beethoven's *Ode to Joy* theme: this is no mere premonition, it is an out-and-out proclamation. The singing throughout the set, by a modest-sized chorus, is vigorous and spirited rather than smooth. We can well imagine that this is the way Mozart heard his works in the performances of his own day.

*Offertorium pro festo Sti. Joannis Baptistae: Inter natos mulierum, K. 72; Kyrie for Four Voices in D minor ("Münchener"), K. 341. SALC & O, Sternberg, Per SPL 519 (*Schütz: Motets).*

These two youthful, but not untypical, works suffer from a nervous, restless approach. The setup of chorus and orchestra seems calculated to emphasize this, for the accompanying figures assume a prominence that really should belong to the vocal parts. The reproduction is loud and coarse.

Requiem, K. 626. Pech, boy-s; Breitschopf, boy-c; Ludwig, t; Progl-

hof, bs; VH, Krips, 10" L LPS 230/1 [2]. *Laszlo, s; Rössl-Majdan, c; Munteanu, t; Standen, bs; VKC; VSO, Scherchen, W WL 5233. Ciannela, s; Okerson, c; Carringer, t; Keast, b; SC; RCAO, Shaw, V LM 1712. Gueden, s; Anday, c; Patzak, t; Greindl, bs; SACC; SAL, Messner, Rem R 199-96. Tassinari, s; Stignani, m-s; Tagliavini, t; Tajo, bs; EIARC & O, Sabata, 10" Cet 1001* [2].

Here is satisfaction for a variety of tastes. If you want your *Requiem* done in the style of the old operatic Sunday night concerts, then there is no question but that you will enjoy the Italian group under Sabata. But this is not so much Mozart as vocal display. Again, if you want some good singing (along with some not quite of the best), are not particular about the quality of the recording (which is rather coarse), and like a bargain price, then the Remington version, made at a festival performance in 1951, will appeal. If you enjoy the singing of boys (which many people do not), you will certainly enjoy the sensitive and nicely styled performance of Krips. The two adult soloists, whose voices are naturally lusty enough, have managed to keep themselves down to the proper size to match their companions. On the other hand, there is a real virtuoso performance by Scherchen, bringing out the drama from the hushed orchestral introduction and the thrilling climax shortly thereafter to the hollow chord at the end. As a recording this is certainly the best version available, and it has some fine solo singing, especially by the two women. But if you want to strike somewhere in the middle of all these styles, the Shaw recording has both a warmth and earnestness that have not always characterized his performances, and some terrific climaxes. The solo singing is modest but competent.

Vesperae de Dominica, K. 321. Stader, s; Fischer, c; Häfliger, t; Schey, bs; RCZ; WINC & O, Reinhart, CH CHS 1033.

Vesperae solennes de Confessore, K. 339. Bak, s; Münch, c; Brünner, t; Linz, b; BAVRC & O, Kugler, 10" Mer MG 15014.

The *"Laudate Dominum"* from the *Vespers*, K. 321, is included in Collette Lorand's Mozart recital (Mer MG 15026). Stader, a more mature artist, provides the high spot in this complete performance with her singing of the same movement. Indeed, the performance is more than complete, for the conductor has interpolated a soprano aria of his own composing. Again, it is the *"Laudate"* that will remain in the memory after a hearing of K. 339, though Bak's singing is by no means the best we have heard of the Psalm. Older collectors will recall the soaring soprano solo in a close-to-perfect performance by Ursula Van Diemen and chorus, under the direction of Siegfried Ochs, recorded many years ago. The best choral work in the *Vespers* is accorded the stunning *"Magnificat"*; throughout the recording there is more evidence of enthusiasm than of warmth, and the soloists just about get by. This must have been a public performance, for one hears occasional page-turnings and coughs.

Operas

Bastien und Bastienne. Hollweg, s; Kmentt, t; Berry, bs; VSY, Pritchard, C ML 4835. Nentwig, s; Plümacher, c; Neidlinger, bs; STO, Reinhardt, Per SPL 542.

The Columbia recording uses recitatives not in the original score (the opera is the work of a twelve-year-old boy), but supplied by Mozart for a "revival" in Salzburg; Period favors spoken dialogue. In the Stuttgart production, a contralto sings the tenor role of Bastien; otherwise there is little over which to quibble in either recording, though the decision in favor of Columbia is easy enough. It is the difference between a happily poised and stylish reading of the score, distinguished by an exceptional soprano and two excellent men, and a quite satisfactory run-of-the-mill job. Columbia's reproduction is not quite perfection, but it is fuller and richer in sound than Period's.

*La Clemenza di Tito. Nentwig, s; Plümacher, c; Weikenmeier, t; etc.; SWS; STO, Lund, Per SPLP 550 [3] (*Les Petits Riens).*

The name of Mozart's *Titus* has been kept alive through the years by a couple of magnificent arias *"Non più di fiori"* and that old favorite of Schumann-Heink, *"Parto, parto!"* The work belongs to the old school of *opera seria;* there is little chance of success for it on the modern stage. For such works, LP is the ideal medium for revival, for here the music's the thing, the absurdity and unnaturalness of the plot counting for little. The present set, with informative background notes and a literate translation of the libretto, is good enough to make its points. The conductor has a nice sense of pace and line, and he imparts these to the singers. Most pleasing voice is Plümacher's; Weikenmeier's tone has size and roundness, and he manages the florid passages amazingly well. All in all, here is an admirable, if not distinguished, performance. The reproduction is full and clear.

Così fan tutte. Souez, s; Helletsgruber, s; Eisinger, s; Nash, t;

Domgraf-Fassbänder, b; Brownlee, b; GFC & O, Busch, V LCT 6104 [3]. *(In English) Steber, s; Peters, s; Thebom, m-s; Tucker, t; Guarrera, b; etc.; MOC & O, Stiedry, C SL 122* [3]. *(Highlights) Jurinac, s; Thebom, m-s; Lewis, t; Kunz, b; Boreiello, b; GFO, Busch, V LM 1126.*

Victor's *Così* is, of course, the famous set of the thirties, remarkably well transferred to LP. The cast is incomparably the finest yet offered. The most impressive voice is that of Souez, who has the sense of style if not quite the agility to put her in the class with famous predecessors in her role of Fiordiligi. Nash and Domgraf-Fassbänder are also outstanding, and Brownlee in his prime does a fine job of characterization. But chief honors go to Fritz Busch, who molded and held the spirited performance together. The ensemble, indeed, is greater than the sum of its parts. Against this we must weigh the superior modern reproduction of the official Metropolitan offering, done in English. The production was a popular success, and the recording has the expected virtues, though it is hardly pure Mozart. Those who prefer opera in the vernacular will be satisfied with it; others will prefer to accept the older recording. The men of the cast sing with notably clear diction, and the voices are generally good, but stylistically, not one of the singers is a match for his Glyndebourne counterpart. A third complete recording, emanating from Stuttgart, is eliminated by the competition (Rem R 199-117 [3]). Here we have a conscientious group of German artists singing fairish Italian. The postwar Glyndebourne "Highlights" is spirited and reasonably well carried out. But not all the detail of the music comes through in the singing. Jurinac, for example, is not up to her best, though the voice is still attractive.

Don Giovanni. Souez, s; Helletsgruber, s; Mildmay, s; Pataky, t; Brownlee, b; Baccaloni, bs; etc.; GFC & O, Busch, V LCT 6102 [3]. *Grob-Prandl, s; H. Konetzni, s; Heusser, s; Handt, t; Stabile, b; Poell, b; Pernerstorfer, bs; etc.; VSOC & O, Swarowsky, HS HSLP 2030* [4].

A number of arguments may be advanced to favor the Haydn Society recording in this choice. The original Prague version is strictly adhered to (whatever may be said of the improvements later made for Vienna, some of which were matters of expediency to suit the available cast, this does establish a special standard). Indeed, the additions for the Vienna *première* are included on the last record side as a kind of supplement; the only difficulty is for those who would fit them into their now accustomed places. No expense or effort has been spared to make the set effective. Still, with the exceptions of the aging Stabile, long a famous Don, and Poell as Masetto, the singers can be praised only with reservations, and in some cases only for good intentions. Here, where distinguished vocalism and mastery of style count for everything, and where a standard has long since existed in the Glyndebourne set, the modern recording adds up to a disappointment.

As for the classic, it would be too much to say it has survived the transfer to LP with its glories untarnished; still it meets the general standards of such revivals. Chief among its virtues is the guidance of Fritz Busch, who gets a remarkably integrated performance from his international cast. And the singers, though they may not be the brightest stars ever to appear in their roles, are never less than admirable. John Brownlee in his vocal prime was an excellent Don; Ina Souez, a rich-voiced Anna; Koloman von Pataky, a much better than usual Ottavio, to mention only a few.

Die Entführung aus dem Serail. Lipp, s; Loose, s; Ludwig, t; Klein, t; Koreh, bs; VSOC; VPH, Krips, L LLA 3 [3].

In its casting, this is one of the finest opera recordings ever offered, and one not likely to be bettered. Wilma Lipp has an unusually appealing voice, and she makes up with an unusual dramatic flair for the few degrees she may lack of technical perfection in Constanze's cruelly difficult arias. Emmy Loose sings Biondchen's music with just the right touch of sophistication; Walter Ludwig and Peter Klein are well balanced in the two tenor roles. The one weak spot in the cast is the Osmin of Endre Koreh, who could sing with greater subtlety and more cleanly; but this is notable chiefly because the others are so good. Krips holds the work together in masterly fashion. The only criticism of the recording is that the singers are too close to the microphone, especially in the passages of spoken dialogue.

La Finta Giardiniera. Guilleaume, s; Plümacher, c; Hohmann, t; Neidlinger, bs; STO, Reinhardt, Per SPL 531 [3]; (Abridged) Per SPL 532 (*Der Schauspieldirektor).

This youthful Italian work is sung to a German text which, the annotator tells us, Mozart himself knew in performance. The singers, all well known in numerous recordings, have pleasing voices and sing with good style. There is admirable enthusiasm in evidence throughout, if no transfiguring distinction.

Idomeneo. Hopf, s; Grob-Prandl, s; Handt, t; Taubmann, t; etc.; VSOC;

VSY, Zallinger, HS HSLP 2020 [4]. (Highlights) Jurinac, s; MacNeil,
s; Lewis, t; Young, t; GFO, Busch, V LHMV 1021.

Almost simultaneously with the complete set, a recording was issued of the drastic Wolf-Ferrari revision, sung in German, and
very severely cut (Mer MGL 5 [2]); it was definitely outclassed by
the Haydn Society performance, which strives for authenticity and
omits very little of the score. The strong and knowing hand of the
conductor holds this production together; the singers strive vali-
antly to conquer the lost art that lies beneath vexing problems of
style. This music demands mastery of florid song as well as big
utterance for its noble recitatives. It cannot be said that the
present group has all that this implies; indeed, no member of the
cast stands out as a model in these respects. Grob-Prandl works
against a rather backward vocal production in the role of Elettra;
Hopf, as Ilia, is also weighted down. The young American Herbert Handt shows magnificent vocal equipment and real promise,
but his singing is not yet even. The lovely choral passages are
well done. The generally satisfactory reproduction is variable.
The Highlights disc represents the postwar Glyndebourne, including a good deal of the finest music. Jurinac is outstanding in a
competent and dedicated cast, reasonably well recorded.

Le Nozze di Figaro. Rautawaara, s; Helletsgruber, s; Mildmay, s;
Domgraf-Fassbänder, b; Henderson, b; etc.; GFC & O, Busch, V LCT
6001 [2]. Gatti, s; Gardino, s; Noni, s; Tajo, bs; Bruscantini, bs;
Corena, bs; etc.; RIC & O, Previtali, Cet 1219 [3]; Schwarzkopf, s;
Seefried, s; Jurinac, s; Kunz, b; London, b; etc.; VSOC; VSY, Karajan,
C SL 114 [3].

Many readers will disagree (as many critics already have) with the
order of preference listed above. If high-fidelity recording is de-
manded, Victor's prewar Glyndebourne set is third on the list, but
it remains by all odds the best-integrated performance, the most
complete realization of the Mozart style, and it is acceptably
transferred to LP. The voices, as voices, are bettered by the Viennese group, who, however, being mostly Germans and Austrians,
sing the Italian text like an adopted language. The men project
their words well enough; the ladies are inclined to coo. I have
listed the cast of native Italians above the Viennese partly because theirs is the only recording complete with recitatives, so
essential a part of the drama, and musically important too. On
first playing the Cetra recording, I was bothered by Previtali's

leisurely tempos; coming back to it after the rather rushed presentation of Karajan, I found Previtali's the more satisfactory. Italians, traditionally, are not the finest interpreters of Mozart (because of their tendency to spread themselves); but this group may be commended for exemplary taste. Still, for pacing that *is* right, and a cast at the very least consistently satisfactory, and with certainly the best Figaro of the three recordings, one returns to Glyndebourne and accepts the less vital reproduction. None of the performances is uncut: the most serious omission is in the Cetra version: the Count's aria *"Vedro mentr' io sospiro."* The balance is generally best with Cetra, though Columbia's recording is more even.

A collection of arias presents Greindl singing *"Non più andrai"* and *"Aprite un po'"* in surprisingly effective Italian, Trötschel in *"Venite inginocchiatevi,"* and Kupper in *"Porgi amor"* (10" D DL 4065). Trötschel sings with considerable charm, but Kupper's voice is inclined to spread.

Il Re Pastore.   Giebel, s; Nentwig, s; Plümacher, c; Hohmann, t; Weikenmeier, b; STO, Lund, P er SPLP 553 [2].

The best that can be said for this recording is that it provides the chance of a lifetime to hear the great aria *"L'amerò, sarò costante"* in its setting. This is not, however, one of the great Mozart operas, and the singers, with their sweet and modest voices, are not equal to the music's demands.

Der Schauspieldirektor (The Impresario).   Nentwig, s; Guilleaume, s; Hohmann, t; von Rohr, bs; STO, Reinhardt, P er SPL 532 (*La Finta Giardiniera, abridged).   (In English) Gordon, s; Hunt, s; Vellucci, t; Bauman, speaker; O, Herz, 10" Mer MG 15025.

The second of these listings is done in the literate English translation of George and Phyllis Mead, and with its spoken dialogue it will make more immediate sense to non-Germans who would look for a story in Mozart's bit of fluff. There is a question in my mind, however, as to how often such a performance will bear repeating—which is to say, was it really worth recording? There is considerably more style in the rival recording, a presentation as authentic as need be. The voices in the cast are good. At first it seemed to me that Nentwig was singing tentatively, but she warmed up. Both she and Guilleaume prove equal to the high flights Mozart has required of them. The reproduction has the quality of sound we used to associate with studio recordings;

there is no sense of space in it; but within its rather confining
limits, the sound is clear and good.

*Thamos, König von Aegypten—Incidental Music. Neidlinger, bs; PRC
& O, Reinhardt, Vox PL 7350.*

This fine music was written as background for a now justly forgotten drama. The performance is passable, with Neidlinger's
singing lending it a certain distinction. The chorus is veiled in
reproduction. It would have helped the listener to have been provided with a text.

*Zaïde. Dobbs, s; Cuenod, t; Demigny, b; etc.; PPO, Leibowitz, Pol
PRLP 901/2 [2].*

Zaïde, an early work, was left unfinished by Mozart. Hence the
performance is more like a concert than a dramatic presentation.
There are several lovely arias, notably *"Ruhe sanft,"* remembered
in the fine record of Barbara Troxell (WCFM 8). The outstanding
singing here is done by Cuenod, who delivers his German text with
distinction. The American Mattiwilda Dobbs shows a lovely voice
and a promising sense of style. There are evidences of hasty
preparation.

*Die Zauberflöte. Lemnitz, s; Berger, s; Roswaenge, t; Hüsch, b;
Strienz, bs; etc.; BSOC & O, Beecham, V LCT 6101 [3]. Seefried, s;
Lipp, s; Dermota, t; Kunz, b; Weber, bs; etc.; MFC; VPH, Karajan, C
SL 115 [3].*

Victor's *Magic Flute* has long been rated among the finest of
phonographic achievements. Beecham's conception of the score
is rightly acknowledged a classic, and in its day the recording
was outstanding. Although I never could accept each individual
member of the cast as absolute perfection, I find that as a group
they stand up even against formidable rivalry from Vienna. Hüsch
remains unsurpassed as Papageno, though Kunz runs him a race;
Roswaenge's Tamino is healthier and more solid than Dermota's.
Although Berger's Queen of the Night is the more proficient, I
find Lipp's more exciting; and the Sarastro of Strienz is not quite
so poised as Weber's. As Pamina, Lemnitz is no more appealing
than Seefried, and tonally she is less steady. The Victor set, in
transfer to LP, has lost something in brilliance, but it sounds acceptable enough. Columbia's reproduction is inevitably better,
though the voices suffer occasionally from over-exposure to the
microphone.

Arias

Die Entführung aus dem Serail—Hier soll ich dich denn sehen; Konstanze, dich wieder zu sehen; Im Mohrenland gefangen war; Don Giovanni—Nur ihrem Frieden; Folget der Heissgeliebten; Die Zauberflöte—Dies Bildnis ist bezaubernd schön. Anders, t; GOH, Schmidt; Isserstedt, 10" Cap L 8084.

Anders is a lyric tenor of the Tauber type, German in style and training, but freer in production than most of his colleagues. These arias are sung competently, without the touch of gracefulness which would have given them distinction. The *Don Giovanni* arias, especially *"Il mio tesoro"* in German, furnish an excellent argument against translating everything into the vernacular. These words simply do not match the music. As it happens, too, Anders is less than perfectly poised in the long, florid phrases. The reproduction is on the rough side.

Ma che vi fece, o stelle, K. 368; Mia speranza adorata, K. 416; Regina Coeli, K. 127. Bak, s; MC & O, Graunke, Mer MG 10085 (*Handel: In Praise of Harmony).

This disc is listed for the repertory it contains, though the second concert aria is better sung by Hollweg (10" L LPS 250) and by Stich-Randall (Col CLPS 1035). Bak's is another of those high, clear voices that dazzle above the staff, but do not afford much pleasure in the lower registers. Her singing of lyrical passages leaves much to be desired.

Le Nozze di Figaro—Tutto 'e disposto; Non più andrai; Die Zauberflöte—In diesen heil'gen Hallen; Così fan tutte—Donne mie la fate a tanti; Don Giovanni—Madamina, il catalogo; Ah! pietà, signori miei; Le Nozze di Figaro—Se vuol ballare; La vendetta. Corena, bs; SCO, Erede; SR, Maag, 10" L LS 671.

Today's reigning buffo basso not only can act with his voice, but also can sing. Touching on the variegated roles of Figaro, Sarastro, Guglielmo, Leporello, and Bartolo, he strikes a masterly balance between vocalism and projection. His *"Madamina"* is well contrasted, avoiding some of the elaboration almost traditional in it these days, and the less usual *"Ah! pietà"* is happily not overdrawn. *"Se vuol ballare"* may be an instant slow in commencing, but it has a new angle, starting off more in anger than in craftiness, leaving the insinuating tones for the last repeat. One must exclaim over the singer's superb diction in *"Aprite un po',"* and the fine swing of *"Non più andrai."* It is interesting to hear this Swiss-Italian sing the *Zauberflöte* piece in good firm German; stylistically little is lacking, though there is a suggestion of clipping the well-articulated words, just a shade of weight wanting in the singer's utterance. The *Così fan tutte* piece is magnificent.

Non temer, amato bene, K. 490; Le Nozze di Figaro—Voi che sapete; Deh vieni, non tardar; Idomeneo—Se il padre perdei. Gueden, s; VPH, Krauss, 10" L LPS 485 (*Verdi: Rigoletto—Arias).

Exsultate, jubilate; Die Zauberflöte—Ach, ich fühl's; Le Nozze di Figaro—Venite, inginocchiatevi; Il Re Pastore—L'amerò, sarò costante. Gueden, s; VPH, Erede, 10" L LPS 681.

Gueden is one of the most musical and appealing of present-day lyric sopranos; she has the poise and the style for Mozart. The infectious lilt of her *"Voi che sapete"* is not interrupted, for all the effective shading and word-coloring she gets into it. The *"Deh vieni,"* done without *appoggiaturas,* is only less good for want of a similar lilt. The *Idomeneo* aria, and *"Non temer,"* composed to be interpolated into that opera, have both style and brilliance. In *Exsultate* (the solo motet ending with the celebrated *"Alleluia"*) she strikes the note of jubilation so often missing; hers is certainly among the better recordings of this work. The *Re Pastore* aria is also beautifully sung.

Mia speranza adorata, K. 416; No, no, che non sei capace, K. 419. Hollweg, s; LSO, Krips 10" L LPS 250 (*Strauss: Ariadne).

Hollweg is gifted with a phenomenal voice, but she is a better singer than most who can be thus characterized. While I do not find that she brings any very personal touch to these concert arias, she tosses them off with little concern for their fiendish difficulties.

Va, dal furor portata, K. 21; Si mostra la sorte, K. 209; Con ossequio, con rispetto, K. 210; Per pietà, non recercate, K. 420; Se al labbro mio non credi, K. 295; Misero! O sogno!, K. 431. Kmentt, t; VSY, Paumgartner, Ep LC 3076.

The first of these concert arias was composed when Mozart was nine; as the Köchel numbers show, the program ranges pretty well over his active musical life. If there is nothing here comparable to the best of the soprano arias, the pieces are all typical and splendidly vocal. Kmentt's voice may be a little heavy for them—he has his troubles in the florid passages of the first aria—but he sings with taste, and he is spaciously recorded.

Ah, lo previdi, K. 272; Chi sà, chi sà, qual sia, K. 582; Vado, ma dove?, K. 583; *Ch'io mi scordi di te?*, K. 505; *Bella mia fiamma*, K. 528. *Laszlo, s; VSO, Quadri, W WL 5179.*

Laszlo's bright and soaring voice is well suited to this kind of music; an occasional tendency to shrillness will not, I think, be found too much. Outstanding on her program is the aria with piano obbligato *"Ch'io mi scordi di te?"*—also recorded (but not quite so happily) by Käthe Nentwig (Vox PL 7370) and the too somber-voiced Jennie Tourel (Columbia ML 4640) as part of the Casals-Perpignan series. Laszlo seems at home in the Italian language, though diction is not her strongest point.

Le Nozze di Figaro—Se vuol ballare; La vendetta; Non più andrai; Vedrò, mentr'io sospiro; Aprite un po' quegl' occhi; Mentre ti lascia, o figlia, K. 513; *Per questa bella mano,* K. 612; *Rivolgete a lui lo sguardo. London, b; COL, Walter, C ML 4699.*

In his five arias from *Figaro*, London presents three different characters, carefully differentiating among them. Because of the weight of his voice, he comes off better as Bartolo and the Count than as Figaro. Perhaps we should blame the recording that his tones seem bigger and more overpowering than ever in real life. Otherwise the pieces are all intelligently and competently done, though the last section of the Count's *"Vedrò, mentr' io sospiro"* seems a little scrambled. The singing is nothing if not virile. The three concert arias have been heard perhaps to better advantage from such subtler singers as Pinza and Tajo, but they are always welcome and certainly not overdone. The voice here seems too forward in recording. The double-bass obbligato in *"Per questa bella mano"* has unfortunately been given to a cello. The recording is very live and not free of echo.

Dulcissimum convivium, K. 243; *Ergo interest,* K. 143; *Panis vivus,* K. 125; *Laudate Dominum,* K. 321; *Die Zauberflöte—O zitt're nicht; Der Hölle Rache. Lorand, s; SAL, Fekete, 10" Mer MG 15026.*

This twenty-five-year-old (at recording) Swiss soprano discloses an admirably healthy voice, somewhat lacking, perhaps, in color and variety, but distinctly promising. Her account of the *Magic Flute* arias, hardly in the great tradition, is better than we usually hear nowadays. I wish she had controlled her rhythm more strictly in the second air—one has the feeling she is about to run away. The church arias are well worth knowing. The *Vespers*, from which the *"Laudate"* is taken, are available in their entirety (CH CHS 1083).

Ombra felice; Io ti lascio, K. 255. *Michaelis, c. Ah, lo previdi,* K.

*272; Ch'io mi scordi di te?; Non temer, amato bene, K. 505; Bella mia
fiamma. Resta, o cara, K. 528; Nehmt meinen Dank, ihr holden
Gönner, K. 383. Nentwig, s; PRO, Reinhardt, Vox PL 7370.*

> Nentwig duplicates three of the arias recorded by Laszlo, and it
> must be conceded hers is the less vibrant and telling voice. She
> is, however, a capable artist, and her record is worth having.
> Michaelis sings her one aria with taste and good style.

*Die Zauberflöte—Possenti numi; Qui sdegno non s'accende; Le Nozze
di Figaro—Non più andrai; Se vuol ballare; Don Giovanni—Madamina,
il catalogo; Deh vieni alla finestra; Finch'han dal vino. Pinza, bs; O,
Wallenstein, V LM 1751 (*Verdi: Arias).*

*Don Giovanni—Madamina, il catalogo; Mentre ti lascia, o figlia, K.
513; Die Entfürung aus dem Serail—Osmin's Aria; Die Zauberflöte—
Qui sdegno non s'accende; Le Nozze di Figaro—Se vuol ballare;
Aprite un po' quegli occhi. Pinza, bs; MOO, Walter, C ML 4036.*

> One can only conclude that Pinza was not satisfied with his Co-
> lumbia recital: he has repeated much of it for Victor. It is sad to
> be reminded so forcibly that these high days of the basso's popu-
> larity have not coincided with the period of his greatest vocal
> splendor. The choice of records is between smoother (if not, even
> then, completely controlled) singing and richer, more refined re-
> cording. As for the background, I prefer the spirit of Walter,
> though just as surely Wallenstein has the better orchestra to work
> with. The recitative preceding *"Se vuol ballare"* is definitely im-
> proved by more harpsichord and less bass. But those of us who
> remember Pinza in the days of his Don Giovanni and Figaro will
> not be satisfied for a moment with this performance. It is amusing
> to compare his recording of the *"Serenade"* and *"Champagne
> Song"* from *Don Giovanni* (V 1467) dating back to the first years
> of his Metropolitan Don. Even then the *tessitura* of the former
> played tricks with his intonation; taking the latter at breakneck
> speed, he was never able to articulate its musical notes as Mo-
> zart wrote them.

*Le Nozze di Figaro—Non più andrai. Sammarco, b. Il Re Pastore—
L'amerò, sarò costante. Ritter-Ciampi, s. Don Giovanni—Finch' han
dal vino. d'Andrade, b. Don Giovanni—Serenata. Renaud, b. Die
Zauberflöte—Queen of the Night arias. Ivogün, s. Die Entführung
aus dem Serail—Hier soll ich dich denn sehen; Konstanze, Konstanze.
Slezak, t. Osmin's Entrance; Ha! wie will ich triumphieren. Hesch,
bs. Et ELP 479.*

In sum, this is a good representation of a "golden age" embracing the first thirty years or so of the present century. Some of the singing is truly distinguished, some less than Mozartean. In the former class is Maria Ivogün, who gives us the two arias of the Queen of the Night with wonderful facility, firm style, and tones that remain melting all the way to the top of her register. Gabrielle Ritter-Ciampi, in an electrical recording with the most prominent of hums, sings a superb *Re Pastore* aria. In the opera house, hers was a tiny thread of tone; it emerges naturally in well-balanced reproduction. Fine, too, are the four *Entführung* numbers by Slezak and Hesch—the latter sometimes called "the German Plançon," though his style bore little resemblance to that of the French mastersinger. The one published recording of Frencesco d'Andrade (the Don of the famous Lilli Lehmann production at Salzburg) is something of a curio, with its cheering studio audience demanding, and receiving, an encore. The voice is remarkably clear and neat, and for all his inordinate speed, he does articulate the eighth notes so many baritones miss. Sammarco sings *"Non più andrai"* with open tone and lots of spirit, but I suspect the recording-speed has not been reproduced accurately. Renaud's *"Serenata,"* sung in French and extended in Italian, is fair neither to the singer nor the composer. The artist made far better records than this one.

Le Nozze di Figaro—Porgi amor; Deh vieni non tardar; Don Giovanni —Vedrai, carino; Batti, batti, o bel Masetto. Sayão, s; O, Leinsdorf, Breisach, Cimara, 10" C ML 2152 (*Sayão Recital).

This singer never descends below a certain admirable standard, but not all these performances are equally interesting. Her *"Porgi amor"* is sung at an unusually slow tempo, one, I am afraid, at which it would be impossible to give the melody the lift it needs. The voice, too, is definitely too light to make a Countess, though in recording it has been built up. *"Deh vieni"* is more her meat, and my dissents are matters of taste. The recitative seems to me too slow again; I miss the crispness that Bori, for instance, used to give it. And I miss the *appoggiaturas*, necessary to the complete realization of the melody. *"Vedrai carino"* and *"Batti, batti"* are good proficient jobs.

Don Giovanni—Madamina, il catalogo; Le Nozze di Figaro—Non più andrai. Schoeffler, b; VPH, Böhm. Die Zauberflöte—Dies Bildnis ist bezaubernd schön; Don Giovanni—Dalla sua pace; Il mio tesoro. Dermota; VPH, Böhm. Nozze di Figaro—Porgi amor; Dove sono. Rein-

ing, s; VPH, Krips. Zauberflöte—Ach, ich fühl's; Nozze di Figaro—
Voi che sapete. Della Casa, s; SR, Reinhagen. L LLP 457.

This disc is a bargain-counter display, with the four artists in
their accustomed roles, and Schoeffler taking over Leporello's
aria for good measure. The singing is all good in the German manner; we are not told that it is all done in that language.

Le Nozze di Figaro—Deh vieni, non tardar; Porgi amor; Voi che sa-
pete; Non so più; Dove sono; Don Giovanni—Vedrai, carino; Non mi
dir; Batti, batti; Idomeneo—Zeffiretti lusinghieri. Schwarzkopf, s;
PHI, Pritchard, An 35021.

Exsultate, jubilate; Il Re Pastore—L'amerò, sarò costante; Die Ent-
führung aus dem Serail—Welche Kummer; Warnung, K. 433. Schwarz-
kopf, s; PHI, Susskind; VPH, Krips; Moore, pf; C ML 4649.

The first of these recitals reveals Schwarzkopf skipping lightly
from one to the other of the chief female characters in *Don Gio-*
vanni and *Figaro.* Her great achievement is the differentiation between the voices of the various ladies and of Cherubino. Her
singing is always distinguished. I would have liked a little more
snap in the recitative leading into *"Deh vieni,"* and I miss the
appoggiaturas in that air. *"Vedrai, carino"* is a little precious,
and the Countess of this *"Porgi amor"* is not one to sing out. I
can only admire the coloratura in the second part of *"Non mi dir,"*
though I do not feel in it much dramatic impact. But the phrasing
of *"Dove sono"* might serve as a model. The reproduction lacks
clarity. Of the Columbia program, I especially liked the little
piano-accompanied song at the end. Her *Exsultate,* admirable as
it is, is not so jubilant as Troxell's or Gueden's.

Der Schauspieldirektor—Bester Jüngling; Die Entführung aus dem
Serail—Durch Traurigkeit; Le Nozze di Figaro—Dove sono; Die
Zauberflöte—Ach, ich fühl's; Don Giovanni—Mi tradi; Non mi dir;
Così fan tutte—Per pietà. Steber, s; COL, Walter, C ML 4694.

Steber's program strikes a good balance between the familiar and
the rarer arias. Her singing is capable and conscientious, though
she has not found the secret of imparting dramatic meaning to the
florid passages. Those who have collected some of her older recordings may find it interesting to trace the singer's development,
notably in *"Dove sono,"* one of several Mozart arias she sang
some years ago for Victor. Bruno Walter, at the podium, imparts a
certain geniality and warmth to this recording.

Mia speranza adorata, K. 416. Stich-Randall, s; SCAO, Paumgartner,
C CLPS 1035 (*March; Scarlatti: Sulle sponde del Tebro).

From Italy comes this performance by one of our Fulbright Fellows, a singer of delicious voice and outstanding artistic promise. A present tendency to sing inwardly is overcome at the climaxes, where the music becomes genuinely exciting.

Mentre ti lascio, o figlia, K. 513; Un bacio di mano, K. 541; Per questa bella mano, K. 612; Così dunque tradisci, K. 432; Rivolgete a lui lo sguardo, K. 584; Alcandro, lo confesso, K. 512. Tajo, bs; RIO, Rossi, Cet 50019.

Tajo was first in the field with these concert arias, and most of them have not been done again. Most intriguing is *Per questa bella mano,* with its high, agile double-bass obbligato. The singer's voice is a rather light *basso cantate* of good range and pleasing quality. He has the proper style for this music, and his unhackneyed program shows him to advantage. Three of the arias are somewhat abbreviated.

Zaïde—Ruhe sanft; Exsultate, jubilate. Troxell, s; NGO, Bales, WCFM 8 (*Concerto for Horn).

The long motet is sung with more of the jubilant spirit its title implies than has often been the case in recordings. Troxell sings in it a cadenza written by Richard Strauss for Elisabeth Schumann. However, the real feature of the disc is the heavenly *Zaïde* aria, long unaccountably neglected. The soprano's voice is lovely in the broadly sweeping melody.

Don Giovanni—Or sai, chi l'onore; Non mi dir. Welitch, s; de Paolis, t; MOO, Reiner, 10" C ML 2118 (*Welitch Recital).

Welitch is at all times an interesting singer, and in the opera house this goes far to make up for what she lacks in sheerly sensuous tone, facile technique, and musicianly style. She may not, for example, manipulate the roulades and runs in *"Non mi dir"* after the manner of the greatest Donna Annas, but on the stage she manages to keep acting, really addressing Don Ottavio, while she sings these passages. In recording, naturally, we miss the visual aid, and are therefore likely to be more critical of her singing. The first striking fact is that she is not altogether at home in the Italian language; her recitatives lack crispness, and she does some peculiar things with the phrasing. Secondly, in the cantilena she wants rhythmic solidity. She cuts corners, and her coloratura bogs down rather badly. The voice itself is strangely more attractive than I remember it at the Metropolitan.

Songs

Das Veilchen; Abendempfindung; Dans un bois solitaire; An Chloe.
Danco, s; Agosti, pf, 10" L LS 699 (*Strauss: Songs).
An Chloe; Warnung; Abendempfindung; Die Zufriedenheit. Rogers, t;
Mitrani, pf, 10" All AL 13 (*Haydn: Songs).
*Dans un bois solitaire; Das Lied der Trennung; Als Luise die Briefe
ihres ungetreuen Liebhabers verbrannt; Abendempfindung; Das Veil-
chen; An Chloe.* Warner, s; Rupp, pf, C ML 4365 (*Schubert: Songs).

It will be noted that the best-known songs are duplicated here, in
some cases sung three times. Of the singers, Danco is the most
mature and artistic, though Warner has the warmest voice and
sings the most generous program. Danco's singing is inclined to
be careful, rather studied than spontaneous, while Warner's is a
little underdeveloped, not free of monotony. There is not a great
deal of color in the light tones of Earl Rogers.

*Trios: Grazie agl' inganni tuoi, K. 532; Più non si trovano, K. 549; Mi
lagnerò tacendo, K. 437; Due pupille amabili, K. 439; Se lontan ben
mio, tu sei, K. 438; Luci care, luci belle, K. 346 (439a); Ecco quel
fiero istante, K. 436; Caro bell' idol mio, K. 562; La Clemenza di Tito
—Vengo! Aspettate!; Zaïde—O selige Wonne; Mandina amabile, K.
480 (from Bianchi's La Villanella Rapita); Das Bandel, K. 441.* The
Mozart Trio (Hansel, s; Collins, b; Yard, b); Reese, pf, Den DR 1.

Three competent artists have joined forces to resurrect a whole
Mozart repertoire that has remained for many years virtually unknown. The voices are not remarkable, but the spirit and the style
are here.

MUSSORGSKY, MODEST PETROVICH (1839-1881)

Operas

Boris Godunov. Zareska, c; Gedda, t; Christoff, bs; etc.; POC & O,
Dobrowen, V LHMV 6400 [4]. Maksakova, m-s; Nelepp, t; Pirogov, bs;
Mikhailov, bs; Yankuschenko, bs; etc.; BSIC & O, Golovanov, Col
CLPS 124026 [3]. (Same performance) Per SPLP 554 [3].

The first of these two performances represents the expatriate Russian tradition; the second brings us the great national opera as it
is given in the Soviet Union. The first had the benefit of the best
modern recording techniques; the second is typical of the better
grade of Russian tapes. Boris Christoff, hailed as heir to the

Chaliapin tradition (and with a voice at times almost frighteningly like that of his great predecessor), sings not only the title role, but two other bass parts as well, and several others in Dobrowen's cast do likewise. This must be set down as questionable practice, however well these artists bring it off. Otherwise, the HMV recording is superior to its rival in every way. The Rimsky-Korsakov edition is used. The Bolshoi Theater disclaims Rimsky, but he is actually not ignored in its production. Pirogov's Boris, a characterization very much admired, is convincing and sonorous, if tonally not too steady. The other basses in the cast are good, though there is some stiff tone on occasion. Nelepp as the false Dmitri shows a serviceable if not overmodulated voice, and a good style of singing; but Maksakova's Marina did not give me much pleasure. Apparently she is bent on characterization to the point where one wonders how the young Pretender could be taken in. A special word is due Mikhailov's delivery of "Pimen's Narrative" in the Duma Scene, and Kosslovsky's heart-rending singing of the Simpleton's music. All the voices have it their own way over the orchestra.

Of special interest is a set of Highlights assembled from Chaliapin's rich legacy (10" V LCT 3). Though a great deal of the effect of his celebrated performance was visual, these samples demonstrate that it need not have been so. Even those whose memories do not go back to the original will acknowledge that this is great vocal acting. The recordings are uneven: a more judicious selection might have been made of the available material. The weak point is the "Coronation Scene," with its poorly reproduced chorus. Ezio Pinza, who took over the role a decade or so after the great Russian's incumbency at the Metropolitan, was a strong, if distinctly Italianate Boris. His series of Highlights is a good memento (C ML 4115). RCA Victor has recently done due honors to Alexander Kipnis, the other great Boris of the thirties, in transferring his fine set of Russian Highlights to LP (V LBC 1082).

From the sound-track of the Russian film-biography of Mussorgsky comes another set of Highlights (Col CRLP 117) featuring the basso Orlov as Boris. The main interest centers in the use of the original Mussorgsky score, without benefit of Rimsky. Both as to performance and as to reproduction, it has its ups and downs. A mostly orchestral selection is offered by Stokowski with the San Francisco Opera Chorus and Orchestra, featuring Rossi-Lemeni's admired Boris in the episode of the clock and the "Death Scene." The conductor has supplied whatever Rimsky-Korsakov may have overlooked by way of making the music effective, and the basso's singing verges, a good deal of the time, on straight declamation. Use of Mussorgsky's original is claimed again for Raphäel Arie's recording of the "Death Scene" (L LPS 98; or 10" LD 9018), which is well sung, but not so impressive technically as it was when it first appeared several years ago.

The Marriage. Desmazures, c; Mollien, t; Agroff, bs; Popovitzky, bs; Paris Radio SO, Leibowitz, Oc OCS 36.

Mussorgsky completed only the first act of this curious opera; the second and third, supplied by Ippolitov-Ivanov, are not included here. The orchestration is attributed to Antoine Duhamel. What we have amounts to little more than several long dialogues in recitative; as it is sung in Russian, there is little for the casual listener to take hold of. One has the impression that the words are well matched to the music, and that the singers, especially the big-voiced Agroff, are delivering them in the proper spirit.

Songs

The Nursery. Kurenko, s; Pastukhoff, pf, Cap P 8265 (*Rachmaninoff: Songs).

So far as I can trace, this is the only complete recording as yet made of the children's cycle. Two pre-LP performances, both in English translation, lacked a song each of completeness. Kurenko never ceases to amaze, not only by the bright and youthful quality her voice retains, but by her ability to enter into any song she sings and bring it to life. One can well imagine the home in old Russia containing the nursery she so vividly portrays for us.

Songs and Dances of Death. Tourel, m-s; Bernstein, pf, C ML 4289 (*Ravel: Shéhérazade).
Songs and Dances of Death; Yeremoushka's Cradle Song; Gopak; The star; To the Dnieper; Reverie of the young peasant; The orphan; Mushrooms; The goat; Ballade; Savishna. Rosing, t; Foggin, pf, D DL 9577.
Songs and Dances of Death (in French). Rehfuss, b; Haeusslin, pf, 10" L LS 9070.

Like most singers who attempt the cycle, our three interpreters use the Rimsky-Korsakov edition, with its various changes and revised order. Singing in Russian, Tourel has the necessary authority and every appearance of conviction, but her rhythm is rather free, and of course no woman's voice is ideal for this music. Rosing, whose reputation was considerable a couple of decades ago, was a distinctly dramatic singer with a limited voice. Some listeners will feel that he paints with too broad a brush. The recording, of course, is not new. Rehfuss, singing in quite beautiful French, delivers the songs robustly and dramatically. Tonally and musically his performance is good, though of course he misses what the other singers gain by singing the original texts.

NEBDAL, OSCAR (1874-1930)

Polenblut. Seegers, s; Mentzel, s; Groh, t; etc.; RBC & O, Dobrindt, U URLP 215 [2].

Seekers after unhackneyed light music will enjoy this product (vintage 1913) of an expatriate Czech who had absorbed the Viennese operetta style and traditions. This excellent performance is built around the Tauber-like Herbert Ernst Groh. The reproduction is powerful and clear.

NICOLAI, OTTO (1810-1849)

Die lustigen Weiber von Windsor. Beilke, s; Schilp, s; Hoffmann, s; Ludwig, t; Hann, bs; Strienz, bs; BCOC; RBO, Rother, U URLP 214 [3].

An earlier recording made in Leipzig boasted the excellent Falstaff of Kurt Böhme, but the rest of the cast was no more than passable, and Kleinert's conducting was on the heavy side (Oc OCLP 303 [2]). Amends are made in this Berlin production, with its well-focused, generally clean recording, its mellifluous and spirited singing. Outstanding voices are those of Lore Hoffmann as Anne Page, the veteran Walter Ludwig as Fenton, Wilhelm Strienz as Falstaff, and the late Georg Hann as Ford. There are certain less fortunate moments: one of them comes with the lyric gem of the opera—Fenton's serenade, *"Horch, die Lerche singt im Hain"*—which is well sung, but too closely recorded (Ludwig is more successful with it in his operatic recital, 10" D DL 4073). The succeeding duet is altogether happy, with its long cadenza and its violin *obbligato*. In the Titania section of the final scene, the music again is close upon us, and, to complete the catalogue, the last chord of the opera is sour. But these are minor blemishes.

OFFENBACH, JACQUES (1819-1880)

La Belle Hélène. Linda, s; Dran, t; Mollien, b; etc.; PPC & O, Leibo-witz, Ren SX 206 [2]. *(Abridged) Dessy, s; Devos, t; Demigny, b; etc.; RSPC; LAM, Gressier, Vox PL 20500.*

Both conductors get spirited co-operation from their casts of sea-soned, able singers. Leibowitz has the gifted Janine Linda as a Helen of Troy to conjure with, and he is also the more spaciously recorded. But a choice between the sets might well be determined by the portion of Offenbach one desires.

Les Contes d'Hoffmann. Doria, s; Bovy, s; Geori-Boué, s; Jobin, t; Bourdin, b; Musy, b; Soix, b; etc.; OCC & O, Cluytens, C SL 106 [3]. *(In English) Bond, s; Grandi, s; Ayars, s; Rounseville, t; Dargavel, b; etc.; Sadlers Wells Ch; RPO, Beecham, L LLPA 4* [3]. *(In German, abridged) Berger, s; Streich, s; Langhammer-Klein, s; Anders, t; Pro-haska, b; etc.; RBC & O, Rother, U URLP 224* [2].

These three sets are hardly comparable, for they are aimed at three quite different audiences. The Cluytens performance, in the authentic French tradition, enlists some of the most distinguished contemporary singers of that school. Least good of the principals is Jobin, who has done other things better. Here his voice sounds more nasal and thin than I have ever heard it on records or in the opera house. Generally the singers are closer than they should be ideally, and toward the center the records are not one-hundred-per cent clear. The Beecham version is the sound-track of the suc-cessful film. As it was a double production (the action carried on by dancer-mimes, while the singers provided the music), we have every right to expect well-planned, evenly reproduced singing, and we are not disappointed. Over all one feels the consistent, vital hand of Sir Thomas, who can bring such a score to life as can no one else today. Rounseville does a musical and intelligent job, though his voice sometimes runs toward blattiness, and his patently American diction assorts strangely with that of his Brit-ish colleagues. Bond as Olympia climbs successfully to the altitudes of the part, but I found Ayars disappointing for both her not altogether tidy vocalism and her quite indistinguishable dic-tion. Grandi has not the vocal freshness she once had, but her temperamental utterance is enough reason for her presence in the cast. Among the others, the big-voiced Dargavel in the various villainous roles makes the strongest impression. The score has been edited, cut down, and rearranged for the special purpose, but I doubt that the Offenbach purists (if any) will be outraged at such procedures. A card in the album recommends that the set be played at full volume; the singers' voices come out perhaps too strongly if this is done, but the orchestra is always solid behind them. I am sure there is a German faction to welcome the Urania abridgment, but to ears such as mine the opera sounds strange in the heavy tongue. The chief distinction in the cast is lent by Berger and Prohaska. In the title role, Anders seems past his prime.

Le Mariage aux lanternes (in English). McGarity, s; Thomas, c; Chelsi, t; etc.; O, Kramer, MT MLP 1005.

This is opera produced on a shoestring, sung in clear and not too blatant English by pleasant bright voices, and accompanied by a very small group that passes as an orchestra. It adds up to a good amateur production through which the tunes emerge prettily, but without a suggestion of French piquancy. The recording is good enough.

Orphée aux Enfers. Collart, s; Linda, s; Dran, t; Mollien, b; *etc.*; PPC & O, Leibowitz, Ren SX 204 [2]. *(Abridged)* Collart, s; Devos, t; Roux, b; RSPC; LAM, Gressier, Vox PL 21200.

The two recordings share the same Euridice, and a charming singer she is. Leibowitz's "complete" set omits the famous overture, but does include beautifully clear French dialogue. His is the more spirited performance, with the brisker tempos; and it is all in all the more clearly reproduced. On the other hand, some of the ensemble work is better in the Gressier version, which includes no dialogue.

La Vie parisienne (Abridged). Renaux, s; Dachary, s; Roux, b; etc.; LAM, Gressier, Vox PL 21000.

This is another spirited, expansive, and authentic performance. The music—an abridged edition of the operetta, properly in order —gives the singers a run for their money, but their nimble tongues get around the problems beautifully. Several of the melodies will come as pleasant surprises with their texts, for they are familiar to all balletomanes.

Selections

La Périchole—O mon cher amant, je te jure; Mon Dieu, que les hommes sont bêtes; Je t'adore; Les Contes d'Hoffmann—Entr'acte and Barcarolle. Tourel, m-s; O, Abravanel, 10" C ML 2024 (*Rossini: Arias).

La Vie parisienne (arr. Rosenthal). Tourel, m-s; COL, Morel, C ML 4608 (*Bizet: Carmen).

Tourel is at her polished best in these delightful bits from *La Périchole*. At least one air is familiar to all ballet audiences; another has been identified among collectors with the singing of Maggie Teyte. If Tourel hasn't all of Teyte's charm in it, she may possibly be more authentic, and she is handsomely recorded. We seldom hear music of this kind done in such good style. The all-too-celebrated *"Barcarolle"* is also well sung; the stunt duet recording is unusually successful, though one wonders why with all the rest of Offenbach to choose from, the program had to be filled out in that way. The *Vie parisienne* is a potpourri specially arranged for Tourel, which includes some of the music from the "name" operetta, but some from other sources. It is sparkling music, excellently done.

ORFF, CARL (1895-   )

Carmina Burana. Trötschel, s; Kuen, t; Braun, b; Hoppe, b; BAVRC & O, Jochum, D DL 9706.
Catulli Carmina. Roon, s; Loeffler, t; four pfs; VKC, Hollreiser, Vox PL 8640.

The *Carmina Burana* created a mild sensation on its release. Taking his text from manuscripts of thirteenth-century poetry in the collection of the Benediktbeuren Monastery in Bavaria, Orff has applied his own new musical principles, by which repetition takes the place of variation. The result is music of striking novelty and tremendous drive, music that will not let you alone, once you start to listen to it. The performance is as full of life as the music itself; the total effect is exhilarating. There are a few technical slips, a blurt or two from the horns, but such things count for little. *Catulli Carmina*, based on the love poetry of Catullus, is a sequel to the *Burana* (a third work, *The Triumph of Aphrodite*, has not yet been recorded). The translator whose work appears on the jacket of the second work has been obliged to leave some of the text untouched, for "obvious" reasons. Perhaps because of the tremendous odds against recapturing such impact as the *Burana* possessed, the second recording is a bit of a let-down. The performance misses the triumph of its predecessor, though it has lots of drive and vitality.

PALESTRINA, GIOVANNI PIERLUIGI DA
(1525 - 1594)

Magnificat quarti toni; Missa Sacerdotes Domini—Pleni sunt coeli; Missa O Rex gloriae—Crucifixus; Missa Descendit angelus Domini— Benedictus; Jesu, Rex admirabilis; Tua, Jesu, dilectio; Adoramus te, Christe; Confitemini Domino; Salve Regina; Hodie Christus natus est. Period Ch Soc, Strassburg, Per SPL 513.

This program is made up of music for high voices, sung not by boys this time, but by women. There may be some question as to the value of stringing together separate movements from various Masses, along with the motets and the *Magnificat*. But the record's main weakness, to my mind, is in the vibrancy of the voices, one reason for preferring boys in this type of music. Some vagaries of pitch are chargeable to the engineers.

Missa Iste confessor; Missa sine nomine (super modulum "Je suis deshéritée"). Welch Ch, Ly LL 49.

Missa brevis; Missa Ascendo ad Patrem. Welch Ch, All 3097.

James B. Welch and his Chorale steer a middle course between the overpowering type of performance and that in which perfect poise is the ideal. The *Missa brevis*, best known of the four Masses, being musically the straightest and most grateful, naturally gets the smoothest performance. On the whole, the singing of the Chorale may lean too much toward the expressive, and the women's voices are rather full-blown.

Missa Papae Marcelli. Netherlands Cham Ch, Nobel, Ep LC 3045 (*Netherlands Chamber Choir Concert). Wagner Ch, Cap P 8126.

For clarity of contrapuntal lines, solid and clean reproduction, surely the full-blooded Netherlands recording must have the preference here. The singing is neither driven nor relaxed, but reflects the musical details of the Mass as they reflect the meanings of the text. The chorus responds to its sensitive conductor with rarely equaled freedom and flexibility. The climaxes are full and sonorous: the Amens that finish the "*Credo*" are ear-filling, the "*Sanctus*" and "*Benedictus*" splendidly solid. After this, the slower tempos, the more deliberately polished singing, of the Wagner Chorale seem long-drawn-out. Still, theirs is a cleanly phrased and nicely balanced performance. The intonation, if not quite perfect, is certainly above average, the reproduction quite acceptable, though it loses clarity in some of the softer passages. An earlier recording, from a French Pathé original, offers the performance of the St. Eustache Choir under Martin (Vox PTL 6790). It is the least sensitive and most energetic of the three. The reproduction is bass-heavy.

Offertories: Exaltabo Te, Domine; Bonum est confiteri; Laudate Dominum. Motets: Super flumina Babylonis; Dies sanctificatus; Pueri Hebraeorum; Tota pulchra es; Hodie Christus natus est; Tribulationes civitatum—Peccavimus; Exsultate Deo; Vox dilecti mei. Improperium: Popule meus. Sistine Chapel Ch, Bartolucci, Ren X 55.

Those who think of Palestrina's music as detached and otherworldly are not likely to care greatly for these hearty, energetic performances. The choral tone is full and sonorous, but never quite blended; the lusty boy voices are not restrained by association with their elders.

PEPUSCH, JOHN CHRISTOPHER (1667 - 1752)

The Beggar's Opera. A double cast, singers and actors; O, Goberman, Des 1 [3].

This production of the great English ballad opera lays claim to both completeness and authenticity. In order to make the most of the dramatic and the musical aspects of the work, a double cast has been used. Whether in the long run hearing John Gay's amusing dialogue with each repetition will give more satisfaction than the prewar Glyndebourne set (Victor M 772) is an individual question. Anyway, some will prefer this unadorned Pepusch score to Frederic Austin's edition. In either case, one always wishes that the songs were not so brief. The style of performance here is decidedly American, but as such it is good.

PERGOLESI, GIOVANNI BATTISTA (1710 - 1736)*

Oratorio

Stabat Mater, Augenstein, s; Plümacher, c; SCS; STO, Grischkat, Per SPL 530.

It is a little difficult to say why this performance fails to come

*Perhaps no other composer has been credited with so many other men's works as the short-lived Pergolesi. Although I have listed them under his name, recent researches of Frank Walker have established *La Contadina Astuta* as actually the work of Hasse, *Il Geloso Schernito* as that of Pietro Chiarini, and *Il Maestro di Musica* as that of Auletta. The arietta *Nina*, which has done so much to keep Pergolesi's name alive, has long been denied him by the musicologists, who found evidence in favor of Legrenzio Vincenzo Ciampi. However, Walker doubts Ciampi's claim, and so is inclined to give *Nina* back to Pergolesi.

to life. The singing is a little lethargic and lacking in spark; neither here nor in the orchestra is there much contrast in tone or color. The orchestra sounds full and bright, the chorus apparently somewhat dulled by distance. Plümacher is the better of the soloists, but even her singing is plodding. Here and there I noted some peculiar Latin pronunciation.

Operas

La Contadina Astuta. Tuccari, s; Mineo, b; RSQC & O, Senatra. *Per SPL 592.*

This pleasant little opera shows the company in its best light. Tuccari sings pleasingly with her pretty voice, and the supporting cast is effective if in no degree subtle. The reproduction is all rather on a fairly high dead level.

La Serva Padrona. Tuccari, s; Bruscantini, b; RIO, Simonetto, *Cet 50036.*

This famous little intermezzo must be tossed off with joyous ease, or there is little point in presenting it. Tuccari and Bruscantini show what can be done by two skilled and seasoned artists who take obvious pleasure in their work. Not so much can be said for another recording (Vox PL 660) in which some of the singing is downright uncomfortable.

Cantatas

Orfeo. Bianchini, t; ICO, Jenkins, HS HSL 76 (*Cambini: Andromaque; Galuppi: Overture No. 2).*

This cantata was composed for a *castrato;* it is an unanswerable question whether the sponsors have done well in giving it to a tenor, for though the sentiments expressed are masculine, they were originally proclaimed in the soprano register. What seems important to me, however, is that unlike so much *castrato* music, this work does not tax the singer unmercifully. Bianchini sings it with conviction. His voice is a high, not particularly sensuous tenor, well able to get around in the music.

Salve Regina. Neway, s; ACS, 10" *All 4019.*

It would be pleasant to praise the singing of this attractive work as we must the enterprise of the artist who chose to record it. But obviously the flowing, lyrical lines of this music are not in this particular soprano's vocabulary.

Arias

Lo Frate 'Nnamorato; Il Geloso Schernito; Il Maestro di Musica; L'olympiade; Catone. Faull, s; Rogell, pf, CH CHC 41.

Ellen Faull is known as a good stylist, and she has found some unusual repertoire here. Still, the recital is a disappointment, because she sings to the piano, thus losing the variety of tone color the original instrumental combinations might have given. The voice in itself is lovely.

PEROTIN (Twelfth-Thirteenth Centuries)

Viderunt omnes; Salvatoris hodie; Vetus abit littera. DC; NY Brass Ens, Boepple, CH CHS 1112 (*Anon.: Nobilis humilis; Alle psallite bonum).

The labeling here is misleading: it is necessary to pore over the descriptive notes in order to establish that all five works are not by Perotin. Indeed, his authorship of *Vetus abit littera* is not certain. The objection to performing the older music with so overwhelmingly large a chorus seems less valid here than it often does, for these pieces have great sonority. Additional weight is given by the brass ensemble, and there are also some definitely foreign sounds—do these musicians carry some other kinds of instruments with them? The recording is effectively roomy. Some more adequate explanation might have been provided as to the text-underlaying.

PLANQUETTE, ROBERT (1848-1903)

Les Cloches de Corneville (Abridged). Angelici, s; Dens, b; Peyron, b; RSPC; LAM, Gressier, Vox PLP 20100.

Though the once-popular *Chimes of Normandy* seems pretty well forgotten in this country, its gay and haunting tunes still survive with their original text in Paris. The recording is Michel Dens's show; you can picture him as you listen, the strapping, handsome, imposing man he is on the stage. Among his colleagues, Angelici sings with her customary lyrical appeal.

PONCHIELLI, AMILCARE (1834-1886)

La Gioconda. Callas, s; Barbieri, m-s; Amadini, c; Poggi, t; Silveri, b; Neri, bs; etc.; CC; RIO, Votto, Cet 1241 [3]. Corridori, s; Pirazzini,

m-s; Cavallari, m-s; Campora, t; Colzani, b; Corena, bs; etc.; SCAC &
O, Parodi, U URLP 229 [4].

The sensational Callas is the feature of Cetra's recording. Hers
is a voice with registers, powerful as a contralto in the chest,
light as a coloratura in the head, most beautiful in the lyrical
medium. For myself, I do not complain that it is not all perfectly
equalized, for she has temperament and the kind of imagination
that makes something new of a war-horse like the "*Suicidio*" aria.
The vivid Laura of Barbieri provides an excellent foil, and of
course Silveri and Neri are in their element. Poggi sounds like
a young man not yet grown up to his assignment, and Amadini's
"*Voce di donna*" could do with greater poise. The several big
ensembles are impressively reproduced. Another quite acceptable
recording of the opera is cast into the shade.

From older masters, Cetra has assembled a set of highlights (Cet
50020), featuring Gina Cigna in "*Suicidio*" and, with Cloe Elmo,
the Gioconda-Laura duet; Stignani in a temperamental "*Voce di
donna*"; Reali and Prandelli in the "*Enzo Grimaldo*" duet and
Barnaba's "*O monumento*"; Masini in "*Cielo e mar,*" and Siepi
in Alvise's unpleasant aria. But best of all is a stunning "*Stella
del marinar*" by Elmo. Returning further into the past, we have
another set of highlights (Et 483), fairly comprehensive except for
the conspicuous absence of Laura. The mezzo-contralto Parsi-
Pettinella contributes the oldest recording (1904), a vivid, strongly
Italianate "*Voce di donna*" (one misses the incomparable poise of
the old Matzenauer recording). Zenatello and Amato give a dramatic account of the Enzo-Barnaba duet, piano accompanied,
though recorded as late as 1908. After De Luca's "*O monumento,*" Baklanoff's "*Barcarolle,*" and Pertile's "*Cielo e mar,*"
the selection is crowned by Boninsegna's magnificent "*Suicidio.*"
The dubbings are very successful.

POULENC, FRANCIS (1899-   )

*Mass in G. SC, Shaw, V LM 1088 (*Britten: Ceremony of Carols).*

Shaw's singers are a remarkably proficient group, but I wonder if
they spent enough time on the preparation of this music. Especially the "*Kyrie*" seems not to have quite "jelled." Matters
improve as the Mass progresses, and the solo work of the soprano,
Florence Fogelson, in the high-lying "*Agnus Dei,*" merits a word

of praise. The recording is hardly a model of clarity; a little more emphasis might have been given the basses.

Les Mamelles de Tirésias. Duval, s; Legouhy, c; Giraudeau, t; Rousseau, b; etc.; OCC & O, Cluytens, An 35090.

This strange *opéra-bouffe,* combining a 1917 Apollinaire play with 1944 Poulenc music, is something for the musical epicures. Underneath the facile and amusing surface, the program annotator tells us, lies the "profound and unique originality of one of the most genuine musical personalities of our present school." And this we can believe, as the outrageous story unfolds, though we need more than a textbook knowledge of French to understand the libretto. The performance leaves little to be desired. The voices are clean and appropriate—in the case of Denise Duval, at least, quite beautiful—and everyone concerned seems to be having a high time.

Le Bal masqué. Galjour, b; Ens, Fendler, Es ES 518 (*Françaix: Sérénade BEA).

This "secular cantata," on a nonsense text by Max Jacob, dates from 1932, and stands as a reminder of that strange period. The superlative recording has the advantage of the authoritative direction of Fendler, who conducted the world *première. Galjour* sings cleanly and accurately, with an uncommonly sturdy voice and admirable French diction.

Songs

Banalités; Chansons villageoises. Bernac, b; Poulenc, pf, C ML 4333 (*Ravel: Songs).

Quatre Poèmes de Guillaume Apollinaire; Tu vois le feu du soir; Main dominée par le coeur; Calligrammes de Guillaume Apollinaire. Bernac, b; Poulenc, pf, C ML 4484 (*Chabrier, Debussy, Satie: Songs).

Bernac, Poulenc's "official" interpreter, never could have been described as a generously gifted singer, though his art of song projection has for many hearers compensated for what he lacks in voice. He has for years worked closely with the composer-pianist, not a few of whose songs have been written for him. Mannerisms he certainly has; still, he is "headquarters" for these songs.

PROKOFIEV, SERGEI (1891-1953)

Alexander Nevsky. Tourel, m-s; Westminster Ch; PHO, Ormandy, C ML 4247. Iriarte, m-s; VSOC & O, Rossi, Van VRS 451.

The first of these recordings was made nearly a decade ago; at the time of its release the set was mechanically sensational. The work is sung in English. The newer version is very full and powerful in reproduction, with a pronounced echo to add to its atmosphere. The sound is very live, yet the singers are too close in effect to make for concert hall illusion. The language used is the original Russian, and in one passage the basses sound like the genuine native variety. The setup seems to have been worked out to favor the orchestra as the most important component, so that the chorus is less distinct in sound. Because of the sparseness of the choral writing, there is a good deal to be said for this treatment. Iriarte, the soloist, has an unusually rich and even voice; she seems happier, on the whole, than Tourel, who may have been embarrassed by the English translation, and who is occasionally guilty of pushing her voice. On the other hand, Ormandy seems to have sunk himself more deeply into the score than has Rossi; his reading is more subtly shaded. Recording-wise, his set is nothing to be ashamed of; the chorus stands out in bolder relief than in the Vanguard record, and the English text is not too hard to follow. On the whole I find myself favoring the Columbia disc.

On Guard for Peace. Dolukhanova, m-s; Talanov, boy-alto; USSRC & O, Samosud, Van VRS 6003.

This is a late work, and one, I am afraid, whose interest is at least as much in the "cause" as in the music, though so thorough an artist as Prokofiev could not help writing in his own recognizable and effective style. The performance is broad and sonorous, the recording very good.

PUCCINI, GIACOMO (1858-1924)

Messa di Gloria. SCAOC & O, Rapalo, Col CLPS 1053.

It would be too much to describe this recently discovered youthful work as a masterpiece, but it would be equally foolish to talk down its appealing melodiousness. Let it be added that the "Cum sancto spiritu" section is an elaborate and effective fugue, which the composer must have mightily enjoyed writing. There is evidence in the recording that the performance was prepared with care and dedication. The baritone solo "Crucifixus" is both dramatic and expressive, the "Agnus Dei" beautiful and eloquent.

Operas

*La Bohème. Tebaldi, s; Gueden, s; Prandelli, t; Inghilleri, b; Arie,
bs; etc.; SCC & O, Erede, L LLP 462/3* [2]. *Albanese, s; McKnight, s;
Peerce, t; Valentino, b; Moscona, bs; etc.; Ch; NBC, Toscanini, V LM
6006* [2]. *Carteri, s; Ramella, s; Tagliavini, t; Taddei, b; Siepi, bs;
etc.; RIC & O, Santini, Cet 1237* [2]. *Sayão, s; Benzell, s; Tucker, t;
Valentino, b; Baccaloni, bs; etc.; MOC & O, Antonicelli, C SL 101* [2].

London's set seems to me the best of these, especially because
of Tebaldi's Mimi and the fine Musetta of Gueden, a far cry from
the too-frequent coquettish caricature. Prandelli proves a romantic Rodolfo, and the other men are well in the picture. Against
the set I must hold Erede's slow tempos. Toscanini's performance
(recorded from his 1946 broadcasts) has the familiar clean-cut
precision, but it is marred by inadequacies of reproduction and by
obtrusive singing on the part of the conductor. No rival can match
the Maestro's credentials as a *Bohème* authority—he conducted
the world *première* just fifty years before this recording—but I
suspect some of his rapid tempos were dictated by exigencies of
the broadcasting schedule. Albanese is appealing, McKnight less
so; Peerce, Valentino, and the rest are in good form. The Cetra
set also has some good singing and a nice spirit among the cast,
especially the attractive-voiced Carteri. Tagliavini is in excellent form; Taddei and Siepi are outstanding. The "official" Metropolitan recording shares some of Toscanini's singers, along
with Sayão's fragile Mimi, Tucker's forthright Rodolfo, and Benzell's all-too-kittenish Musetta. The reproduction is good;
Sayão's light, well-carrying voice is allowed to sustain itself
without undue amplification. The conducting is routine.

A popular-priced recording, starring Ilitsch as Mimi, has little
beyond economy to recommend it (Rem R 199–80 [3]; another with
Schimenti (Rem R 199–99) derives interest from the presence of
the veteran Lauri-Volpi in the cast; but his is not the most poetic
of Rodolfos, and the rest of the singers are hardly more than
adequate.

For those who would settle for less than the whole opera, we have
an excellent set of highlights with Di Stefano as the best of
modern phonographic Rodolfos, and Albanese in top form; Munsel
and Warren round out the cast (V LM 1709). And a Maria Cebotari
memorial disc contains the first-act duet and *"Mimi's Farewell,"*
sung in German with the tenor Peter Anders. The soprano's voice

is very lovely, but it is strange to hear the third-act quartet sung
by two singers—Musetta and Marcello are simply omitted (U
URLP 7105).

*La Fanciulla del West. Gavazzi, s; Campagnano, t; Savarese, b; etc.;
RIC & O, Basile, Cet 1215 [3].*

The cast assembled to perform Puccini's "American" opera is as
thoroughly Italian as the music itself, so that the little bits of
local color emerge the more amusingly. This is as it should be.
The principals are known for their work in other recorded operas;
there are several fine voices, but no outstanding vocalism. The
recording is clear enough, though the voices are too close upon
us.

*Madama Butterfly. Tebaldi, s; Rankin, m-s; Campora, t; Inghilleri, b;
etc.; SCC & O, Erede, L LLPA 8 [3]. Dal Monte, s; Palombini, m-s;
Gigli, t; Basiola, b; etc.; ROC & O, Fabritiis, V LCT 6006 [2]. Steber,
s; Madeira, c; Tucker, t; Valdengo, b; etc.; MOC & O, Rudolf, C SL
104 [3].*

If all that mattered were rich, sonorous, well-balanced recording,
the choice here would go to the official Metropolitan-Columbia
set, but as a performance it must take third place. If one's conception of Butterfly is a smooth Italian voice rather than a simulated
Japanese quality, one will favor London, which is not too far behind Columbia in quality of sound. The Victor performance is in
the historical class, dating from the thirties (though its reproduction is not bad); its cast is headed by Dal Monte, in her day a top-
flight coloratura soprano, whose aging voice, paradoxically, has
an appropriately thin and girlish quality in this music. This
appeals to some connoisseurs like a heady wine, but very definitely antagonizes others. Tebaldi, after an uncomfortable start,
does so much lovely singing in the course of the opera that I feel
sure most listeners will find her more satisfactory. Her soft
beginning of *"Un bel dì"* is the work of a true artist. Her supporting cast is good, with Campora a mellifluous Pinkerton,
Inghilleri an adequate Sharpless, and, for his one moment, Corena
a terrifying Bonzo. Rivaling these are Gigli in his best form, the
smooth-voiced Basiola, and Dominici. In the Columbia set, Steber
is only tolerable in the first act, improves in the second, and ends
with unwonted conviction. Tucker sings lyrically and well,
Valdengo quite eloquently.

Albanese, Browning, and Melton join in a group of Highlights, first issued in 1946 (10" V LM 2). Included are the Love Duet, *"Un bel dì,"* the Flower Duet, and Pinkerton's *"Addio, fiorito asil."* Unfortunately the first rapturous number ends with the singers going their separate ways—Albanese up, Melton down— and the orchestra cutting the postlude, as if in protest. The Butterfly-Suzuki duet seems to me the best feature of the set. A curious choice is offered to those who do not mind hearing the Love Duet in German. In both cases the soprano is the late Maria Cebotari, the conductor Artur Rother. The earlier recording has Walther Ludwig as a finely lyrical Pinkerton (U URLP 7036), the later Helge Roswaenge, a less appealing one (U URLP 7105). The reproduction of the second version is vastly superior, and as a dividend it includes Cebotari's *"Un bel dì."*

Manon Lescaut. Petrella, s; Campagnano, t; Meletti, b; etc.; RIC & O, Del Cupolo, Cet C 1243 [3]. *Zamboni, s; Merli, t; Conati, b; etc.; SCAC; MISO, Molajoli, C SL 111* [2].

There is nothing to compare between the two performances listed above, the one a well-recorded and reasonably satisfactory present-day production, the other a run-of-the-mill revival. One thing the old set has: the tenor Merli boasted a freer and steadier tone than Cetra's Campagnano. In the title role, on the other hand, Petrella, though not a completely even singer, has more timbre in her voice than Columbia's Zamboni. It should be added that in the big moments the new singers rise nobly to the occasion, the tenor's somewhat earthy voice taking the high B's and C's more easily than it manipulates the legato passages. Meletti is an excellent baritone who makes the most of Lescaut's moments. The handling of crowds, the ensembles where a voice or two should stand out clear and distinct above a chorus, is exceptionally happy in the Cetra set. The ending of Act 1 is very lovely as we have it here.

Tosca. Callas, s; di Stefano, t; Gobbi, b; Luise, bs; etc.; SCAC & O, Sabata, An 3508-B [2]. *Tebaldi, s; Campora, t; Mascherini, b; Corena, bs; etc.; SCC & O, Erede, L LL 660/1* [2]. *Caniglia, s; Gigli, t; Borgioli, b; etc.; ROC & O, Fabritiis, V LCT 6004* [2]. *Dall'Argine, s; Scattolini, t; Colombo, b; Poell; etc.; VKC; VSO, Quadri, W WAL 302* [3]. *Guerrini, s; Poggi, t; Silveri, b; Badioli, bs; etc.; RIC & O, Molinari-Pradelli, Cet 1230* [2].

To some listeners, the "historical" performance on this list will always remain *the* recording of *Tosca.* Even those unmoved by Caniglia's vibrant voice and Gigli's fulsome expressiveness will grant that the still-reasonably-effective reproduction preserves a style of singing which should not be lost. The Westminster and Cetra versions, produced in 1951, offer well-paced readings of the score, good voices in the various roles, but hardly an outstanding characterization between them. Both are amply and roundly reproduced, with Westminster the more even, as well as the better balanced. Dall'Argine is the more satisfying Tosca, though neither soprano altogether lives up to the promise of her voice; Scattolini, despite some vocal pushing, is the more eloquent Mario. Colombo's Scarpia is routined, if not very subtle, easily preferable to Silveri's. Cetra's Badioli makes the character of the Sacristan more real than his counterpart; both Angelottis are good, especially Westminster's versatile Poell. On a higher plane is London's recording with Tebaldi; it still offers magnificent competition for the somewhat later Angel set. As a vocalist pure and simple, Tebaldi is more even than Callas, and hers remains one of the loveliest sopranos in action today. She has both temperament and intelligence, a rare combination. And her supporting cast is good. Still, Angel has not only Callas, but the fiery maestro Sabata to make one of the great operatic recordings, not to mention Di Stefano in his most lavish voice, and Gobbi contributing both characterization and real singing as Scarpia. At best the Callas voice is almost painfully beautiful; one can question, not quite condemn, a certain hollow sound that creeps in from time to time. One feels from her first entrance, and throughout the first-act duet, not simply a voice, but an imagination at work. In the second act she warms up to an enormous tension, taking fire, perhaps, from the conductor and his seething orchestra. Her pronouncement of the word *"Assassino!"* is bloodcurdling. In the *"Vissi d'arte"* the river nearly overflows its banks; the big tones pour out almost to the extinction of the very solid orchestra. For the most part, however, she conveys emotion without extra-musical means. The smaller roles are well portrayed, especially the sacristan of Luise, which is sung as well as delineated. For the most part the balance is better than good, though here and there, as noted above, the voices have it too much their own way.

A souvenir of the Tosca of Ljuba Welitch is to be had in the "Love Duet," with Richard Tucker, and *"Vissi d'arte"* under the direction of Max Rudolf (C ML 4795). Strangely, for one trained in the German language, she slides over her diction in Italian; her singing consequently lacks dramatic weight and musical profile. Tucker is more authentic as Cavaradossi.

Il Trittico:

Il Tabarro. Petrella, s; Scarlini, t; Reali, b; etc.; RIO, Baroni, Cet 50029.

Suor Angelica. Carteri, s; Truccato Pace, m-s; etc.; RIC & O, Previtali, Cet 50030.

Gianni Schicchi. Rapisardi, s; Savio, t; Taddei, b; etc.; RIO, Simonetto, Cet 50028.

Of the three one-acters, first heard at New York's Metropolitan in 1918, *Gianni Schicchi* has firmly established itself as a repertory piece, *Il Tabarro* turns up occasionally, and the fragile *Suor Angelica* is rarely awakened from its peaceful sleep. The somber *Tabarro* posed geniune problems for the recording engineers: much of its effect depends on stage locations. A real effort has been made to give a sense of distance and of relative positions, though sometimes the offstage voices and the automobile horn are not *"lontano"* enough. The singing is mostly good, though Reali as Michele does not always find the *tessitura* comfortable, and the distinctly attractive Petrella is not fully mistress of her fine voice. There is a curious echo in evidence from time to time, and some noises such as we hear in "actual performance" recordings. *Sister Angelica*, with its half-tints and all-feminine cast, demands a more nearly perfect production. Again the voices are good in themselves, though some of the vocalism is untidy and the reproduction seems to some extent crowded. Here is no attempt at stage-depth; the voices are all too close.

The wonderful comedy of *Gianni Schicchi* fares better than its companions. Taddei is capital in the title role; Rapisardi and Savio are passable, if no more, as the young lovers; and there are various other effective characterizations. The pacing is convincing (though I wish the conductor had allowed a trifle more of a pause before "*O mio babbino caro*"), and the balance is such that the orchestra can be clearly heard. Here again some stage effects have been made to help the illusion.

Turandot. Cigna, s; Olivero, s; Merli, t; Poli, b; Neroni, bs; etc.; EIARC & O, Ghione, Cet 1206 [3]. Grob-Prandl, s; Ongaro, s; Zola, t; Rossi, b; Scott, bs; etc.; FOC & O, Capuana, Rem R 199–169 [3].

The first of these recordings dates from the thirties; it is an exceptionally successful convert to LP, but there is no escaping the fact that it was not ever thus. Still, for all its tubby bass, it left me convinced that *Turandot* is Puccini's masterpiece. The cast may contain no Eva Turner, no Antonio Cortis, and no Eidé Norena, which means that certain portions of the score have been better done on imported 78-rpm discs; but Cigna is at her best— uneven, but on the whole acceptable—Merli is a meatier-than-most tenor, Oliveri is at least competent; the supporting artists and very important chorus and orchestra are thoroughly equal to their tasks. The much more recent Remington version does not meet the standards of this performance. I would be less critical of the cast were the reproduction better, but in its own way this is nearly as inadequate as its rival. A good deal of adjustment is needed to balance the power and the accentuation of the highs, and no amount of playing with the controls will bring the singers into proper relation with the orchestra. Such a scene as the wonderful *"Nessun dorma"* quite loses its magic with so modest a chorus and orchestra; nor does the death of Liù have its essential poignance, despite the sweet, easy-voiced singing of Ongaro. Zola, too, is a good Calaf, and one feels that experience will add to the impressiveness of his utterance. Ping, Pang, and Pong are excellent, the first showing a fine rich baritone. Grob-Prandl as Turandot has the power and the cutting high tones needed for the part, but hers is a less effective voice, because less Italian, than Cigna's. In the lower registers the tone does not seem quite solid: one is not always sure of her intonation. In the high unison with Zola she covers him almost to the point of suffocation. There are a few minor cuts in the score. And I noted a persistent pre-echo through a good deal of the recording.

A pendant to these performances is offered by Anne Roselle, a famous Turandot of two decades ago, unfortunately accompanied sketchily at the piano, and not too well recorded (10" Rem PL 2-149). Still, this disc, made long years after her great days, gives some idea of the size and altitude of her voice.

Arias

Gianni Schicchi—O mio babbino caro; Tosca—Vissi d'arte; Madama Butterfly—Un bel dì; Tu, tu? piccolo iddio!; La Rondine—Ore liete divine; Turandot—Tu che di gel sei cinta; Manon Lescaut—Sola, perduta, abbandonata. Kirsten, s; MOO, Cleva, 10" C ML 2200.

Kirsten's luminous voice does not in itself express drama. There is no need for it to do so in the graceful *Rondine* waltz song, which I found her best offering. She gives herself with admirable earnestness to the *Turandot* and *Manon Lescaut* scenes, but I found the *Gianni Schicchi* rather fussy than distinguished. Those from *Tosca* and *Madama Butterfly* are on the placid side.

*Tosca—Recondita armonia; E lucevan le stelle; La Fanciulla del West—Ch'ella mi creda; Manon Lescaut—No! pazzo son!; Turandot —Non piangere, Liù. Del Monaco, t; SCO, Erede, 10" L LS 670 (*Verdi: Arias).*

Del Monaco pours his tones out prodigally in this selection of arias, only the last of which calls for anything like intimacy. Vocally, he is in fine estate.

PURCELL, HENRY (ca. 1659 - 1695)

Choral Works

Te Deum and Jubilate in D; The "Bell Anthem"; O sing unto the Lord. Purcell Performing Society, King, All ALG 3027.

The nine-voice choir of the Old Stone Church in Cleveland, with a small group of instrumentalists, makes a specialty of this kind of music. We are indebted to the members' enterprise for the rare opportunity to hear these fine pieces. They are not, however, easy pieces to sing, and especially in the *Te Deum* the various solo voices (the members of the choir alternate) are obviously taxed by the elaborate melodic lines. Whether or not the recording was made in the church, it is not very atmospheric.

Stage Works

Dido and Aeneas. Flagstad, s; Schwarzkopf, s; Hemsley, t; etc.; Mermaid Singers & O, Jones, V LHMV 1007.

An earlier LP performance (Per SPLP 546) and two very much older ones at 78 rpm are all cast into the shade by this famous recording. Needless to say, Flagstad's voice is big, noble, rich, and incomparably beautiful, her style impeccable. One criticism, applying both to the great star and to Schwarzkopf, is that for all the clarity and intelligibility of their English, it is not quite conversational. They do not make the big points with the text. Hemsley's mealy-mouthed Aeneas is no match for this Dido, and

the delivery of Mandikian's properly strident Sorceress is marred
by some sort of accent. One wishes the lusty Sailor's Song were
more raucous than David Lloyd makes it. The over-all ensemble
is hardly the acme of precision, and the reproduction is uneven:
comparison of Flagstad's first solo and her singing of the great
"Lament" suggests that a veil might have dropped over the stage
in the course of the performance. But, after all, the merits of
this *Dido* are unlikely to be bettered.

*The Fairy Queen—Selections; Masque in Timon of Athens. Ritchie,
s; OLO, Lewis, OL OLLD 16.*

*The Fairy Queen—Excerpts. Curtin, s; Davis, m-s; Tibbetts, bs;
Cambridge Fest Ch & O, Pinkham, All ALL 3077.*

*Masque in Timon of Athens (arr. Woodhouse). IMS, L LLP 292 (*Arne:
Thomas and Sally).*

The first record is nicely enough turned by one of the best present-
day English lyric sopranos, but it offers no more than a taste of
either work represented. Which makes it the more disappointing
that the Allegro disc should give so generous a sampling of *The
Fairy Queen* (the book of which is an adaptation a long way after
Shakespeare's *A Midsummer Night's Dream*) without giving us the
whole. The sponsors have in laudable honesty noted the number-
ing of sections as they appear in the score, by which we can tell
even where the original order has been changed, but there is little
in the nature of continuity here, so that the effect is rather of a
Purcell concert. The excerpts are done with style by the three
admirable singers, well supported by chorus and orchestra. The
members of the Intimate Opera Company are a bit beyond their
depth in the *Timon* music, in which adaptation has gone to the
length of reducing the choruses to solo trios.

King Arthur. Ellsperman, m-s; Chelsi, b; Ch, Kramer, MT MLP 1006.

This performance is sketchy in intent, with its Hammond organ
and piano for orchestra, its generous cuts and tentative singing.
Nor is the recording very good. Indeed, the copy reviewed was so
off-center that the pitch wavered nearly a half-tone. And this is
a *King Arthur* performance without the most famous song—"*Fairest isle.*" What it has to give, then, is no more than a hint of
the music's beauty.

*The Masque in Dioclesian; or The Prophetess. Lloyd, m-s; Avery, t;
etc.; Kramer, pf, MT MLO 1013.*

The voices concerned in this performance are good enough to

cause a genuine regret that a more careful and authentic presentation was not attempted. For, alas, the company strides right
through the score (or most of it) to a piano accompaniment. It is
well enough to hear such a work done sketchily in a semi-amateur
production, but if one is buying a record, one expects something
more.

Songs, etc.

*Why should men quarrel; Two in one upon a ground; How pleasant is
this flowery plain; What can we poor females do?; Whilst I with grief;
When the cock begins to crow; What a sad fate; Strike the viol.
NYPMA, Greenberg, Es ES 519 (*Blow: Ode on the Death of Mr. Henry
Purcell).*

This is a selection of songs for various voices, and a trio, frequently done by three men, but here by soprano, counter-tenor,
and tenor: *When the cock begins to crow.* The voices are attractive; the style is sensitive and convincing. The feature of the
disc, however, is the touching tribute by John Blow to his more
famous pupil.

*Music for a while; I'll sail upon the dogstar; The knotting song; Strike
the viol; Evening Hymn; The queen's epicedium.   Langstaff, b;
Chessid, hpsd; Soyer, cello; Ren X 27 (*Dowland: Songs).*

*I'll sail upon the dogstar; On the brow of Richmond Hill; There's not a
swain on the plain; Man is for the woman made; The message; Come
unto these yellow sands; I attempt from love's sickness to fly; Cease,
o my sad soul; More love or more disdain I crave; Ah! how pleasant 'tis
to love; The owl is abroad; Arise, ye subterranean winds. Brownlee,
b; Harper, pf, Roy 1404 (*Franz, Mendelssohn: Songs, E. Schumann).*

*Saul and the Witch of Endor; Bess of Bedlam; My song shall be alway
of the loving kindness of the Lord.   Popeski, s; Kisch-Arndt, c;
Howard, t; Eby, bs; EMC & O, Hauptmann, Ren X 14.*

John Brownlee, in the earlier stages of his career, might have
made a real contribution with his program, for the songs are delightful, and his voice and style should have suited them well.
how much of the disappointment is due to the singer, and how
much injustice he has been done by the recording, I am not sure.
Still, there is not a spark of humor in the delivery, and of course
his voice no longer has the original bloom on it. The first four
songs are done in harmonizations by Benjamin Britten. Some of
these songs are duplicated in the Langstaff recording, more au-

thentically accompanied by the harpsichord, with the cello rein-
forcing the bass. The singing, too, is more sensitive. Musical
and poetic intelligence here do much to triumph over a somewhat
throaty tone. Two of the very finest Purcell songs are included:
Music for a while and the magnificently devotional *Evening Hymn.*
The cantata *Saul and the Witch of Endor* needs an exceptionally
finished and devoted performance, a better one than it gets on the
Renaissance recording. The voices are not well matched, and
there is no sign of outstanding interpretive talent. *Mad Bess* (as
Bess of Bedlam is sometimes called) does not fare much better.
The best piece on the disc is the anthem, sung by Kisch-Arndt
and the ensemble.

RACHMANINOFF, SERGEI (1873 - 1943)

Choral Work

*The Bells, opus 35. Moscucci, s; Anthony, t; Malfatti, b; Rach C & O,
Rachmilovich, RS 8.*

Rachmaninoff called this setting of Russianized Poe a symphony,
and such it really is, with the solo and choral voices simply
taking their part and publishing the message of the work. We are
told that the composer favored this above all his other compositions. Though written in 1913, it has not had many performances,
owing largely to the difficulties of production. The present performance was recorded in Italy, with two American soloists and
one Italian, and an Italian chorus. The text used being Fanny S.
Copeland's translation back into English from Konstantin Bel-
mont's Russian, it is not surprising that the two American men
show up best for diction—and a very fine best it is—or that the
soprano and the chorus cannot be followed easily. Moscucci's
voice, however, is clear in tone and uninhibited in delivery. The
general sound is good, and there is vitality in the performance.

Operas

*Aleko. Pokrovskaya, s; Orfenov, t; Petrov, b; etc.; BSIC & O,
Golovanov, CH CHS 1309.*

Rachmaninoff's first opera, a product of his nineteenth year, is
surprisingly dramatic and vital. The recorded performance also
is alive; in most of its roles it is well sung. The big exception is
Pokrovskaya, as the heroine, with one of those intense Russian

sopranos, neither steady nor well focused. The men show her up with good healthy tones and a sense of the drama.

*The Miserly Knight—Act 2. Siepi, bs; LOS, Scherman, C ML 4526 (*Arensky: Variations).*

This act of a little-known opera is a long monologue for bass. One wonders why it was revived in English for a singer with a thick Italian accent.

Songs

*In the silence of the night; Lilacs; Summer nights; The alder tree; O cease thy singing, maiden fair; Sorrow in springtime; The soldier's bride; Vocalise. Kurenko, s; Pastukhoff, pf, Cap P 8265 (*Mussorgsky: The Nursery).*

On the death of a linnet; Melody; I ask mercy; Night is mournful; Arion; Music; I remember that day; Vocalise; At night in my garden; To her; Daisies; The rat-catcher; A dream; A-ou. Kurenko, s; Pastuk-hoff, pf, RS 2.

The fountain; Yesterday we met; The changing wind; Fragment from Alfred de Musset; It is pleasant here; Two partings; What happiness; Everything is taken from me; The ring; I am alone; We will rest; The muse; Dissonance. Kurenko, s; Rosenthal, pf, RS 5.

*O cease thy singing, maiden fair; The soldier's bride; All things depart; In the silence of the night; The answer; Before my window; Sorrow in the springtime; Floods of spring; Lilacs; The drooping corn. Tourel, m-s; Kahn, pf, C ML 4357 (*Villa-Lobos: Seréstas).*

Kurenko has supplemented her two Rachmaninoff Society recitals, in which the familiar repertoire was avoided, with the Capitol disc made up of favorites. As will be noted, in doing so she has to a large extent duplicated the Tourel program, even to the song "*Before my window*," disguised on her list as "*The alder tree.*" In one instance she has duplicated herself, though her treatment of the "*Vocalise*" has undergone a change since the first Society disc was issued. In the Capitol version she favors more rapid tempos, though her phrasing of the wordless song and the inner rhythmic pulse are as masterly as before. In the Russian repertoire, Kurenko has no superior, and her voice retains to an amazing degree its pristine clarity and radiance. The versatile Jennie Tourel is also more than satisfactory, so that preference between the two may well be determined by the listener's predilection for a high or a medium voice. For those who wish to explore the lesser-known repertoire, the two Society records offer much of interest.

RAMEAU, JEAN-PHILIPPE (1683-1764)

Operas

Hippolyte et Aricie—Selections. Verneuil, s; Wend, s; Moizan, m-s; Amade, t; Ch; SO, Désormière. OL OLLD 10.

This is only a fraction of Rameau's first, and sensational, opera, beginning, indeed, not before the third act. Complete information as to the contents is supplied on the labels, but not on the container, which may prove confusing. The performance is authentic in spirit, and charming, but vocally impressive only in the very high tenor of Amade. As Rameau gave a very heavy assignment to the horns, it is hardly surprising that there are some loose ends in the orchestral playing.

Les Indes galantes—Excerpts. Joachim, s; Mauranne, t; Malvasio, b; GC; HCO, Hewitt, D DL 6080.

A cross-section of the opera-ballet first produced in 1735, recorded some time before the very spectacular and successful revival at the Paris Opéra in 1952. Of the soloists here, the baritone is outstanding; the soprano sings prettily as to tone, but not quite neatly enough. Some of the solo parts are recorded too close, but the slightly clouded choral effects are good, and the orchestra comes through successfully.

Arias, etc.

Dardanus—Act 2, Introduction; Tout l'avenir est présent à mes yeux. Conrad, bs.; Ens. Castor et Pollux—Prologue, Minuet. Sautereau, s; Wend, s; Derenne, t. Hippolyte et Aricie—Rossignols amoureux. Wend, s. Dardanus—Act 3, O jour affreux! Kolassi, m-s. Les Indes galantes—Entrée 2, Clair flambeau du monde. Demigny, b; Ens. Hippolyte et Aricie—O disgrace cruelle; Overture; Fanfare; Ballet figuré. Kolassi, m-s; O. Castor et Pollux—Séjour de l'éternelle paix. Derenne, t. Les Fêtes d'Hébé—Volons sur les bordes de la Seine; Acanthe—Entr'acte. Sautereau, s; Wend, s. Platée—Chantons Bacchus! Derenne, t; Ens. Voc & Inst Ens, Boulanger, D DL 9683.

This is a curiously unsatisfactory disc, despite its rich promise. As always, Boulanger is the all-pervasive and all-persuasive guiding spirit of the enterprise, and of course everyone performs at his or her best. But the program is too fragmentary, and some of the best is not quite good enough. Chief exceptions are Irma Kolassi, who has both temperament and dignity, and Bernard Demigny, whose performance really takes fire. Paul Derenne is stylistically very fine, but has some difficulty with the long phrases. Sautereau and Wend contribute gracefully, the latter having the especially charming nightingale song to sing. The whole collection is too miscellaneous.

Cantatas

Diane et Actéon; L'Impatience. Cuenod, t; Ens, Pinkham, Ly LL 44.
Cuenod is one of the few singers practicing today who are really at home in the Rameau style and can sing this kind of music with the ease and grace it needs. The changing moods of the protagonist are expressed in a series of recitatives and arias; the challenge for the singer is to introduce sufficient tonal and expressive variety to keep the works from showing their length. In Cuenod's hands they are colorful and satisfying. The small ensemble accompanying him is made up of first-rate musicians; the *rapport* among them is excellent.

RAVEL, MAURICE (1875-1937)

Operas

L'Enfant et les Sortilèges. Sautereau, s; Angelici, s; Michel, m-s; le Marc'Hadour, t; Peyron, b; etc.; RDFC; ONA, Bour, C ML 4153.
All sorts of musical styles are welded into this fantastic but harmonious whole, as indeed there must be for a tale peopled by armchairs, teakettles, squirrels, dragonflies, trees, etc., not to mention a fairy princess escaped from a book. The duet of the two cats is an incredible feat of imagination and virtuosity. Obviously, all this must add up to a particularly challenging assignment for a cast of opera singers. It seems scarcely likely that we will hear the score better realized than it is by this French group. Special mention is due Sautereau as the Child, Angelici as the Princess, and le Marc'Hadour in several roles.

L'Heure espagnole. Danco, s; Derenne, t; Rehfuss, b; etc.; SR, An-sermet, L LL 796. Duval, s; Giraudeau, t; Vieuille, b; etc.; OCO, Cluytens, Ang 35018. Linda, s; Dran, t; Hoffman, b; etc.; RDFO, Leibowitz, Vox PL 7880.

These three recordings which appeared in the matter of a few months, pose a real problem for the prospective buyer. When the Ansermet version arrived, I was inclined to hail it as definitive, for a subtler, more beautifully balanced, smoother-sounding performance is hard to imagine. No detail is missed, nor is there one unbeautiful or unmeaningful tone. The cast is well-nigh perfect, technically at least, and the singers have obviously been rehearsed to the point where they actually live the opera. Danco, to be sure, is rather much of a lady to be the ideal Concepcion, but except for the outburst *"Oh la pitoyable aventure,"* a kind of outraged "credo," she wins us over completely. In that one scene I wanted more edge, perhaps a less lovely sound. The final quintet is masterly and irresistible, with its concerted roulades and trills. The Leibowitz performance, which seemed more than satisfactory before I had heard this one, is of coarser grain. Linda provides what Danco does not have; her Concepcion may be described by a five-letter word, which is really what the story calls for. The balance here is no match for the London recording. If one's mind is now made up, the third version comes to upset the conclusions. Duval is a Concepcion who sings more beautifully than Linda, and characterizes more successfully than Danco; the supporting cast could hardly be improved upon. Orchestrally the set is second-best, but as comedy it bows to none. Still, the balance is not so good as London's.

Songs

Don Quichotte à Dulcinée. Singher, b; CBSO, Abravanel, C ML 4152 (*Debussy: Ballades de Villon; Operatic Arias). Souzay, b; PCO, Lindenberg, 10" L LD 9091 (*Debussy: Songs).

Pride of place goes to Singher, who has made these songs peculiarly his own (one of them is dedicated to him). One would respond more enthusiastically to this recording, however, were it not that he did them once before in the presence of the composer, at a time when his voice was very much fresher than it sounds here. The two old Victor discs are hard to come by nowadays, but those who have them will not quite accept the new, for all the advantages of LP. Souzay, for his part, does a gentlemanly and dignified piece of work, especially admirable in the quiet second song.

Histoires naturelles; Deux Épigrammes; Chansons madécasses; Chants populaires. Singher, b; Ulanowsky, pf; etc.; CH CHS 1124.

Histoires naturelles. Souzay, b; Bonneau, pf, 10" L LS 536 (*Falla: Canciones Populares Espanolas).

Chansons madécasses. Tourel, m-s; Reeves, pf; etc.; 10" C ML 2184 (*Debussy: Chansons de Bilitis). Chansons madécasses. Jansen, b; Bonneau, pf, L LL 644 (*Debussy, and Chabrier: Songs).

Of the songs on Singher's disc, the best are the *Épigrammes*, one of which, "*D'Anne jouant l'espinette,*" is among the most charming of modern French songs. His *Histoires naturelles* lack the spark of warm humor Povla Frijsh (for one) used to find in them; on the whole I prefer the easy, almost conversational approach of Souzay. In the *Chansons madécasses* Singher misses the elemental quality Ravel caught from the amazing poetry of Evariste Parny; he is altogether too polite. Here I prefer Jennie Tourel (though the sentiments of the songs are decidedly masculine), and again my memory runs back to the fine performance of Madeleine Grey, which has not been made available on LP. Tourel has every mechanical advantage, of course. As for Jansen, his singing is neat enough, but rather careful. The piano tone on his disc seems muffled.

Mélodies populaires grecques. Kolassi, m-s; Bonneau, pf, 10" L LS 568 (*Kolassi Recital).

Mélodies populaires grecques; Quatre Chants populaires. C. Panzéra, b; M. Panzéra, pf, Mer MG 10098 (*Panzéra Recital).

Kolassi sings the Greek songs in their, and her, native tongue, one of several points in her favor. She is a singer of attractive voice, good diction, and a real sense of style—in short, a distinguished interpreter of songs. Panzéra gives the same set in French, with waning voice but superb penetration. Anything this artist does is worthy of study, and at the same time productive of enjoyment. Still, if one wants the songs for themselves, Kolassi's version must be given preference.

Shéhérazade. Tourel, m-s; COL, Bernstein, C ML 4289 (*Mussorgsky: Songs and Dances of Death).

Tourel sings this exotic music very well, if rather darkly. One regrets that the even finer version by Danco, issued not long before LP came in, has not been re-recorded. That performance, under

Ansermet, still seems very nearly definitive, but this is not to discount the fine singing of Tourel.

REVUELTAS, SILVESTRE (1899-1940)

Five Songs of Childhood: The little horse; The five hours; Nonsense Song; Cradle Song; Mr. and Mrs. Lizard; Two Songs; Serenade; It is true; The owl; Bull frogs. Greissle, s; Wolman, pf, SPA 9 (*Ives: Songs).

These songs are all done in English translation, and in a rather unimaginative manner. There may be something more in them than appears in this treatment.

RIMSKY-KORSAKOV, NIKOLAI (1844-1908)

Operas

May Night. Maslennikova, s; Lemeshev, t; Krasovsky, bs; etc.; BSIC & O, Nebolsin, Van VRS 6006/7/8 [3].

Rimsky-Korsakov's *May Night,* to most of us, means an overture with a theme curiously reminiscent of the like-named song of Brahms. Beyond the fact that this theme turns up again in one of the principal arias, the opera will be of interest chiefly to the specialist. The performance is routine, the leading lady somewhat less than that.

Mozart and Salieri. Mollien, t; Linsolas, b; Paris Radio SO, Leibowitz, Oc OCS 32.

Rimsky's tribute to Mozart derives a certain interest from the reverently borrowed melodies woven into the score. This performance (in French) has life and spirit; Mollien sings well, Linsolas a little stiffly. The recording level is not altogether even.

Sadko. Shumskaya, s; Davidova, m-s; Antonova, c; Nelepp, t; Krasovsky, bs; Reizen, bs; etc.; BSIC & O, Golovanov, CH CHS 1307 [3].

As opera recordings from Moscow average, this is a good performance, and certainly it ranks among the best in reproduction. The sound of the orchestra is bright and clear; the main weakness is the usual over-amplification of voices. But at its best the singing would hardly pass muster in our own opera houses. There are exceptions in the cases of the three one-aria "guests," who perform their limited assignments with good voices and assured style. Nelepp, in the title role, is quite unfocused at the outset, and though he improves as he goes along, his singing is never distinguished. Shumskaya has good material, and some of her singing is attractive, but she is uneven. Antonova is especially coarse and unsteady. In short, the level of vocalism is not very high in Russia, to judge by such samples as this. And the opera, remembered as one of the outstanding spectacles of Gatti's regime at the Metropolitan, is a little wearisome done in this way. There are a number of cuts in the performance.

Arias

Le Coq d'or—Hymn to the sun. Pantofel-Netshetskia, s. May Night— Levko's Arietta; Snegourotchka—Czar Berendey's Cavatina; Sadko— Song of India; Czar's Bride—Lykov's Aria. Lemeshev, t. May Night —Levko's Aria. Kolzlovsky, t. Snegourotchka—Mizguir's Aria. Ivanov, b. Czar's Bride—Duet, Czar Berendey and Koupava. Ivanova, s; Lemeshev, t. Sadko—Song of the Viking. Freitkov, bs. Sadko— Volkhova's Lullaby. Kazantseva, s. Czar's Bride—Marfa's Aria. Shpieler, s. Czar's Bride—Liubasha's Aria. Maksakova, m-s. Kashtchay the Immortal—Kashtchaievna's Aria. Preobrajenskaya, m-s. BSIO, Orloff, Kondrashin, Golovanov, Col CRLP 121.

This group of arias sung by prominent Soviet artists averages better in vocalism than many of the opera performances from the same source, but one has to accept a good deal of sub-standard recording throughout the program. None of the reproduction is more than passable. Lemeshev, reputed the best tenor in Russia, appears several times to substantiate his claim, acquitting himself in each instance with credit. The too familiar "Song of India" has rarely been so pleasingly sung, and the *May Night* air has considerable charm. Shpieler, too, is outstanding in the soprano aria from *The Czar's Bride*. Maksakova, with a richer natural voice, is only less satisfying artistically. Pantofel-Netshetskia shows good quality and vocal proficiency in the "Hymn to the Sun," but she is treated worst of all by the recording. Kozlovsky's light, high tenor sounds thin after Lemeshev, and Preobrajenskaya is uncomfortably unsteady in her aria.

ROSSINI, GIOACCHINO *(1792-1868)*

Choral Works

Messe solennelle. Tuccari, s; Salvi, c; Besma, t; Catalani, b; RSQC & O, Vitalini, Per SPL 588.

A more or less casual hearing of this recording is apt to leave one impressed by Rossini and by his interpreters. Only when following the Mass with a score can we grasp what a chasm exists between the intentions of the composer and the achievement of the performers. In the first place, the work is cut unmercifully. The long orchestral introductions to the arias are habitually trimmed, and huge chunks are missing within practically every number. Some of the pruning seems altogether unnecessary, as for instance lopping off a couple of measures at the end of a piece. Granted, the Mass without abridgment would be very long, and perhaps boring; still, the present major operation seems like butchery. Like Verdi, Rossini put plenty of expression and dynamic directions into his score; no one could guess at them on the basis of this presentation.

Stabat Mater. Steingruber, s; Hermann, c; Dermota, t; Schoeffler, bs; VKC; VSO, Sternberg, Oc OCS 24. Seefried, s; Anday, c; Fehenberger, t; Frantz, bs; SACC; SALO, Messner, Rem R 199–111 [2].

That the Salzburg recording occupies four sides to Vienna's two is an indication of vast differences in pacing. Sternberg's tempos, to be sure, are on the brisk side; Messner's are unconscionably slow. The Cathedral Choir sings without too great precision, and the soloists vary from Seefried's superb projection of the *"Inflammatus"* to Anday's leaden *"Fac ut portem."* This is a work to stand or fall by its soloists, and Sternberg's quartet is, except for the soprano, superior to Messner's. They do not overcome all the difficulties Rossini has set for them, but their voices have the ring of conviction and sincerity. The Salzburg performance has its complement of audience noises; the Vienna has a dead studio quality. Seefried's *"Inflammatus,"* which I have admired, and Fehenberger's *"Cujus animam,"* to which I can give more moderate praise, are available in a Salzburg Choir concert, along with selections from the Verdi *Requiem* and the Haydn *Seven Last Words* (Rem R 199–121).

Operas

Il Barbiere di Siviglia. Simionato, m-s; Infantino, t; Taddei, b; etc.; RIC & O, Previtali, Cet 1211 [3]. *De los Angeles, s; Monti, t; Bechi, b; Luise, bs; Rossi-Lemeni, bs; Ch; MISO, Serafin, V LM 6104. Capsir, s; Borgioli, t; Stracciari, b; Baccaloni, bs; etc.; SCAC; MISO, Molajoli, C EL 1* [3].

The Columbia recording listed is a document, for Stracciari was a famous Barber, and Borgioli, exponent of a vanishing art, was equal

to the coloratura of Count Almaviva's part. Capsir too enjoyed a
reputation, but to this reviewer's ears her voice was not especially
pleasing. The sound as we hear it from LP is on the thick, heavy
side, though one adjusts to this, and those who enjoy hearing a
"golden age" baritone go through a whole opera will have much
pleasure from the set. The other two versions offer a problem.
Both are distinguished by superlative Rosinas, both of whom sing
the music in the original mezzo key. Simionato seemed an approach
to the ideal before I heard De los Angeles. But the latter's roulades
and trills, her lyrical *cantilena,* no less than the humor of her performance, are altogether winning, enough so to put her admirable
rival in the shade. Unfortunately, the Victor set has a very loud
and unsubtle Figaro in Bechi, while Cetra's Taddei is first-rate.
The others in both casts are good, though Rossi-Lemeni in the
Victor set seems bent on recalling the disproportionate Basilio of
Chaliapin. The pacing of Previtali is more traditional than Serafin's, but both are spirited performances. Monti is a promising, but
not altogether ripe, Almaviva; Infantino is a better than average
one.

*La Cambiale di Matrimonio. Tuccari, s; Gentile, t; Catalani, b; etc.;
RSQC & O, Morelli, Per SPL 583.*

The name of Rossini's first opera has been kept alive by its overture. This first opportunity to make the acquaintance of the comedy
as a whole at least convinces us that the score is worthy of a better performance. There are some very attractive numbers in it, done
here with spirit and enthusiasm, if without precision.

*Il Cambio della Valigia. Russo, s; Salvi, s; Besma, t; Catalani, b;
etc.; RSQC & O, Morelli, Per SPL 595.*

The Societa del Quartetto (by which strange name these performers
are identified) rates commendation at least for intentions. However,
the singing has little of the "zip" necessary for the realization of
Rossini's recitatives, and there is not much evidence of authority
in the performance. Russo, the soprano, is gifted by nature with a
good voice, but her vocalism is uneven.

*La Cenerentola (Abridged). Simionato, m-s; Rovero, s; Valletti, t;
Meletti, b; Dalamangas, bs; RIC & O, Rossi, Cet 1208 [2].*

This Cinderella opera calls for two things in its interpreters: extraordinary vocal technique, and a sense of humor. Cetra's cast
qualifies on both counts, with special honors earned by Giulietta
Simionato in the title role. Hers is a true Italian mezzo-soprano,
smooth, flexible, and wonderfully steady. Her part has undergone

some simplification, along with some of the others, but its musical character is unchanged. It is her opera, and she has good support in Cesare Valletti and the *buffo* Christiano Dalamangas particularly. The volume level of the set is somewhat uneven, but not enough to be troublesome.

Guglielmo Tell. Carteri, s; Filippeschi, t; Taddei, b; etc.; RIC & O, Rossi, Cet 1232 [4].

William (here *Guglielmo*, though more properly *Guillaume*, as the original libretto is French) *Tell* is an acknowledged if rarely preformed masterpiece, full of stirring melodies and magnificent ensembles, opportunities for singing in the grand manner. The cast assembled for this performance is probably as good as could be found in Italy today. Taddei's Tell is really first-rate, with a voice as expansive as it is rich, and with real dramatic ring in his delivery. Filippeschi as Arnold has the needed powerful high notes, though stylistically he is not fully mature. Carteri is too vibrant in the recitatives, but she can spin a nice neat line when *cantilena* is called for. Sciutti's Jemmy is appealing, and the various basses are excellent. The balance is reasonably good as such things go, though the big ensembles go too much to the singers—the trio for Mathilda, Jemmy, and Hedwig in the last act is a notable example —and the orchestra is a little restricted in sound. There is a fine dynamic range, from the subdued singing of the conspiracy to the big ensembles.

La Scala di Seta. Tuccari, s; Gentile, t; Besma, t; Catalani, b; etc.; RSQC & O, Morelli, Per SPL 591.

Another little comedy remembered by its overture is here given a performance of more spirit than polish. Rossini is a composer easily damned with faint phrases.

Il Signor Bruschino. Ribetti, s; Pontiggia, t; Capecchi, b; Maugeri, b; etc.; MIPO, Gerelli, Vox PL 8460.

Il Signor Bruschino is remembered chiefly as the opera Rossini wrote unwillingly, and in which he pulled all sorts of tricks by way of revenge. The most striking of his special effects is in the overture, where the violins are required to tap upon the wood of their instruments, but there are some far knottier problems set for the singers. In the present performance there are superior voices and a general spirit of clean fun. The "find" of the cast is Pontiggia, a lyric tenor with more than ordinary facility and an admirable sense of style. His first duet with Ribetti is turned with neatness and simple charm. The soprano, however, fails to maintain this standard throughout the opera; she just misses distinction in her various solos. Capecchi handles the *buffo* part with unction, and the florid music holds no terrors for him. There are some generous cuts in the score, but enough is left to represent the comedy and its music. There is plenty of *recitativo secco*, which the singers handle expertly. The reproduction is on the whole good, though I noted a pre-echo shortly after the beginning. If anything, for once, the voices are swamped by the orchestra. I think some quality and some steadiness of pitch have been sacrificed toward the center of the first side in the interests of including 31:30 minutes of music.

Arias

Il Barbiere di Siviglia—Una voce poco fa; Contro un cor che accende amore; L'Italiana in Algeri—Oh, che muso; Per lui che adoro; La Cenerentola—Signore, una parola; Non più mesta. Supervia, m-s; Manurrita, t; Ederle, t; Scattola, bs; Bettoni, bs; O; D DL 9533.
Il Barbiere di Siviglia—Una voce poco fa; L'Italiana in Algeri—Cruda sorte. Tourel, m-s; MOO, Cimara, 10" C ML 2024 (*Offenbach: Arias).

The late Conchita Supervia's following grows with the years; it is fortunate that she recorded well. The singer's almost overpowering exuberance is still very much with us on LP, and her ability to negotiate Rossini's florid melodic lines is still a matter for wonder. Her assisting artists are capable and well seasoned, though one of the basses has more than enough wobble. A very different mezzo is Jennie Tourel, always solidly musical and satisfying, never sensational. With just a touch of Supervia's verve, she would be terrific in this music. It is a shame that in transferring this program to LP two more Rossini arias were dropped. Surely her recital was worth a twelve-inch side!

Guglielmo Tell—Ah! Mathilda (German). Slezak, t; Demuth, b. *Troncar suoi dì; La gloria infiammi.* Escalaïs, t; Magini-Colletti, b; Luppi, bs. *Resta immobile.* Battistini, b. *O muto asil; Corriam, corriam.* Gilion, t. *Il Barbiere di Siviglia—Una voce poco fa (French).* Ritter-Ciampi, s. *La Cenerentola—Miei rampoli.* Badini, b. *Semiramide—Bel raggio.* Alessandrini, s. Et 707.

This disc is evenly divided, the first side being all acoustically recorded, the second side electrically. The first side, too, is entirely devoted to *William Tell*. Linguistically, the selection is a hodge-podge, but there is some excellent singing. Most interesting on the *Tell* side is the trio, in which three terrifically healthy voices join and give their all. This amounts to an impressive display; if some of the intonation seems less than perfect, it may be that the old recording failed to pick up an overtone or two. The Slezak-Demuth duo shows these fine artists in good form, and Battistini pours out his tone generously, if not very rhythmically. The Gilion is obviously a later recording; the tenor had strong high tones. Ritter-Ciampi's voice is unusually warm and attractive in Rosina's air, and she is recorded with plenty of space around her. The Badini selection is good vocal characterization. Alessandrini shows unusual agility, if also a prominent *vibrato* and a tendency to shrillness.

RUBBRA, EDMUND (1901-   )

Missa in honorem Sancti Dominici. FSC, Lawrence, L LL 805 (*Vaughan Williams: Mass in G minor).
This performance has a melancholy interest in that the conductor died midway in the recording. His work was finished by the composer. I find I have to get used to the British manner of pronouncing Latin all over again every time I hear such a work performed. The recording seems a little close, and toward the end of this Mass it comes perilously near to overloading. The acoustics of the hall where it was made seem a little strange.

SAINT-SAËNS, CAMILLE (1835-1921)

Oratorio de Noël. Surian, s; Huff, m-s; Rogers, c; Huff, t; Mullen, b; San José State College Ch; San José SO, Jessen, ML MLR 7008.
This is a pleasant work, if not an overwhelming one, by a master of musical resources. The performance is in English, and is representative of good, typical church choir singing, with competent, unexciting soloists. The contralto avoids some of the low notes in the score, and the soprano has an inclination to stridency. The reproduction is brilliant and shallow, with the balance best in the final chorus.
Samson et Dalila. Bouvier, c; Luccioni, t; Cabanel, b; Cambon, bs; Médus, bs; POC & O, Fourestier, Vox PL 8323 [2].
Originally issued in this country by Columbia before the days of

LP, this recording has passed into the hands of Vox, and has been notably improved in its second transfer to the slow speed. Something has been done to give the orchestra and chorus a greater richness and power, and the soloists have increased "presence," perhaps a little too much for the good of the balance. The performance might be called "typical" in the sense that it could have been taken directly from the repertoire without extra preparation for recording. There is neither great animation nor a notable standard of precision in the choral singing (so important in this oratorio-opera). Bouvier, a good artist with a rich, but hardly sinuous, voice, is musically well suited to the leading female role, though she does not delineate much of a character. For this the conductor may well be to blame, for the chorus of maidens is no more seductive than she. José Luccioni, as his name suggests, seems to combine the salient features of the Italian school of singing with the French; his Samson has stature and power. He delivers his lines well; again it may be the conductor who holds him back. The low-voiced men are all excellent and authentically French.

SAMMARTINI, GIOVANNI BATTISTA (1701 - 1775)

Fifth Cantata for the Fridays in Lent. Tyler, s; Amadini, c; Bianchini, t; ICO, Jenkins, HS HSL 75.

This interesting devotional work well demonstrates how thin was the line between sacred and secular music in the eighteenth century. The moods are by turns dramatic and lyrical; the casual listener today would hardly find his thoughts turning toward the church. The playing of the orchestra in this recording is notable for its precision and verve; the singing is, on the whole, good. Amadini, well known to collectors, cannot guide her big round voice about with all the required agility, but she is musical, and she shows her admirable intelligence in her lovely aria. Tyler is none too tidy in the recitative, but she comes through gloriously in her air, the gem of the entire work. Here the tone of the orchestra is quite melting. Bianchini is adequate in the part of the angel.

SATIE, ERIK (1866 - 1925)

Socrate. Journeaux, s; Lindenfelder, s; Pebordes, s; Carpenter, s; PPO, Leibowitz, Es ES 510.

Perhaps it is not a matter for surprise that Satie, the musical original and wit, should have conceived his music based on the *Dialogues of Plato* all in the soprano range. But this is only one of the idiosyncracies of a strange and perhaps wonderful work. The various ladies perform their parts well, and Leibowitz is thoroughly at home in this music.

SAUGUET, HENRI (1901-   )

*Visions infernals.   Conrad, bs; Garvey, pf, REB 2 (*Mouvements du coeur, a cycle by Sauguet, Milhaud, Poulenc, Auric, Françaix, and Preger).*

Our only recorded example of Sauguet's music suffers from heavy treatment at the hands of the singer. The cycle on the reverse holds a special interest: Doda Conrad, in observance of the Chopin centennial, commissioned a group of outstanding French composers to write a set of songs in a style reminiscent of his great compatriot.

SCARLATTI, ALESSANDRO (1659-1725)

Choral Works, etc.

*Motetto di Requiem.   Tinayre, b; ACS, Morgenstern, All AL 87 (*Porpora: Salve Regina).*
Stabat Mater.   Giancola, s; Truccato Pace, c; Ch, SVO, Ephrikian, Vox PL 7970.

Tinayre built his reputation on his ability to locate and rehabilitate old, forgotten scores. The present motet is a good example of his way of adapting such music to his own requirements. Unfortunately, he was not in good form when the record was made. The notes accompanying the *Stabat Mater* go to some length to establish a parallel between this and the later setting by Pergolesi. Beyond question the popularity of the latter work is well founded; this one would stand quite comfortably beside it, were the performance less lethargic. Perhaps the singers are weighted down by the solemnity of the occasion. The recording is also weighted.

Passio D.N. Jesu Christi secundum Joannem.   Stern, t; Laurent, b; Borden, t; St Thomas Ch, New Haven; Yale U O, Boatwright, Ov LP 1.

This striking work was recently discovered in manuscript, and the performance here recorded represents in all probability its first since the lifetime of the composer. The Passion is reputed to date from between 1680 and 1685; the recording was made in 1953. Surely this must be the most compact of all Passions; the Latin text is scrupulously set, with no expansion, no repetition, and none of the meditations introduced by Bach. The bulk of the work falls on the Evangelist (as usual, a tenor), with the other voices and the chorus taking their appointed parts in the drama. The narrative line is of extraordinary eloquence and beauty; Blake Stern sings it with tremendous expressiveness. The not very strong reproduction has caught something of the atmosphere of the church in which it was recorded, with nothing too close upon us.

Opera

Il Trionfo dell' Onore. Zerbini, s; Pini, m-s; Berdini, t; etc.; RIO, Giulini, Cet 1223 [2].

The Triumph of Honor, the first full-length opera of Alessandro Scarlatti to reach discs, is a gay, melodious comedy. The performance gives evidence of rehearsal; everything seems to come off, with especial distinction in the priceless second- and third-act quartets.

Cantata

Sulle Sponde del Tebro. Stich-Randall, s; SCAO, Paumgartner, Col CLPS 1035 (*Mozart: Mia speranza adorata).

This disc was made by Teresa Stich-Randall while a Fulbright Fellow in Italy. Since the recording, she has enjoyed enviable success on the opera stages of various European capitals. Hers is an uncommonly fine voice, and her artistry, as evidenced, needs only further ripening. She is inclined to be reticent, but that she can overcome this is indicated strongly at the climaxes of this cantata.

SCHILLINGS, MAX VON (1868-1933)

Glockenlieder. Anders, t; Prussian St O, Heger, U URLP 7104 (*Britten: Les Illuminations).

Schillings has here given us an impressive Wagnerian piece, very rich and sonorous. Anders, surrounded by the full and glowing orchestra, and powerfully recorded, sounds wonderful. The Carl Spitteler text is missing from the jacket notes, though a prose translation is given.

SCHMITT, FLORENT (1870-   )

Psaume XLVII. Duval, s; BC; PCO, Tzipine, An 35020.

This *Psalm* has been hailed as "among the most grandiose conceptions of modern French music." The recording is "official" in that it was made under the composer's supervision; it would seem that his conception must be completely realized. A special word of praise is due the solo of Denise Duval.

SCHNABEL, ARTUR (1882-1951)

*Waldnacht; Sieh mein Kind, ich gehe; Tanzlied; Das Veilchen an den spanischen Flieder; Dann; Frühlingslied; Marienlied; Dieses ist ein rechter Morgen; Hyazinthen; Die Sperlinge. Francoulon, s; H. Schnabel, pf, SPA 55 (*Concerto for Piano and Orchestra).*

Those who know the great Beethoven interpreter by his later atonal compositions will have a fresh surprise in these youthful romantic lieder. Francoulon's voice is rich, her delivery good, so that we are made to feel the effectiveness of the word-setting. The composer's daughter-in-law is the authoritative pianist.

SCHOENBERG, ARNOLD (1874-1951)

Gurre-Lieder. Semser, s; Tangeman, m-s; Lewis, t; Riley, bs; etc.; NSSPC & O, Leibowitz, HS HSL 100 [3]. Vreeland, s; Bampton, c; Althouse, t; Robovsky, b; etc.; Ch PHO, Stokowski V LCT 6012 [2].
*Gurre-Lieder—Lied der Waldtaube. Lipton, m-s; NYPH, Stokowski, 10" C ML 2140 (*Berg: Wozzeck—Selections).*

There is, of course, no comparison between the two full recordings. Stokowski's is the famous set made at a Philadelphia performance in 1932. The occasion itself was memorable, and the recording, by one of those happy chances, caught not only an amazing amount of the music, but a good deal of charged atmosphere. The three leading singers still sound impressive, and the balance with the orchestra is quite remarkable, considering the record's vintage; the choral parts, not unnaturally, were too much for the recording of those days. All in all, this is an exciting presentation of some magnificently ripe romantic music. The new version has all the advantages of expansive modern reproduction, and it works its spell under the guidance of a gifted and versatile conductor, also one of the world authorities on Schoenberg. Richard Lewis sings the main part with solid tone and an all-pervading intelligence. Ethel Semser does her best recorded singing to date, but is hardly in a class with the radiant-voiced Jeannette Vreeland. Nell Tangeman is an eloquent Wood Dove, comparing not unfavorably with Rose Bampton, who gave the performance of her career on the great occasion. It is interesting to watch the score as Morris Gesell performs his speaking part, for he follows faithfully the rise and fall indicated by Schoenberg's notes—sketched out in the manner of the later-Schoenbergian *Sprechstimme*. The choral parts are splendidly sung; I am sure it is by well-considered design that these passages seem distant. Only at the end it seemed to me as if more sheer sound were needed. There is one place where the orchestra covers a singer's voice, and this to poor advantage: the text sung by the Bauer seems to me too important to be thus lost. A fine effect in the orchestra is the sound of the ghostly huntinghorns. All in all, this is a monumental set, and should win many friends for at least the early Schoenberg. In the *Waldtaube* excerpt, Martha Lipton sings with considerable vocal beauty, once her voice is warmed up. Her delivery of the words *"Tove ist stumm"* is very lovely indeed.

Buch der hängenden Gärten. Kibler, c; Albersheim, pf, Ly LL 42.
These fifteen settings of Stephan George poems represent the Schoenberg of 1907–8. Kibler brings to them a pleasing voice and an accurate ear, which enables her to move around cleanly among the difficult intervals. Only occasionally, when the composer takes her above her best range, does she seem ill-at-ease. The voice is well reproduced; not so the piano.

Erwartung. Dow, s; NYPH, Mitropoulos, C ML 5424 (*Křenek: Symphonic Elegy).
This monodrama is a *tour de force*, and a cruel assignment for any singer. The morbid text—depicting a girl who comes into the woods to meet her lover, then, after a long and anxious wait, stumbles over his corpse—may have limited appeal in our generation. Schoenberg has well matched this effusion in his music, and the performance is terrific.

Songs

Erwartung; Jesus bettelt; Erhebung; Waldsonne; Hochzeitslied; Frei-
hold; Traumsleben; Alles; Mädchenlied; Verlassen; Ghasel; Am Wegrand
Lockung; Der Wanderer; Ich darf nicht dankend; In diesen Wintertagen.
Steingruber, s; Haefner, pf, SPA 32.

These are all early songs (*"Erwartung"* is not to be confused with
the later monodrama). The favorite poet is Dehmel, and the hot
romanticism of his texts finds eager collaboration in the music.
The vocal lines are sometimes angular, and there are long skips,
but Steingruber can make such devices seem natural. The piano
parts are not simple, nor are they virtuoso pieces like those of
Strauss. The soprano's tone is crystalline, round, and enveloping
at times, occasionally a bit inclined to whiteness in the lower
register, but never unpleasantly so. One feels that she and her
pianist have thoroughly mastered the songs.

Ode to Napoleon. Adler, speaker; Ens, Leibowitz, Dia 3 (* Trio, opus
45).

A survivor from Warsaw; Kol Nidre. Jaray, speaker; VKC; VSY, Swa-
rowsky, C ML 4664 (*Chamber Symphony No. 2).

The combination of Byron and Schoenberg may seem ironic, even
as the composer's intention was ironic in implying a parallel between Napoleon and a certain dictator of our own times. Miss
Adler's voice is excellent for her assignment; its very softness
heightens the effect of the poem. She is so placed that every word
and every nuance is clear to the listener, yet she never dominates
the ensemble, seeming to come from within it. *A Survivor from*
Warsaw has an English text by the composer himself, delivered
here, perhaps not inappropriately, in a thick accent. I would hesitate to recommend this disc to anyone but a complete Schoenbergian.

Pierrot Lunaire. Stiedry-Wagner, speaker; Ens, Schoenberg, C ML 4471.
Adler, speaker; Ens, Leibowitz, Dia 16.

Columbia's LP release of the classic recording brings back a document of first importance in modern music. Less forward in reproduction than the original 78-rpm discs, the recording has also developed some undesirable peaks. Though the surfaces are not
silent, they are less assertive than in the older version. The
estimable Leibowitz performance lacks not only the superb delivery of Mme Stiedry-Wagner, but the personal value and interest

of the late composer's direction. It is, of course, vastly superior as a recording.

SCHUBERT, FRANZ PETER (1797-1828)

Choral Works

Gesang der Geister über den Wassern. VSOC; VSY, Krauss, Vox PL 6480 (*Beethoven: Choral Fantasy).

This little-known Goethe setting, somber in tone, will come as a surprise even to most more or less complete Schubertians. It is well presented under the knowing hand of Clemens Krauss.

Mass in E flat. Rathauscher, s; Hofstaetter, c; Planyavsky, t; Equiluz, t; Berry, bs; VKC; VSY, Moralt, Vox PL 7840.

This very Viennese Mass receives a dedicated performance at the hands of competent musicians. Some of the solo singing is tentative, some lovely. Chorus and orchestra evince a healthy enthusiasm, if not always perfect precision. For the most part the reproduction is effective, though in spots the solo voices come out too strongly.

Mass in G. Ciannella, s; Keast, bs; SC; RCAO, Shaw, V LM 1784. (*Bach: Motet, Komm, Jesu, komm; Brahms: Choruses).

Mass in G; Miriams Siegesgesang; Hymne an die Sonne. Dutoit, s; Planyavsky, t; Buchsbaum, bs; Neulinger, s; VKC; VSY, Grossmann, Vox PL 7510.

It has been noted that in all his Masses Schubert omitted the passages in the *"Credo"* about the Church, an omission emended in the Shaw performance by a simple change of note-values. Shaw's reading is less imposing and passionate than Grossmann's. To the advantage of the Chorale, the American voices are less vibrant than the Viennese; the effect of both chorus and orchestra is neater, smoother. But the soloists who have their say in the lovely *"Benedictus"* show less assurance than those with the Austrian group. The soprano, especially, needs to come out of her shell, for she has fine vocal material. *Miriam's Song of Triumph* is a kind of extended anthem, which Schubert never got around to orchestrating. The *Hymn to the Sun* is a pleasing, wholly neglected, repertoire piece.

Widerspruch; Nachthelle; Liebe; Psalm 23; Geist der Liebe; Der Gon-

delfahrer; Die Nachtigall; Das Dörfchen; Im gegenwärtigen Vergangenes:
Kmentt, t; VKC, Grossmann, Vox PL 6870.
An den Frühling; Widerspruch; La Pastorella; Ständchen; Sehnsucht.
Krebs, c; SC; pf, Shaw, 10" V LM 81.
Psalm 23; Ständchen; Der Gondelfahrer; La Pastorella; Die Nachtigall.
Vienna Choir Boys; pf, Grossmann, Cap P 8085 (*German Folk Songs).

Considerable duplication will be noted here. But hearing the lovely setting of the *Twenty-third Psalm* sung first by men, then by boys, amounts to two different experiences. With all due respect to the men, I find the Wiener Sängerknaben very moving in this music. Schubert arranged many of his choruses for varying groups, so no question of correctness concerns us here. But whereas the voice of Beatrice Krebs is appealing enough in the *"Ständchen"* (not to be confused with the celebrated song in the *Schwanengesang*), that of the Viennese boy is irresistible. A more recent Vienna Choir Boys concert, including *"Ständchen"* and *"La Pastorella,"* is technically an improvement on the recording considered here, but I felt less magic, somehow, in the performance of these pieces (C ML 4873).

Opera

Der häusliche Krieg. Steingruber, s; Dutoit, s; Roon; s; Berry, bs;
etc.; VKC; PRCO, Grossmann, Vox PL 8160.

This disc takes in the entire musical score of Schubert's opera. Presumably there must be a good deal of spoken dialogue to bring the work to normal length. The cast performs capably and with spirit. Outstanding, perhaps, is Elisabeth Roon, to whom falls the very pretty romance, *"Ich schleiche bang und still herum."* The reproduction is acceptable, though not without an edge. Neither libretto nor any sort of translation is provided with the record.

Incidental Music

Rosamunde—Incidental Music. Rössl-Majdan, c; VKC; VSO, Dixon,
W WL 5182.

Though the drama by Helmine von Chézy, for which Schubert wrote this music, is long since lost, the overture and ballet music remain among the all-time favorites of the concert hall. Here the whole musical score is performed with controlled energy and nice balance. The lovely *"Romanze"* is not unknown on recital programs; Rössl-Majdan sings it tastefully. The choruses are especially delightful. The overture played is not the better-known one (originally composed for another work, *Die Zauberharfe*) but that borrowed from *Alphonso und Estrella* for the disastrous *Rosamunde* production of 1823.

Songs

Die schöne Müllerin. Fischer-Dieskau, b; Moore, pf, HMV ALP 1036/7 [2]. Schiøtz, t; Moore, pf, V LCT 1048. Ludwig, t; Raucheisen, pf, D DL 9648. Munteanu, t; Holetschek, pf, W WL 5291. Singher, b; Ulanowsky, pf, CH CHS 1114. A. Dermota, t; H. Dermota, pf, L LL 971.

Of the six singers here listed, three have the range to perform the songs in their original keys. Schubert wrote the cycle for tenor, and the burden of interpretation is just that much heavier on a baritone. But in speaking of tenor Aksel Schiøtz and baritone Fischer-Dieskau, such considerations count for little. Each is a musician of the first rank; each has the penetration and the mastery of diction to make his points with the text. Both are well matched in these recordings with the piano-playing of Gerald Moore. Unfortunately, Schiøtz's recording is a transfer from the 78-rpm set made a decade or so ago, and it is not so successful in its new form. Some of the songs are incomparably performed, but a great deal has been lost. Fischer-Dieskau, on the other hand, benefits from the most recent recording (all the better for the spacing on two discs instead of one), so that every tone of his handsome voice, every inflection, and every color with which he illuminates the poems, come through will full effect. The reproduction is somewhat less kind to Moore, for the tone of the piano is not altogether natural. Of the other four singers, Ludwig has the most beautiful voice, and he is a sensitive artist, though perhaps more at home in opera than in lieder. Munteanu has less of tonal charm; his voice has a somewhat "flabby" quality, a lack of hard core. The contrasts between his loud and soft singing are altogether too marked. With this equipment, his singing of the cycle is admirable, if not particularly ingratiating. As for Singher, he has undoubtedly absorbed a good deal of the essential German style from his father-in-law, the late Fritz Busch, but he is less in his element than are his tenor rivals. His is an interesting performance, but in the long run less satisfying. Dermota, another opera singer, should have given a better account of himself than he has. His tones are marred by an occasional bleaty quality, and his treatment of the songs is often free where it should be steady.

Since the above was written, the Fischer-Dieskau recording has
been given domestic release (V LHMV 6), but on a single disc.

*Schwanengesang. Herbert, b; Waldman, pf, Al All 3089. Munteanu, t;
Holetschek, pf, W WL 5165.*

*Das Fischermädchen; Die Stadt; Am Meer; Der Doppelgänger; Die
Taubenpost. Lichtegg, t; Haeusslin, pf, 10" L LD 9093.*

In reality *Schwanengesang* is no cycle at all, but a group of fourteen Rellstab, Heine, and Seidl settings published after Schubert's
death. Although they group effectively, there is actually no connection between them. Among the songs are several of the most
famous in the entire literature. The two singers who have recorded the whole set are real artists, but neither is particularly
persuasive here. Herbert's is a solid voice, heavy for some of
the songs; Munteanu's is on the light side. Whereas Herbert is
the more successful in the dramatic *"Doppelgänger,"* Munteanu is
better suited to *"Liebesbotschaft."* Westminster's is the better
recording. Lichtegg is another light tenor: he sings the most somber songs he has chosen in an open tone of voice, pleasant enough
in itself, but not long on color and nuance. His best offering is
the final song, *"Die Taubenpost,"* a piece that wears its heart on
its sleeve. The piano is quite overbalanced by the voice throughout the set.

The English edition of Fischer-Dieskau's recording of Beethoven's
An die ferne Geliebte (HMV ALP 1066) is coupled with the five
Heine songs from this set, only three of which are included on the
American disc (V LHMV 1046). The performances are masterly,
and the less crowded record is clearer in sound.

*Die Winterreise. Carne, t; Moore, pf, W WL 5087/8 [2]. Hotter, bs;
Raucheisen, pf, D DX 111 [2]. Schmitt-Walter, b; Giesen, pf, L LL
702/3 [2].*

Our first consideration here should concern original keys: of the
three singers listed, only one is a tenor, and, for all their somber
coloration, these songs were composed for high voice (to be sure,
manuscripts exist of some of them transposed). I believe one reason why the cycle so often tends to be dull, monotonous, and un-
relievedly gloomy is that as a rule only heavy-voiced singers attempt it. Aside from this generality, Victor Carne has other points
in his favor. Not a professional singer, he is an official of the
EMI concern in England. His is not a sensuous voice, but, a
pupil of Elena Gerhardt, he quite obviously understands and feels

what he is singing about. Failing a reissue of the classic performance of Gerhard Hüsch, something can be said for both bass-baritones. Neither artist is any longer in his vocal prime; tonally Schmitt-Walter is the more ingratiating because the quality of his voice is lighter. Hotter, one of the great singing-actors of our day, is dramatic without being quite operatic. Schmitt-Walter has a tendency to mouth his words; Hotter, too, is somewhat "loose" in his diction. Hotter holds the attention more firmly, but Schmitt-Walter is the more even vocally. An earlier selection of six songs from this cycle sung by the latter (Cap P 8123) is altogether less satisfactory.

Liebesbotschaft; Der Erlkönig; Ständchen; Der Tod und das Mädchen; Gretchen am Spinnrade; Die Forelle; Ave Maria. Anderson, c; Rupp, pf, 10" V LM 98.

Most of these Schubert interpretations have long been known to us. The singer is best in the lighter songs, though she has obviously put much admirable thought and care into her *"Erlkönig."* She has recorded *"Der Tod und das Mädchen"* a number of times, here not quite so successfully, I think, as in the first essay, back in the early thirties.

Suleika, I & II; Der Hirt auf dem Felsen. Berger, s; Schick, pf; Oppenheim, clar; 10" V LM 133 (*Mozart: Il Re Pastore—Aria).

The two Suleika songs are rarely heard; the second one, especially, is top-flight Schubert, and one must be grateful to Erna Berger for recording it. She has the field to herself, so far as LP goes, in the long piece with clarinet *Der Hirt auf dem Felsen*. The singing is cool and proficient, most effective, to my ears, in the *allegretto* section of *Der Hirt*. The voice tends to overbalance the piano.

Dem Unendlichen; Erlafsee; Der Wachtelschlag; Im Walde; Die Liebe hat gelogen; Ellens zweite Gesang; Das Lied im Grünen. Glaz, m-s; Mueller, pf, MGM E 3055 (*Schumann: Songs).

Fahrt zum Hades; Schäfers Klagelied; Fischerweise; Die Männer sind mechant; Du liebst mich nicht; Des Mädchens Klage; Wehmuth; Seligkeit. Glaz, m-s; Rosenstock, pf, Ren X 15.

There is a good deal of variety in these two programs: were there as much in the singing, indeed, the two discs would place among the great ones. But ideally so broad and noble a song as *"Dem Unendlichen"* demands a bigger voice than that of Herta Glaz; the combination of intelligence and amplification do not quite overcome the essential lack. On the other hand, *"Erlafsee"*

wants lighter treatment, a less serious approach. So on through
the recitals: the darker songs emerge the more successfully; the
gayer moods need an extra lift. Perhaps the major contribution is
"*Fahrt zum Hades*," an inexplicably neglected song. The MGM
reproduction is considerably better than the Renaissance.

*Goethe Songs: Heidenröslein; Gesänge des Harfners; Geheimes; Rast-
lose Liebe; An Schwager Kronos; Meeres Stille; Ganymed; Wanderers
Nachtlied; Der Musensohn; Jägers Abendlied; Erlkönig.   Herbert, b;
Waldman, pf, All AL 27.*

Herbert, whose voice is by all odds too heavy for "*Heidenröslein*,"
strikes a norm somewhere between this and the blustering of "*An
Schwager Kronos*." Obviously out of his element in the first of
these, whether through his or Waldman's inclination, he cuts the
latter into even squares. Perhaps his most successful song is
"*Der Musensohn*," which he allows to gallop its own way.

*Viola; Die Blumensprache; Der Blumen Schmerz. Lemnitz, s; Rauch-
eisen, pf, U URLP 7013.(*Lemnitz Recital).*

*Heimliches Leben. Lemnitz, s; Raucheisen, pf. Hoffnung; Der Jüngling
an der Quelle; Nachtstück. Erb, t; Reutter, pf. Tischlied; Tischlerlied;
Der Goldschmiedgesell. Strienz, bs; Raucheisen, pf.   U URLP 7047
(*Schumann: Songs and Duets).*

Lemnitz's first three songs take up one entire record side, running, so the label tells us, to twenty-one minutes. Most of this is
consumed by "*Viola*," a song covering fifteen pages in the Peters
edition. Variously described as a "floral pageant...no more than
a curiosity" (Capell) and "not the longest of all Schubert's songs,
though it is by far the most perfect and beautiful of the long ones"
(Tovey), this work could easily lead us into boredom if done with
less exquisite art. The singer is less happy in her contribution to
the joint program, for here her tone is infirm. Karl Erb, whose
years entitle him to be called patriarchal, has found an interesting
little piece in "*Hoffnung*," but his singing is almost entirely
staccato, a fact that proves the undoing of "*Der Jüngling an der
Quelle*." After a more promising start, "*Nachtstücke*" suffers
from the same ailment. Strienz's three songs are of a more hearty
type; nothing in them calls for subtlety. The piano is weakly recorded in most of the songs, and in one or two I heard suggestions
of the old vibraphone effect, once all too common on discs.

*Dithyrambe; Lachen und Weinen; Du liebst mich nicht; Das Wirtshaus;
Auf dem Wasser zu singen; Nacht und Träume. Niemela, s; Koskimies,
pf, WCFM 10 (*Haydn: Songs).*

This program does not tax Niemela's lyric voice seriously, though a bigger tone would make more of a song like *"Dithyrambe,"* and we usually associate a male voice with *"Das Wirtshaus,"* from *Die Winterreise.* *"Lachen und Weinen"* is delightfully done, *"Nacht und Träume"* beautifully sustained; the smooth-flowing *"Auf dem Wasser zu singen"* is perhaps best of all.

Wohin?; Ungeduld; Eifersucht und Stolz; Erstarrung; Die Post; Die Krähe; Rückblick; Frühlingstraum; Der Wanderer an den Mond; Das Lied im Grünen; Im Frühling; Der Kreuzzug; Der Musensohn; Gott im Frühlinge; Totengräber-Weise. Schey, b; Reyners, pf, Pol PRLP 1009.

This program contains enough of the less usual to warrant acquiring the disc—the superb *"Wanderer an den Mond,"* the moving *"Der Kreuzzug,"* the reverent *"Gott im Frühlinge,"* and the nostalgic *"Totengräber-Weise."* But it would be too much to say Schey's singing of these songs is a revelation. His voice is past its best days; his artistry does not quite succeed in obscuring this patent fact.

Die Forelle; Du bist die Ruh'; Horch, horch, die Lerch'!; Heidenröslein; Das Lied im Grünen; Rosamunde—Romanze; Ave Maria. Schumann, s; Moore, pf, V LCT 1126 (*Schumann: Frauenliebe und Leben).

This recital has been pieced together out of the rich legacy left us by Elisabeth Schumann. Most of the recordings date back to her wonderful days in the thirties, though the *Rosamunde* piece is later. Almost all of the recital is exquisite—did anyone ever give *"Du bist die Ruh' "* more beautifully, or was ever singing so invigorating as *"Das Lied im Grünen"*? My one reservation concerns the *"Ave Maria,"* with its orchestral background. Fine as Schumann's performance is, this accompaniment is neither appropriate nor matched with the rest of the program.

An die Musik; Im Frühling; Wehmuth; Das Lied im Grünen; Ganymed; Gretchen am Spinnrade; Nähe des Geliebten; Die junge Nonne; An Sylvia; Auf dem Wasser zu singen; Nachtviolen; Der Musensohn. Schwarzkopf, s; Fischer, pf, An 35022.

Schwarzkopf is inevitably charming, best in the lighter songs despite the rather dark characteristic color of her voice. She is an artist with imagination, sometimes going too far in the underlining of words and the careful turning of phrases. One feels occasionally, as in her rather fussy *"Im Frühling,"* that the long line of the whole composition is lost in detail. *"An die Musik"* she conceives on a smaller scale than many singers, making it intimate rather than noble. Her *"Wehmuth"* is dark and somber; *"Das Lied im Grünen"* is light, but not as infectious as Schumann's. Nor is *"Nähe des Geliebten"* held together with a wizardry comparable to that great artist's. Her *"Die junge Nonne"* is in the passionate tradition. The fact that Edwin Fischer assists at the piano holds out more promise than fulfillment. Apparently he believes an accompanist should provide only a modest background for the singer, and in this he is abetted by rather weak recording. Nor does he make much of the spinning wheel figure in *"Gretchen am Spinnrade."*

Der Jüngling und der Tod; Der Jüngling an der Quelle; Der Wanderer an den Mond; Ihr Bild; Liebesbotschaft; Der Schiffer; Ganymed; Erster Verlust; Die Forelle; Nacht und Traüme. Souzay, b; Bonneau, pf, 10" L LS 655.

Gesang des Harfners, no. 1; Fischerweise; Der Wanderer; Der Doppelgänger; Heidenröslein; Der Erlkönig. Souzay, b; Bonneau, pf, L LLP 245 (*Fauré: Songs).

Souzay's voice is too light, too characteristically French in texture, to be ideal in Schubert, though some may find this a relief from the characteristic somberness of so much German singing. In the heavier songs, such as *"Der Wanderer"* and *"Der Doppelgänger,"* he is obviously miscast, and he is as out of place as are most men in *"Heidenröslein."* His *"Erlkönig"* is best described as an interesting try. On the other hand, *"Fischerweise"* comes through gaily, and I liked best of all the folksy little ballad *"Der Fischer."* The balance is good on the whole, but the voice overwhelms the piano in *"Erlkönig,"* of all songs!

L'incanto degli occhi; Il traditor deluso; Il modo di prender moglie; Der Kampf. Symonette, bs; Masiello, pf, Col CLPS 1002. (*Brahms: Ernste Gesänge).

Symonette impresses even more in the light-weight Italian arias Schubert wrote for the great basso Lablache than in his better-than-presentable singing of the Brahms overdisc. For their rarity these pieces are doubly welcome. There are some not quite comfortable high tones in *"Der Kampf."*

Lied der Mignon; An die Nachtigall; Im Frühling; Im Abendroth; Gott im Frühlinge; Die Gebüsche. Warner, s; Rupp, pf, C ML 4365 (*Mozart: Songs).

Simply as a program, this is one of the best records we have had: each song is a gem, and not one is over-familiar. Warner's voice is unusually rich and appealing; given a little more time to mature, she may become a distinguished singer of songs. At present her performance is very listenable but not strong in profile, so that a whole side of these lieder may seem monotonous. Taken one at a time, the songs will be found charming.

SCHUMANN, ROBERT (1810-1856)

Songs

Dichterliebe. Schiøtz, t; Moore, pf. Panzéra, b; Cortot, pf. V LCT 1132 (two performances coupled on one disc). Ludwig, t; Raucheisen, pf, 10" D DL 7525. Lehmann, s; Walter, pf, C ML 4788 (*Frauenliebe und Leben). Bernac, b; Casadesus, pf, 10" C ML 2210.
Dichterliebe; Du bist wie eine Blume; Geständnis; Der Nussbaum; Der Sandmann. Souzay, b; Bonneau, pf, L LL 940.

The best two performances are the oldest, now issued on two sides of one disc in Victor's "Treasury" series. Pride of place goes to Schiotz, because his voice is right for the original keys, but his finely conceived and executed performance, ably partnered by the indispensable Gerald Moore, is no longer the last word in recording. Perhaps even more sensitive, certainly freer in conception, is the companion performance by Panzéra. Here is a Frenchman who has thoroughly assimilated the style and language, and he was in his prime when the recording was made. Cortot, a Schumann interpreter of great and deserved reputation, gives, if not technically the most perfect account of the piano part, surely the most penetrating one. Among the more modern recordings, Ludwig is the singer with the right voice, and the one most securely in character. He shows best in the more lyrical moods, just as Mack Harrell, on still another recording, now withdrawn (10" V LM 29), did his best in the dramatic ones. Souzay has carefully and skillfully planned his interpretation; his German diction is for the most part excellent, his understanding unimpeachable. But his voice remains French and foreign. The recording listed is his second of the cycle, the first having been coupled with four Hugo Wolf songs instead of the extra Schumann (L LL 535). The second try shows a considerable improvement in reproduction and balance; at the same time the singer's diction has been touched up to advantage. Personally, I have never been able to accept Lotte Lehmann in this masculine cycle, especially as her recording is poorly balanced with Walter's reticent piano-playing. For Bernac I can say even less, though many admire his singing of these songs. To me it is mannered to the point of caricature, and, of course, nowadays little is left of his voice.

Frauenliebe und Leben. Ferrier, c; Newmark, pf, L LLP 271 (*Brahms: Ernste Gesänge). Graf, s; Newmark, pf, 10" All Al 4034. Schumann, s; Moore, pf, V LCT 1126 (*Schubert: Songs). Lehmann, s; Walter, pf, C ML 4788 (*Dichterliebe). Flagstad, s; McArthur, pf, V LM 1738 (*Flagstad Recital). Höngen, c; Leitner, pf, D DL 9610 (*Loewe: Songs).

Kathleen Ferrier's noble instrument is a joy to hear in these songs, but her singing is a little too grand for the intimacy of Schumann's expression. Still, with the superiority of London's recording, hers must be the preferred *Frauenliebe.* If Ferrier's voice stood in the way of her performance, the same is more true of Flagstad's. It is remarkable that the soprano learned the cycle only for a couple of her farewell recitals. The Schumann recording is a memento for her admirers to treasure, but I am not sure it should ever have been issued. Inevitably, there are certain points in the performance no other singer could match, little felicities of expression in her own very personal manner, but as a whole the cycle is hardly a success. Lehmann's presentation is of course very much admired, but she and Bruno Walter are subjected to weak and poorly balanced recording. Höngen's voice is fluttery in her performance; the chief value of the disc is Greindl's singing of Loewe on the reverse. Which leaves Uta Graf, a fine sensitive artist with the imagination to point up the words and make them count. She, too, is poorly recorded, For some reason Marian Anderson's intelligent performance has not been put on LP, and the very excellent singing of Astra Desmond on 78-rpm London is all but forgotten.

Liederkreis, opus 39. Danco, s; Agosti, pf, 10" L LS 590. Warfield, b; Herz, pf, C ML 4860 (*Brahms: Ernste Gesänge). Sydney, m-s; Loibner, pf, Van VRS 411 (*Brahms: Songs).

Danco's singing of this Eichendorff cycle is easily the best; her style is excellent, her tone lovely. Only here and there she misses a point a German singer might have made. It is a pleasure to hear so limpid a voice float through the ethereal lines of *"Mondnacht,"* and all the quieter songs are beautifully performed. William Warfield is not really happy in the cycle, which is certainly better suited to a woman's voice. Listening to his *"Waldesgespräch"* is enough to give an idea of what the baritone lacks: there simply is no drama in the dialogue. And in *"Mondnacht,"* where Danco's tone so beautifully envelops us, Warfield's is hardly exciting. Sydney's voice and style should equip her for this music, but she has obvious and persistent faults that detract from the total effect. Concentrating, apparently, on vocal richness rather than purity of line, she commits the sin of so many deep-voiced ladies, padding the upper reaches, where she should point the tone, with a consequent sag in pitch and a lack of support.

*Im Wald; Die Spinnerin; Die letzten Blumen sterben; Die Soldatenbraut; Erstes Grün, Zigeunerliedchen; Ich wand're nicht; Aufträge; Melancholie. Glaz, m-s; Mueller, pf, MGM E 3055 (*Schubert: Songs).*

*Märzveilchen; Schneeglöckchen. Lemnitz, s; Raucheisen, pf. Wiegenlied; Unter'm Fenster; Familiengemälde. Lemnitz, s; Anders, t; Raucheisen, pf. Die Kartenlegerin; Lust der Sturmnacht; Frühlingsnacht. Klose, c; Raucheisen, pf. U URLP 7047 (*Schubert: Songs).*

*Lied eines Schmiedes; Meine Rose; Kommen und Scheiden; Die Sennin; Einsamkeit; Der schwere Abend. Schloss, s; Brice, pf, IRCC L-7000 (*Franz, Strauss, Wolf: Songs).*

All this neglected repertoire is well worth hearing. Glaz, always a proficient and serious artist, is a little too much the latter in her recital, for she fails to get the needed lift into her gayer moods, with a resulting impression of monotony. Taken in smaller doses, her record is a very worthy one. Lemnitz is at her best in *"Schneeglöckchen,"* but somewhat fluttery in *"Märzveilchen."* Her duets with Anders are pleasant to hear, but not exciting. Klose, though essentially an opera singer, does a neat job on *"Die Kartenlegerin"* and *"Frühlingsnacht."* The opening of *"Lust der Sturmnacht"* is a bit out of focus, but in the middle section her tone and line are lovely. The piano is weakly recorded. Schloss is an unusually satisfactory artist, whose ample and appealing voice is always put at the service of the composer. She conveys a good deal of the mood of a song simply by the quality of her tone.

SCHÜTZ, HEINRICH (1585-1672)

Choral Works

Historia von der Auferstehung. Lindemeier, s; Muench, c; Berling, t; Liebl, t; etc.; Munich Ch & Viol Quint, Schleiffer, Mer MG 10073.

This *Resurrection Story* is easily one of the best Schütz recordings. As in the Passions, and in the *Christmas Story*, the burden of the work is carried by the tenor Evangelist, other soloists and chorus taking their parts as the story unfolds. Berling, the Evangelist in this performance, is exceptionally sensitive. The choral parts are a few degrees less satisfactory.

Johannes-Passion. Stemann, t; Hohmann, t; Müller, bs; SCS, Grischkat, Ren X 26.

This wonderful work should be required listening for all who would study the Passions of Bach. Here the story is told in the simplest, most direct manner, mostly, of course, by the tenor Evangelist. There are no arias, no chorales, not even any accompaniment, but the impact is tremendous. The performance is not all it might be. The Evangelist, Stemann, has a way of halting between phrases which might make a good effect were it not overdone. The reproduction is for the most part good, though clouded toward the end.

Matthäus-Passion; Symphoniae Sacrae: No. 9, Frohlocket mit Händen; No. 10, Lobet den Herrn. Meili, t; etc.; BCC, Koch, ·BG 519/20 [2].

Matthäus-Passion. Stemann, t; etc.; SCS, Grischkat, Ren X 49.

The Stuttgart presentation is painstaking and sincere, with creditable work by the Evangelist, Klaus Stemann. Still, though the tenor sings with more freedom here than in the *St. John Passion*, his tendency to cut the narrative into yard-lengths again makes for monotony. Max Meili's voice shows signs of age, but his artistry is intact. His performance is in another world from Stemann's; he knows the value of every word, and he sings with the greatest expressiveness, intensity, and a controlled elasticity within the musical structure. The other soloists measure up well, especially the high-voiced Judas and a Pilate's Wife who leaves an enduring impression with her one line. The Berlin chorus, on its mettle, makes us realize once more the towering genius of Bach's great forerunner. The odd side of the set is filled with two *Symphoniae Sacrae* beautifully sung by Meili.

Musikalische Exequien. Bloecher, s; Brainerd, s; Pierce, c; Hess, t; Squires, t; Matthen, bs; Cass, bs; Cantata Singers, Mendel, REB 9.

This is a forgotten masterpiece, composed in memory of a lamented royal friend and patron. The text is made up of scriptural passages that had been favorites of the departed, and were carved in the marble of his tomb. Schütz's work is among the most memorable tributes ever paid in music. The final section, with the text of the *"Nunc dimittis"* (in German) set against that of "Blessed are the dead" in the two choirs, is unutterably beautiful. In this

recording the first choir part is taken by the soloists; there are
some lovely solo passages. The duet for two basses is especially
delightful.

Die sieben Worte Jesu Christi am Kreuz; Selig sind die Toten; Also
hat Gott die Welt geliebt; Der Engel sprach; Ich sterbe, siehe, nun
sterbe ich; Das ist je gewisslich wahr. Rathauscher, s; Hofstaedter,
b; Berry, bs; VKC; VSY, Grossmann, Vox PL 6860.

This tempting assortment turns out to be somewhat square in
performance. The music is lovely in all conscience, but there
are better Schütz recordings.

Weihnachts-Historie. Bloecher, s; Hess, t; Matthen, bs; Cantata Sing-
ers; O, Mendel, REB 3. (In Italian) Rizzo, s; Filacuridi, t; Clabassi,
bs; Ch; SCAO, Caracciolo, Col CLPS 1034.

The Cantata Singers recording was made following a performance
of the *Christmas Story* given at the Metropolitan Museum of Art in
New York. The work benefits by excellent soloists, especially
William Hess, whose Evangelist may be hailed as a masterpiece.
The reproduction is spacious and clear. It is amusing to turn to
the Italian version of the same music. Despite a curious statement in the rather more than curious program notes, the text
sounds strange indeed in this translation, hardly in keeping with
Schütz's style as we know it. We are not told what edition is
used, but clearly it is not Arthur Mendel's. In contrast to the
Mendel performance, Caracciolo favors bigness and sonority; the
Evangelist's part is hardly recognizable. For the rest, the work
is done well enough, though the basso representing Herod seems
an extremely mild man for the part. The Angel is assisted by a
choir of cherubs, who add a little background and help out on the
long sustained final notes of phrases. The last chorus is rather
square-cut. Noises indicate that this recording may have been
made at a public performance.

Die Worte der Abendmahlseinsetzung; Ich weiss, dass mein Erlöser
*lebet. SCS, Grischkat, Per SPLP 519 (*Mozart: Offertorium).*

These two beautiful motets are among the best-performed of the
Stuttgart offerings. They are rather incongruously coupled with
a fairish Mozart performance, but on their own merits they can be
recommended.

For Solo Voices

Kleine geistliche Konzerte—Eile mich, Gott, zu erretten; Bringt her
dem Herrn; O Süsser, o Freundlicher; Ich will dem Herrn loben allezeit;

Symphoniae sacrae—Nos. 1, 3, 6, 7. Cuenod, t; VSY Ens, Pinkham, W WL 5043.

Kleine geistliche Konzerte—Eile mich, Gott, zu erretten; Was hast du verwirket; Ich danke dem Herrn von ganzem Herzen; O Süsser, o Freundlicher; Ich liege und schlafe; O misericordissime Jesu; Die Furcht des Herren. Hess, t; Matthen, bs; Beaven, org, REB 10.

Erbarm dich. Tinayre, b; ACS, All AL 79 (*Telemann: Feste pentecostae; Kreidel: Die Liebe, Die Englein).

It will be noted that the Cuenod and Hess-Matthen discs overlap considerably. More than that, *Eile mich, Gott, zu erretten* is also available in the miscellaneous programs of William Warfield (C ML 4545) and Suzanne Danco (10" L LS 698), not to mention Max Meili's performance in the old 78-rpm Anthologie Sonore (AS 28), which might possibly be slated for transfer to LP by the Haydn Society. In this piece Hess gives the most intense and dramatic performance, singing with fine freedom, unimpeachable musicianship, and the high intelligence that always marks his work. Cuenod's program may sound less churchly than that of Matthen and Hess, because he sings to an ensemble including harpsichord, while they are accompanied by the organ. All three artists sing with distinction. Cuenod is especially impressive in the height and flexibility of his voice, Matthen in the richness and sincerity of his. For me the gem of the two programs is Matthen's *Ich liege und schlafe*, but there is not a performance in the lot one would willingly sacrifice. The final number on the REB disc is a duet. Tinayre's voice had lost something of its cunning when his recording was made. The music he sings is well worth having, but it is merely sketched in this performance.

SHEPHERD, ARTHUR (1880-)

Triptych. Kraft, s; Walden Str Qt, SPAM R 1 (*Koutzen: Quartet No. 2).
This cycle of Tagore settings is a product of the twenties. If today we seem somewhat removed from it, this is true in the same sense of the poetry itself. It is interesting, at the very least, to go back to these things today. Marie Kraft is a "composer's singer," a dependable and understanding musician with a sweet, modest voice.

SHOSTAKOVICH, DMITRI (1906-)

Song of the Forests. Petrov, t; Kilichewsky, bs; USSRC & O, Mravinsky, Van VRS 422.

Written to glorify the composer's homeland and its achievements, this cantata is conservative and not too imaginative. There is no gainsaying Shostakovich's skill in the use of voices and instruments, but the fine sonorities he achieves do not strike the ear with any great degree of novelty. The performance is filled with zeal impressively reproduced.

SIBELIUS, JEAN (1865-)

Säf, säf, susa; Svarta rosor; På veranden vid Hafvet; Im Feld ein Mädchen singt; Diamenten på Marssnön. Rautawaara, s; BPO; Leitner, pf; 10" Cap L 8041 (*Rautawaara Recital).
Im Feld ein Mädchen singt; Varen flyktar hastigt; Illalle; Var det en dröm? Niemela, s; Koskimies, pf, WCFM 5 (*Grieg, Kilpinen: Songs).

Aulikki Rautawaara's recital has a special interest, for no singer has more consistently championed Sibelius than this countrywoman of his, or been more closely identified with his music. In this recording the soprano maintains a good norm, making dramatic and emotional points without quite producing a major thrill. The recording, in its original form, is prewar, some of it, at least, going back well into the thirties. Heard thus continuously, it is not consistent in volume or sense of space, for something has been lost in the transfer to LP. The patchwork effect is furthered by the fact that some of the songs are sung to the piano, some orchestrally accompanied. None has too much realism; in those with piano there is some wavery pitch. One of Rautawaara's offerings is repeated in the more modern recording of Niemela. Her lyric voice is always sweet and expressive, and she has a generous share of style and interpretative talent. One curious shortcoming is a lack of support in some of the softer and lower passages, a fault probably magnified by the microphone.

SMETANA, BEDRICH (1824-1884)

The Bartered Bride (Prodana nevesta). Musilova, s; Kovár, t; Kalas, bs; etc.; Prague Nat'l Th Ch & O, Vogel, U URLP 231 [3]. (In German)

Richter, s; Hauser, t; Böhme, bs; etc.; BCOC & O, Lenzer, U URLP 210 [3].

Here is a demonstration of the effect of translation on an opera. If one accepts the German language in this very Czechish music, the second performance is excellent. Especially notable is the Kezal of Kurt Böhme. The reproduction is extremely full and roomy, rather on the loud side, but very clear. The balance, though not altogether consistent, is better than that of many opera sets. Coming to the Czech performance is like emerging from shade into broad sunlight. One does not need to understand a word of the language in order to join the fun: the very sound of the text is often uproariously funny. The cast is eminently satisfactory, longer on teamwork than on *prima donna* show, but all possessed of better than average voices. The tempos are lively and bright—almost perilously fast in the overture—and, to mention but one scene, the sextet has much of the great beauty Smetana conceived in it. The recording sound is excellent.

SPOHR, LUDWIG (1784–1859)

Six Songs for Mezzo-Soprano, Clarinet and Piano. Howland, m-s; Weber, clar; Mittman, pf, STR 609 (*Grand Nonette).

I suspect that this nostalgic reminder of the high days of nineteenth-century romanticism could have a stronger appeal than it exerts in this competent recording. Alice Howland's dusky voice blends well with the clarinet, and she sings the music cleanly enough. However, no score or text was available to me as I listened to the record, and I had no more than the very sketchy program notes to guide me as to the meaning of the songs. Only a very occasional word came over to me in the singing.

SPONTINI, GASPARO (1774–1851)

La Vestale. Vitale, s; Nicolai, m-s; Gavarini, t; Ferrein, bs; etc.; RIC & O, Previtali, Cet 1224 [2].

La Vestale, a classic of the post-Gluck generation, is remembered in America as one of Rosa Ponselle's great starring operas. Its melodies are conceived along broad, noble lines; a like nobility in performance is a major requirement, which accounts for the infrequency of Spontini revivals. The recording cast is not equal to this requirement, but manages to convey an impression of the composer's music. Fortunately, Ponselle left us two of the arias in

one of her great recordings, now available in an LP recital (10"
V LCT 10).

Arias

*La Vestale—Sinfonia; Inno della sera; Inno mattutino; Milton—Se
stesso amor; Aria di Carlotta; Romanza; Triste destin; Olympia—
Sinfonia; Auprès d'un amant; Fernando Cortez—O Liberia mia.* Flery,
s; Ferrigno, m-s; Pirino, t; Ch; SCAO, Caracciolo, Col CLPS 1030.

This cross-section of Spontini contains some beautiful singing,
especially by Mirella Flery, and some that is at the least presentable enough. The recording, especially of the orchestral
parts, is variable, at best rather restricted in range.

STAINER, SIR JOHN (1840-1901)

Crucifixion. Van der Gucht, t; Noble, b; Whitehall Ch; org; Helliwell,
CH CHS 1110 [2].

This is a fairly typical church rendering, even to the tenor with
the over-careful diction, the baritone showing signs of age, and
the organist to whom registration is more important than rhythm.
The Anglican hymns, which occupy a place similar to that of
Bach's chorales, are sung with familiar earnestness, and with a
good pause for breath before each new stanza—never a stanza is
omitted. I have no doubt that the elemental appeal that has kept
the work popular, the acceptance of Stainer's music and Sparrow-
Simpson's text because of what they stand for—these things may
well make another best-seller of this recording.

STRAUS, OSKAR (1870-1954)

Ein Walzertraum. Opawsky, s; Christ, t; etc.; Ch & O, Straus, Per RL
1903.
Die letzte Walzer. Opawsky, s; Christ, t; etc.; Ch & O, Straus, Per
RL 1904.

It must have been a satisfaction to the late composer to leave behind these two productions, with blue-ribbon casts under his own
direction. The better-known of the two works, and by all odds the
better, is the perennial *Waltz Dream*, with its infectious title
theme, enough in itself to keep the score alive. The two leading
singers in both casts are known for recordings of far different
types, but seem very much in their element here. Rudolf Christ is

the real star of both operettas; his voice is pleasantly open in quality, his style at times recalling Tauber. His are a beautiful diction and an easy delivery—his handling of the famous melody with the words *"Leise, ganz leise"* is magical. Opawsky pushes her voice, perhaps in the interests of characterization; her singing is more or less typical of continental *prime donne* in this type of show. The choral passages have their ragged edges, but the orchestral sound is powerful and lush. The recording is a shade raw.

STRAUSS, JOHANN (1825-1899)

Die Fledermaus. Gueden, s; Lipp, s; Wagner, c; Patzak, t; Dermota, t; Poell, bs; etc.; VSOC; VPH, Krauss, L LLP 281/2 [2]. (In English) Welitch, s; Pons, s; Lipton, c; Tucker, t; Kullman, t; etc.; MOC & O, Ormandy, C SL 108 [2]. (In English; Abridged) Resnik, s; Munsel, s; Stevens, m-s; Melton, t; Peerce, t; Merrill, b; etc.; SC; RCAO, Reiner, V LM 1114.

The Viennese version is one of the great modern recordings, a well-nigh perfect cast attuned to the style of the music and entering into the spirit of the comedy with rare good humor and sense of the theater. This is *Fledermaus*, no two ways about it. Wilma Lipp is a wonderful Adèle; she gets just the right injured tone into *"Mein Herr Marquis,"* and *"Spiel ich die Unschuld"* is knowingly delivered. The clear but delicate orchestra background to the first of these airs is one of the features of the set. Gueden's *"Czardas"* is tremendous, and the beginning of the great ensemble *"Brüderlein und Schwesterlein"* is almost beautiful enough to bring tears. One realizes in listening how perfectly this music fits its text. The Metropolitan version was a popular success, and is said to have made possible more serious productions in the house. We should therefore treat it with respect. The truth is, however, that translators Dietz and Kanin have made a Broadway show out of this Viennese operetta. And aside from the glamour of their names, one can think of no reason why some of the stars were assigned the roles they sing. Victor, using the translation of Ruth and Thomas Martin, may be a little less wide of the mark, and its cast seems to me considerably better vocally. As a set of highlights rather than a performance, this recording has little continuity, but it does contain the best-loved tunes.

Eine Nacht in Venedig. Rethy, s; Bösch, s; Schober, s; Friedrich, t; Jerger, b; etc.; Bregenz Fest Ch; VSY, Paulik, C SL 119 [2].

This is not quite Grade-A Strauss, and though it is sung with relish, it is not quite a Grade-A performance (so high is the standard set by London's *Fledermaus*). It is, however, full of waltzes, and this will be enough to give a lot of pleasure.

Tausend und eine Nacht. Seegers, s; Mentzel, s; Groh, t; Carell, b; etc.; RBC & O, Dobrindt, U URLP 203 [2].

This operetta, which began life as *Indigo* in 1871, was the composer's first success in the theater. It was transformed after his death by the substitution of a reputedly much-improved libretto. It is given an excellent idiomatic performance in this recording, the company including several bright young soprano voices, a second tenor with the usual thin tone but lots of style, and of course the star, Herbert Ernst Groh, who recalls Tauber. The last side is filled in with an orchestral performance of the Strauss waltz *Seid umschlungen, Millionen.*

Wienerblut. Beilke, s; Richter, s; Streich, s; Hauser, t; Hoppe, b; etc.; BCOC & O, Lenzer, U URLP 209 [2].

This is a *pasticcio* on which Strauss was working at the time of his death. It was completed by his musical executor, Adolf Müller. The score is full of familiar tunes and whole waltzes, delightful enough in themselves, but not adding up to a strongly integrated whole. Given as it is here, without dialogue, it does not make much sense, but it can be enjoyed for the exuberant music. The performance is pleasant, headed by the attractive-voiced Irma Beilke, with Traute Richter as an able second. Sebastian Hauser is a Viennese tenor in the right tradition, with a voice inclined toward nasality. As usual with Urania, the recording is strong and brilliant.

Der Zigeunerbaron. Zadek, s; Loose, s; Anday, c; Patzak, t; Poell, bs; etc.; VSOC; VPH, Krauss, L LLP 418/19 [2]. *(Highlights)* Barabas, s; Siebert, s; Milinkovic, c; Christ, t; Edelmann, b; Braun, bs; etc.; VKC; VSY, Moralt, Ep LC 3041.

A cast essentially identical with that of London's *Fledermaus* does similar honors to the second-best Strauss masterpiece. Patzak makes a superb Barinkay, singing with éclat and charm, but Loose walks away with the honors for exceptional singing. I found Zadek disappointing; she has neither the spark nor the vocal finish to do justice to the *"Gypsy Song."* She has a tendency to sag below the center of the pitch. Anday, a real veteran, sounds like one, though she is in better voice than in some other recent recordings. Poell is splendid. There are a number of cuts, including the second stanzas of two of the principal numbers. Hearing the Epic abridgment, we realize that actually it was Clemens Krauss who made the London set, for Moralt has neither his mastery of detail nor his rhythmic lift. Christ is a good operetta tenor, but he lacks Patzak's subtlety; Barabas has even less of the needed vocal brilliance than Zadek; Milinkovic, however, has more voice to give than Anday. An even tighter abridgment enlists the competent services of Maud Cunitz, Walther Ludwig, and Hans Hopf, acceptably recorded (10" Mer MG 15005). In none of these performances is the lovely duet *"Wer uns getraut"* given its full due.

STRAUSS, RICHARD (1864-1949)

Choral Works

Taillefer. Cebotari, s; Ludwig, t; Hotter, bs; LC; RBO, Rother, U URLP 7042 (*Divertimento after Couperin).
Wanderers Sturmlied, opus 14. VKC; VSY, Swoboda, W WL 5081 (*Brahms: Gesang der Parzen; Nänie).

Taillefer dates from 1903, following the famous tone-poems but antedating the great operas. It has the earmarks of both, telling in its Uhland text the story of the battle of Hastings, with unabated excitement throughout. There is fine solo singing by Ludwig and Hotter, the late Cebotari sounding only somewhat less well. The coupling of the *Wanderers Sturmlied* with Brahms's last two choral pieces—generally acknowledged among his best—gives us an opportunity to observe how the younger composer picked up where the older man left off, his own romantic ardor not quite making up for the serene mastery of his model. The Strauss gets the better singing on this disc.

Operas

Elektra. 4. Konetzni, s; Ilitsch, s; Mödl, c; Klarwein, t; Braun, b; etc.; FMC & O, Mitropoulos, Cet 1209 [2].
Elektra—Final Scene. Schlüter, s; Welitch, s; Widdop, t; Schoeffler, b; etc.; Ch; LPO, Beecham, V LCT 1135.

Elektra—Highlights. *Goltz, s; Höngen, m-s; Frantz, b; BAV, Solti, D DL 9723.*

All three of these recordings are outstanding in separate ways; all are uncommonly exciting, though the first two, at least, would no longer stand up under scrutiny simply as recordings. The complete set was made at a public performance, with audience noises and applause. It has the aura of presence, with the feeling of stage depth and the reproductive inequalities that go with these things. The singing is not exceptional, but the orchestra makes up for whatever the vocalists lack, the conductor being altogether in his element. The Beecham and Solti selections overlap; but whereas the former dispenses with the part of Klytemnestra, the latter has no Chrysothemis. The second side of the Beecham disc is all material after the end of the Solti. Beecham's Elektra, Erna Schlüter, makes a haunting thing of the repeated name *"Orest'."* Goltz, on the other hand, has what seems a bigger voice, and is more consistently steady tonally. Höngen, in the Solti performance, does a miracle of characterization with a voice not quite impressive enough; both Frantz and Schoeffler are sonorous and dignified as Orestes. Welitch's Chrysothemis is a good foil for Schlüter's Elektra. The balance in the Decca set is not natural, but effective: the voices stand out a little more than they could in life, but this is to the benefit of the singers' diction. In the Victor recording the balance was exceptional when the set was first issued, and even today is impressive. The Strauss connoisseur perhaps will want to own all three of the *Elektra* recordings.

Der Rosenkavalier. *Reining, s; Jurinac, s; Gueden, s; Weber, bs; Dermota, t; etc.; VSOC; VPH, Kleiber, L LLA 22 [4]. Bäumer, s; Lemnitz, s; Richter, s; Böhme, bs; etc.; DOC; SAX, Kempe, U URLP 201 [4]. Ursuleac, s; Milinkovic, m-s; Kern, s; Weber, bs; etc.; MSOC & O, Krauss, Vox PL 1774 [4]. (Abridged) Lehmann, s; Olszewska, c; Schumann, s; Mayr, bs; etc.; VSOC; VPH, Heger, V LCT 6005 [2].*

Der Rosenkavalier—Finale, Act 1; Finale, Act 3. *Lemnitz, s; Milinkovic, m-s; Trötschel, s; WSTO, Leitner, D DL 9606.*

Der Rosenkavalier—Presentation of the Rose, Act 2; Finale, Act 2. *Schwarzkopf, s; Seefried, s; Hermann, c; Weber, bs; VPH, Ackermann, 10" C ML 2126.*

The Marschallin, central figure though not the title role in this opera, is a lady beset with the realization that she is beginning to age. There may be some justice, therefore, in the selection of singers for this part in all three of the "complete" sets, though only one of them provides much in the way of aural pleasure. Bäumer and Ursuleac were fine singers in their day, and at one time must have been more than acceptable Marschallins; but in these recordings realism is carried too far. Both are victims of the wide tremolo. Reining, though past the first bloom of her sweetly lyrical voice, is magnificent when the range of the music does not tax her. There are a few high notes at which she rather pecks, but in the lower-lying conversational passages she delivers with dignified authority. There are plenty of memorable details—for example, her disillusioned *"Mein lieber Hyppolyte,"* her understated *"Ich hab' ihn nicht einmal geküsst,"* and her beautifully poised tone on *"die silberne Rose"* at the end of the first act. Of the three Oktavians, only one is the mezzo-soprano specified by Strauss, but she is also the least appealing of the three. Jurinac gets off to a slightly twittery start, but for the most part she sings beautifully. Lemnitz is also excellent, though her voice is less youthful and fresh. Gueden seems to me the best of recent Sophies, though Kern is still a good one and Richter is more than acceptable. Weber, whose Ochs is shared by Vox and London, does more legitimate singing than I have heard from any other in the part, notably some *mezza voce* one would hardly expect in this music. Böhme is effectively unctious. Dermota's singing of the tenor aria in the London set is worth special mention. Of the three sets, only London's is actually uncut; it is also the most recent and the most satisfactorily recorded. One might have expected the most revealing reading of the score from Clemens Krauss, but he is hampered by the quality of some of the singing. London's balance is sometimes less than perfect: in the second-act Oktavian-Sophie duet, *"Mit ihren Augen voll Tränen,"* the voices are too strong. But the set is not only the best of the three: it is an outstanding performance.

The Victor abridgment is a classic. The cast was the finest that could be assembled in the thirties, with Lehmann, Schumann, and Mayr in roles that will always be associated with their names. Olszewska may not have been the very prince of Oktavians, but was deservedly famous in the part. The transfer to LP is reasonably successful. Decca's selections take over Urania's Oktavian —Lemnitz—for the Marschallin role, and share the Vox Oktavian, Milinkovic. Lemnitz has the imagination and style for the new

role, but the whole performance seems scaled down to match her
limited volume. She never strains. This may be called a "dreamy"
performance. The Columbia disc, with the "Presentation," is interesting, but not really satisfactory. The lyric voices of Schwarzkopf and Seefried are too similar: one who is not intimate with the
score will have difficulty visualizing boy-meets-girl in their tonally lovely singing. In the second scene it is good again to hear
Weber's genuine and unspent voice as Baron Ochs. The name of
the conductor is omitted on the first side of the record; it might
better have been from the second, where the orchestral playing
should have been better.

Salome. Goltz, s; Kenney, m-s; Patzak, t; Dermota, t; Braun, b; etc.;
VPH, Krauss, L LL 1038/9 [2]. Wegner, s; Milinkovic, m-s; Szemere,
t; Metternich, b; etc.; VSY, Moralt, C SL 126 [2].

The late Clemens Krauss left himself a masterly memorial in his
recording, one of the finest reproduced operas we have had. Goltz,
whose Salome has been familiar for several years in a now superseded earlier recording (Oc OCS 302 [2]), has grown even beyond
the intensity of that performance, and she is aided by superlative
reproduction. Not only does the tone of her voice convey the
character of Herodias's daughter, but details in the text stand out
as I have never heard them before. The final apostrophe to the
head of Jokanaan is magnificent. But this is not altogether
Goltz's show, for Patzak presents a consummate Herod. If Goltz's
diction is admirable, his is superb. Every word he sings stands
out as if spoken by a great actor (it must be admitted Strauss made
this easier for him than it could ever be for the soprano). His ca-
joling speech before Herod finally breaks down and grants Salome's request calls for further superlatives. Braun's Jokanaan
has dignity to afford relief in the tension of the psychopathic
drama; if some of his high tones are not too easily produced, this
is somehow in keeping with the character. A special word is due
Dermota, whose Narraboth is as complete a delineation as those
of the principals. Kenney, as Herodias, is acceptable, if not up
to this standard. When all is over, she has left little impression.
The smaller parts are taken mostly by singers thoroughly familiar
to record-buyers in this country, artists often cast in stellar roles.
And through it all, the orchestra plays with a splendor neither
earlier recording in any way approaches. This is, after all,
Krauss's performance. Only one small criticism seems in order:
the break before the last side occurs at the tense moment when

Herod is about to give way to Salome; something is lost by the necessary pause.

The Columbia recording is by no means so beautifully balanced as the London, though it remains a good job. Wegner's voice sounds smaller and less intense than Goltz's, and she is less genuinely at home in the part of Salome (I understand the recording was her debut in it). Her tone has a curious way of thinning out in the upper reaches. It must be conceded, however, that her intonation is more secure than her rival's. The Herod is admirable until we have heard Patzak's, and the Jokanaan is good and solid, though he sets no standards for breadth of utterance. The Herodias is light-weight; she does not have enough tone for the climaxes. To make Jokanaan sound sufficiently sepulchral, he seems actually to have been put in a cistern or a sounding-chamber. There is some unevenness in the reproduction, and the voices are certainly too prominent.

At the time of Ljuba Welitch's debut at the Metropolitan, she and Fritz Reiner (who made his bow the same evening) made a recording of the finale (C ML 4795). Much of the excitement of the great occasion has thus been preserved. One regrets that the entire opera was not recorded or, at least, that Herod's final disgusted speech was omitted. A more surprising performance was left us by the late Maria Cebotari, under the direction of Arthur Rother (U URLP 7036). The soprano had no trouble encompassing the wide range of the music, but hers was essentially a lighter voice, less suggestive in quality than that of Welitch or Goltz. She was spaciously recorded. There is a curious orchestral concert ending to the scene.

Aria

*Ariadne auf Naxos—Zerbinetta's Recitative and Aria. Hollweg, s; LSO, Krips, 10" L LPS 250 (*Mozart: Arias).*

This is the first recording, I believe, of the incomparably taxing coloratura aria in the original unsimplified version. It is carried off with diabolical glee; the voice is really exciting.

Songs

*Six Songs on Poems by Clemens Brentano, opus 68. Berger, s; Raucheisen, pf, D DL 9666 (*Brahms: Songs).*

This cycle is something of a specialty with Erna Berger. Few singers, indeed, could attempt to compete with her in singing it. The flashes of coloratura recall Maria Ivogün. The songs are tremendously long and elaborate, and it may be charged that they rove beyond the proper limits of the lied. Still, if a singer can carry off the showy passages of the second song, then sustain the elevated, very Straussian mood of the third, the listener is not likely to be bothered with considerations of formal propriety. Certainly Erna Berger has recorded nothing finer than her singing of these songs.

*Morgen; Ständchen; Traum durch die Dämmerung; Zueignung; Freundliche Vision. Danco, s; Agosti, pf, 10″ L LS 699 (*Mozart: Songs).*

Danco, as always, is the complete musician; her singing of the quieter songs has admirable poise and reserve. She does not leave the beaten track in her repertoire, but treats the songs to an unusual display of sheer effective vocalism.

Hat gesagt—bleibt's nicht dabei; Ach Lieb', ich muss nun scheiden; Die Nacht; Schlagende Herzen; Schlechtes Wetter; Einerlei; Morgen. Felbermayer, s; Graef, pf. Winterliebe; Ruhe, meine Seele; Waldseligkeit; Das Rosenband; Im Spätboot; Nichts; Traum durch die Dämmerung; Mein Herz ist stumm. Poell, b; Graef, pf. Van VRS 431.

Here is a program well balanced between the familiar and the virtually unknown Strauss. Anny Felbermayer, according to the jacket notes aged twenty-four when the recording was made, has a meltingly lyrical voice and the right simple approach for lieder singing. If the gift of penetrating humor could be added to her assets, she might well be spoken of as a logical successor to the late Elisabeth Schumann. Perhaps her best efforts are *"Ach Lieb', ich muss nun scheiden,"* and the exuberant *"Schlagende Herzen"*; I am grateful, too, for her unsentimental treatment of the often abused *"Morgen"* and for the unexaggerated flexibility of her *"Heimkehr."* Dr. Poell, who might be to Schlusnus what Felbermayer is to Schumann, is always the intelligent artist, though occasionally a high note taxes him noticeably or a lower one finds him a little insecure. His *"Ruhe, meine Seele"* has weight and authority, and the rhapsodic *"Waldseligkeit"* comes off brilliantly.

Breit über mein Haupt dein schwarzes Haar; Allerseelen; Zueignung; Cäcilie; Pilgers Morgenlied; Hymnus. Janssen, b; Mayer, pf; Taubman, pf; O, 10″ Et ELP 491.

This collection is made up of previously unavailable recordings, some apparently taken from broadcasts. The recording quality is inevitably variable both as regards the voice itself and as to general acoustics, which suggest the old-fashioned "studio take." Most unusual, and in all respects most valuable, are the two big orchestral songs on the second side of the disc, which allow the singer's voice to spread itself.

Four Last Songs; Arabella—Aber der Richtige; Das war sehr gut, Mandryka. Della Casa, s; Gueden, s; Poell, b; VPH, Moralt, L LL 856. Four Last Songs; Capriccio—Closing Scene. Schwarzkopf, s; PHI, Ackermann, An 35084.

Capriccio, along with the four last songs, constitutes Strauss's farewell to the music of the human voice. The combination on the Schwarzkopf disc is, therefore, particularly felicitous. The singing is tonally lovely, and splendidly poised, recorded with beautiful clarity. If this singer has a fault, it is a tendency to sing "inwardly." This is noticeable more in the songs than in the finely sustained projection of the *Capriccio* scene. Of the many lovely and moving details, I would single out the horn passages, as at the words *"Langsam tut er die müdgeworden Augen zu,"* in *"September."* In the final song—*"Im Abendroth"*—the soprano recalls rather strangely the voice of the late Elisabeth Schumann. Lovely as Schwarzkopf's singing is, that of Della Casa is more so; she climbs to the higher reaches with greater buoyancy; whereas Schwarzkopf seems at times to be holding in, Della Casa gives the impression of masterful reserve. Though Angel's recording is richer and brighter than London's, I find myself preferring the Della Casa version. The *Arabella* selections, in which the soprano is joined by Gueden and Poell, are altogether lovely. Not since the original recording of some of this music by Marta Fuchs, Elsa Wieber, and Paul Schoeffler has this captivating music been so ravishingly sung.

Melodrama

Enoch Arden, opus 38. Rhodes, narrator; Manley, pf, NR NRLP 501 [2]. (*Liszt: Consolations).

It is curious to hear this melodrama with Strauss's music, though there is some question how often one will want to repeat the experience. Curious, too, is the fact that the composer left long stretches of Tennyson's poem unaccompanied. The emphasis, we note, is definitely on the poem. The speaker does his part with dignity and without undue parade; the pianist scores his points, such as they are.

STRAVINSKY, IGOR (1882-   )

Choral Works, etc.

Cantata on Anonymous 15th- and 16th-Century English Lyrics. Tourel, m-s; Cuenod, t; Concert Ch; PHC, Stravinsky, C ML 4899 (*Symphony in C).

> Stravinsky tells us he composed this cantata after completing *The Rake's Progress*, having become fascinated by the problems of setting English poetry to music. One wishes he had gone into more detail as to his distinctly individual view of these problems. His writing for the voice is never "grateful," avoiding, apparently quite carefully, two of the chief attributes of vocal music: melodic curve and color. Tourel and Cuenod perform with great precision, holding their own as parts of the ensemble, though their task is not easy. If their vocalism is on a straight line, so is the music it fits. And if their phrasing is not always just what the text seems to call for, this is not to be laid to the singers' charge. The Concert Choir is equally successful with the *Lyke-Wake Dirge*, which serves as introduction, interlude, and postlude.

Symphonie des Psaumes. RDFC; National O, Horenstein, An 35101 (*Strauss: Metamorphosen). LPC & O, Ansermet, L LL 889 (*L'Oiseau de feu—Suite). CBSC & O, Stravinsky, C ML 4129 (*Symphony in Three Movements). RIASCC & O; St Hedwig's Cath Ch, Fricsay, 10" D DL 7526.

> The composer's reading is notably clear and precise, alive and exciting. As always, he strives for a dry, crisp sound. He is, however, not so well recorded as Horenstein and Ansermet. The latter goes in for a good deal more shading and polish, and is given roomy reproduction. Somewhere between his point of view and Stravinsky's is that of Horenstein, who is even better recorded. Fricsay's playing is careful, not altogether convincing; it lacks the drive and purposefulness of the composer's, as well as the poise and finish of the other two. The safest choice is Horenstein.

Operas, etc.

Mavra. Curtin, s; Warren, c; Carmine, c; Harmon, t; NY Wind Ens & O, Craft, Dia 12.

> One hesitates to pronounce too positively on this performance,

which presumably was made with the composer's approbation, and certainly is by a conductor who has a reputation as a Stravinsky interpreter. The singers, too, are well-known and able. But whether the English translation gets in the way of the very Russian music or whether Craft falls short of true grasp of the piece, the results are only moderately invigorating.

*Les Noces. Steingruber, s; Kenney, m-s; Wagner, t; Waechter, bs; VKC; Ens, Rossi, Van VRS 452 (*L'Histoire du Soldat).*

Les Noces; Mass; Pater Noster; Ave Maria. Addison, s; Okerson, c; Price, t; Burrows, b; Concert Ch; O, Hillis, Vox PL 8630.

A group of proficient singers from Vienna presents the colorful vocal ballet in the original Russian, while the American artists sing the work in English. The Viennese performance is somewhat more relaxed and more richly recorded. Surely little is lost to the English-speaking listener, as not much of the other generally admirable presentation comes through in the words. It is amusing that the annotator introducing this mixed-voice performance of the Mass should tell us Stravinsky himself prefers an all-male choir. Failing this requirement, he should be satisfied with this presentation.

Oedipus Rex. Mödl, m-s; Pears, t; Rehfuss, b; Cocteau, speaker; etc.; Cologne Radio SO, Stravinsky, C ML 4644.

This is a composite recording, for the musical portions were taped in Cologne in October 1951, and Cocteau's speeches added some eight months later in Paris. The poet speaks in French, while the language of his tragedy is Latin. The recorded sound is powerful, with the voices rather in the lead; there is not much room-resonance, but a very clean and well-defined tone. At one spot the music fades momentarily, but this is quickly past. Outstanding among the singers is Martha Mödl, at the time of recording in the transition stages between contralto and soprano; the music does not tax her, and the rich opulence of her tones carries the weight of eloquent expressiveness. Pears displays his musicianship in a new light; his delivery of the text is more remarkable than the voice itself.

Pulcinella. Simmons, s; Schnittke, t; MacGregor, bs; Cleveland O, Stravinsky, C ML 4830.

This is the first complete performance of the Pergolesi-inspired score, the first, indeed, to include the vocal parts. The songs interspersed throughout the ballet are mostly straight Pergolesi with a dash of Stravinsky, just enough to make them amusing. The performances by the singers are no more than acceptable, especially that of the tenor. Still, it is pleasant to hear the familiar *"Se tu m'ami"* in this strange context. Orchestrally, the performance is good.

The Rake's Progress. Gueden, s; Thebom, m-s; Lipton, c; Conley, t; Harrell, b; Scott, bs; etc.; MOC & O, Stravinsky, C SL 125 [3].

The Metropolitan production, put on under the composer's eyes, was taken over by him for recording, which would seem to guarantee authenticity. For those who take to the opera, it is hard to imagine what could be left to desire. Gueden, given a role perhaps intended to have more tenderness than comes through in the music, does all that can be done with appealing lyricism and melting tone, though she has trouble making herself understood in English—a fact I blame on Stravinsky rather than on the singer. Conley is vocally strong and pleasant, if not very subtle—perhaps he too has been given less than an even break by the composer. The three characters whose words are most naturally set happen to be impersonated by the three singers with the best diction; and so to a larger extent than was probably intended, the performance belongs to Harrell, Thebom, and Paul Franke. Thebom, to be sure, would hardly be recognized as the possessor of much vocal beauty, but what she does is in the spirit of the opera. Technically, the set is admirable.

*Renard. Hess, t; Harmon, t; Galjour, b; Lishner, bs; O, Craft, Dia 10 (*Suite No. 1, for Orchestra; Song of the Volga Boatmen; Elegy for Viola Alone; Berceuse du chat).*

Though this performance of the little known opera-ballet would seem to be something of a triumph for all concerned, and certainly is in all ways more successful than the *Mavra* recording, it too suffers from translation trouble. Even in the mouths of such experts as these singers, this text would never convince the listener that the music could have been written to match it. The reproduction is very clear and bright. Among the miscellany on the reverse of the disc is one song, quite beautifully sung in Russian by Arline Carmine: *"The Cat's Lullaby."*

Songs

Spring; Pastorale; A song of the dew; Forget-me-not; The dove; Akahito; Makatsumi; Tsaraiuki; Tilim-boum; Ducks, swans, geese; The bear; The cat's lullabies; The drake; Toasting Song; The sparrow; The dissident; Mavra—Song of Parasha. Kurenko, s; S. Stravinsky, pf, All AL 64.

Stravinsky's songs present a lesser facet of his art, but they can be effective, as Kurenko has often demonstrated in her recitals. Such a program as this, however, is perhaps best heard in installments, as the expressive range is limited and the admirable singer's voice has not been too well recorded. The balance and the piano tone could be better.

SULLIVAN, SIR ARTHUR SEYMOUR (1842-1900)

The Mikado. Bennett, s; Curtis, c; Oldham, t; Fancourt, b; Green, b; etc.; Ch & O, Godfrey, V LCT 6009 [2].
H.M.S. Pinafore. Lewis, s; Baker, b; Robertson, b; Fancourt, b; D'Oyly Carte Op Ch & O, Sargent. Trial by Jury. Lawson, s; Oldham, t; Baker, b; Sheffield, b; etc.; D'Oyly Carte O, Sargent. V LCT 6008 [2].
The Pirates of Penzance. Harding, s; Osborn, t; Green, b; Fancourt, b; etc.; D'Oyly Carte Op Ch & O, Godfrey, L LLP 80/1 [2].

The sample of the new recordings by the authorized company has not the spirit that went into the mementos of the thirties. The voices in the company, generally speaking, could always have been more sumptuous, and, of course, modern recording can do more in the way of atmosphere, but in the old *Mikado, Pinafore,* and *Trial by Jury* Gilbert's priceless lines come through with stunning freshness; there is, however, no dialogue. Mechanically, *Mikado* is the better of the two sets, as it was a remake after the original series had been completed. The postwar *Pirates* shows a decline in singing, despite the excellent diction of all concerned. Only Martyn Green as the Major General is altogether satisfactory. The recording is spotty.

Selections

Mikado—I've got a little list; Trial by Jury—The Judge's Song; Pirates of Penzance—A modern Major General; Mikado—Willow, tit willow; Iolanthe—Nightmare Song; Mikado—The flowers that bloom in the spring; H.M.S. Pinafore—When I was a lad; Yeomen of the Guard —I've jibe and joke; Mikado—There is beauty in the bellow of the blast; Princess Ida—If you give me your attention; Whene'er I spoke; Yeomen of the Guard—I have a song to sing; Patience—Am I alone?;

Iolanthe—When I went to the bar; The law is the true embodiment; Yeomen of the Guard—Oh! a private buffoon. Green, b; COLC & O, Engel, C ML 4643.

Martyn Green, assisted where needed by members of the "opera company," here gives us a cross-section of his famous roles, singing all with superb diction, rhythm, style, and no voice. He is able to make a separate character of each he represents; all, of course, are presented with verve.

SUPPÉ, FRANZ VON (1819-1895)

Boccaccio—Highlights. Roon, s; Hermann, c; Kmentt, t; Berry, bs; etc.; Vienna Volksoper Ch; VSO, Paulik, C ML 4818.

Boccaccio is consistently melodious and grateful to the singers. The outstanding air, "*Hab' ich nur deine Liebe*," is one of those unforgettable things, and an infectious string of waltzes played by the orchestra in the last band of the present disc can hardly fail to win new friends. This is a de-luxe performance, with singers who can not only maintain a musical line, but make the words count as they do it.

TCHAIKOVSKY, PETER ILICH (1840-1893)

Operas

Eugene Onegin. Kruglikova, s; Antonova, s; Kozlovsky, t; Norzoff, b; etc.; BSIC & O, Orlov or Melik-Pashayev, Col CRLP 127/8/9 [3].
Eugene Onegin—Letter Scene. Welitch, s; PHI, Susskind, C ML 4795 (*R.Strauss: Salome; Puccini: Tosca; J.Strauss: Fledermaus, Zigeunerbaron).

The "complete" performance was available in this country even before the days of LP. Russian techniques have improved considerably since then, so that it cannot even be described as one of the better Soviet products. Its first appearance on LP was by way of Period (SPLP 507). Colosseum has been able to brighten up the dull reproduction to some extent, but nothing has been done to correct the speed, with resulting high pitch and added vocal shrillness. Under the circumstances it is not fair to judge the singers too critically; they are obviously competent and seasoned artists. But the big scenes, such as the *Polonaise*, are messy and unclear, the solo ensembles like so many catfights. But if it is

Onegin we want, this will have to be it. Welitch's German version of the *"Letter Scene"* dates from about the time of her American debut and catches her at her very best. The temperament of the artist and the glowing tone she brings to the impassioned music are ably seconded by conductor and orchestra. The recording is still very good.

Mazeppa. Pokovskaya, s; Davidova, m-s; Bolshkov, t; Ivanov, b; Petrov, bs; etc.; BSIC & O, Lukovnikov, CH CHS 1310 [3].

This is an excellent performance by present-day Russian standards. The voices, especially those of the men, are sturdy and well-modulated, Ivanov in the title role doing especially stylish and expressive singing. Pokovskaya, the leading lady, is over-vibrant at the start, and one fears her tremolo may become excessive. On the contrary, however, she ends in better form, making a good effect with the final cradle song. All this is heard through recording that may most charitably be described as uneven. There is plenty of power, and at times the sound is reasonably clear, but refinement is not a characteristic, and there is considerable variation from one side to the next.

Pique Dame. Smolenskaya, s; Verbitzkaya, m-s; Nelepp, t; Ivanov, b; etc.; BSIC & O, Melik-Pashayev, CH CHS 1305 [3]. *Djerzhinskaya, s; Zlatogorova, c; Hanaiev, t; Baturin, b; etc.; BSIC & O, Samosud, Col CRLP 130/1/2/3* [4]. *(In German) Grümmer, s; Klose, c; Schock, t; Prohaska, b; etc.; BCOC; RBO, Rother, U URLP 207* [2].

The most recent of these three performances is incomparably the best, musically and mechanically. The German recording is considerably abridged and thoroughly Teutonic; the well-known singers in its cast unquestionably have finer voices than their Russian counterparts, but have been badly treated by the engineers. Klose's noble contralto is no match, characterwise, for either of the Russian Countesses, partly because the recording creates no illusion for her. Only in the Concert Hall version do we get a real *pianissimo* as the old aristocrat sings the little Grétry air, one of the tremendous moments in Russian opera. Something similar can be said of every character and every scene in the score. Only the Concert Hall recording is smooth and refined enough to do Tchaikovski anything like justice. Nelepp, a more virile tenor than many from his land, gains in vocal control as the opera progresses, ending up impressively; the baritone Ivanov makes a healthy Tomsky. Smolenskaya as Lisa shows ample power; her tone is vibrant but focused. Though some of the ensembles are not free from a suggestion of confusion, the singing of the entire cast is well above average.

Songs

Warum?; Es war auf dem Balle; Warum sind die Rosen so blass; Wiegenlied; Ob heller Tag. Lichtegg, t; Haeusslin, pf, 10" Cap LS 799 (*Mendelssohn: Songs).

The singer's *métier* is musical comedy; he is not the most subtly insinuating of lieder singers. His tone is good, however, and he enunciates with great clarity. It is all just a little obvious.

Romeo and Juliet. Fenn, s; Manton, t; Los Angeles O, Waxman, Cap P 8189 (*Gounod: Roméo et Juliette—Non, ce n'est pas le jour).

This long duet is Taneyev's completion of sketches left by the composer, using thematic material from the famous Overture-Fantasy. It has been recorded once before, by two popular Soviet singers (Griffon 1002, withdrawn). The present restrained and tonally pleasing presentation in French is better supported by a better-sounding orchestra.

TELEMANN, GEORG PHILIPP (1681-1767)

Pimpinone. Fuchs, s; Lassner, b; Salzburg Str Qt; Sternberg, hpschd, Oc OCS 27.

This little intermezzo (otherwise known as *Die unglückliche Heirat*) shows Bach's more famous contemporary is an unfamiliar and amusing light, but the performance sets no standards. The soprano hardly rises above the amateur class.

Ihr Völker hört (Cantata No.1, in G). Hennecke, c; Ens, 10" D DL 7542 (*Handel: Della guerra amorosa).

Hennecke displays a clean, attractive voice, a little on the heavy side, especially after we listen to the agile bass in the Handel cantata overdisc. The recording is good.

THOMAS, AMBROISE (1811-1896)

Hamlet—Mad Scene. Robin, s; PCO, Blareau, 10" L LPS 676 (*Donizetti: Lucia—Mad Scene).

This scene can be made dramatic by sheer vocal brilliance, as Melba proved long ago in her various recordings of it. Robin, who is said to sing higher than any other present-day soprano, is not yet prepared to carry on in the old tradition.

Mignon. Micheau, s; Moizan, m-s; de Luca, t; Bianco, b; etc.; La Monnaie Ch; Brussels O Nat de Belge, Sebastian, L LLA 15 [3].

Mignon requires a better than adequate performance, for as a drama it is preposterous, and even the "hit" songs are not too easy to sing. I wonder if part of the trouble may not be that the heroine, who is nothing at all if not sweetly innocent, is usually impersonated by a mezzo or a contralto, a voice suggesting maturity altogether out of character. This newest presentation does not escape such pitfalls. Moizan has a handsome voice and understands the proper style, yet she never for a moment makes us feel what manner of girl Mignon was supposed to be. Still her singing of *"Connais-tu le pays?"* is genuinely beautiful, especially the words *"C'est là"* in the second stanza. Micheau, a charming lyric singer, seems strangely cast as the brilliant Philine, for she has neither the technique nor the upper voice to dazzle in such a piece as the *Polonaise*. De Luca does some admirable singing, and some uneven: *"Adieu, Mignon"* starts beautifully but does not sustain, and again in *"Elle ne croyait pas"* he falls short. Bianco as Lotharic reveals a rather hoarse high voice, well enough in character. The rest are adequate. The overture gives promise of exceptional recording, but this is not altogether realized. Much of the singing is too close, the ensembles in particular lacking the desired aura. The crowd and stage noises are generally good. The contralto role of Frédéric is made more credible by the tenor voice.

A set of Highlights from the thirties has been reissued, featuring Germaine Cernay, André d'Arkor, and M. Demoulin (C RL 3093). There is little continuity, and though the cast includes a Philine (Lucienne Tragin), the *Polonaise* is omitted. Nor is there any overture. Not an exciting production, it is at least authentically French. There are times when the recording belies its years.

THOMPSON, RANDALL (1899-)

The Testament of Freedom. Eastman Rochester Ch & O, Hanson, Mer MG 40000 (*Hanson: Songs from Drum Beats).

The reputation of this stirring setting of selections from the patriotic writings of Thomas Jefferson was helped in the prewar years by a monumental recording enlisting the Harvard Glee Club and the Boston Symphony Orchestra under Koussevitzky. Sensational as that performance was in its day, Hanson has matched it in terms of High Fidelity. It would seem that little more could be said in this music.

THOMSON, VIRGIL (1896-   )

Four Saints in Three Acts (Abridged). Robinson-Wayne, s; Matthews, s; Holland, t; Matthews, b; etc.; Ch & O, Thomson, V LCT 1139.

Though the recording was made some fourteen years after the original production, the "creators' cast" was kept practically intact; most of these singers have taken part in almost every revival the opera has had. With the recent tragic death of the St. Ignatius, Edward Matthews, an important figure must be missing from any future production. The recording appeared in 1948, shortly before the development of LP, which may account, among other things, for the fact that the score is abridged. That the composer, and not Alexander Smallens, who first conducted the work, is at the podium, changes surprisingly little and adds a special note of interest. The transfer to LP is very successful.

Stabat Mater. Tourel, m-s; New Music Str Qt. Capital, Capitals. Male Qt; Thomson, C ML 4491 (*Harrison: Two Suites).

Jennie Tourel brings to the moving Max Jacobs setting all the penetrating musicianship and warm vocalism for which she is noted. *Capital, Capitals*, on a text by Gertrude Stein, is tossed off with amazing virtuosity by a quartet of male voices.

TOCH, ERNST (1887-   )

The Chinese Flute. Mock, s; Pacific Symphonette, Compinsky, Alc Y 1006.

The Chinese Flute, "a series of mood pictures inspired by ancient Chinese poems treated, as it were, in tender pastoral colors," dates from 1923. It is not a series of songs, but of instrumental pieces in which the voice serves as a part of the ensemble. The fact that the voice in the present performance, tasteful and musical as it is, is of modest proportions and hardly notable for "bite" is not necessarily a flaw, except that it effectively minimizes the significance of the poems. Alice Mock easily tosses off the more florid passages of her part; but as it was considered worth while to translate the texts into English, it seems not unreasonable to expect more conviction in their delivery. The whole ensemble is magnified in reproduction, not a bad way to have it in this type of music. The details of scoring and of contrapuntal lines are well brought out.

VAUGHAN WILLIAMS, RALPH (1872-   )

Mass in G minor. FSC, Lawrence, L LL 805 (*Rubbra: Mass).

This important modern Mass was recorded some years ago by the same choir; this replacement was among the last works of T. B. Lawrence, who died during the recording of the companion Mass by Vaughan Williams's pupil Rubbra. There is something a little strange and difficult to account for in the acoustics of this disc. One wonders in what sort of hall it was made, and whether the microphones were not placed a little too close to the singers.

Five Mystical Songs. Ronk, b; Schaefer, org, Den DR 2 (*Buxtehude: Cantata, Chorale Prelude).

This is the kind of performance one might happen on almost any Sunday in a music-minded church, or at least at some kind of special service. It is good to have an example of this side of Vaughan Williams's genius, but that one would want to repeat such a recording very often is unlikely.

Five Tudor Portraits. Rankin, m-s; Anderson, bs; Pittsburgh Mendelssohn Ch; PSO, Steinberg, Cap P 8218.

This hearty, and at times malicious, music is set to poems of John Skelton (1460-1529), Poet Laureate of England. The spirited performance, made at the first Pittsburgh International Contemporary Music Festival, catches a great deal of the unction of both words and music. It is heartily recommended.

VECCHI, ORAZIO (1550-1605)

L'Amfiparnasso. Lecco Acad Ch, Camillucci, Cet 50066.

This performance was prepared in 1950 to celebrate the composer's 400th birthday. Obviously a good deal of care and thought went into it. Every student of musical history knows the name of Vecchi and of his comedy-in-madrigals; we are fortunate that so good a realization of the work as this has been preserved for us. The reproduction varies from slightly cloudy at the outset to clear at the end.

VERDI, GIUSEPPE (1813-1901)

Choral Works

Quattro Pezzi Sacri. Aachen Cath Ch; Aachen O, Rehmann, D DL 9661. VKC; VSO, Swoboda, CH CHS 1136.
Stabat Mater only. BAVRC & O, Kugler, 10" Mer MG 15011 (*Brahms: Choruses).

Of the two complete recordings of Verdi's last four works, that of the Aachen choir is the more sensitive, though it is the less impressive in matters of sheer sound. The recording was made at a rather low level, and, possibly because of the cathedral acoustics, the tone is somewhat diffused. The curious *Ave Maria*, based on an "enigmatic scale" which is sung as a *cantus firmus* by the various voices in turn, is clear and even in sound, though somewhat removed. The other three pieces are increasingly better, building up to a really impressive *Te Deum*. If one is inclined to mix one of these pieces with some rather slipshod Brahms, the performance of the Bavarian Choir in the Verdi is reasonably satisfactory. What the recording lacks in atmosphere and perspective is made up by an impression of dedication.

Requiem. Nelli, s; Barbieri, m-s; di Stefano, t; Siepi, bs; SC; NBC, Toscanini, V LM 6018 [2]. Caniglia, s; Stignani, m-s; Gigli, t; Pinza, bs; ROC & O, Serafin, V LCT 6003 [2].

The Toscanini recording is his broadcast of January 27, 1951. We must accept certain inequalities and more than the usual quota of coughs along with the music. The fault in the balance is an error in the right direction; for once the orchestra is not dominated by the singers, but rather covers them at times. The instrumental detail is at some points almost too much. But it is good to note that the Maestro, for one, has regard for Verdi's frequent expression and dynamic markings, though in the finished product four *p*'s do not always spell the extreme of softness. The orchestral opening, however, is so delicate that there is some danger that the controls may be set too high, which will cause a shock at "*Te decet hymnus.*" The soloists are unusually eloquent; if ever they feel the urge to overdo expressiveness, they overcome it most admirably. Nelli easily tops the chorus with her high C's, and for once the crucial unaccompanied *"Requiem"* solo with chorus is controlled and in tune. Barbieri has the temperament and the vivid vocal color to make her part effective, and Di Stefano combines the desired lyrical quality with plenty of power. Siepi has rarely sung with such dignity. But the chorus carries the chief honors. The *"Sanctus"* touches greatness, and the magnificent fugue on *"Libera me"* is enormously exciting.

Serafin's recording has long been famous for its all-star cast, though I must confess I have never been one of its admirers. Of the quartet, only Pinza maintains any sort of dignity; the others are in effect so many unbridled operatic temperaments, each out to make the most of the drama in Verdi's music. The standards of intonation are hardly a cause for rejoicing, and the aforementioned expression marks might as well never have been written into the score. A more modern recording, made in Rome under the baton of Luigi Ricci (U URLP 213 [2]), merits the same criticism. The soloists, who share the vices of their more celebrated colleagues, do not, alas, rival their beautiful voices.

Two last-minute arrivals change the picture somewhat. Fricsay, leading the RIAS Symphony Orchestra with St. Hedwig's Choir and a quartet consisting of Stader, Radev, Krebs, and Kim Borg, gives the most reverent and refined performance on records (D DX 118 [2])—rivaled in my experience only by the masterly reading of Bruno Walter at the Metropolitan Opera several seasons ago. Reverent and refined as it is, this performance has plenty of excitement; the *"Dies irae"* does not lose its power to raise gooseflesh. The *"Sanctus"* is the fastest imaginable—Toscanini's seems tame in comparison—and the *"Libera me"* fugue is taken at a terrific pace. The quartet is unusually well balanced; each member improves his dramatic opportunities. Krebs's meditative *"Ingemisco"* is an example of the fresh approach of these artists to the familiar work. De Sabata, working with the forces of La Scala, Schwarzkopf, Dominguez, Di Stefano, and Siepi (An 3520-B [2]) combines genuine Italian temperament (missing, for better or for worse, in Fricsay) with clean musicianship and vital, well-balanced reproduction. In this performance, as in Fricsay's, Verdi's indications as to expression and dynamics are respected, though the singers are allowed to spread themselves within the bounds of good taste. The most is made of the dramatic choral movements. The two male soloists appear also in the Toscanini performance; the contrast between their work under different conductors is most revealing. Both were in fresher voice when the Toscanini broadcast took place, yet they sing here in a more relaxed manner, more as though expressing themselves. In matters of intonation, perhaps, they do not always meet the Toscanini standard. Schwarzkopf, like Stader, lacks the characteristic Italian chest tones that seem to be indicated for the *"Libera me,"* but she sings more dramatically than the Swiss soprano. Her treatment of the perilous *"Requiem"* with chorus is almost awesomely reserved, yet it is indescribably lovely in tone and squarely on pitch. The octaves she sings with Dominguez in the *"Agnus Dei"* are the most nearly perfect I have heard. It would be impossible to make a clean-cut choice among the three modern *Requiem* recordings, each so masterly in its own way.

Operas

Aïda. Tebaldi, s; Stignani, m-s; Del Monaco, t; Protti, b; etc.; SCC & O, Erede, L LLA 13 [3]. Mancini, s; Simionato, m-s; Filippeschi, t; Panerai, b; Neri, bs; etc.; RIC & O, Gui, Cet 1228 [3]. Arangi-Lombardi, s; Capuano, m-s; Lindi, t; Borgioli, b; Pasero, bs; Baccaloni, bs; etc.; SCAC; MISO, Molajoli, C EL 3 [3]. Caniglia, s; Stignani, m-s; Gigli, t; Bechi, b; Pasero, bs; Tajo, bs; etc.; ROC & O, Serafin, V LCT 6400 [4].

Of all the complete *Aïdas* yet made, the most exciting was the early electrical Victor set featuring Dusolina Giannini in a performance she herself never matched in my experience, and Aureliano Pertile, at his best an outstanding tenor. Possibly the old recording has offered insurmountable obstacles to LP transfer; in any case it is a collectors' item today. Columbia's set, more or less contemporary with it, featuring Arangi-Lombardi and Lindi, is again available as noted above, and has many votaries. It is a strongly temperamental performance, not very even vocally, rather constricted in reproduced sound.

By far the best of the modern sets is London's, for it has not only Tebaldi most nearly approaching Giannini, but also recording of refinement and power. Tonally, Del Monaco sounds less well than I have sometimes heard him in the opera house, and he is no more successful than usual in modulating his big, lusty voice. The vivid Stignani is not consistently at her best vocally; Protti proves himself a good, dependable Italian baritone. Generally speaking, the pacing is good, though at times Del Monaco seems rushed. The only serious rival to this performance is the Cetra, with Mancini at her by-no-means-consistent best an excellent Aïda, Simionato a disappointing Amneris, and an otherwise serviceable cast stronger in temperament than in disciplined vocalism. I do not find much to admire in the star-studded Victor performance led by Serafin. I discern no sensuous appeal in Caniglia's voice as here revealed; both she and Gigli sing pretty much on a dead level throughout. Stignani and Bechi are better in this respect, but neither deserves a medal for subtle vocalism. Serafin seems unable to lift the performance, and the engineers appear to have conspired with the singers to drown out the orchestra. New York's City Center Opera Company has been drawn on for a single-sided recording of Highlights, coupled with a similar condensation of *Faust* (MGM E 3023). The cast is promisingly talented; there is still some rawness in Camilla Williams's often lovely singing of the title role and in Gari's ample tenor tones. Ibarrondo makes a convincing Amneris, and Winters displays a good strong baritone voice. Among the historical offerings, Victor presents *"Aïda of Yesterday"* (LCT 1035). Gigli's *"Celeste Aïda"* is borrowed from the Serafin performance; other recordings reach back as far as the 1910 *Judgment Chamber Scene* with Louise Homer and Caruso. Most of the recordings thus revived are classics, but it would have been wiser not to mix recording periods to this extent. Two sets of Highlights might easily have been assembled: Gadski, Homer, Caruso, and Amato made enough excellent sides to fill an LP disc. Indeed, in the present selection Gadski and Amato are represented by just one half of their *Nile Scene* recording. An electrically recorded collection might include the entire *Nile Scene* with Rethberg, Lauri-Volpi, and De Luca. One special attraction of the present program is the rare Ponselle-Martinelli duet from this scene.

Un Ballo in Maschera. Caniglia, s; Barbieri, m-s; Gigli, t; Bechi, b; etc.; ROC & O, Serafin, V LCT 6007 [2]. *Semser, s; Kerol, t; Borthayre, b; etc.; PPC & O, Leibowitz, Ren SX 207* [3].

The choice here is between an all-star Italian cast recorded several years back under a conductor to the manor born and a modern recording of an excursion into Italian by a group of competent French artists. The firm hand of Serafin molds a consistent performance for Victor, if perhaps a somewhat slick one, and Gigli is in his best form, though some of the others are a little below theirs. To hear the French performance after this one is to realize the importance of authentic style, even when a little below par.

La Battaglia di Legnano. Mancini, s; Berdini, t; Panerai, b; etc.; RIC & O, Previtali, Cet 1220 [3].

A cast of by now thoroughly familiar Italian singers gives a vital account of this thoroughly unfamiliar early score. Mancini is at her best in the role of Lida. Her voice floats nobly over the chorus in the very Verdian "Prayer."

Don Carlo. Caniglia, s; Stignani, m-s; Picchi, t; Silveri, b; Rossi-Lemeni, bs; Neri, bs; etc.; RIC & O, Previtali, Cet 1234 [4]. (Highlights) Thebom, m-s; Bjoerling, t; Merrill, b; Tajo, bs; RCAO, Cellini, Morel, V LM 1128.

Caniglia shines her brightest in the sometimes splendid complete performance, though her vivid Italian temperament leads her on occasion to play fast and loose with the pitch. Stignani is heavy in her "*Canzone del Velo,*" but superb in "*O don fatale.*" Picchi displays a fresh, strong voice, equal to most, if not all, of Verdi's demands; Silveri is, as usual, competent, and Rossi-Lemeni powerful after the manner of Chaliapin. Neri's Grand Inquisitor is tremendous. There are some insignificant cuts, and the recording balance is not altogether even. Victor's Highlights set memorializes all too briefly the fine achievement of Bing's first production at the Metropolitan (though, to be sure, Thebom joined the cast after the first performance, and Tajo had left the company before the presentation). The best singing is provided by the mezzo, who brings exceptional lightness to the "*Canzone del Velo,*" and, despite some difficulty with the highest notes, manages "*O don fatale*" only less magnificently than Stignani. Bjoerling and Merrill are at their best, but Tajo tends to overdramatize King Philip's great soliloquy. This is a performance without a heroine: the loveliest moment in the score is missing: Elisabetta's "*Tu che le vanità.*" For a single highlight, Raphaël Arie may be heard in "*Ella giammai m'amò*" (10" L LD 9018), giving a good substantial characterization of the unhappy King, somewhat muffled in reproduction. If one can accept Verdi in

German, Martha Mödl's *"O don fatale"* has much to commend it
(10" Tel TM 68009).

*Ernani. Mancini, s; Penno, t; Taddei, b; Vaghi, bs; etc.; RIC & O,
Previtali, Cet 1210* [3].

Even in the not too distant days when *Ernani* was part of the
domestic repertoire, we rarely heard it satisfactorily because of
that intangible called performing style. For that reason, if for no
other, we should be grateful that this set is as good as it is. The
cast is headed by Mancini, an almost Ponselle-like soprano (of
course, some immaturity is implied in that "almost"); Penno, a
good robust tenor; and Giuseppe Taddei, who proves that he can
do the old-style recitative and *cantilena* as well as the music of
Falstaff and Gianni Schicchi. Only in his big third-act aria did I
feel some disappointment in his failure to make the scene as
lyrical as some older baritones have done. The weakest principal
is Vaghi. It is good to hear Verdi's orchestra and chorus in good
balance and unusually clear and clean in the spacious reproduction. Volume is not even throughout the set, but this weakness
is minor.

*Falstaff.   Nelli, s; Stich-Randall, s; Merriman, m-s; Elmo, m-s;
Madasi, t; Valdengo, b; etc.; SC; NBC, Toscanini, V LM 6111* [3].
*Carteri, s; Pagliughi, s; Canali, m-s; Renzi, t; Taddei, b; etc.; RIC
& O, Rossi, Cet 1207* [3].

The Toscanini recording preserves the famous broadcasts of
April 1 and 8, 1950. *Falstaff* is an old specialty of the Maestro;
it hardly needs saying that the lightness of his touch is the
despair of all comers. The transfer of the broadcasts to discs is
a triumph for all concerned. It is true that the voices come over
to us more strongly than could ever be possible in the opera
house, but though they may over-balance the orchestra, they never
overwhelm it. It is also true that the acoustics of the broadcasting studio were such as to produce a dry, clean sound, with
no atmosphere save that which breathes in the music itself. In
effect, we are in the room with the music, and only the music can
transport us beyond the four walls. In some spots this is unfortunate: the snatches of love duet for Nanetta and Fenton in the
second act are close upon us, even when the stage direction
reads "within." However, there is some offstage singing in the
last act. I doubt that the great concluding fugue has ever been
performed with such transparency. Toscanini seems to have

picked his cast carefully for their youthful voices as well as for their musical dependability; if they have a general fault, it is that they sound young for their parts. Valdengo, in the title role, is always more than pleasing to the ear, and always in character; yet he cannot do, for instance, what a more mature, perhaps rougher voice can in such a passage as the "Honor Monologue" (*cf.* the 1909 Scotti performance on V LCT 1039). Even more pronounced is the youth of Madasi, but in the part of Fenton this is not against him. Still, one would prefer a smoother delivery of his burst of solo in the last act. Teresa Stich-Randall floats some lovely tones as Nanetta. Guarrera as Ford shows careful coaching, but carries characterization by vocal color a bit too far. The quality of his voice is lighter than we know it today. Outstanding among the women is Cloe Elmo, whose very Italian mezzo is just right for Mistress Quickly. Her proclamation of the oft-repeated "*Reverenza*" is masterly, her "*Povera donna*" quite heart-breaking. Nelli is tonally ingratiating, though she does some sliding, and Merriman fits well into the ensemble. There are bursts of applause at the ends of the acts.

The Cetra recording, conducted by Rossi, still ranks among the best complete operas to come out of Italy, and in many ways it complements the Toscanini set. Here is no attempt at such pinpoint perfection, no comparable lighter-than-air buoyancy, but here is more genuinely distinguished singing. Foremost in the cast, appropriately, is Taddei, whose Falstaff has the unction we miss in Valdengo, whose voice, indeed, is the richer of the two. Renzi, the Fenton, has his resources better in hand than Madasi, and Meletti's Ford is a more mellowed characterization than Guarrera's. The women, led by Carteri and Pagliughi, are admirably seasoned artists.

La Forza del Destino. Caniglia, s; Stignani, m-s; Masini, t; Tagliabue, b; Pasero, bs; etc.; RIC & O, Marinuzzi, Cet 1236 [3]. Guerrini, s; Pirazzini, m-s; Campora, t; Colzani, b; Modesti, bs; Corena, bs; etc.; SCAC & O, Parodi, U URLP 226 [3].

The choice here is by no means an easy one, for both sets are uneven; neither boasts a Ponselle or a Milanov in the leading role, and neither is satisfactory mechanically. The Cetra performance was by no means new when it was brought out on LP, and is therefore the less imposing as a recording. Caniglia walks off with the honors, though (save occasionally in matters of pitch) Stignani is also in her best stride. The basses in the cast are satisfactory, the tenor and baritone a little too outspoken emotionally. The great *"Madre pietosa"* scene is on the fast side. Urania's better-reproduced cast does not match the best work of Cetra's.

If the possibility of a complete *Forza* with Milanov seems remote, we do have in her aria recital (V LM 1777) a large slice of the Convent Scene, as well as *"Pace, pace."* The record, a must for her admirers, is likely to increase their numbers. The German soprano Traute Richter gives us *"Madre pietosa"* and *"Pace, pace"* in her own language (Tel TM 68006). Though the translation is all but fatal here, the singer's fine intelligence is as welcome as the subtle shading of her vocal line. Her vibrato, however, would be more effective were the language Italian, and the lack of a chorus detracts considerably from the impressiveness of the Convent Scene.

Un Giorno di Regno. Pagliughi, s; Capecchi, b; Bruscantini, bs; etc.; RIC & O, Simonetto, Cet 1225 [2].

Verdi's one early comedy has not been heard often; on the evidence of this recording, it has deserved a better fate. The performance enlists the services of several well-known singers, all firmly grounded in the Italian traditions and all equal to the demands of the music. The recording is not consistent in perfection of balance, but it is on the whole good.

I Lombardi alla Prima Crociata. Vitale, s; Pirazzini, m-s; Gallo, t; Bertocci, t; Petri, bs; Frosini, bs; etc.; RIC & O, M. Wolf-Farrari, Cet 1217 [3].

The cast here brings together some excellent voices, but the vocalism is uneven. Vitale ranges from exquisite to nasal in quality; despite a tendency to slide, she has a way of getting successfully to where she is going. Petri, though somewhat mouthy, does some notable singing, and Gallo, though inclined to lachrymosity, reveals a genuine Italian tenor voice. The reproduction, marred by a hum, is fuller in the later sides than in the first.

Luisa Miller. Kelston, s; Lauri-Volpi, t; Colombo, b; Vaghi, bs; etc.; RIC & O, Rossi, Cet 1221 [3].

This performance introduces a skillful American soprano, Lucy Kelston, who has been singing for some years in Italy. Hers is a rich, creamy voice; great things may be expected from her. The veteran Lauri-Volpi, who sang the leading tenor role in the opera when it was presented at the Metropolitan with Rosa Ponselle in 1929, still has moments of the old-time splendor, though for him life begins at *forte*. The celebrated *romanza*—*"Quando le sere al placido"*—has been more tellingly given by younger voices. The rest of the cast is adequate, though not outstanding.

Macbeth. Höngen, c; Ahlersmeyer, b; etc.; VSOC; VPH, Böhm, U URLP 220 [3].

The wisdom of bringing out Verdi operas in German is always open to question. In this case, *Macbeth* is not otherwise available. Though the performance is announced as abridged as well as translated, the cuts are not more serious than is often the case in the opera house. This middle-period work is a curious mixture, reaching such tremendous heights as the "Sleepwalking Scene," and descending to such ordinary Italian operatics as that of the Witches, with the three Weird Sisters converted into a chorus. Höngen sings Lady Macbeth with firmer tone than she has shown in some other recordings. For the most part she negotiates the high *tessitura* in a manner to suggest that she belongs up there rather than in the mezzo-contralto range more familiar to her. Of characterization, however, she does not give us much, a point emphasized by comparison either with the old Margherita Grandi recording, so magnificently founded on Beecham's expressive orchestra (HMV DB 6739–40, 78 rpm only), or with the more recent German performance of Martha Mödl (10" Tel TM 68009). In Höngen's florid passages we must often take something for granted. The men's voices are good, but again there is no real characterization among them. The balance favors the singers, and there are some slight uncertainties of pitch.

Nabucodonosor (Nabucco). Gatti, s; Mancini, s; Binci, t; Silveri, b; Gaggi, bs; etc.; RIC & O, Previtali, Cet 1216 [3].

The outstanding singing here is contributed by Gabriella Gatti in her all-too-brief role. The others have their fine moments, but there is a general tendency to spread tones, with the consequent uncertainties of pitch. The worst offender is Mancini, who has done good work in other Verdi operas, but finds her part in this decidedly taxing. On the whole, the performance can be commended for its vital spirit.

Otello. Nelli, s; Vinay, t; Valdengo, b; etc.; Ch & NBC, Toscanini, V LM 6107 [3]. La Pollo, s; Sarri, t; Manca Serra, b; etc.; ROC & O,

Conca, U URLP 216 [3]. (Selections) Steber, s; Vinay, t; Guarrera, b; MOO, Cleva, C ML 4499.

When Toscanini's *Otello* was broadcast in December 1948, his reading was hailed as the final and definitive revelation of Verdi's score and a demonstration of the composer's exact intentions. Of course, it was nothing of the kind, for in the very nature of things a concert performance or a broadcast of an opera can never be quite the same thing as a stage production, and Verdi was writing for the stage. Add to this the fact that the distinguished conductor was compelled by the clock and by the ways of radio to make his timing come out even, and it becomes obvious that the final results are not what they might have been in the opera house. Perhaps because of the influence of the clock, the interpretation, from the opening crash and tempest to the final collapse of the Moor on his sword, has an almost unbearable drive and nervous vitality. Exciting as the recording is simply as drama, it is also a historical document, one of the supreme examples of the clarity and mastery that have been Toscanini's secrets. The carefully chosen cast on the whole justifies the conductor's judgment and faith. Vinay, hardly created by nature for the part, triumphs over his limitations in a manner altogether admirable; Valdengo is in superb voice and has been admirably coached, though one is conscious that he is actually a very young man. He is led into the *"Brindisi"* at a terrific clip, but he manages to make it ring. Nelli sings with nice line and pleasing tone, if little characterization. The others perform creditably. A word should be added for the chorus, and the lightness with which the *"Fiocca di gioia"* is presented. Those who remember the broadcast will miss a false entrance at the beginning of the second act; this has been skillfully eliminated. The impressively turned-out libretto provided with the set has not only the text and translation, but a column of Shakespearean sources. Since the release of the Toscanini recording, there seems little likelihood that the rival venture under Conca will continue in great demand, though it was welcome enough when it was first released. Here was a more standard performance that did not miss distinction by too wide a margin. The main fault was with the microphone placement. Desdemona, especially, was much too close; as a result her voice was consistently shrill and unpleasant. The Otello was good as Otellos go, the Iago passable. The orchestra played competently; one would have liked to hear it more. Columbia's Highlights are the first- and third-act duets for Desdemona and Otello, the *"Credo,"* the great scene between Otello and Iago concluding in *"Si, pel ciel,"* Otello's "Monologue," and the "Willow Song" and *"Ave Maria"* and Otello's death. Vinay had grown in the role between the Toscanini broadcast and this recording; he achieves a certain vitality, as Martinelli used to do, by saving his rather limited voice for the climaxes. Steber sings musically, if not very warmly; Guarrera sounds well, but has not the subtlety for a real Iago.

Rigoletto. Pagliughi, s; Colasanti, c; Tagliavini, t; Taddei, b; Neri, bs; etc.; CC; RIO, Questa, Cet C 1247 [3]. Berger, s; Merriman, m-s; Peerce, t; Warren, b; Tajo, bs; etc.; SC; RCAO, Cellini, V LM 6101 [3]. Capsir, s; Bassi, c; Borgioli, t; Stracciari, b; Dominici, bs; etc.; SCAC; MISO, Molajoli, C EL 2 [2]. Orlandini, s; Melani, c; Sarri, t; Petroff, b; etc.; TCC; FM, Ghiglia, Rem RLP 199–58/9/60 [3]. (In German) Berger, s; Klose, c; Roswaenge, t; Schlusnus, b; etc.; BSOC & O, Heger, U URLP 222 [2].

Cetra's Italian recording scores a number of points over Victor's American production; its superiority is clinched by the more mellow approach of the conductor. Cellini's work suffers from what seems like streamlining: we are no sooner through with one scene than we are in the middle of the next. As for the casts, Pagliughi is the most lyrically appealing of the Gildas listed above. Her voice is warmer than Berger's, and she is an equally proficient singer. Her meltingly lovely treatment of the line *"Se non volete di voi parlarmi"* in the second act duet with Taddei is a measure of her artistry. Taddei is for the most part splendid; his is a more supple voice than Warren's, more plastic in expression, and he easily equals the American's impressive dramatic talents. He has a bad moment just before *"Si, vendetta,"* when his voice sags momentarily, but his performance is superior. Tagliavini is less conspicuously successful. His voice is a little below its best; his singing inclines to be precious. Colasanti is very right for Maddalena, and Neri is an effective Sparafucile. Victor's cast is the better for Jan Peerce, who puts more into his full-throated singing than Tagliavini manages to convey, and for Italo Tajo, who shows a genuine flair for characterization. In neither set is the recording balance perfect; it is better in the Cetra.

Columbia's set has enjoyed great popularity, indeed was considered *the* recording of *Rigoletto* for many years. Stracciari, Borgioli, and Capsir make a star cast, and at least the baritone's performance has something of the classic about it. The sound in its LP version is not bad, though, of course, the ear must adjust itself after the high fidelity we have become accustomed to hearing. Remington's recording is a good buy at the price. The performance is well routined, and the voices are mostly good. The reproduction is among the best to come from this company.

Urania's German performance shares Victor's Gilda, again singing in musicianly and proficient style. The strangeness of the language is most apparent in the tenor arias, for Roswaenge, no more than any other singer, can give *"Questa o quella"* in German with requisite lightness. He is in good voice, however, and carries an effort to be idiomatic to the point of sobs and tears. Schlusnus, vocally resplendent, manages to sing with some fire, and without loss of smoothness. The opera is crowded onto two discs, and the breaks are unfortunate. Also the numbers are run together in a manner to make the Victor performance seem leisurely. The reproduction is if anything too roomy: there is some tonal diffusion and consequent messiness.

A collection of "Arias and Duets" call forth some expert and expressive singing by Pagliughi and Sved (Cet 50003), and Hilde Gueden, an authentic, appealing Gilda, gives us *"Caro nome"* and *"Tutte le feste."* I am sorry she cut the coda of the first aria, for her singing is very beautiful (10" L LPS 485).

Simon Boccanegra. Stella, s; Bergonzi, t; Silveri, b; Petri, bs; etc.; RIC & O, Molinari-Pradelli, Cet 1231 [3].

The striking thing about this performance is the unusual attention paid by cast and conductor to Verdi's dynamic markings. It is a pleasure to hear an Italian group with not only the ability, but also the will, to sing *pianissimo*. Still though the spirit of the performers is admirable and their style idiomatic, the production is not above criticism. Stella must have been very young when the recording was made, for her exceptional voice has its raw spots; the rhythmic pulse of her big aria is all too obviously beaten out. Silveri is a good artist, but his voice is on the dry

side. And *"Il lacerato spirito"* has been sung with richer tone
than Petri's.

*La Traviata. Callas, s; Albanese, t; Savarese, b; etc.; RIC & O,
Santini, Cet C 1246* [3]. *Albanese, s; Peerce, t; Merrill, b; etc.;
Ch; NBC, Toscanini, V LM 6003* [2]. *Guerrini, s; Infantino, t; Silveri,
b; etc.; ROC & O, Bellezza, C SL 103* [3]. *(Highlights in German).
Cebotari, s; Roswaenge, t; Schlusnus, b; BSOC & O, Steinkopf, U
URLP 7011.*

Cetra's *Traviata* is a nicely paced production typical of the
better-grade present-day Italian opera stage. The Prelude is admirably reserved at the start, and is allowed to expand; the first
scene, with its bits of conversation on stage, is properly kept on
a quiet level. In matters of balance, it is the best of the *Travi-
atas*. And it has Maria Callas in the title role. Not that the
soprano is at her best: the vocal line we have so often admired
is not always in evidence. Sometimes she shades her phrases
very beautifully; sometimes her voice has a tendency to spread.
The recitative preceding *"Ah, fors' è lui"* is not as crisp as I
would like it, and the cadenza of the aria is heavy. Nor is her
"Sempre libera" as animated as it should be. In a word, despite
some superior singing, this is not Callas's best performance.
But if the soprano falls short on shading, so does her partner,
Francesco Albanese. His tenor voice is a little stiff in the medium and low registers, and often its quality is too open, but he
has strength and brilliance on the top. He hits his best stride in
the second act, where he has a chance to expand, but at best he
is an uneven singer. Savarese's is a rather thick baritone not
transfigured with imagination. He is most successful, as is Callas, in *"Dite all giovine,"* which scene the singers bring to a
brilliant close. His *"Di Provenza"* is nicely conceived, if tonally somewhat uncertain. The acid test (both figuratively and
dramatically) of a Germont is the withering *"Di sprezzo degno,"*
at which point other baritones have risen to greater heights.

The much-heralded Toscanini recording is his famous broadcast
of 1946. After the performance considered above, this one seems
smooth and streamlined. It has the inevitable polish and orchestral detail, but the singers are all below their best. One feels
they have little chance, led through their arias at such a pace.
In the good old Italian tradition, they want to spread themselves
in their big moments, but the conductor keeps them strictly in

line. In spots his voice is heard, helping them out. The Columbia
set has a soprano with possibilities hardly realized, a good
(though also immature) tenor, best in the dramatic moments, and
a serviceable baritone whose career at the Metropolitan has been
made since this recording. There is not much characterization
in the performance, nor any first-rate vocalism. For distinguished
singing one must look to the German Highlights. The lamented
Cebotari furnishes the best reasons for acquiring the set. Remington also has a Traviata made in Rome under Ricci, featuring
Schimenti, Pola, and Chesi (R 199–98 [3]). The vocal material
is a good average, the lungs are healthy, finesse is in short
supply.

*Il Trovatore. Milanov, s; Barbieri, m-s; Bjoerling, t; Warren, b; etc.;
SC; RCAO, Cellini, V LM 6008 [2]. Scacciati, s; Zinetti, m-s; Merli,
t; Molinari, b; etc.; SCAC; MISO, Molajoli, C SL 120 [2]. Mancini, s;
Pirazzini, m-s; Lauri-Volpi, t; Tagliabue, b; etc.; RIC & O, Previtali,
Cet 1226 [3].*

Victor's *Trovatore* is something very close to a masterpiece.
Milanov, at the top of her form, leads the cast with a generous
portion of that vocal cream no other practicing soprano today can
rival.   With her are the finest Manrico the Metropolitan has
boasted in many years and an Azucena with both voice and temperament. Warren, for his part, is at his best as Count di Luna.
The balance is satisfactory, and the tempos are lively, perhaps
even a bit slick. The resurrected Columbia set was never too
good, even when it was new. The singing is mostly strident and
sloppy, with the Leonora the worst offender. After this one,
Cetra's set sounds well, though it is not one of that company's
proudest offerings. Mancini shows surprising agility in the florid
parts of the work, and Lauri-Volpi demonstrates that time has not
taken away his lungs. But this contest of vivid Italian temperaments is hardly bearable after the Victor set.

Arias

*Luisa Miller—Quando le sere al placido; Traviata—Dei miei bol-
lenti spiriti; Macbeth—Ah! la paterna mano.   Del Monaco, t; SCO,
Erede, 10" L LS 670 (*Puccini: Arias).*
*Aïda—Pur ti reveggo; O terra addio; Trovatore—Miserere. Ilitsch,
s; Baum, t; MOC & O, Rudolf.   Un Ballo in Maschera—Teco io sto;*

Otello—Già nella notte densa. Ilitsch, s; Tucker, t; MOO, Rudolf,
C ML 4230.

Ernani—Ernani involami; Otello—Salce, salce; Ave Maria; La
Traviata—Ah, fors' 'e lui; Sempre libera; Don Carlo—Tu che le
vanità; La Forza del Destino—Pace, pace, mio Dio. Steber, s; MOO,
Cleva, 10" C ML 2157.

For the most part Del Monaco is at his best in these arias, and
his enterprise in selecting the out-of-the-way *Luisa Miller* and
Macbeth pieces is heartening. His is a real voice and a loud one.
Ilitsch was briefly a member of the Metropolitan Opera Company,
at which time she was teamed with two of the tenor mainstays
for these recordings. The soprano's voice was big and fine in
itself, easily equal to the demands of the music, and at times
lovely in quality. She was not, however, an even singer, nor did
she convey any great degree of warmth. In volume, Baum was a
better match for her than Tucker, but he was never a singer of
great imagination either. Tucker certainly made more of his
material, though it was a strange idea to put him into the *Otello*
duet. The recording balance is not exemplary, though Baum is
properly removed to suggest the offstage dungeon in the *"Mis-*
erere." I wish the chorus had been similarly removed. The
voice of Gladys Zieher is heard as a rather too eager Amneris in
the *Aïda* finale. The larger arias in Steber's set suffer from some
forcing and unsteadiness; while the quieter ones have lovely
tones, they do not carry much conviction. Hers is not the gift
of simplicity. It seems strange in considering Italian arias to
speak of singing less and talking more, yet this is just what, for
example, the opening of *"Salce, salce"* needs.

La Traviata—Questa donna conoscete? Zenatello, t; Otello—Ora
e per sempre addio. Rayner, t. Otello—Dio! mi potevi scagliar; Niun
mi tema; Rigoletto—Ella mi fu rapita.   Pertile, t.   Requiem—
Ingemisco. Piccaver, t. Rigoletto—Questa o quella; Trovatore—Ah
si, ben mio. Lauri-Volpi, t. Ballo in Maschera—Ma se m'è forza
perderti. Vignas, t. Trovatore—Di quella pira. Lois, t. Et 703.

This collection of tenor arias shifts back and forth between
electric and acoustic reproduction, though only the Zenatello and
Vignas seem to be genuinely "old" (1906). As it happens,
these two are outstanding: Zenatello's is a splendidly clear,
piano-accompanied performance showing the artist at his best;
Vignas has both vocal fullness and fine style. Rayner and Pertile

divide the honors as Otello, both electrically recorded, and both in good form. Piccaver's recording is as good as any I have heard of this Viennese idol. The young Lauri-Volpi shows curiously undependable intonation, and of course the lyricism of *"Ah si, ben mio"* was never his longest suit. I know nothing of Vittorio Lois, whose recording is electrical, but his is a strange performance. To compensate for his lack of melodic articulation, he gives a certain dramatic stress. As for his intonation, his aim is consistently high.

Songs

Il poveretto; In solitaria stanza; Il mistero; Il tramonto; Stornello; Deh pietoso, o adolorata; Ad una stella. Lucca, s; R. Malipiero, pf, 10" Col CLPS 1028.

Italian song is nicely represented by this set of seven Verdi pieces, simple, grateful, and little known. One of them, interestingly, is a setting of translated Goethe, Gretchen's *"Ach neige, du Schmerzenreiche."* Lucca's singing is rich and controlled.

VICTORIA, TOMÁS LUIS DE (ca. 1549-1611)

Masses: O Magnum Mysterium; O Quam Gloriosum. Welch Ch, Ly LL 46.

The two Masses here recorded are based on themes from Victoria's own like-named motets. Some will find the performing style a little free here—too much variety of tempo—but the Masses are cleanly and honestly delivered with generally admirable tone.

Officium defunctorum (Missa pro defunctis); Magnificat IV toni. Lecco Acad Ch, Camillucci, Vox PL 8930.

The rather long and somber *Requiem* (whose more proper title has been restored above to distinguish it from another *Missa pro defunctis*) is given a very energetic performance, too obviously measured by the bar-lines. There is no suggestion in the singing of the eternal mysteries pondered in the text. The *Magnificat* ("in IV tones," as the labeling has it!) is a solider composition, more susceptible to this kind of treatment. Still, one wishes the singers were a little more relaxed.

VILLA-LOBOS, HEITOR (1887-   )

Mass of Saint Sebastian. U of Cal Ch, Janssen, C ML 4516.

Villa-Lobos's Mass, says Alfred Frankenstein, "is not beholden so much to Bach as to the Spanish and Portuguese choral composers of the sixteenth century...." A curious effect is achieved by the doubling of the three voice parts among the men and women. The music moves ahead impressively; several of the movements end in tremendous climaxes. The reproduction is notably expansive and clear.

*Bachianas Brasileiras, No. 5. Sayão, s; Eight Cellos, Villa-Lobos, 10" C AL 3 (*Verdi: Traviata—Arias).*

This recording has enjoyed tremendous popularity at 78 rpm; indeed, it is accountable for the public appreciation of the music, perhaps to a large extent for the composer's reputation in this country. The principal melody, a wordless vocalise, is hauntingly expressive, and in Sayão's voice it found its perfect vehicle. The great days of the recording are by no means over.

VIVALDI, ANTONIO (ca. 1676-1741)

Beatus vir. Sailer, s; Kiefer, s; Graf, t; Müller, bs; Werdermann, bs; SSAC; PRO, Grischkat, Vox PL 7140.

Vivaldi's psalm is a work of great dignity and no little purely musical beauty, with perhaps the *"Jocundus homo"* section outstanding, a soprano solo with obbligato for organ in the manner of Bach's chorale preludes. The work is handsomely done in this performance, though the choral tone is diffused in reproduction.

Dixit. Giancola, s; Piovesan, s; Amadini, c; Cristinelli, t; Ferrein, bs; SVC & O, Ephrikian, Per SPLP 537.

This setting of the 110th Psalm is preceded by a long and elaborate tenor solo. The performance is good, with special credit going to Cristinelli for his mastery of the florid style.

*Gloria. EVP; O, Jouvé, W WL 5287 (*Charpentier: Midnight Mass). Zanolli, s; Giordano, m-s; Lecco Ch; MITN, Pedrollo, Vox PLP 6610.*

This fine work seems now to be generally known as *Gloria Mass*, though in fact it is not a Mass at all, but the *"Gloria in excelsis"* section so elaborately set that the experts question that it ever was a part of a larger whole. The Vox recording, acceptable in its day, is cast into the shade by the later Westminster. The

Italian soloists hardly sound professional: were their names not given, we might easily take them for boys. Their counterparts in the French performance remain anonymous, but are vastly superior. This recording as a whole is more carefully realized, more polished, cleaner, and more refined in sound. That Jouvé's tempos are more vital than Pedrollo's is indicated by the fact that he uses only one side of the disc to his rival's two.

Juditha triumphans. Giancola, s; Amadini, c; Cristinelli, t; Cortis, b; Ferrein, bs; FOC; SVO, Ephrikian, Per SPLP 557.

This *Judith* is an oratorio, and an extremely dramatic one. The performance is in many ways excellent, if uneven. The best of the singers is Cortis (the Holofernes), a fine flexible Italian baritone with style as well as technical assurance. Amadini (Judith) possesses a rich, ample contralto somewhat inclined to fatness. One might wish for more subtlety in her delivery, though she sings with taste. Giancola and Ferrein are good in their parts, Cristinelli less so: his light voice here seems too open. The recording balance is not altogether satisfactory: the solos are often overloaded and not matched with the choruses.

Laudate pueri, I & II. Giancola, s; SVO, Ephrikian, Ren X 50.

Though a "choral ensemble" is listed on the labels, this disc actually contains two solo settings of the 113th Psalm, both sung by Rosanna Giancola. Of the two, the second is at once the more brilliant (making more than ordinary demands on the singer), the more effective, and the better sung. The artist has a sweet, clear soprano, but it is not perfectly even in quality; occasionally a high tone will slip out of line. This tendency is more apparent in the first than the second setting. She does not toss off the long passages with complete ease, nor does she always manage to pronounce her words very clearly when Vivaldi takes her into the higher registers. But she does leave the impression of some very beautiful music.

Stabat Mater. Amadini, c; AC & O, Gerelli, Vox PL 7180 (*Carissimi: Jonas).

Vivaldi's *Stabat Mater* is a contralto solo of considerable beauty, fairly well done here by the rather ponderous voice of Amadini. The delightful Carissimi oratorio overdisc is better done.

Serenata à Tre. Rapisardi, s; Zanolli, s; Bianchini, t; MIC, Loehrer, Vox PL 7990.

The three singers in this charming little pastoral clearly have a grasp of what is going on, and the performance is held together by the conductor. The voices as such are nothing much.

WAGNER, RICHARD (1813-1883)

Operas

Der fliegende Holländer. Kupper, s; Wagner, c; Windgassen, t; Metternich, b; Greindl, bs; etc.; RIASC & O, Fricsay, D DX 124 [3]. Ursuleac, s; Willer, c; Ostertag, t; Hotter, b; Hann, bs; etc.; BAVOC & O, Krauss, Mer MGL 2 [4].

The Fricsay reading is exciting from first to last. The singing is mostly on a high level of competence, the recording clear and credible, if not perfectly balanced in the solo parts. The choral shouts in the first act are like waves rolling over the listener. The exception among the fine singers is Kupper, whose voice is not steady. She has a sense of style, and her "Ballad" is by no means bad, but at best her tone is on the dry side. Metternich's voice is light for the Dutchman, and he has nothing like the power of Hotter's delivery in the rival set. Greindl is an unusually sympathetic Daland, and Windgassen does more than most tenors with the character of Erik. Indeed, at times his energy is overwhelming. The few cuts are of little more than repetitions; a couple of bad breaks between sides are more unfortunate. Despite the efforts of Clemens Krauss, the Mercury set has little to recommend it beyond Hotter's justly famous Dutchman. Ursuleac and Willer are both past their prime and their vocal steadiness; whatever is admirable in the singing of others in the cast is nullified by very loud, coarse recording. A better-reproduced sample of Hotter's characterization may be had in his Wagnerian Recital (D DL 9514), which includes *"Die Frist ist um."*

Eterna offers a set of Highlights, more nearly unified than most of its kind (Et 481). The role of Senta is shared by two sopranos, Emmy Bettendorf and Elisabeth Ohms. The former gives a vocally rich but not very exciting "Ballad," acoustically recorded; the latter joins with Theodor Scheidl in an eloquent version of the great duet, which, however, ends inconclusively. Scheidl was one of the best German baritones between the wars; his delivery of the long first-act monologue is dramatically powerful and vocally fine. Michael Bohnen has to contend with poor reproduction (acoustic) in Daland's aria. A separate recording of the

"Ballad" is offered by Maud Cunitz (10" Tel TM 68001). The soprano sings in a big, even voice, dark in quality, perhaps a little heavy. Except occasionally, when she pushes it, her tone is commendably steady.

Lohengrin. Cunitz, s; Klose, c; Schock, t; Metternich, b; Frick, bs; etc.; NWDRC & O, Schüchter, HMV ALP 1095/6/7/8 [4]. Kupper, s; Braun, m-s; Fehenberger, t; Frantz, b; Rohr, bs; etc.; BAVRC & O, Jochum, D DX 131 [4]. Schech, s; Klose, c; Vincent, t; Boehm, b; Böhme, bs; etc.; MSOC & O, Kempe, U URLP 225 [5]. Steber, s; Varnay, s; Windgassen, t; Uhde, b; Greindl, bs; etc.; BFC & O, Keilberth, L LLA 16 [5].

Of these four *Lohengrins* not one is completely satisfactory. To some extent this is the composer's fault, for his opera is exceptionally difficult to cast. The ideal singer for the title role must be both robust and tender; the *tessitura* of the part is as trying as anything in Wagner. Then there is Ortrud, usually sung by a contralto who cannot ascend the heights or a soprano without sufficient weight. Telramund, a bass-baritone, has some high passages to sing, and even the genuinely basso King needs a good upper voice. Elsa must rely on infinite lyricism, for there is little shading in her blond German character. At the same time, very nearly everything depends on a good strong hand at the podium. The rhythmic patterns throughout the score are cut to a definite measure, and the opera can seem interminable. In casting, each of the four recordings has a point or two in its favor; in vitality and dramatic insight on the part of the conductor, the best is easily the HMV. Schüchter may be accused of keeping the tempos too fast; at least he keeps them alive. This most recent recording is also the most atmospheric, natural, and refined in reproduction, from the shimmering strings of the Prelude to the biggest of the climaxes. For all their sonority, the ensembles are exceptionally clear: the individual voices stand out. Sensitive ears will sometimes be bothered by the singers' intonation, but in this respect none of the sets will be found innocent.

Schock, the HMV Lohengrin, is better on the robust side than the tender. Though he does not find all the music comfortably within his voice, and his tone quality is a little hoarse, his style is praiseworthy. Windgassen, in the London set (made at a public performance at Bayreuth in 1953), is the best of the Lohengrins, once he gets warmed up. Decca's Fehenberger makes an effective entrance at the proper distance, and he succeeds fairly well in lightening his somewhat heavy voice in the "Bridal Chamber Scene." Vincent, of Urania, is a young American of promise, not quite ready for his assignment when the recording was made. The most successful Telramund, vocally and histrionically, is Decca's Frantz. He delivers his envenomed lines and shades his words with all the power of mastery. Metternich in the HMV set is admirably dramatic, too, especially in the poisonous aria at the beginning of the second act. Andreas Boehm of the Urania set was a young singer of solid achievements who died shortly after the recording was made. HMV's King, Gottlob Frick, is more alive than most operatic royalty; his singing of the "Prayer," though perhaps a little rushed by the conductor, has weight and tonal beauty. Greindl and Rohr are satisfactory in this part; the usually admirable Kurt Böhme seems to be singing above his best range. Margarete Klose, the Ortrud of the HMV and the Urania sets, is a veteran, surely, of many *Lohengrins*, and her singing has the true dramatic ring. Her voice does not, naturally, sound its best in the upper reaches, but the kind of shrieking tone she gets is not out of character. Vocally, she may have lost something between the two recordings. The other Ortruds are sopranos. Helena Braun's voice is on the light side, and does not contrast strongly enough with that of the Elsa. It is also somewhat taxed by the weight of the role, though she compensates for this by "singing with her brain." Varnay's vocal production is not forward enough for the most telling diction, a fact, I think, emphasized by the exigencies of the stage recording. None of the Elsas is able to float her tone into the night as Wagner invited her to do in *"Euch Lüften, die mein Klagen."* Of the four, the rather brittle-voiced Maud Cunitz is the best, because her tone is the steadiest, and at least it never gets out of hand, though it has an inclination to spread in the high register. She is at her best in the "Bridal Chamber Scene."

A set of highlights dubbed by Eterna is more modern in sound than many this company has used (Et 0-472). Electrically reproduced, Olszewska and Schipper have the whole of the first side for a rousing Ortrud-Telramund duet. This contralto's voice ascends impressively to the altitudes of her part. Emmy Bettendorf has the needed quality for *"Euch Lüften,"* and Karin Branzell delivers Ortrud's outburst, *"Entweihte Götter,"* quite tremendously. Finally, the Elsa-Ortrud duet, by Bettendorf and

Branzell, crowns the program, splendidly sung and still effective in reproduction.

Three separate issues of the "Bridal Chamber Scene" are worth listing. The Flagstad-Melchior recording (V LCT 1105) is a treasurable souvenir despite the fact that the singers were more closely identified with other roles than these, and that the recording was never well-balanced nor the orchestra eloquent. Traubel and Baum (C ML 4055) make a majestic Elsa and a somewhat stiff Lohengrin. Neither of these recordings captures much in the way of tenderness and warmth; both have moments of ingratiating tone. Both versions are somewhat cut. Lemnitz and Völker (U URLP 7019), for their part, do not continue all the way to the end. The soprano's voice is very lovely, that of the tenor not in its best estate.

Die Meistersinger. Schwarzkopf, s; Malaniuk, c; Hopf, t; Unger, t; Edelmann, b; Kunz, b; Dalberg, bs; etc.; BFC & O, Karajan, C SL 117 [5]. Lemnitz, s; Walther-Sachs, c; Aldenhoff, t; Unger, t; Frantz, b; Böhme, bs; etc.; DOC; SAX, Kempe, U URLP 206 [6]; (Episodes) Frantz, b; O, Kempe, U URLP 7067. Gueden, s; Schürhoff, c; Treptow, t; Dermota, t; Schoeffler, b; Edelmann, b; etc.; VSOC; VPH, Knappertsbusch, L LLA 9 [6].

Die Meistersinger—Act 3. Teschemacher, s; Jung, m-s; Ralf, t; Kremer, t; Nissen, b; Fuchs, bs; etc.; DOC & O, Böhm, V LCT 6002 [2].

The Bayreuth performance has the element of excitement we get only in actual public performance recordings, but it has also the usual unevenness of such "takes." The Dresden presentation of Urania has greater brilliance, clarity, and sonority, but not perfect consistency throughout. Sometimes the singers are too close, sometimes about right, sometimes weak. In the London set the voices are definitely too near, and for this reason lose something of their appeal. The best Sachs, all things considered, is Urania's Frantz, though, of course, London's Schoeffler is a firstrate artist, and Columbia's Edelmann (who is also Pogner for Urania) draws a creditable character with a less warmly attractive voice. Lemnitz is a sweet-voiced Eva, but overpowered in the climaxes, for which reason Schwarzkopf is preferred. Urania and Columbia share the David of Unger and the Watchman of Faulhaber. The Beckmessers are all good, and none is too much caricatured, the best probably being the Bayreuth Kunz. The big, rich voice of Böhme easily makes the best Pogner. None of the

Walters is ideal, but Hopf seems to me definitely the best. Victor's revival of the old Dresden Act 3 remains remarkable for its ensemble.

Parsifal. Mödl, s; Windgassen, t; London, b; Weber, bs; Uhde, bs; etc.; BFC & O, Knappertsbusch, L LLPA 10 [6].

This "actual performance" recording, made in the Bayreuth Festspielhaus during the summer of 1951, really took fire. This time we have ample compensation for all the coughing and other audience noises. George London, the Amfortas, does some of the finest singing of his career to date. His voice is rich and expressive, if anything too young and healthy, and he is not made to sound like a giant. Martha Mödl has an insinuating vocal quality, and obviously there is a mind working behind it. Perhaps her top tones are not so strong as one could wish, but this is understandable in a Kundry who started as a contralto. Her besetting sin is a habit of sliding up to a note; but one forgives her readily in gratitude for the general excellence of her performance. Windgassen may well be the best of current German tenors; his voice, to be sure, is a little stiff at first, but from the point where Kundry kisses him it takes on authority and body. Weber's Gurnemanz has humanity and warmth, though he is not too finical about the notes he sings. Uhde, a properly villainous Klingsor, seems to be singing most of the time in a cave. The flower-maiden scene does not come off too happily, for the young ladies come too close—one wants a little more perspective. There is a strange effect, like a pre-echo, when Kundry's voice is first heard in this scene. One especially unfortunate between-sides break occurs in the midst of the garden scene, cutting Kundry's narrative in mid-course.

Every Wagnerian role interpreted by Flagstad and by Melchior has now passed into history; therefore their recording of the duet in garden scene (V LCT 1105) has special value, despite an orchestra that does not support them too well and poorly balanced recording. There is considerable sheer vocal beauty in their performance.

DER RING DES NIBELUNGEN (Das Rheingold, Die Walküre, Siegfried, Götterdämmerung)

Die Walküre—Act 1. Müller, s; Windgassen, t; Greindl, bs; WSTO, Leitner, D DX 121 [2] (*Götterdämmerung—Act 2, Scene 3. Greindl,

bs; MPH, Rieger). Lehmann, s; Melchior, t; List, bs; VPH, Walter,
V LCT 1033.
Die Walküre—Act 1, Scene 3. Traubel, s; Darcy, t; NYPH, Rodzinski.
Act 3. Jessner, s; Traubel, s; Janssen, b; etc.; NYPH, Rodzinski,
C SL 105 [2].
Die Walküre—Act 3. Varnay, s; Rysanek, s; S. Bjoerling, bs; etc.;
BFO, Karajan, C SL 116 [2].

Here are two complete first acts and one love duet, the latter
taking in what many consider the cream of the act. As a recording, the most recent—the Decca—is incomparably the best, and
it is a good performance by well-routined singers. Maria Müller,
obviously past her best days, sings with exemplary care, holding
her voice to greater steadiness than has marked the more recent
of her previous efforts. But she hardly gives the impression of
abandoning herself to the ecstasy of the moment. Windgassen
rates certainly among the better German tenors, and Greindl sustains his reputation. The voices seem to be in a chamber separated from the orchestra. The Victor recording is a classic.
Lehmann's Sieglinde is legendary, and Siegmund was one of
Melchior's best parts. List and Walter, too, were in top form when
the recording was made. We must accept the fact that the once-
superlative reproduction has faded somewhat, though it may still
be heard without pain. For their part, Traubel's Sieglinde is on
the majestic side and Darcy's pleasing voice is too light to cut
impressively through the Wagnerian orchestra. Act 3 was one of
Columbia's outstanding achievements of the mid-forties, featuring
the best cast available at the Metropolitan in its day, under a
conductor of authority and power. A remarkable feature at the
time of release was the stage effect: though this was a concert
performance, the singers were so placed as to give some dramatic
illusion. The thing may even have been overdone, but I have always liked it. Traubel, back in her own proper role of Brünnhilde,
is in top form, and Janssen proves himself a good, if rather light-
voiced, Wotan. However, he has a tendency to dominate the orchestra, especially in the *"Abschied."* Stage effect really comes
into its own in the Bayreuth Act 3, which was taken during a
public performance. More than the usual amount of fading is
caused by movement on the stage during the first scene: the
Wotan-Brünnhilde part stays much more in line. Varnay's Brünnhilde is not of the steadiest, but Sigurd Bjoerling's Wotan is exceptional. The total effect is magnificently vital and exciting.

Siegfried—Awakening Scene. Flagstad, s; Svanholm, t; PHI, Sebastian, V LHMV 1024 (*Götterdämmerung—Immolation Scene).

One of the penalties a soprano of Flagstad's gifts must pay is never to sing with a tenor of comparable endowment. Even Melchior, though his voice was adequate, never matched the soprano's accurate musicianship. The tenor in the present case is about as good as most these days, but his stiff production is oddly assorted with the easy outpouring of the Flagstad tone. Her part in the duet is in her best postwar voice, and she even attacks the high C's, which she used to skip when in her prime. The balance with the orchestra is unusually good, and the orchestra plays well; but the performance does not rise above good routine.

Götterdämmerung—Hagen's Wacht; Hagen's Ruf. Hoffmann, bs. Song of the Rhinedaughters, Act 3, Scene 1. Siegfried's Narration. Schubert, t, Death of Siegfried. Schmedes, t. Immolation Scene. Leider, s. Et 480.

Götterdämmerung—Act 2, Scene 3. Greindl, bs; MPH, Rieger, D DX 121 [2] (*Walküre, Act 1).

Götterdämmerung—Immolation Scene. Flagstad, s; PHI, Furtwängler, V LHMV 1024 (*Siegfried—Awakening Scene).

Götterdämmerung—Funeral Music and Immolation Scene. Harshaw, s. Tristan und Isolde—Prelude, Liebesnacht and Liebestod. PHO, Ormandy, C ML 4742.

Götterdämmerung—Brünnhilde's Immolation; Siegfried Idyll. Traubel, s; NBC, Toscanini, V LCT 1116.

The "historical" record is justified on the grounds that most of the music it contains is not otherwise available on LP. But most important on its musical merits is the splendid *Immolation* by Frida Leider, an electrical recording magnificent in its day and still not killed by the array of rivals listed below it. The other singers assembled from various recording periods are good of their kind, and the reproduction is up and down. The barbarous music of *Hagens Ruf* is more excitingly done by the admirable Josef Greindl, with the impressive assistance of conductor Rieger and the modern engineers. Flagstad's *Immolation* is sung with poise and majestic tone, always riding the orchestra, yet never dominating it after the manner of too many recordings. Her voice may be less fresh than it was when her earlier recording was made, but there is no question as to the superiority of this one.

Furtwängler seems to have been just the conductor to make the wonderful voice glow. Harshaw's (or rather Ormandy's) perform-ance begins with the so-called *"Funeral March,"* continuing through the entrance of Gutrune, then skips to the measures pre-ceding Brünnhilde's peroration. The conductor draws from his orchestra a mass of seething sound; in his hands the music be-comes exciting and real. Harshaw, who is not allowed to dominate the ensemble unduly, gets off to a rather tremulous start, but warms up effectively, though she does not succeed in imparting much drama to her singing. The Traubel-Toscanini collaboration produced one of the great records of the late pre-LP era, and one well worth bringing back, though there has been some loss of brilliance in the transfer. So here we have a choice of four Brünnhildes, each outstanding in her day. Flagstad and Furt-wängler give us the most complete satisfaction; Leider's is still to me the most exciting vocally; but the Traubel-Toscanini re-cording has a grandeur of its own.

Tannhäuser. Schech, s; Bäumer, s; Seider, t; Paul, b; Rohr, bs; etc.; MSOC & O, Heger, U URLP 211 [4].

Admirers of *Tannhäuser* have to content themselves with a choice of one, a performance more or less typical of what is done for this opera on European stages today. The conductor is an old, skilled hand; the reading is authentic; chorus and orchestra are experienced and efficient. Schech as Elisabeth performs no wonders, but sings sweetly enough. Bäumer, however, is a dis-tressingly unsteady, unseductive Venus, Seider typically a Ger-man tenor. Paul does well as the all too saintly Wolfram, Rohr makes a sonorous Landgrave, and the rest are in the picture.

Tristan und Isolde. Flagstad, s; Thebom, m-s; Suthaus, t; Fischer-Dieskau, b; Greindl, bs; etc.; ROOC & O, Furtwängler, V LM 6700 [5]. Bäumer, s; Westenberger, m-s; Suthaus, t; Wolfram, b; Frick, bs; etc.; MRC; LGO, Konowitschy, U URLP 202 [5]. (Abridged) Larsen-Todsen, s; Helm, s; Graarud, t; Bockelmann, b; Andrésen, bs; etc.; BFC, El-mendorff, C EL 11 [3].

By one of those happy strokes of fortune, the complete *Tristan* crowning the career of Kirsten Flagstad is all we could reasona-bly hope it would be. Rarely in the opera house has the soprano given so eloquent a performance of this music, because rarely has she worked in complete *rapport* with so masterful a conductor as Furtwängler. One is tempted to call the recording his masterpiece as well as hers. The opening of the Prelude is almost frighteningly soft, but before we know it, Furtwängler has built up terrific tension, and this hardly relaxes throughout the ten long record sides. At first I noted some lack of incisiveness in the string tone, but I quickly forgot such things. Later on there are wonderful effects, recordingwise, such as the instrumental definition in the "Love Duet." Once or twice the reproduced sound becomes slightly clouded, but this is never serious. I thought I heard some extraneous noises, such as might have been made by hitting of music stands, and in my copy there is a mechanical knocking toward the end of side 5. The orchestral balance is cause for rejoicing: for once, working with the unique Flagstad voice, the engineers have not been afraid of drowning out the singing. Some of the offstage voices, as that of the Sailor at the beginning, sound as though they were in a neighboring hall, but at least they are offstage. On the other hand, Brangäne's call is way off there where it should be, and the effect with the orchestra is magical. The story of a couple of high C's Flagstad could no longer produce, and of Schwarzkopf's stepping into the breach, has been given such currency that it scarcely needs repeating here. Aside from that, there is little evidence that the soprano's career is about to come to its end. It would be too much to expect that a Tristan could be found to match such an Isolde; it is good to note, therefore, that Suthaus is an unusually good one. I was struck by the intelligence with which he enunciates Wagner's text, so well in keeping with the character. The fact that he occasionally bleats and slides diminishes in importance. Of course, the ideal Tristan voice would have a keener cutting edge than his does. He rises to real distinction in the third act, reaching his top in the section *"Wie sie selig."* Only Melchior at his best has sounded better in the "Love Duet" in my experience. Suthaus has the usual trouble with that ticklish spot *"Nie wieder erwachen,"* and his *"Lass mich sterben"* is detached. Though he was also the Tristan in the Urania recording, he is incomparably more impressive in the later Victor set. Thebom is a good Brangäne, though she shines less brightly in this company than she has often done. Her voice, indeed, seems lighter than Flagstad's, which somewhat throws the balance. Fischer-Dieskau, by nature and training a lieder singer, learned the role of Kurwenal for this recording, and he adds another reason for admiring his artistry. He is a more human, younger, less gruff retainer than some I have known, though he is not over-gentle in the lusty parts. He does some beautiful singing in the last act, and I can charge him with only one less-than-first-rate high tone. Greindl brings admirable dignity to the speeches of King Mark, though his voice is on the light side.

• After all this, there is little to say of the rival recording, with its tremulo-ridden Isolde ("After all," a friend of mine remarked, "she is on shipboard!"), though cast and recording are otherwise acceptable. As for the Bayreuth abridgment, it is hard to believe, as we listen to the Prelude, that this set was made in 1928. As the records progress, however, the quality of the reproduction proves decidedly uneven. Its existence on LP is justified as a cheap reprint and as a memento of the various distinguished artists who took part in it. Larsen-Todsen was a justly admired Isolde, but vocally variable when the set was made; Graarud and Andrésen were accomplished and popular in their day. The outstanding performance, however, is the Kurwenal of Rudolf Bockelmann. One has to be really interested in the artists to listen with anything better than toleration to the unatmospheric "Love Duet" herein contained.

Flagstad, in an earlier recording, presents the "Narrative and Curse" from Act 1 and the "Love Duet" from Act 2. The assisting artists—Höngen the Brangäne of the first selection, Shacklock in the second, and Svanholm the Tristan—are no more than foils for the star, and Dobrowen does not prove himself another Furtwängler (V LM 1151). The balance with the orchestra is far from ideal in the "Love Duet," and the Brangäne is too close. Helen Traubel, singing the "Curse," stands up to her great rival, though we must discount a few uncomfortable top tones (V LM 1132). There is no Brangäne in this performance, and there is a little less of the music than in Flagstad's. Also included is the *"Liebestod,"* but in this Traubel sounded better when she recorded it with Rodzinski for Columbia several years ago. Here the singing lacks the old surge, and again some of the high notes are a trial to her. Singing superbly in the "Love Duet," Traubel has a light-weight Tristan in Torsten Ralf, and in Herta Glaz an appealing Brangäne whose tower is located altogether too conveniently in relation to the microphone. The late Fritz Busch favors tempos not without a suggestion of rush (C ML 4055). Martha Mödl and Wolfgang

Windgassen, with Johanna Blatter as Brangäne, have also recorded the duet (Tel LGX 66004). The singing is tonally beautiful, cleanly reproduced, but not exciting, because conductor
Rother is unable to strike a spark. To emphasize this pedestrian
tendency, the balance is shamelessly thrown in favor of the
singers. Still, one listens fascinated to the intelligent vocalism
of Mödl. More especially in the Liebestod (10" Tel TM 68003)
there are reminders that this singer was once a contralto; but if
now and then she strains, and if her tones are not always steady,
she nevertheless stands forth as one of the most convincing
recent Isoldes.

Arias

*Die Meistersinger—Was duftet doch der Flieder; Wahnmonolog;
Schusterlied; Euch macht ihr's leicht; Verachtet mir die Meister
nicht; Tannhäuser—O du mein holder Abendstern; Der fliegende
Holländer—Die Frist ist um; Parsifal—Nein! lasst ihn unenthüllt!;
Tannhäuser—Blick' ich umher. Edelmann, bs; VSY, Loibner, Moralt,
Ep LC 3052.*

Otto Edelmann, the Sachs of Columbia's *Meistersinger* and the
Pogner of Urania's, has one of those big, heavy German bass
voices which can ride so easily over the largest orchestra in recording and are all too frequently encouraged to do so. That is
mainly what is wrong with these selections from *Meistersinger*.
Beckmesser might scratch up another mark against the tempos or
lack of vital pulse in the two monologues. On the evidence of
this recording, I would have said that Edelmann's voice was
better fitted to the role of Vanderdekken (the Flying Dutchman)
than to that of Sachs, but of course we know that he *can* sound
effective in the latter part. The *Parsifal* excerpt is recorded at
a lower level.

*Der fliegende Holländer—Die Frist ist um; Die Walküre—Wotans
Abschied; Die Meistersinger—Was duftet doch der Flieder; Wahn,
Wahn, überall Wahn. Hotter, b, O, D DL 9514.*

Hans Hotter is a great singing-actor, as will be immediately apparent, no matter where one comes in on this recital. The voice
itself is not first-rate, though he often surprises with a beautifully controlled *mezza voce*, and his vocalism is always expressive. There have been Wotans and Sachses with warmer, mellower
tones, but Hotter is today without a peer as the Dutchman.

Lohengrin—Nun sei bedankt; Höchstes Vertraun; Gralserzählung; Lohengrins Abschied; Tannhäuser—Lied an die Venus; Romerzählung; Meistersinger—Am stillen Herd; Preislied. Slezak, t, Et 499.

The *Lohengrin* selections, in many ways better than we often hear them, are hardly Slezak at his greatest. His voice must have been a trial to the engineers in the days of acoustic recording, for it was so big and hefty that it could easily shatter the apparatus. In these selections he does not seem comfortable. The *Tannhäuser* pieces are better, especially the piano-accompanied "Hymn to Venus." The first-act recital from *Meistersinger* is, if anything, even better; the "Prize Song" is vocally admirable, its pace a little leisurely.

Lohengrin—Höchstes Vertrau'n; In fernem Land; Die Meistersinger— Am stillen Herd; Preislied; Die Walküre—Siegmund's Monologue; Siegmund's Spring Song; Tannhäuser—Rome Narration. Svanholm, t; RCAO, Weissmann, V LM 1155.

The Swedish tenor sounds in this recital a little better than his best, thanks to the microphone buildup. Happily, his voice is not allowed to overwhelm the orchestra. He sings his various scenes with assurance and authentic style.

Tannhäuser—Elisabeths Gebet; Lohengrin—Euch Lüften, die mein Klagen; Tristan und Isolde—Curse; Liebestod. Traubel, s; RCAO, Weissmann, V LM 1122.

Die Walküre—Der Männer Sippe; Du bist der Lenz; Fort denn, eile; Lohengrin—Elsas Traum; Parsifal—Ich sah das Kind; Der fliegende Holländer—Traft ihr das Schiff; Götterdämmerung—Helle Wehr! Traubel, s; RCAO, Weissmann, V LM 1123.

It is understandable that Helen Traubel should have wanted to group together some of her most effective scenes in a couple of LP recitals, but I cannot help regretting that she has duplicated so much that she recorded when her voice was a few years younger. I will concede, nevertheless, that this *"Du bist der Lenz"* is more comfortable for her than that in the *Walküre* set (C SL 105), where she may have felt the conductor was rushing her. Certainly this performance is better poised. The *Tannhäuser* Prayer does not escape the eternal pitfall of dullness, and the *Lohengrin* excerpts present a rather too majestic Elsa. The rest of the program is good Traubel, though there are weaknesses: the sinuous lines of the *Parsifal* passage, for example, would have come through more effectively had the big voice been allowed a little more distance from the microphone. With this reservation on balance, I have only praise for the recording.

*Der fliegende Holländer—Overture; Die Frist ist um; Senta's Ballad;
Die Meistersinger—Was duftet doch der Flieder; Die Walküre—Der
Männer Sippe. Varnay, s; Schoeffler, b; ASO, Koslik, Loibner, Weigert,
Rem R 199–137.*

This disc is put forth as highlights from *The Flying Dutchman;*
presumably the *Meistersinger* and *Walküre* selections are to be
considered encores! After a so-so overture under Koslik,
Schoeffler sings the Dutchman's big monologue with great eloquence, but is not too clearly reproduced. Here and in the Ballad
the choral parts are included, which leads me to suspect that
these may be excerpts from a complete recording. Varnay's work
is assured and conscientious, if not tonally ingratiating. The
quality of her voice is inclined to be over-dark. The soprano is
most at ease in the *Walküre* scene; Schoeffler is admirable in
the *Meistersinger.*

*"Wagner Treasury." Lehmann, s; Leider, s; Rethberg, s; Gadski, s;
Schumann-Heink, c; Melchior, t; Schorr, b; Witherspoon, bs; V LCT
1001.*

*"Wagnerian Baritones." Rhode, b; Zador, b; Manowarda, b; Bohnen,
b; Schwarz, b; Et ELP 0–474.*

Victor's treasury program contains nothing that did not merit reissue, nor any singer unworthy of so impressive a memorial. Still,
one wishes matters had been managed differently. The Lotte
Lehmann bit is a side from the *Walküre, Act 1,* now available in
its entirety on LCT 1033. Here is only a fragment. Frida
Leider's *Parsifal* is a thing of great beauty, and one rarely hears
"Dich, teure Halle" proclaimed with the authority and sweep of a
Rethberg. Schorr's two *Meistersinger* monologues, however, have
been offered as four selections, with breaks between the old
original twelve-inch sides, indicating that the editor did not know
Wagner's score. The more's the pity, for these are among the
great Wagnerian recordings of the thirties. Schumann-Heink's
early *"Weiche, Wotan,"* with incidental responses by Herbert
Witherspoon, sounds odd among these electrical recordings; one
wonders why her quite magnificent later disc was not used in this
place. The Schorr *Dutchman* piece—*"Wie aus der Ferne"*—was
never released on domestic Victor, which makes it doubly welcome, but Gadski, magnificently as she sings *"Ho-jo-to-ho!,"* is
at a disadvantage in the acoustic recording. I do not think a
mixture of the two types of reproduction is generally wise, especially in a Wagner program.

Something similar may be said of the Eterna baritone collection.

Rhode displays a well-seasoned style and a voice well in character for the Dutchman's monologue, if only under control up to ·a point. He does not find the going easy in the higher register, for which reason other performances of this music will be found more satisfactory. Zador does the venomous passage from *Rheingold* known as "Alberich's Curse" in as bitter and evil a manner as anyone could wish. Schwarz, on the other hand, is disappointing in the great *Rheingold* finale, mostly for mechanical reasons. His voice is big and rich, but is so exposed by distance from the inadequate orchestra that it creates no illusion. Manowarda does the *"Wache, Wala"* passage from *Siegfried* well enough, and Bohnen demonstrates that as Hans Sachs (*"Verachtet mir die Meister nicht"*) and Gurnemanz (*"Titurel, der fromme Held"*) he could curb his bubbling energies and sing with dignity.

Songs

Fünf Gedichte. Farrell, s; SO, Stokowski, V LM 1066 (*Tannhäuser —Overture and Venusberg Music). Lemnitz, s; Raucheisen, pf, U URLP 7019 (*Lohengrin: Love Duet; Tannhäuser—Dich, teure Halle).

Wagner's five songs to texts by Mathilde Wesendonck (two of which are designated as studies for *Tristan und Isolde*) were composed for voice and piano, though the composer always thought in grand terms, and they take naturally to the Mottl orchestration with which they are generally associated. It is proper, therefore, that we should be given a choice between two performances at present (with always the possibility that the admired Flagstad-Gerald Moore recording may be added to the American lists): one with piano, the other with orchestra. The qualities of the two interpretations are appropriate to their presentation, for Tiana Lemnitz, piano-accompanied, brings out the lyrical qualities of the songs, while Eileen Farrell, against Stokowski's lavish orchestral background, plays them for drama. Lemnitz, who recorded them once before for Polydor, back in the thirties when she was in fresher voice, still commands an appealing tone, though she hardly matches Farrell's temperament.

WALTON, SIR WILLIAM (1902-   )

Belshazzar's Feast. Noble, b; LPC; Phil Prom O, Boult, W WL 5248.

With this intense Biblical setting, produced at the Leeds Festival in 1931, Walton made one of the really important modern contributions to the list of oratorios. I note that the excellent HMV-Victor recording, made some years ago under the composer's direction, has been reissued in England despite this powerful competition. Boult has caught, no less successfully than Walton, the tremendous drive of the music, and of course he is far more brilliantly reproduced. Dennis Noble is the soloist in both performances; his splendid delivery will undoubtedly furnish the model for all interpreters to come. The choral diction in the Boult recording is remarkable: note the final t's on such words as "wept." In the final Hallelujah's there is an obtrusive sound which I take to be Sir Adrian singing in the manner of Toscanini, to spur his forces on.

WEBER, BEN (1916-   )

Symphony on Poems of William Blake. Galjour, b, O; Stokowski, V LM 1785 (*Harrison: Suite for Violin, Piano and Small Orchestra).

Whether one likes it or not, Ben Weber's *Symphony* is an unusual experience. In the first place, it is a striking idea to set the poetry of Blake in twelve-tone rows; in the second, the composer's method of setting is the kind that takes poetry apart, pretty much line by line, pronounces it, then lets the instruments take over for comment. This means there is nothing left of the lyrical lines or of the form of the verses. Something is happening all the time—usually several somethings. With Stokowski at the helm, it hardly needs saying that the details of the score come through with marvelous clarity, if with little "hall" effect. Galjour, whose voice is treated as a part of the ensemble rather than as the center of attraction, has little chance to modulate his tone, but sings with the most exemplary diction. It is hardly his fault that the inflections do not seem to have much to do with Blake.

WEBER, KARL MARIA VON (1786-1826)

Choral Work

Kampf und Sieg. Schmidt-Glänzel, s; Fleischer, c; Lutze, t; Krämer, b; Radio Leipzig Ch & O, Kegel, U URLP 7126.

This curious work is a patriotic outburst occasioned by the news of the victory at Waterloo in 1815. Aside from its rousing finale, the chief interest lies in its premonitions of the greater Weber who was still to come, the Weber of *Freischütz* and *Oberon*. The cantata is performed here with considerable fervor and some good vocalism, though the bass soloist is rendered ineffectual by a bothersome wobble. Chorus and orchestra perform competently, and all are well recorded.

Operas

Abu Hassan. Schwarzkopf, s; Witte, t; Bohnen, bs; RBC & O, Ludwig, U URLP 7029.

This harmless little work has a delightfully ridiculous plot; this, however, is not the concern of the recording, which omits the spoken dialogue. The three well-known singers play the comedy in their music for all it is worth. It is good to hear from Michael Bohnen again, and to note that he retains much of his voice and all his old unction.

Der Freischütz. Trötschel, s; Beilke, s; Aldenhoff, t; Böhme, bs; etc.; DOC; SAX, Kempe, U URLP 403 [3]. Cunitz, s; Loose, s; Hopf, t; Rus, b; etc.; VSOC & O, Ackermann, L LLA 5 [3]. Paludan, s; Löser, s; Wehofschütz, t; Kral, bs; etc.; ASO, Doehrer, Rem R 199–100 [3]. (Abridged) Müller, s; Spletter, s; Seider, t; Hann, bs; etc.; BSOC & O, Heger, D DX 112 [2].

The Remington performance may be dismissed at once with acknowledgments for its good intentions and its popular price. There are good spots—Wehofschütz's *"Durch die Wälder"* is creditable, and Paludan's *"Und ob die Wolke"* surprisingly mellow after her none-too-steady *"Leise, leise."* But the conductor is heavy-handed, and the whole performance not very neat. Of the other two complete versions my preference is for the Urania, though the choice is by no means easy. Either would please me better than the abridged Decca performance, made, I understand, during the late war. Neither boasts a first-rate Max; Urania has the better Kaspar. Both Ännchens are good; Urania's is the better Agathe. The Dresden company makes more of the *Wolf's Glen Scene*, and the theater effects generally are better in the Urania set. In the abridgment we hear a Maria Müller still able to remind us of her ten successful seasons at the Metropolitan, stylistically superb and capable of some thrilling phrasing, but guilty of some acid high tones and too much unsteadiness. She is ably seconded by the light soprano of Carla Spletter; their duet is very charming.

The tenor August Seider seems to have one of those German voices trained beyond their natural size; his tones are big but not steady. The large brassy baritone of Georg Hann is just right for the role of Kaspar. The fly in the ointment is the cuts, for nothing seems complete except Agathe's two big arias, and orchestrally something is missing even there. The spoken dialogue, some of which is included, might have been forgone in favor of more music. The overture, available in many other recordings, is omitted altogether.

Oberon. Bader, s; Sailer, s; Muench, m-s; Fehringer, t; Liebl, t; etc.; SDRC & O, Müller-Kray, Per SPL 575 [2].

Although *Oberon* was composed to an English text, I suspect Weber always thought in German, and so his opera somehow seems more natural in his own language. At any rate, if we hear the music at all, it is usually in German, and the work is rarely given outside Germany. But even in Germany Weber is not very well performed, such is the virtuosity he demands of his hero and heroine. In the present cast the soprano is afflicted with a wide tremolo, and the tenor just does not have the facility to manipulate the florid passages and sustain the high *tessitura* of his part. The rest of the cast is more or less of the same stripe, with the exceptions of Muench, who sings Fatima's airs acceptably, and Sailer, who outshines all her colleagues in the small part of the Mermaid. The orchestral sound is reasonably good, though for once there is rather too much impression of space, and the tone is somewhat shallow. The conductor's part in the proceedings is competent rather than masterly.

WEBERN, ANTON VON (1883 - 1945)

Four Songs, opus 12. Beardslee, s; Monod, pf, Dia 17 (*Concerto; Variations; Quartet).*

The four very brief songs take up only a fraction of one side of this disc. No titles are furnished either on the jacket or on the label. The first text is a folk song, *"Der Tag ist vergangen"*; the second, from Hans Bethge's *Chinesische Flöte,* is *"Die geheimnisvolle Flöte"*; the third is *"Schien mir's als ich sah die Sonne,"* from Strindberg's *Gespenstersonate,* and the fourth Goethe's *"Gleich und Gleich."* This is our only recorded example of songs by a leading modernist: the singing is surprisingly appealing.

WEIGL, KARL (1881 - 1949)

*O cricket sing!; Woe to eyes!; O blessed darkness, heavenwide. Howland, m-s; Woodstock Qt, Tri 1 (*Sonata, Viola and Piano; Quartet No. 6).*

Weigl, a Viennese and a younger contemporary of Schoenberg, spent the last decade of his life in America. The three songs recorded are characteristic of his solid workmanship and his late-romantic style. Alice Howland sings them richly in her dark-hued voice, against the close-textured playing of the string quartet. The German poems are sung in English translation.

WEILL, KURT (1900 - 1950)

The Threepenny Opera. Lenya, s; Sullivan, s; Arthur, s; Merrill, t; Wolfson, b; etc.; O, Matlowsky, MGM E 3121.
Die Dreigroschenoper—Highlights. Lenya, s; Gerron, b; etc.; O, Mackeben, Cap P 8117.

The first listing is the *Dreigroschenoper* in Mark Blitzstein's adaptation and translation, as presented in New York in 1954. Beyond question, his is one of the successful operatic translations; though his text is by no means a literal rendering of the ideas in the original, it fits the music so well that one forgets that it has not always been there. The cast could hardly be better. Though voice for its own sake counts for little in this style of music, here are several authentic singers, as well as an impressive group of *diseurs*. Outstanding is Lotte Lenya, the widow of Kurt Weill, singing the role of Jenny, which has belonged to her since the world *première*. Her subtle delivery of the English lines may well stand as a model. For those who would compare English with German, Americans with Central European performers, and—most interesting of all—Lotte Lenya then and Lotte Lenya now, we have the original-cast performance still available. The reproduction carries its more than twenty years exceedingly well, and in their quite different way the singers match their counterparts. Lenya is again the outstanding artist among them.

WILBYE, JOHN (1574-1638)

Flora gave me fairest flowers; Adieu, sweet Amaryllis; And though my love abounding; As fair as morn; I fall, o stay me; Weep, o mine eyes (three voices); Hard destinies are love and beauty parted; Fly not so swift, my dear; Oft have I vowed; Sweet honey sucking bees; Yet sweet, take heed; Happy, o happy he; Ye that do live in pleasures; O what shall I do?; Thus saith my Chloris bright; All pleasure is of this condition; Weep, weep, mine eyes. Randolph Singers, W WL 5221.

Among the groups that specialize in the madrigal literature, the Randolph Singers have enjoyed an enviable reputation in recent years. I am grateful to them for making this fine music available, but I suspect they prepared for the recording in something of a hurry. Several of the madrigals seem to be brushed through without particular relish, and in too many of them there is a lack of poise. The individual singers remain too strongly individual in intonation as well as quality.

WOLF, HUGO (1860-1903)

Opera

Der Corregidor. Fuchs, s; Teschemacher, s; Erb, t; Hermann, b; Böhme, bs; Frick, bs; Hann, bs; etc.; DOC; SAX, Elmendorff, U URLP 208 [3].

Those of us who have known and admired Wolf's songs had hardly dared to hope for an opportunity to hear his reputedly un-stage-worthy opera, much less to have it in a recording. To be critical of the results, then, may seem like carping. Or is it honorable to wish the conductor had been Bruno Walter? Elmendorff is an old hand, but the listener will miss many details in the orchestral web, even though he follows the records with the score. This is not to be blamed entirely on the conductor, however, for in the approved manner of reproduced opera, the singers are given the better of the balance. The best of the singers is Josef Hermann in the role of the Miller. The distinguished sopranos, Teschemacher and Fuchs, sound very lovely indeed. Karl Erb tends to overdo, and he plays fast and loose with the notes as Wolf wrote them. None of the other singers will disappoint. Numerous cuts in the score in some cases amount to mutilation.

Songs

Frühling über's Jahr; Auf eine Christblume; Die Geister am Mummelsee; Mausfallensprüchlein; Nachtzauber; Morgenthau; Der Genesene an die Hoffnung; Denk es, o Seele; Blumengruss; Du denkst mit einem Fädchen; Anakreons Grab; Nimmersatte Liebe; Und willst du deinen Liebsten sterben sehen; Lied vom Winde. Bothwell, s; Meyer, pf, Roy 1310.

> The singer (whom I have never otherwise heard) can scarcely be done justice in this noisy recording. As it comes to us, the voice seems modest but serviceable, the singing always tasteful. But even at the bargain price, one wishes the record were better mechanically.

Fussreise; In der Frühe; Lied eines Verliebten; Gesang Weylas; Der Tambour; Nachtzauber; Der Musikant; Verschwiegene Liebe; Heimweh (Eichendorff). Calder, b; Carley, pf, 10" All AL 4045.

> The recording here is reasonably good, though the piano tone lacks depth and richness. Calder has a pleasant voice, and proves himself a serious and tasteful singer. But one does not get excited.

Verborgenheit; Anakreons Grab; Blumengruss; Gleich und gleich; Frühling über's Jahr. Danco, s; Agosti, pf, 10" L LPS 335 (*Brahms: Songs).

> Danco has the discrimination always to choose songs suited to her voice and style. Such airy pieces as "*Gleich und Gleich*" and "*Frühling über's Jahr*" or the almost painfully lovely "*Blumengruss*" are naturals for her. Few vocalists sing as musically or as accurately as she, though some may bring greater warmth to their songs.

Italienisches Liederbuch—Sixteen Songs. Fischer-Dieskau, b; Klust, pf, D DL 9632.

> This disc contains a number of the composer's most priceless miniatures. Fischer-Dieskau has few rivals to the title of finest contemporary lieder singer; his voice is at once powerful and tender (one does not sense in his recordings all the power he actually has at his command), and his mind works through his magnificent diction on every subtle word-coloring or turn of phrase.

Michelangelo Lieder; Cophtische Lieder, 1, 2; Grenzen der Menschheit; Prometheus; Harfenspielerlieder; Geselle, wir woll'n uns in Kütten hüllen. Hotter, b; Moore, pf, An 35057.

> Hotter's program embraces some of the strongest and most mascu-

line songs in the Wolf repertoire. His is not a sensuous voice. I doubt that it ever was, and certainly now it has lost such bloom as it once had. Still, he amply compensates by the penetration of his interpretations, and he does have an amazingly effective *mezza voce*. His quiet opening in the first *Michelangelo Lied* is both novel and striking, and gives him a magnificent opportunity for a climax. Perhaps the finest moment in the recital comes at the end of the first *Harfenspieler Lied*, *"Denn alle Schuld rächt sich auf Erden."* The recording is not notable for liveness, though it is well balanced and intimate; the piano tone is not of the best.

Fussreise; Anakreons Grab; Über Nacht; Auf einer Wanderung; Und steht ihr früh am Morgen auf; An eine Aeolsharfe; An die Geliebte; Gesegnet sei; Gesang Weylas; Der Musikant; Der Rattenfänger; Verborgenheit; Der Gärtner; Abschied. Poell, b; Holletschek, pf, W WL 5048.

This amazingly versatile baritone can be heartily recommended in these songs. From the morning joyousness of *"Fussreise,"* through the profound quiet of *"Anakreons Grab,"* the rapt adoration of *"Und steht ihr früh,"* and the ebullient spirits of *"Der Rattenfänger,"* to the malicious humor of *"Abschied"* is a musical excursion calling for varied expression, and Poell is equal to it. The voice has power and tenderness, both poise and temperament.

Bedeckt mich mit Blumen; Gesegnet sei das Grün; O wär' dein Haus; Ihr jungen Leute; Wie glänzt der helle Mond; Du denkst mit einem Fädchen; In der Frühe; Sie blasen zum Abmarsch; Blumengruss; Nun wandre, Maria; Als ich auf dem Euphrat schiffte; Ein Ständchen Euch zu bringen; Verborgenheit; Phänomen; Anakreons Grab; Nimmersatte Liebe. Schumann, s; Reeves, pf, All AL 98.

It is sad to have to report this record a failure: it does not catch the essential thing at all. This I blame more on the recording than on the undeniable fact that the singer was past her best days when it was made. She was, after all, still a great artist, as all who heard her last recitals well remember. Several of the songs can still be found on earlier imported 78-rpm discs, which tell quite a different story.

Herr, was trägt der Boden hier; Wenn du zu den Blumen gehst; Wer tat deinem Füsslein weh?; In der Frühe. Souzay, b; Bonneau, pf, L LL 535 (*Schumann: Dichterliebe).

Souzay sings in the careful, intelligent manner characteristic of his interpretations in German, but somehow never succeeds in convincing us that he belongs in this repertoire.

Der Feuerreiter; Gesellenlied; Denk' es, o Seele; Im Frühling.
Roswaenge, t; Raucheisen, pf. Über Nacht; Gesang Weylas; Rat einer
Alten. Klose, c; Raucheisen, pf. In der Frühe; Nixe Binsefuss;
Mignon; St Nepomuks Vorabend; Elfenlied; Tretet ein, hoher Krieger;
Wie glänzt der helle Mond; Er ist's. Simon, s; Ulanowsky, pf. U
URLP 7025.

This joint recital of two veterans and a neophyte has much to
recommend it, especially on the first side of the disc. Older
collectors will remember Roswaenge's interpretations of the
grisly ballad of the "Fire-Rider," and the Meistersinger-like song
of the apprentice, both included in the sixth volume of the old
Hugo Wolf Society. He has certainly lost nothing of the powerful
virtuosity that made him a good choice for these big songs, and
his voice has withstood remarkably well the ravages of time.
The disturbing philosophy of *"Denk' es, o Seele"* is vividly
realized, and the previously unrecorded *"Im Frühling"* shows
that strength is not the singer's only asset. Klose sings *"Über*
Nacht" and the bardic *"Gesang Weylas"* operatically, but with
telling effect, though she works too hard at giving advice to the
young in *"Rat einer Alten."* The voice is at its superb best.
The American Annemarie Simon presents a nicely varied program with admirable taste and musicianly phrasing. She too
has the usual tendency to make too much of her songs, the lovely
and little-known *"St. Nepomuks Vorabend"* suffering the most
from this. I have still to hear a realization in performance of
the special kind of barbed humor inherent in *"Tretet ein, hoher*
Krieger." In sum, this is commendable if not completely communicative singing by a voice lovely at its best, but inclined to
shrillness.

Die Nacht; Liebesglück; Ob auch finstre Blicke glitten; Morgenstim-
*mung. Schloss, s; Brice, pf, IRCC L-7000 (*Franz, Schumann,*
Strauss: Songs).

This disc is valuable on two counts: first for the unusual and
worth-while repertoire of four composers, and second for the pre-
eminently satisfactory singing. Schloss's voice is ample and
pleasing, with the unusual capability of suggesting the mood of a
song simply by tone color. Above and beyond this, she is a
musician with real understanding of the texts she sings, especially those in darker moods. Her four Wolf songs are not other-

wise available; but they have more than their rarity to recommend them.

*Italienisches Liederbuch—Twenty-two Songs. Seefried, s; Werba, pf, D DL 9743 (*Brahms: Songs).*

With these twenty-two songs and the sixteen recorded by Fischer-Dieskau, Decca has given us all but nine of the forty-six *Italian* lieder (one song is duplicated in the two sets). As the collection divides itself into masculine and feminine poems, it would seem that an opportunity had been missed by the producer, with twó singers so well equipped, in producing so nearly complete a performance. Seefried is always admirably musical, always the comprehending artist. Her voice is appealingly bright and lyrical in quality, just cool enough to suit these sophisticated dramas in miniature. She is best where pathos is required—the ironic songs have been more bitingly sung by others. But this recital adds up to a more than satisfying whole. I liked especially *"Wir haben beide lange Zeit geschwiegen"* and the climactic *"Wenn du, mein Liebster, zeigst zum Himmel auf,"* though I could admire the way in which the singer lifts *"Mein Liebster ist so klein"* above the usual strain of sarcasm. Well as Seefried sings the short Brahms group, I would have liked to hear more Wolf.

*Auf eine Wanderung; Verschwiegene Liebe; Verschling der Abgrund; Um Mitternacht; Cophtisches Lied No. 2; Elfenlied; Schlafendes Jesuskind; Auf dem grünen Balkon. Thebom, m-s; Hughes, pf, V LM 1203 (*Mahler: Lieder eines fahrenden Gesellen).*

Thebom remains an admirable opera singer, and she gives her best in the bigger songs. The exuberant *"Auf eine Wanderung"* rejoices in the singer's fullest tones, and the bitter *"Verschling der Abgrund"* becomes a miniature drama. On the other hand, *"Um Mitternacht"* needs endless reserve and a note of calm that Thebom does not capture, and *"Verschwiegene Liebe"* suffers from fluttery tone.

WOLF-FERRARI, ERMANNO (1876-1948)

I Quattro Rusteghi. Noni, s; Orell, s; Carlin, t; Ulivi, b; Corena, bs; Dalamangas, bs; etc.; RIO, Simonetto, Cet 1239 [3].

Wolf-Ferrari's comedy, in his familiar eighteenth-century manner, has a text in Venetian dialect. The recording is given in the original, which adds a very special flavor to the music. One does not have to understand it all to take pleasure in the sheer sound of this language. The cast, by now mostly familiar, obviously has a wonderful time with the score's bubbling humor, infectious tunes, and shifting rhythms.

ZANDONAI, RICCARDO (1883-1944)

Francesca da Rimini. Caniglia, s; Canali, m-s; Prandelli, t; Tagliabue, b; etc.; RIC & O, Guarnieri, Cet 1229 [3].

Francesca da Rimini, which enjoyed two seasons at the Metropolitan in 1917-19, may be called a lesser *L'Amore dei Tre Re*, lacking only the musical distinction of that fine opera. Caniglia brings to the title role her ripe experience and much of the vocal quality of her best days, only the high reaches taxing her unduly. Prandelli is a satisfactory Paolo. There is occasionally some uncertainty of pitch throughout the cast, but for the most part the singing is good and well recorded.

ZELLER, KARL (1842-1898)

Der Vogelhändler—Medley. Cunitz, s; Loose, s; Terkal, t; Grosskurth, b; etc.; LC; BAVRO, Mattes, 10" Tel TM 68008.

The one thing one in this country is likely to know about Karl Zeller and his little operetta is that the work contains a long popular hit generally called *"The Nightingale Song."* Now that we have this medley, we learn that this was not Zeller's only inspiration: here are two sides packed with tunes. The cast is made up of names well known to opera- and operetta-recording collectors, and the record is satisfying in every way.

ALDEBURGH FESTIVAL, 1953

Ode in Honor of Great Britain—Rule, Britannia (Arne). Pears, t. O grant the Queen a long life (Purcell). Deller, counter-t; Pears, t; Lumsden, bs. Now all the air shall ring (Arne). Mandikian, s; Whitrad, s; Fest O, Holst, L LL 808 (*Oldham, Tippett, Berkeley, Britten, Searle, Walton: Variations on an Elizabethan Theme).

This is a memento of the Coronation year. Of special interest is the singing of "*Rule, Britannia*" in its original form, though one might have wished to hear it in a more imposing and solider voice than that of Peter Pears. The Purcell anthem, with its unusual voice combination, is something of a find. The last piece, by Arne, deserves to be better sung. ·

ALL SAINTS CHURCH CHOIR, WORCESTER, MASS. (William Self)

FIVE CENTURIES OF CHORAL MUSIC: Adoramus Te (Rosselli); Alma Redemptoris mater (Palestrina); I will not leave you comfortless (Titcomb); Hymn of Praise (Self); O Lord most holy (Franck); Gallia— Jerusalem (Gounod); Emitte spiritum tuum (Shuetky); If ye love me (Tallis); Father, thy holy spirit send (M. Franck); Come, blessed death; Subdue us with thy kindness; Jesu, joy of man's desiring (Bach). CE 1023.

CHORAL MASTERPIECES FROM THE RUSSIAN LITURGY: Hear my prayer; Out of the depths (Archangelsky); Alleluia! Christ is risen; Hear my prayer (Kopolyoff); Cherubic hymn; Nunc dimittis (Gretchaninoff); Bless the Lord, O my soul (Ippolitov-Ivanov); To Thee, O Lord (Rachmaninoff); O gladsome light (Kastelsky); Divine praise (Bortniansky). CE 1022.

The historical ring of the cover titles should throw no one off: these are not musicological programs, but a kind of American choir festival. All Saints Church has a boy choir of which it has reason to be proud. Though part of the first program is made up of transcriptions, excerpts, and translations, there are also the Rosselli (often attributed to Palestrina), the Palestrina, and the Tallis, not to mention the contemporary Titcomb and Self, which are authentic enough in performance. The Russian selection

contains many of those works which have achieved popularity in
this country and have become staples in the choir repertory.

· AMATO, PASQUALE, baritone

*Rigoletto—Povero Rigoletto; Cortigiani; Aïda—Ciel! mio padre (with
Mazzoleni,s); I Due Foscari—Questa dunque è l'iniqua mercede
(Verdi); Tosca—Te Deum; Gioconda—Così mantieni il patto (with
Mazzoleni, s). Et 482.*

As a member of the Metropolitan Opera during the second decade
of this century, Amato made numerous Victor recordings that enjoyed great popularity and have never become rare. The present
program is made up of earlier examples, recorded by Fonotipia
beginning in 1906. Most of the numbers were repeated later, but
these early "takes" have special interest for collectors. The
voice is in its full glory, large and round, with a rapid *vibrato* to
give it a peculiar vitality. Recording techniques had advanced
between this version of the big scene from *Rigoletto* and the
Victor performance, but the voice is more opulent here. The same
goes for the *Tosca*, a scene really too much for the best acoustic
recording. The *Aïda* duet is certainly better in the Victor version, because there the partner was Gadski, and she was in superb voice (half of their performance is available on V LCT
1035). Mazzoleni may be more genuinely Italian, but she is also
more shrill.

ANDERSON, MARIAN, contralto

*Deep river; He's got the whole world in His hands; Roll, Jordan, roll;
Go down, Moses; Crucifixion; Sometimes I feel like a motherless
child; Let us break bread together; Plenty good room; Every time I
feel de spirit; If He change my name; O what a beautiful city. Rupp,
pf, 10" V LRM 7006.*
*Nobody knows the trouble I see; Ride on, King Jesus; Hear de lambs
a cryin'; Sinner, please don't let this harvest pass; Soon-a will be
done; My Lord, what a morning; Were you there?; On ma journey; De
Gospel train. Rupp, pf, 10" V LM 110.*

My choice between these two sets would fall on the first because
it contains songs that seem to me outstanding. But though some
of the arrangements Anderson uses are on the elaborate side, her

spirituals are always deeply and sincerely felt. The best, to my mind, are *"He's got the whole world in His hands," "Crucifixion," "If He change my name,"* and the directly eloquent *"Let us break bread together."*

ANGELES, VICTORIA DE LOS, soprano

SPANISH SONGS: El jilguerito con pico de oro (Laserna); Canción de Cuna (Anon.); Minué Cantada (Bassa); Seguidillas Religiosas (Pla); Canción Picaresca (Palomino). Chiasson, hpschd. *El paño Murciano (Trad.); Farruca (Turina); Hablame de amores (Fusta); El retrato de Isabela (Vives); El amor y los ojos ("Canciones Epigramaticas").* Moore, pf, V LM 6017 [2] *(*Falla: La Vida Breve).*

SPANISH FOLK SONGS: La vi llorando; Ya se van los pastores; Canción de trilla; Parado de Valldemosa; Nik baditut; Adregaya; El Rusinyol; Granadina; Playera; El Testament d'Amelia. Tarrago, gtr, 10" V LM 63.

SPANISH FOLK SONGS, VOL.2: El mirar de la maja (Granados); Non quieras avellanas; Jota (Guiridi); La maja dolorosa; El majo discreto (Granados). Moore, pf, 10" V LM 131 *(*Falla: Siete Canciones Populares Españoles).*

The coming of Victoria de los Angeles to the opera houses and concert halls of our feverish postwar period has been something like the breath of spring. Hers is a voice of lovely quality, magnificently under control (witness her Rosina in Victor's *Barber of Seville*) and capable of power as well as softness. Her repertoire spans the nowadays incredible gap between Rossini and Wagner; she shines with equal brightness in Mozart and Puccini. In recital I have not found her the mistress of lieder which she has been acclaimed, but there is no resisting her in the Spanish repertoire, whether sung to guitar, harpsichord, or piano. The first songs listed are Hispanic classics in the modern arrangements of Nin and Subira. *El jilguerito con pico de oro* is particularly attractive. When the piano comes in for the second half of the program the ear needs a moment or two to adjust, but the wizardry of Gerald Moore soon works its spell. The first "Folk Song" record is more aptly titled than the second (which is art from the word go), but it, too, is definitely a concert performance. What one enjoys is the beautiful clear voice in the not too varied Spanish melodies.

ANGLICAN CHANTS, etc.

MUSIC OF THE LITURGY IN ENGLISH: Plainsong; Holy Communion; Evening Prayer; Anglican Chant and Merbecke; Morning Prayer; Holy Communion. General Theological Seminary Ch, Brown; Mixed Ch, Gilbert, C ML 4528.

These Anglican services fill a gap in the recorded repertoire. Coming from General Theological Seminary, they represent traditions that may be accepted as standard. The presentation has dignity and a special kind of beauty.

L'ANTHOLOGIE SONORE

VOL.1: Gregorian Chant to the 13th Century; The 13th and 14th Centuries; The 14th and 15th Centuries; Machaut and Dufay; The 15th Century; Josquin des Pres and Other Composers of the Late 15th and Early 16th Centuries. Pro Musica Antiqua, Cape; Les Paraphonistes de St. Jean des Matines, Van; etc; HS AS 1–5 [5].

VOL.2: (Record 3) Vocal Music of the 15th, 16th, and 17th Centuries; The Italian Madrigal at the End of the Renaissance. Luca Marenzio Ens, Saraceni, HS AS 8.

VOL.7: (Record 4) Orchestral and Vocal Music of the 18th Century; Mozart, Motets. Soloists; Anth Son Ch & O, Duruflé, HS AS 34.

In embarking on a new edition of the famous *Anthologie*, the Haydn Society aims not at complete transferral of the series to LP, but at putting into a new perspective those parts of it which meet modern standards of reproduction, and continuing, meanwhile, to add new material. The chief complaint against the old series was its apparently casual sequence. So many recordings were gathered together representing so many periods of musical history, and in whatever order they happened to be issued, a booklet was prepared to cover them. The new *Anthologie* begins with Gregorian Chant, and each LP side is devoted to a period or some aspect of music history. It may be surprising that so much can be presented in the first issue without even drawing on some of the long-familiar early releases, and the obvious questions about how some of them could possibly survive the change of speed are left mercifully unanswered. What has been used sounds remarkably well. There are also some new things—lots of them, and fine ones, too, notably the Banchieri *Festino* and the Mozart motets.

ARIAS DE ZARZUELAS

El Cabo Primero—Romanza de Pilar (Caballero). Linares, s. El Niño Judio—Cancion Española (Luna). Berchman, s. El Barbero de Sevilla—Me llaman la primorosa (Nieto y Jiminez). Olaria, s. Seguidilla del Barberillo de Lavapies—Cancion de paloma (Barbieri). Rivadeneira, c. Bohemios—Romanza de Cosette (Vives). Olaria, s. Gigantes y Cabezudos—Romanza de la carta (Caballero). Berchman, s. El Duo de la Africana—Romanza (Caballero). Rivadeneira, c. Marina—Rondo (Arrieta). Linares, s. Orquesta Sinfonica Española, Martinez, Mont FM-LD 17.

For a sampling of the *zarzuela* in its arias, this disc could hardly be improved. The music is strangely suggestive of other schools of light opera; the voices for the most part are very appealing; the style is beyond all praise. The singers all record well.

ARIE, RAPHAEL, basso

OPERATIC RECITAL: Boris Godunov—Death of Boris; La Sonnambula —Vi ravviso; Don Carlo—Ella giammai m'amò; Il Barbiere di Siviglia —La calunnia. LSO, Krips; SR, Erede, 10" L LPS 98.
RUSSIAN OPERATIC ARIAS: Eugene Onegin—Everyone knows love on earth; Prince Igor—I hate a dreary life; Sadko—Song of the Viking Guest; A Life for the Czar—They guess the truth. PCO, Erede, 10" L LD 9074.

Arie, remembered for honorable service at New York's City Center, has a good solid voice of the Russian type. He is at his best in the second recital listed, though his voice is sometimes hoarse in the upper reaches, and the reproduction is quite loud. From the first disc, the *Boris* and *Don Carlo* selections, at least, seem to be the recordings issued at 78 rpm several years back, and considered exceptional at the time. Today they are somewhat below par, what with too strong bass and lack of clarity in the highs. The feature of the *Boris* scene is the use of the original Mussorgsky orchestration. The singing is good, if hardly as exciting as that of some other Borises we have known. *"Vi ravviso"* is reasonably well performed, though not in the purest *bel canto* tradition; the record includes at least an abbreviated run through the *cabaletta* which follows the aria. The artist is better in the *Don Carlo* soliloquy; the singing here is tonally richer, more surely characterized, than in the rest of this program. The *Barbiere* interpretation is effective enough.

BARBIERI, FEDORA, mezzo-soprano

OLD ITALIAN SONGS AND AIRS: Un certo non so che (Vivaldi); Piangete, ohimè (Carissimi); Rinaldo—Lascia ch'io pianga (Handel); Serse—Affè! Affè! mi fate ridere (Cavalli); Se tu m'ami (Pergolesi); Nel cor più non mi sento (Paisiello); Arianna—Lasciatemi morire (Monteverdi); Come raggio di sol (Caldara); Demofonte—Ahi! che forse si miei dì (Cherubini); Il Pirro e Demetrio—Le violette (A. Scarlatti); Bella fiamma (Marcello); Gli Zingari in fiera—Chi vuol la zingarella (Paisiello). Marzollo, pf, Vox PL 7980.

Fedora Barbieri, for several years one of the leading members of the Metropolitan Opera, is admired for her big, vibrant voice, for her temperament, and for her abilities as an operatic actress. These qualities have been caught in several recorded operas— notably *Gioconda, Trovatore,* and *Ballo in Maschera*—but they do not make her a *bel canto* artist, and this is what her program of *"Old Italian Songs and Airs"* calls for. The selections are classics in all senses of the word, and some rather famous ones —Handel's *"Lascia ch'io pianga,"* Scarlatti's *"Le violette"*— are not otherwise available on LP; still others—Cavalli's *"Affè! Affè!. mi fate ridere,"* Cherubini's *"Ahi! che forse si miei dì"*— are new to discs.

BATTISTINI, MATTIA, baritone

Pagliacci—Prologo; Ernani—O dei verd' anni miei; Macbeth—Pietà, rispetto, amore; Rigoletto—Sì, vendetta (with Hayes, s); La Favorita —Vien, Leonora; Lucia di Lammermoor—Cruda funesta smania; Don Sebastiano—O Lisbona (Donizetti); Le Nozze di Figaro—Non più andrai. Et 0-462.

These are without exception outstanding Battistini recordings; in every one of them he pours out his fullest tones with superb prodigality. Were I to name a "best," it would be either the *Macbeth* or the *Favorita* aria. In the *Ernani* we have an especially interesting demonstration of his often remarked trick of pushing a sustained high tone a little sharp just before leaving it. Lulu Hayes, his partner in the *Rigoletto* duet, seems to have been a serviceable soprano.

BERGER, ERNA, soprano

Semele—Oh sleep, why dost thou leave me? (Handel); Lachen und Weinen; An die Nachtigall (Schubert); Exsultate, jubilate (Mozart); Geheimnis; Das Mädchen spricht (Brahms); Ophelia Songs from Hamlet (Strauss); Pantomime; Clair de lune; Pierrot; Apparition (Debussy). Raucheisen, pf, U URLP 7060.

Berger, who since the retirement of Lotte Lehmann has been advertised as "the first lady of lieder," made her reputation as an opera singer, and first came to America to join the Metropolitan in 1949. Record collectors had known her voice for nearly two decades before that. Hers is a pure, almost virginal, soprano which has lost little of its bloom in the years of the artist's maturity. Whatever she does is vocally admirable and musically well conceived. She is more at home in the songs of this program than in the piano-accompanied Handel aria and Mozart motet. Somehow or other, in these the essential spark is missing. The Schubert and Brahms lieder are pleasantly turned, but the real value of the disc derives from the unusual Strauss Shakespeare songs and the four little-known early Debussy items. Here she is preferable to Pons (C ML 2135). A Victor recital (10" LM 133) is devoted to Schubert, except for the Mozart *Re Pastore* aria, unfortunately sung in German, with the proper violin obbligato, but piano accompaniment.

BJOERLING, JUSSI, tenor

Die Forelle; Die Allmacht; Ständchen; Wanderers Nachtlied; Die böse Farbe (Schubert); Die Mainacht (Brahms); Es muss ein Wunderbares sein (Liszt); Verborgenheit (Wolf); En Svane; En Drøm (Grieg); Ständchen; Morgen (Strauss); Svarta rosor (Sibelius); Tonerna (Sjöberg); Lilacs (Rachmaninoff); Ideale (Tosti). Schauwecker, pf, V LM 1771.

The importation of the first Bjoerling discs in the thirties caused a stir among those who enjoy Italian opera sung by a strong healthy voice, but regret the emotional excesses that seem to creep into such singing. Bjoerling has proved one of the most dependable of tenors; one can rarely go wrong with his records. This lieder program represents his recent work: it does not present his voice in all its pristine freshness and beauty. There is not enough intimacy in *"Die Forelle"* or in *"Wanderers Nachtlied."* One admires rather the support that makes it possible for

him to sail over the top of the long phrases in *"Die Mainacht"*
(a real vocal challenge), and one thrills to his tonal outpouring in
"Die böse Farbe." In the Scandinavian songs, however, his
soft singing takes on intensity; he throws entirely new light on
Sjöberg's *"Tonerna."* But, on the whole, it is in the full-voice
singing that the tenor sustains his reputation. There is a strangely
indefinite chord, sounding for all the world like an incredible mistake, in Schauwecker's playing of *"Morgen."* More characteristic,
perhaps, is the usual collection of operatic arias (10" V LM 105)
—*Pagliacci, Faust, Cavalleria, Bohème, Africana, Carmen*—
among which the *Faust* deserves special praise. And with Robert
Merrill he does the expected duets from *Forza del Destino, Don
Carlo, Bohème,* and *Pêcheurs de perles,* as well as the (from
them) not expected one from *Otello* (10" V LM 7007). This is
good healthy singing all down the line, but I wish the sponsors
had not seen fit to repeat the *Don Carlo* recording which is part
of the Highlights from that opera (V LM 1128).

BONCI, ALESSANDRO, *tenor*

*Puritani—A te, o cara; Elisir d'Amore—Una furtiva lagrima; Quanto
è bella; Favorita—Spirto gentil; Una vergine; Rigoletto—Parmi
veder; Martha—M'appari; Paride ed Elena—O del mio dolce ardor
(Gluck); Lucia—Tombe degli avi miei; Fra poco; Tu che a Dio;
Andrea Chénier—Un dì all' azzuro spazio; Don Pasquale—Cercherò
lontana terra; Tornami a dir (with Pinkert, s); Bohème—Che gelida
manina. Scala 811.*

In his heyday Bonci's admirers used to pit him against Caruso,
proclaiming that though Enrico might have the greater voice,
Alessandro was the real artist. Like his rival, Bonci was a
prolific recorder, beginning in 1905 and continuing even into the
electrical period, but his records never achieved popularity comparable to that of Caruso's. The reason seems clear: though they
do give an idea of his style, it is hardly credible that they do
justice to the quality of his voice. There is a tendency to tonal
whiteness, and at times his carefully cultivated *vibrato* seems excessive. Still, one admires the grace and skill of his ornamentation and his extraordinary vocal control. This recital shows him
mostly at his recorded best, and there is evidence of care in the
transfer to LP. Perhaps the best number is *"A te, o cara,"* with
its high D flat, though the *Lucia* airs are also very fine. That

he did not have the style for Gluck is demonstrated in his least happy selection. A goodly portion of the program is repeated in a rival LP (GAR 101), which is less rich in sound. The importance of correcting the speeds of these old recordings is to be noted in the two dubbings of *"Spirto gentil."* The GAR disc has the *Barber of Seville* duet with the famous baritone Corradetti, but it is not very successfully reproduced.

BONINSEGNA, CELESTINA, soprano

Trovatore—Tacea la notte placida; D'amor sull' ali rosee; Gioconda —Suicidio; Cavalleria Rusticana—Voi lo sapete; Ballo in Maschera —Love Duet (with Del Ry, t); Morrò, ma prima in grazia: Ernani— Ernani, involami. Et LP 0-468.

Boninsegna is one of the great phonographic enigmas. Her opera career in New York was limited to four appearances at the Metropolitan Opera in the season of 1906–7, and though she sang subsequently with the Boston Opera Company, she was not accepted among the elect in this country. She made records, however, for all the major companies, and from the first the best of them were sensational. She passed into legend as one of the greatest of all operatic artists, and her discs have long been highly desirable collectors' items. Eterna has dubbed a good representative selection, mostly, the notes tell us, from Pathé originals, which makes these particular performances novel even to established collectors of the standard brands. To be sure, the repertoire is not unusual, and all of it figures on her HMV-Victor-Columbia lists. In this case, however, *"Tacea la notte"* is shortened and has the *cabaletta* added, and *"D'amor, sull' ali rosee"* is particularly lovely. Perhaps no voice within memory can match the wonderful glow of Boninsegna's tone, and few of like amplitude have mastered the florid style as she did. It all misses perfection by a margin of varying breadth, and there is always an obvious break between her chest and medium registers; still, so far as her recorded arias are concerned, they are so exciting that one does not take such details into account.

BOULANGER, NADIA

FRENCH RENAISSANCE VOCAL MUSIC: Mille Regretz de vous abondonner (Josquin des Pres); Ce Moys de may (Jannequin); Hélas, mon Dieu (Le Jeune); Bonjour, mon coeur (Lassus); Noblesse git au coeur (Costeley); Quand mon mary vient de dehors (Lassus); A déclarer mon affection (Anon.); Mignonne, allons voir si la roze (Costeley); Hau, hau, hau les boys (Sermisy); Revecy venir du printans (Le Jeune); Vous me tuez si doucement (Mauduit); Tu ne l'enten pas (Le Jeune); Au joli boys (Sermisy); Francion vint l'autre jour (Bonnet); Le Chant des oiseaulx (Jannequin). Vocal and Instrumental Ensemble conducted by Nadia Boulanger, D LP 9629.

"PETIT CONCERT" OF FRENCH VOCAL MUSIC FROM 12TH TO 20TH CENTURY: L'Autre Jour (Consilium); Madrigal (Fauré); Las je n'irai plus jouer au bois (Costeley); Dieu! qu'il la fait bon regarder (Debussy); Pie Jesu (Lili Boulanger); Cantique de St. Jean de la Croix (Preger); S'on me regarde (12th century); Epitaphe du Paresseux (Couperin); L'Oiseau blessé (Manziarly); Musette (Couperin); Amours partez (Sermisy); A pris ai qu'en chantant plour (Troubadour, 13th century); Le Lay des amants (Anon.); Trio d'Amadis (Lully); Quand ce beau printemps (Nicolas de la Grotte); A une demoiselle malade (Françaix); Levez ces couvre-chefs (Françaix); Belaud mon petit chat gris (Françaix). Peyron, s; Holley, c; Derenne, t; Conrad, bs; Instr Ens, Boulanger, Vox PL 6380.

Mlle Boulanger's interpretative genius is well demonstrated by these two programs, the one devoted to music of the older times, the other mixing that music with some of its descendants. It may be just her refusal to be bound by tradition and scholarly research that makes her so persuasive in the Renaissance program, but of course this could only be true of so knowledgeable, thorough, and broad a musician as she. She has lived so long with the works she presents, she knows them so thoroughly, and such is her innate sense of style, that whatever she does comes to exciting life, whether it be Josquin, Monteverdi, Bach, Fauré, or her sister Lily. I think the point she wants to make in the second program is that the fundamentals of music have not changed in the nine centuries represented, that the modern works she performs are important as heirs to the older traditions. It is possible, of course, to quibble about a detail here or there, but I am sure most sensitive listeners will find pleasure in Boulanger's genuine music-making.

BRANZELL, KARIN, contralto

Erlkönig; Der Tod und das Mädchen; Der Lindenbaum (Schubert); Heimliche Aufforderung (Strauss); Die ihr schwebet; Und willst du deinen Liebsten sterben sehen (Wolf); Das irdische Leben (Mahler). Pf, 10" Rem RLP 149–6.

From 1923 to 1944 Branzell was one of the most dependable and satisfactory artists in the Metropolitan company. Gifted with a voice of gorgeous quality and ample size, she was a mainstay not only of the Wagnerian wing, but of the Italian and French sections as well. She also enjoyed a fine reputation as a singer of songs, especially the German lieder and the Scandinavian repertoire. After her retirement from the opera her annual recitals became a feature of the New York season. Unfortunately, her recordings were never numerous; we can be especially thankful for this late one, even though it does not do her full justice. Her "*Erklönig*" must rank among the better ones, and the less familiar Mahler is to be commended.

BRICE, CAROL, contralto

Armida—Lungi dal caro bene (Sarti); In questa tomba oscura (Beethoven); Im Herbst; Im Frühling; Mutter, o sing' mich zur Ruh' (Franz); Seguidilla (Falla); They all dance the samba (Berger); The day is no more (Carpenter); My good Lord done been here (arr. Johnson); On ma journey (arr. Boatner); Witness (arr. Johnson); Ah! may the red rose live alway (Foster). J. Brice, pf, 10" C ML 2108.

Carol Brice has one of the great natural voices of our time— the most gorgeously dark contralto, perhaps, since Sophie Braslau. She is also an intelligent and musical singer, one from whom better than ordinary things are expected and sometimes received. Perhaps it is the very darkness of the voice that most stands in her way as an artist: in the lovely Sarti air, where limpidity and grace should be paramount, she seems bent on showing the full richness of which her voice is capable. The result is heavy and disaffecting. The Beethoven is somewhat better, but here she matches the sepulchral text with a tone wanting in humanity and is guilty of pushing her voice. The three Franz songs are welcome in themselves, and they show decided stylistic improvement.

She is not abandoned enough for the Falla "*Seguidilla*," but she does nobly with the rapid-fire Berger song. It is in the spirituals that she really hits her stride and begins to talk to us. There are some peculiar things in the labeling.

CARTER, SARA, soprano

MODERN AMERICAN ART SONGS: Three Songs from Chamber Music (Citkowitz); Eight Epitaphs (Chanler); Five Songs: The dugout, Heaven haven, Go and catch a falling star, Send home my long strayed eyes, Valentine to Sherwood Anderson (Flanagan); Songs of Innocence (Smith). Weiser, pf, NE 2.

Four American composers have their innings in this program, two of them qualifying, perhaps, for inclusion among the middle-aged and two definitely belonging to the younger generation. Citkowitz and Chanler have long since established themselves particularly in the field of song; indeed, the first piece on this record, "*Strings of the earth and air*," was hailed years ago by William Treat Upton as something of a masterpiece. Flanagan and Smith are genuine talents. Unhappily, this recording only hints at a part of the story, for while the singer produces very pretty sounds, she does not manage to get many of her words across. When composers look for inspiration in the works of Joyce, De la Mare, Hopkins, Donne, Blake, and others of like caliber, they consider the texts important. The reproduction of the piano is not clear.

CARUSO, ENRICO, tenor

Elisir d'Amore—Una furtiva lagrima; Gioconda—Cielo e mar; Africana —O paradiso; Bohème—Che gelida manina; La Juive—Rachel, quand du Seigneur; Aïda—Celeste Aïda; Pêcheurs de perles—Je crois entendre encore; Carmen—Flower Song; Pagliacci—Vesti la giubba; Rigoletto—La donna è mobile. V LCT 1007.
Ballo in Maschera—Di tu se fedele; Tosca—E lucevan le stelle; Vaghissima sembianza (Donaudy); Trovatore—Ah! si, ben mio; Di quella pira; Le Cid—O Souverain; 'A vucchella (Tosti); Bohème— Testa adorata (Leoncavallo); A Granada (Alvarez); Messe Solennelle —Domine Deus (Rossini). V LCT 1034.
O sole mio (Capua); The lost chord (Sullivan); For you alone (Geehl); Ave Maria (Kahn) (with Elman, vln, Kahn, pf); Serse—Ombra mai fù (Handel); Because (d'Hardelot); Elégie (Massenet) (with Elman, vln,

Kahn, pf); Sei morta nella vita mia (Costa) (with Bellezza, pf). 10"
V LCT 2.

No name in the history of recorded music can compare with that of Enrico Caruso. From the season of 1903–4, when he first came to the Metropolitan Opera, until his death in 1921, he was one of the busiest of recording artists, and it was the phenomenal success of his discs that really put the Victor Talking Machine Company (and with it its various rivals) into the world of big business. Most of the records he made held their places in the catalogues through the acoustic period, and several of them were re-recorded electrically with dubbed-in orchestra. Caruso's career divided itself naturally into three periods: he came to this country a light lyric tenor; by 1910 he was so robust a singer that those whose memories did not serve them well used to assert that he was in reality a pushed-up baritone; then, in his final years, he developed into a true heroic tenor, a Samson, an Eléazar, a potential Otello (though he never sang this last role). Not the least valuable thing about his records is that by them we can trace his steady growth down the years. Unfortunately, though his singing still enjoys top sales, his records have been transferred to LP in a helter-skelter manner. The discs listed above are typical samples: though dates are generally given for the recordings, no attempt has been made to keep together the fruits of various years or periods. Thus we often find an early example followed by a late one, then without warning we are transported to the years after his death by the miracle of re-recording (always with a loss in quality). And though the operatic selections are satisfactory on the whole, each of them contains an example of the less admirable Caruso records. Finally, we find too many duplications in these "Treasury" items: we never can be quite sure, when buying a new one, that we have not had half of it before.

CHALIAPIN, FEODOR, basso

Prince Igor—I hate a dreary life; Sadko—Song of the Viking Guest; The Demon—Do not weep (Rubinstein); A Life for the Czar—They guess the truth; Faust—Invocation; Lucrezia Borgia—Vieni la mia vendetta (Donizetti); Sonnambula—Vi ravviso; Norma—Ite sul colle; Ernani—Infelice; Mefistofele—Ave, Signor. Scala SC 801.
The birches; Night; Dubinoushka (Folk Songs); The little nightingale

(Tchaikovsky); Mefistofele—Ave, Signor; Faust—Church Scene (with Michailowa). 10" AM LPA 1002.

For quality of dubbing, the first of these two discs is the more successful, though the Russian folk songs in the second have a special interest. As usual, the best arias are the Russian ones, for Chaliapin was too individualistic to be bound by the rules so essential to French and Italian music. The *Faust* selections are sung in Russian (the first, incidentally, is mislabeled). The second enlists the assistance of Marie Michailowa, the first successful recording soprano, and to this day one of the loveliest to hear, but not otherwise represented on LP. The Scala notewriter gets onto some insecure ground asserting that the basso, for all his contempt for *bel canto* as a way of singing, could hold his own in the older musical styles. Interesting as is his *"Vi ravviso,"* one would hardly compare it with Plançon's. The folk songs, taken from the 1910 HMV series, are sung with unaccompanied chorus.

CHORAL MASTERPIECES OF THE RENAISSANCE

Ave Maria; Ave verum (Josquin des Pres); Jesu dulcis memoria; Gaudent in coelis (Victoria). The Nonesuch Singers, Smith. Vive la serpe et la serpette; Au joli bois (Sermisy); Il est bel et bon (Passereau); La plus belle de la ville (Jannequin); Mignonne, allons voir (Costeley). French Circle Ch of Univ of Bristol, Benham. Ave verum corpus (Byrd); Hide not Thou Thy face; Call to remembrance (Farrant); Magnificat; Nunc dimittis (Gibbons); Rejoice in the Lord alway (Redford). The Open Score Soc, Cameron, Per SPLP 535.

It is good to hear such quiet, unforced singing as that of the Nonesuch Singers, so much spirit, fine diction, and apparent appreciation of the texts by the French Circle group, such honest English cathedral style in the work of the Open Score Society. If I am right in my impression that the last group is a small-sized boy choir, it prompts the old question: why do they do these things so much better in England? I propose a special vote of thanks for the Gibbons *Magnificat* and *Nunc dimittis*.

CHRISTOFF, BORIS, basso

RUSSIAN ARIAS AND SONGS: The Legend of the Invisible City of Kitesh—Prince Youri's Aria (Rimsky-Korsakov); Khovantchina— Dositheu's Aria; Eugene Onegin—Everyone knows love on earth; Song of the Volga Boatmen (Trad.); The Prophet (Rimsky-Korsakov); Softly the spirit flew up to heaven; Field Marshall Death (Mussorgsky); Siberian Prisoner's Song (Trad.); The grave; Song of the Flea (Mussorgsky). PHI, Dobrowen, Scheuchter; Moore, pf, V LHMV 1033.

Boris Christoff seems the favored contender for the mantle of Chaliapin; more than any of the several other current Borises he actually *sounds* like his great predecessor, though neither his voice nor his physical presence is quite so overwhelmingly big. But as Chaliapin never gave the same performance twice, so Christoff sounds like him without ceasing to be himself, and an impressive musical figure he is. As in opera, so in song, he carries on the tradition and the repertoire. His disc contains rarely heard arias and a miscellaneous assortment of songs, all delivered with temperament and intensity. The program annotator makes an attempt to explain away the orchestration of one song accompaniment; the rest are done to Gerald Moore's impeccable piano.

COLLEGIUM MUSICUM (Paul Hindemith)

Lagrime d'amante al sepolcro dell' amata (Monteverdi); O care, thou wilt dispatch me; Hence, care, thou art too cruel; A sparrow-hawk proud (Weelkes); Dolcissima mia vita; Io pur respiro (Gesualdo); Singet dem Herrn ein neues Lied (Bach).
Vol. 2; Organum: Alleluia, Nativitas gloriosae (Perotin); Missa, Ave regina coelorum—Kyrie (Dufay); Missa, Sine nomine—Credo (Palestrina); Lagrime di San Pietro—No. 7, Ogni occhio del signor; No. 17, Ah, quanti gia felice; Im lant zu Wirtenberg (Lassus); Mirabile mysterium (Gallus); Nunc dimittis; Virtute magna (G. Gabrieli). Collegium Musicum of Yale Univ Sch of Mus, OVER 4, 5 [2].

This program was recorded in Sprague Memorial Hall, Yale University, partly at the public performance on May 14, 1953, and partly at the dress rehearsal on May 20, 1950. It represents, then, not a single year's Collegium, but combines two, separated by a couple of years. The recording has its quota of coughs and other extraneous noises, but it has also the kind of vitality and excitement peculiar to the moment of public performance. In his years at Yale, Hindemith demonstrated over and over his uncanny ability to bring out of any performer the best music in him. And though he scornfully rejected the title of musicologist, there can be little question that his success as an interpreter is based on the most practical kind of scholarship. To hear his version of the Monteverdi *Lagrime* is to hear the *sestina* for the first time. We have had a couple of recordings before, one of which indeed was impressively good, but we have not had such lofty expressiveness as this, or such clear and balanced singing. The music is allowed to speak to us: there is no forcing, no loading of emotion. The reproduction is slightly clouded, but not oppressively so. Curiously, in the beautiful Weelkes madrigals, the English is not so easy to follow as it might be, but the conception is admirable. The Gesualdo pieces come as something of a revelation. I am less enthusiastic about the Bach, which, for all its well-differentiated choruses, seems a little square-cut. The cruelly difficult final fugue, however, is the best part of it. The third side affords some interesting contrasts, notably the Dufay and Palestrina works. The last side is somewhat weak in reproduction.

CONCERT CHOIR (Margaret Hillis)

CONTEMPORARY CHRISTMAS CAROLS: The Star Song; Ideo gloria in excelsis; There is no rose; A song against bores (Kraehenbuehl); On the morning of Christ's nativity; The Shepherds' Carol (Jones); The Virgin's Lullaby; Three kings went to call; Rejoice greatly; A King is born (Sasonkin); The Christmas Chanters; Rejoice; The boar is dead (Harris); The birds; Sweet was the song (Gruen). Con AP 122.

It was a good idea for Contemporary Records to commission five young composers to freshen up the Christmas repertoire with some new material. Most of them have drawn on the older poets for their texts, though Manus Sasonkin has written his own verses. A pleasingly light touch is evidenced in most of these pieces (rather loosely grouped together as carols); only Charles Jones's "*On the morning of Christ's nativity*" runs a bit into obscurity, not unnaturally weighted by Milton's text. The small performing group is made up of "first stand" vocalists; their singing is spirited and proficient, though there are signs of hasty preparation.

CORENA, FERNANDO, basso

FAMOUS OPERATIC EXCERPTS: L'Elisir d'Amore—Udite, udite, rustici; Don Pasquale—Ah! un foco insolito; La Gazza Ladra—Il mio piano e preparato (Rossini). SR, Erede, 10" L LS 701 (*Operatic Arias, Protti).

Fernando Corena, a 1953-4 newcomer at the Metropolitan Opera, has a long list of operatic recordings to his credit, and he is well established as one of the finest Italian bassos of the day. As a comedian he has few rivals, but he is a legitimate singer, and can vocalize as expressively as the best of them. The three arias listed are from his *buffo* repertoire. It is a cause for some disappointment that only one side was accorded Corena, for Aldo Protti, a less distinctive artist, has been content with three well-worn numbers from *Trovatore*, *Barber of Seville*, and *Pagliacci*. Corena contributes one sterling performance to a catch-all operatic program (L LL 534): "*A un dottor*" from the *Barber*. The singing of the others on that record is disappointing.

CUENOD, HUGUES, tenor

ITALIAN SONGS OF THE 16TH AND 17TH CENTURIES: Valli profonde (Gagliano); Se l'aura spira (Frescobaldi); Fuggi, fuggi, cuar mio; Con lagrime e sospir (Verdelot-Willaert); Cara e dolce (Scarlatti). *SPANISH SONGS OF THE 16TH CENTURY:* Perdida; Sospiro; Durandarte (Milan); Si me llaman; Triste estaba; Israel (Mudarra). Leeb, lute, W WL 5059 (*Lute Solos by Fiorentino, Milan, Mudarra). *FRENCH SONGS (16th and 17th Centuries):* Psaume 130 (Certon); Psaume 50 (Adrian le Roy); Quand me souvient (Crequillon); Tant que vivray (Attaignant); En quelque lieu; La voila la nacelle; Beaux Yeux (Besard); *ENGLISH SONGS (17th Century):* Flow, my tears; I saw my lady weep (Dowland); When from my love; A pretty duck there was; What thing is love (Bartlett); Rest, sweet nymphs (Pilkington); It was a lover (Morley). Leeb, lute, W WL 5085 (*Lute Solos by Visée, Dowland). *ELIZABETHAN LOVE SONGS AND HARPSICHORD PIECES:* When Laura smiles (Bull); Go to bed, sweet muse; Sweet Kate (Jones); Underneath a cypress tree (Pilkington); Weep you no more, sad fountains (Dowland); Drink to me only with thine eyes; Have you seen but a whyte lily grow? (Anon.); Sorrow, sorrow, stay (Dowland); Why dost thou turn away (Giles Earles's ms); Now, o now I needs must part; Away with these self-loving lads (Dowland). Chiasson, hpschd, Ly LL 37 (*Harpsichord Solos by Bull, Johnson, Gibbons, Farnaby, Peerson).

Cuenod is well established among the most musicianly of singers, and the peculiarity of his high voice (he might, indeed, be classed as a counter-tenor) opens up for him a repertoire not accessible to many. Though he is most at home in the older styles of music (his work is outstanding in several Bach recordings, and he is equally admirable in Rameau, Schütz, and Couperin) he has touched many schools. These programs show his feeling not only for the music he has chosen, but for languages; his English is not without a slight accent, but it is clear enough to shame our native practitioners. And here, for once, is a singer who gives the text of *"Drink to me only"* as Ben Jonson wrote it, and as it must be in order to rhyme. This in itself is a unique and rewarding experience.

CURTIN, PHYLLIS, soprano

AFRO-CUBAN AND LATIN-AMERICAN SONGS: Cinco Canciones *Populares (Ginastera);* Tres Canciones *(Galindo);* Dos Poemas Afro-Cubanos; Bito manué *(Caturla);* Cancion al arbol del olvido *(Ginastera);* Samaritana de Floresta; Noite de Junho; A velha historia; Cançao do mar *(Fernández).* Tucker, pf, 10" Cam CRS 203.

Phyllis Curtin's first considerable reputation was made as a Bach and Purcell singer, though of late she has been heard in operas as diversified as Einem's *The Trial,* Verdi's *Falstaff,* and Strauss's *Salome.* It need hardly surprise us, then, that she has a Latin American string to her bow. She seems thoroughly at home in these variegated songs, making the most of every mood and every nuance. Her voice is an instrument of unusual beauty; wedded to such temperament as she here displays, its effect is tremendously exhilarating. There can be little doubt that this is just what the songs need.

DANCO, SUZANNE, soprano

Louise—Depuis le jour; Traviata—Ah, fors' è lui; Manon—Adieu, notre petite table; Carmen—Micaëla's Air; Alceste—Divinités du Styx; Dido and Aeneas—When I am laid in earth. SR, Erede, L LLP 224.

A RECITAL OF 17TH AND 18TH CENTURY MUSIC: Eile mich, Gott, zu erretten *(Schütz);* Bist du bei mir; Warum betrübst du dich?; Komm, süsser Tod *(Bach);* Paride ed Elena—O del mio dolce ardor *(Gluck);* La donna ancora è fedele—Se Florindo è fedele *(Scarlatti);* Come

raggio di sol (Caldara); Danza, danza (Durante); Amarilli (Caccini).
Demessieux, org; Agosti, pf, 10" L LS 698.

Danco has been one of the most successful recording sopranos in
recent years because the bright, clear quality of her voice re-
produces consistently well, and because she is a broad enough
musician to present a varied and unusual repertoire. Her gift of
languages is impressive: though French is natural to her (she is
Belgian), she is flawless in Italian, and not far from it in German
and English. Though others may bring more personal warmth to
the operatic scenes—and the *Alceste* and *Dido* arias are usually
associated with heavier voices—we rarely hear them done with
such pure vocalism. In the program of early music the Schütz and
Bach are lovely; the little Scarlatti song is delightful. Vocally
"O del mio dolce ardor" is admirable, though in spirit it may
seem to belie its title.

DAVIS, ELLABELLE, soprano

Don Carlo—Tu che le vanità; La Wally—Ebben? ne andrò lontana
(Catalani). NEW, Braithwaite. Wanderers Nachtlied; Lachen und
Weinen; Wohin? (Schubert); Allerseelen; Befreit (Strauss). Greenslade,
pf, 10" L LPS 181.
Nobody knows de trouble I've seen (arr. Burleigh); Good news (arr.
Hayes); On ma journey (arr. Boatner); I'm a-traveling to the grave (arr.
Dett); My soul's been anchored in the Lord (arr. Price). Greenslade,
pf. *I stood on de ribber of Jordan (arr. Burleigh); Plenty good room*
(arr. Boatner); Were you there? (arr. Burleigh); Oh, what a beautiful
city (arr. Boatner). O, Olof, 10" L LPS 182.

Davis brought to the concert stage one of the loveliest voices of
recent years, a veritable Stradivarius of a voice, on which considerably less of an artist than she could have made magnificent
music. These recordings were not taken in the very first blush of
her success, but in that period when, with the tone still untarnished, the intellect was beginning to count for more. Perhaps
this explains the non-success of the opera arias, which are sustained beyond the limits of expressiveness, for no apparent reason
other than her ability to do it. The Schubert lieder are beautifully
conceived, though they communicate little. The Strauss, however,
justify the first disc. After this it requires a true artist to hold us
through a program of spirituals, but Davis does it. Here the essential simplicity is conveyed with an irresistibly melting tone

quality despite some rather fancy arrangements and even some atrocious orchestration.

De PAUR INFANTRY CHORUS (Leonard de Paur)

Swing low, sweet chariot; I want Jesus to walk with me; Nobody knows de trouble I've seen (arr. de Paur); In dat great gittin'-up mornin' (arr. Hairston); Who built de ark? (arr. Johnson); Soon ah will be done (arr. Dawson). 10" C AL 45.

Set an accomplished Negro choir to singing spirituals, and the results are bound to be rousing. The De Paur Chorus has established itself as a virtuoso group of the highest caliber, one might almost say a kind of American Don Cossack Choir—the parallel extends beyond the fact that both groups began in the army, and that both perform musical prodigies. They share, I should say, a certain easy mastery. A special effect is achieved here with *"In dat great gittin'-up mornin'"* by steadily rising pitch.

DEL MONACO, MARIO, tenor

La Juive—Rachel, quand du Seigneur; Pagliacci—Prologo; La Gioconda—Cielo e mar; La Forza del Destino—O tu che in seno agli angeli; Rigoletto—La donna 'e mobile. SCO, Erede, L LLP 880/1 [2]. (*Leoncavallo: Pagliacci, 3 sides).
Loreley—Nel verde maggio (Catalani); Il Tabarro—Hai ben ragione; Andrea Chénier—Un di all' azzuro spazio; La Fanciulla del West—Or son sei mesi; Turandot—Nessun dorma; La Bohème—Che gelida manina. O, Ghione, L LL 990/1 [2]. (*Mascagni: Cavalleria Rusticana, 3 sides).

Mario Del Monaco is potentially one of the great tenors of our time. Indeed, nature might have intended "his tenor note," like that of a greater Mario, to "soothe a soul in Purgatory." But soothing is one thing it does not do. So prodigal are the young man's gifts that we find him mostly giving too much and too early, though an occasional phrase conveys to us an inkling of what an artist he might be. Perhaps he shows at his best in the Verdi and Puccini recitals, listed under the composers' names, especially the former. Those noted above, fillers for opera sets, are mostly standard, though the *Loreley* and *Tabarro* numbers lend novelty. A novelty, too, is his excursion into the baritone regions with the

Pagliacci Prologue, following a precedent set by Richard Tauber. Del Monaco's experiment will cause no suicides among the baritones.

DERMOTA, ANTON, tenor

OPERATIC AND LIEDER RECITAL: Don Giovanni—Dalla sua pace; Il mio tesoro; Die Zauberflöte—Dies Bildnis ist bezaubernd schön; Capriccio—Sonnet: Kein andres, das mir so im Herzen loht. VPH, Böhm. *Der Nussbaum; Die Lotosblume (Schumann); Nimmersatte Liebe; Der Musikant; Auf ein altes Bild (Wolf); Ständchen; Zueignung (Strauss).* H. Dermota, pf, L LP 345.

Anton Dermota, whose Metropolitan Opera engagement several seasons ago was canceled by illness, has been heard as soloist in a number of choral and operatic recordings, notably Scherchen's *B minor Mass* (Bach) (W WAL 301), *Fledermaus* (L LLP 281/2), and *Zauberflöte* (C SL 115). He is a versatile artist, with a light, sweet voice. His breath control is exceptional, and it may be that he exploits his ability to spin a phrase at the expense of musical shape. But he never fails to make his singing interesting. The *Capriccio* number lends special interest to his recital, and his excursion into lieder is rewarding. The Strauss *"Ständchen"* and Wolf *"Der Musikant"* stand out.

DESSOFF CHOIRS (Paul Boepple)

Die mit Thränen säen (Schein); Assumpta est Maria (Palestrina); Mirabile mysterium (Gallus); Lord, how long wilt Thou be angry? (Purcell). CH CHC 44 (*Bach: Motet, Der Geist hilft).

This is a surprisingly effective "public performance" recording made in the Armor Hall of New York's Metropolitan Museum of Art. The reverberation is considerable, which is most effective in the Palestrina, least so in the chromatic Schein motet. A criticism of the Dessoff Choirs has been that the group has grown too large for the good of polyphonic music; in the present program the sound of the chorus is good, and not overloaded.

DESTINN, EMMY, soprano

Aïda—Ritorna vincitor; Cavalleria Rusticana—Voi lo sapete; Pagliacci—Ballatella; Lohengrin—Du Ärmste; Euch Lüften; Bartered Bride

—Marie's Air; Nozze di Figaro—Porgi amor; Carmen—Séguidilla; Chanson bohème; Der fliegende Holländer—Traft ihr das Schiff; Zauberflöte—Ach, ich fühl's; Mignon—Prayer; Madama Butterfly—Sai cos' ebbe cuore; Tu, tu, piccolo iddio; Freischütz—Leise, leise; Und ob die Wolke; Dalibor—Act II Aria; Tannhäuser—Dich, teure Halle; Trovatore—D'amor sull' ali rosee; Faust—Air des bijoux; Alleluia (Hummel); Aus der "Hohenlied" (A. Mendelssohn); Slovaka Pisen (Kovarovic); Robert le diable—Eh' ich die Normandie verlassen; Geh', sprach sie zu mir; Roussalka—Aria, Act I; Damon (Stange). CE 7001 [2].

Der Freischütz—Leise, leise; Cavalleria Rusticana—Voi lo sapete; Aïda—O patria mia; Ave Maria (Gounod); Hallelujah (Hummel); Tosca —Vissi d'arte; Robert le diable—Eh' ich die Normandie verlassen; Geh', sprach sie zu mir; Pagliacci—Ballatella; Der fliegende Holländer—Traft ihr das Schiff; Roussalka—Du lieber Mond. Sca 804.

Destinn's amazing versatility may be fairly judged from these selections, but lovely as some of the singing is, it is an acknowledged fact that her numerous recordings did her scant justice. The dubbings on the Scala disc are more forward and lifelike than those offered by Classic Editions; both programs draw on recordings made at various periods of her career, and for different concerns. Not all the apparent duplications in the two programs turn out to be the same recording, and sometimes there is a wide difference in their quality. In the first program all the opera arias are sung in German except those from *Madama Butterfly* and *Trovatore*; in the second the selections from *Cavalleria Rusticana*, *Aïda*, *Tosca*, and *Pagliacci* are in Italian. As far as I can ascertain, both producers have taken thought on the subject of recording speeds. Some selections may not have come out right, but it is next to impossible to be sure. The *Flying Dutchman* ballad on the Scala disc sounds decidedly high, but a checkup establishes that it is in the original key.

DIDUR, ADAMO, basso

OPERATIC RECITAL: Il Barbiere di Siviglia—La calunnia; Der Freischütz—Drinking Song; No nessun salvar ti puo; Mefistofele—Duet, Act I (with Zenatello, t); Ernani—Infelice, e tuo credevi; La Juive— Malediction; Faust—Dio dell' or; Mefistofele—Ecco il mondo; Boris Godunov—Death of Boris. Et LP 0-467.

Didur's voice was magnificent in range, vitality, and power when these recordings were made. In fact, I get the impression that with so many effects possible to him he could not keep his spirits down. Hence there are all sorts of composing and embellishing in the *Barber* aria, in the Italianized *Freischütz*, and in the piece from *Faust*. That he could sing straight, however, is shown in the *Ernani* aria, and, above all, in the weakly recorded passage from *Boris Godunov*. The voice is well forward in most of these reproductions.

DOBBS, MATTIWILDA, soprano

Die Spröde; Die Bekehrte; Zitronenfalter im April (Wolf); Clair de lune; Notre Amour (Fauré); Si mes vers avaient des ailes (Hahn); Le Colibri; La Cigale (Chausson); Die Entzückung an Laura; La pastorella; Nacht und Träume; Heidenröslein; Liebhaber in allen Gestalten (Schubert); Auf dem Schiffe; Wiegenlied; Nachtigallen schwingen; Botschaft (Brahms). Moore, pf, An 35094.

Mattiwilda Dobbs has obviously grown in stature since her previous operatic records were made: one feels now that she has complete control of her ample resources and that she is developing into an artist of deep sensibilities. Her tones are dulcet and clear in these songs, though unhappily the reproduction is not as clean and firm as it should be. The Wolf lieder are well done: they do not require great expressiveness, and she does not try to give them such treatment. Fauré's *"Clair de lune"* is for the most part good, though she takes a slight unauthorized ritard at the end. *"Notre Amour"* is among the finest of the offerings. The Schubert selections show the singer's best. *"Nacht und Träume"* is beautifully sung, though rhythmically it is cut rather square and weakly reproduced; her nicely sung *"Liebhaber in allen Gestallten"* is hardly so shapely as Schumann's. The three Brahms songs are among the best, especially *"Nachtigallen schwingen."*

DON COSSACK CHORUS (Serge Jaroff)

CHRISTMAS MUSIC AND CAROLS: Hymn for Christmas; Hymn for Virgin Mary; Glory to the Birth of Jesus Christ; Stikh; Hymn to the Virgin Mary; First Irmos from the Christmas Canon; Carol 1, Heaven and Earth; Carol 2, In Jerusalem; Carol 3, Shtchedrivka; Pre-Easter Service. CH CHS 1191.
EASTER MUSIC: Hymn to the Resurrection of the Saviour; Hymn for

Easter; The Great Litany; Kanone (Canticles 1-9); Easter Concert and Hymn. CH CHS 1192.
RELIGIOUS MUSIC: Augmented Litany (Gretchaninoff); Ave Maria (from Evening Service) (Rachmaninoff); Funeral Service (Trad.); In Church (from Album for Children) (Tchaikovsky); Let all mortal flesh (Trad.); Alleluia (from Requiem) (Tchesnokov); Christmas Song (Folk Song). 10" C ML 2163.

For those who do not know the music of the Russian Church, these programs will be interesting; for those who do, they will come as pleasant reminders. Russian singers, of course, get something into their performances which we miss in the familiar American church style. The Don Cossack Chorus has its own peculiar way with the music, which is just a little more Russian than that of any other group. Because of the effective falsetto so generously employed by the highest tenors, the chorus is not confined by the usual considerations of range, and of course there are subterranean basses to provide unmistakable Russian sonorities. The first two records bring us an experience very like attending church. The third, made up mostly of more modern pieces, is more like a concert. The Gretchaninoff *"Litany"* will be remembered from a magnificent old recording by Chaliapin and the Afonsky Choir of Paris, and some may recall the arrangement of the little Tchaikovsky piano piece sung by the Siberian Singers or by the Don Cossacks themselves. The singing of the group is always magnificently drilled, and never without striking, if rather tricky, effects. These things fit into their dealings with sacred as well as secular music.

EDELMANN, OTTO, basso

Tannhäuser—Ansprache des Landgrafen; Fidelio—Ha, welch' ein Augenblick!; Falstaff—Ehi! taverniere!; Der Barbier von Bagdad—Salaam, aleikum. VPH, Moralt, L LLP 427 (*Patzak Recital).

Edelmann, who sang Pogner in London's *Meistersinger* and Sachs in Columbia's, shows himself as one of the most versatile and promising of present-day bass-baritones. His pronouncement of the Landgrave's address is noble and dignified. The *Fidelio* song is well sung, if not quite nasty enough; there is a fine crescendo effect in the choral background. The *Falstaff* scene sounds rather strange in German, but it is well delivered, and the delightful *Bar-*

ber of Bagdad finale caps the Strienz performance on Urania (URLP 7026).

FAMOUS FRENCH TENORS

La Juive—Rachel, quand du Seigneur; Sigurd—J'ai gardé mon âme ingénue. Vezzani, t. L'Africaine—O paradis. Rayner, t. Sigurd— Le bruit des chants; Roméo et Juliette—Salut, tombeau. Franz, t. Il Trovatore—Supplice infame. Escalaïs, t. L'Attaque du Moulin—Le jour tombe; Hérodiade—Ne pouvant reprimer; Lakmé—Fantaisie aux divins mensonges. Friant, t. Werther—O nature. Rayner, t. ET 708.

This collection accomplishes well its purpose of calling attention to an often forgotten group of singers, and this without representation of the three best-known French tenors of recent times—Edmond Clément, Charles Dalmorès, and Lucien Muratore—though reference is made to their names in the jacket notes. Vezzani, remembered as the Faust of Victor's first recording of the Gounod opera, makes a fine showing here. His voice has unusual body along with its lyric quality. Franz, long a favorite in Paris, though virtually unknown elsewhere, is equally admirable. The American Sidney Rayner is included because so much of his career was made in France. He is more effective in the *Werther* number than the *Africaine.* Escalaïs is of an earlier generation, his recording more primitive. Power he had in ample measure, and a really exciting top voice. Friant does his three arias well, making an especially effective *crescendo* at the end of the *Hérodiade* piece.

FAMOUS ITALIAN TENORS

Luisa Miller—Quando le sere al placido; Don Pasquale—Sogno soave e casto. Anselmi, t. Otello—Ora e per sempre addio. Zenatello, t. Don Carlo—Io l'ho perduto. Pollicino, t. Tosca—Recondita armonia; Rigoletto—La donna 'e mobile. Schipa, t. Fedora—Amor ti vieta; Vedi, io piango. Pertile, t. Nerone—Queste ad un lido fatal. Pollicino, t. Paride ed Elena—O del mio dolce ardor; Faust—Salve, dimora. Bonci, t. I Puritani—Vieni fra queste braccia, Lazaro, t. ET 492.

This program opens with some of the best singing I have heard of Anselmi, and perhaps the finest performance on records of the

Luisa Miller aria. The phrasing is a model, the *legato* a thing of thrilling beauty. The *Don Pasquale* number is nearly as fine in its way. Zenatello is heard as of 1907, in an exciting bit from *Otello,* after which the Pollicino seems less imposing. The Schipa pieces show the voice in its youthful days, fuller and apparently less powerful than the quality we know best. These, I take it, are from Pathé originals. Pertile sings with fervent style and an intense *vibrato,* very effectively in *"Amor ti vieta,"* but to my taste too tearfully in *"Vedi, io piango."* Pollicino gives us a chance to hear a bit from Boïto's *Nerone,* in which his voice is of good size and quality. I care less for Bonci's Gluck, which has little of the true classic style; he is much better in his Italianized Gounod, showing unusual sensitivity to the text. His treatment of the words *"questa povertà"* carries a thrill of its own. Lazaro shows the power of his voice, and demonstrates his high D, which is not as secure as his reputation would lead us to expect, but in the opera today would certainly bring down the house.

FERRIER, KATHLEEN, contralto

FOLK SONGS: Blow the wind southerly; Ma bunny lad; The keel row (arr. Whittaker); Have you seen but a whyte lily grow? (arr. Grew); Willow, willow (arr. Warlock); The lover's curse; Down by the Sally Gardens (arr. Hughes). Spurr, pf, 10" L LS 48.
KATHLEEN FERRIER SINGS BRITISH SONGS AND FOLK SONGS: Ye banks and braes (arr. Quilter); Now sleeps the crimson petal (Quilter); Over the mountains; Drink to me only with thine eyes (arr. Quilter); Fair house of joy (Quilter); O waly, waly (arr. Britten); I have a bonnet trimmed with blue (arr. Hughes); My boy Willie (arr. Sharp); I know where I'm going; I will walk with my love; The stuttering lovers (arr. Hughes). Spurr, pf, 10" L LS 538.
SCHUBERT: Gretchen am Spinnrade; Die junge Nonne; An die Musik; Der Musensohn; SCHUMANN: Volksliedchen; Widmung. Spurr, pf, 10" L LD 9099.

The late Kathleen Ferrier was one of the most generously gifted, one of the most musically dependable, and one of the most sincere singers of our time. Hers was the true English contralto voice, big, rich, and as imposing as the diapason of a cathedral organ. The two collections of British songs (with the altogether too free use of the phrase folk songs) are tonally magnificent. In the first set *"Blow the wind southerly"* (sung without accompaniment) and the infectious *"The keel row"* seem to me outstanding. *"Willow, willow"* deserves mention, too, as a drama in miniature. The *"Whyte lily"* and the *"Sally Gardens"* are less happy. The second recital contains a whole side of Roger Quilter's most popular songs and arrangements. The singer is best in such a trumpet call as the old English *"Over the mountains."* Two of the Schubert songs were released several years ago; the other lieder were not issued until after the singer's tragic death. The best singing in the set is in *"An die Musik,"* a tonally lovely and meltingly musical reading of the famous song. *"Der Musensohn"* is essentially healthy in approach, and has more gaiety in it than we usually associate with Ferrier; still, I think I know why it was not released in the artist's lifetime: the high tones at the repeated climax are not perfect. I am sure she would have done them better in her last years. Schumann's *"Volksliedchen"* is properly simple, but the contrasts in *"Widmung"* are overdone. The middle section is very slow, and loses the ecstatic feeling it should maintain. *"Gretchen"* and the *"Nonne,"* which I have known before, are tonally attractive, but not exciting. It is the pianist here who misses the point. This Gretchen, so contained in her singing, was apparently unable to operate her spinning wheel steadily.

FISCHER-DIESKAU, DIETRICH, baritone

An die ferne Geliebte (Beethoven); Ständchen; Das Fischermädchen; Erlkönig; Nacht und Träume; Am Meer; Der Atlas; Der Doppelgänger (Schubert); Mondnacht; Die beiden Grenadiere (Schumann). Moore, pf, V LHMV 1046.

Though he has yet to make his debut in this country, there is little doubt among collectors of lieder recordings or those who have heard him abroad that Dietrich Fischer-Dieskau is the finest singer of songs in the postwar generation. As one who is numbered among both groups of admirers, I can report that the voice is bigger both in volume and in range than I had thought on hearing his earliest recordings, that it is a beautiful instrument in itself, and that the artist uses it strictly for purposes of musical communication. If one were to pick a flaw it would be in the too sudden contrast between his *pianissimo* and *fortissimo*. But his is unquestionably the best *An die ferne Geliebte* since Gerhard Hüsch's, and the Schubert and Schumann songs coupled with it show what may come of an interpretive intellect playing upon poetry in music. What he and Gerald Moore can do with the familiar Schubert *"Ständchen"* and the delicately folksy *"Fischermädchen"* is an object lesson, while such heavier fare as *"Der Atlas"* and *"Der Doppelgänger"* are laden with excitement. His also is the best Brahms *Ernste Gesänge* on records at any speed (DL 9668) and his Wolf disc (DL 9632) is a must for every song collection.

The English edition of the Beethoven cycle (HMV ALP 1066) is less generous in its coupling than the American version listed above. Instead of eight Schubert songs and two Schumann, we find simply the five Heine settings from Schubert's *Schwanengesang*. As only three of these appear on the American label, this makes a difficult choice. In quality, however, the less crowded British disc is superior.

FLAGSTAD, KIRSTEN, soprano

SONG RECITAL: Frauenliebe und Leben (Schumann); An die Musik; Ganymed (Schubert); Von ewiger Liebe; O wüsst' ich doch den Weg zurück (Brahms); Ich liebe dich; Ruhe, meine Seele (Strauss); At parting (Rogers); Morning (Speaks); We have turned again home (McArthur); When I have sung my songs (Charles). McArthur, pf, V LM 1738.

GERMAN SONGS (arr. Dørumsgaard): Ich lass dich nicht (Schemelli Gesangbuch); Es ist vollbracht (Freylinghausen Gesangbuch); Auf, auf, mein Herz mit Freude (Crüger); Geh' ein, mein Leib, in deine Kammer (Böhm); Die Güte Gottes; Busslied; Passionslied; Preis sei dem Gotte (C. P. E. Bach); Vergiss mein nicht; O finstre Nacht; Liebster Herr Jesu; Komm, süsser Tod; Dir, dir, Jehova (Bach); Wie seh' ich dich, mein Jesu, bluten; Sei nur still; Auf, auf! zu Gottes Lob! (Franck). Moore, pf, V LHMV 1070.

Flagstad was one of the vocal miracles of the century, a voice sufficient unto itself, needing nothing but its glorious sound to hold any audience. As we all know, she was more than that: she was a musician of rockbound solidity and integrity; she had the gift of languages and the perfect diction needed to make plain the message of what she sang. Her retirement caused much regret, for it was felt she had years of service left in her voice, and the magnificent endurance which kept her going in the Wagner operas showed no signs of diminishing. That she did not have all that once she possessed is evidenced by the Song Recital, made at the time of her Carnegie Hall farewell. Some of the songs, notably the

Strauss *"Ich liebe dich,"* carry her into altitudes beyond easy vocal production, and some seem rather square-cut and lacking in melodic curve. We can only deplore the English group at the end of the recital, for these songs are not likely to appeal to lieder enthusiasts who want the Schumann, Schubert, Brahms, or Strauss. The singer pours out her voice with ear-filling prodigality in the early German sacred songs. Again, it is undeniable that some of the broad and noble melodies tax her resources, but they have a ring of truth and sincerity to show a mellowing of the soprano's artistry. Dørumsgaard has made concert-hall arrangements of the songs, frankly translating their accompaniments into terms of the modern grand piano. He has also added, in a number of instances, long introductions and postludes. The results are grander than anything the composers had in mind, but present-day audiences will find them decidedly effective. Certainly the playing of Gerald Moore presents the strongest possible case for them.

GEDDA, NICOLAI, tenor

OPERATIC ARIAS: La Gioconda—Cielo e mar; Rigoletto—Ella mi fu rapita; Martha—Ach, so fromm; L'Elisir d'Amore—Una furtiva lagrima; Favorita—Spirto gentil; L'Arlesiana—E la solita storia; Eugene Onegin—Faint echo of my youth; Werther—Pourquoi me reveiller?; Les Pêcheurs de perles—Je crois entendre encore; Manon—En fermant les yeux; La Muette de Portici—Du pauvre seul ami fidele; Roméo et Juliette—Ah! lève-toi, sòleil. PHI, Galliera, An 35096.

As other recordings have shown, Gedda is very likely *the* coming operatic lyric tenor, but one whose talents extend beyond the opera. Such a program as this, taken in one dose, may seem long and a little tiresome, even when the artist is able to make it up of so many schools and languages. Born in Sweden of Russian stock, Gedda sings after the manner of his forebears; his basic style and production suggest his Russian background, though he is at home in various other types of music. Especially in the Italian arias one appreciates his thoughtful approach, his considered dwelling upon phrases and individual words. A native Italian would pour out more tone than he does in *"Cielo e mar,"* but would not do so much by pure artistry. His *diminuendo* on the final tone is very effective. In such a piece as *"Una furtiva lagrima,"* the best of the Italians would caress the melodic lines more than he does, but few would make it more appealing. The *"Lament"* from *L'Arlesiana* is beautifully reserved, Lenski'a aria from *Eugene Onegin* given with fine artistry. His French is less natural in sound than his Italian, and in the *Werther* and the *Roméo* arias we could do with a more outspoken approach. The *Pêcheurs de perles* aria is a mite slow, but does not fall apart; his tone floats through the melody in a lovely manner. The *Manon* is nicely spun out, but the real find of the program is the *Slumber Song* from *La Muette de Portici*, a winning number exquisitely sung. The recording is generally good.

GEORI-BOUÉ, soprano

RECITAL: Faust—Ballade du roi de Thulé; Air des bijoux; Hérodiade —Il est doux, il est bon; Louise—Depuis le jour; Mandoline; Il pleure dans mon coeur; Green (Debussy); Clair de lune; Les Roses d'Ispahan; Au bord de l'eau (Fauré); Chanson triste; Phidylé (Duparc). POO, Sebastian, Faure, pf, U URLP 7070.

Famed in France for her embodiment of the favorite operatic heroines and no less for her tasteful singing of the song repertoire, Geori-Boué is best known here as the Marguerite in the Beecham *Faust* recording (V LCT 6100). Collectors of 78-rpm discs may have had the luck to pick up some of her earlier song recordings or her light-opera duets with her husband, Roger Bourdin. Her Recital shows the two aspects of her art, the operatic side of the disc sampling a Beechamless *Faust* and what must have been a charming *Louise*, the song side devoted to France's three most famous writers of *mélodies*, well accompanied by the dependable Maurice Faure. Like most French sopranos, the lady inclines to shrillness, a fact emphasized, perhaps, by very roomy recording.

GHENT ORATORIO SOCIETY (Marcel De Pauw)

*FLEMISH CHORAL MUSIC: O la, o che bel eccho; Serenade van de Landsknecht (Lassus); Mille Regretz (Josquin des Pres); In't groene (Jan van Belle); Maria de soude naer Bethlehem gaen; Het was een Maghet uutvercoren (arr. De Pauw); Ic sag Caecilia komen (Boeck); Ic seg adieu (Clemens non Papa); Amoreus Liedekijn (Meulemans); Fantasia (Tinel); Hymne aan de Schoonheid (Meulemans). Es ES 514 (*Guitar Solos, Anon., Rore).*

It was an inspiration to go to Ghent to pick up this recording, so many of the great Renaissance masters having been Flemish. Indeed, the idea has here been carried so far that even so familiar a piece as Lassus's *"Matona, mia cara"* is sung in the Flemish language (though the *"Echo"* appears in Italian). The program has added value in that it includes a couple of anonymous songs in good solid arrangements, and some modern works. Outstanding among the latter is a *"Hymn to Beauty"* by Arthur Meulemans. The guitar interludes played by Max Demasse lend variety.

GLORIA, SARITA, soprano

BRAZILIAN SONGS: Côco peneruê (Henrique); Rolinha (Henrique); O'Kinimbá (Braga); Dansa de cabôclo (Tavares); Azulão (Ovalle); A Gatonha parda (Villa-Lobos); Abaluaiê (Henrique); Casinha pequeinia (Mesquita); Querer bem não é pecado (Sousa); Estrela do mar (Ovalle); Baianinho (Oliveira); Cancao das mares pretas (Mignone); D. Juanina (Mignone). Chanaka, pf, V LM 1737 (*Sandi: Ballet Bonampak).

Sarita Gloria, a soprano with a clear, sweet, true voice, gives us a generous portion of the Elsie Houston repertoire, along with a couple of songs recorded by Bidu Sayão and Jennie Tourel. The program has been well chosen to give variety and to demonstrate that something of both character and value is being produced below the Equator. Some of the songs may be classed as folk songs, though in all the arrangers have done their work elaborately enough to lift the pieces out of that class; others are genuinely composed, though they have something of the same quality and atmosphere. There is an attractive sparkle in the singer's art.

GOLDEN AGE OF OPERA

Don Giovanni—Batti, batti. Farrar, s. White sea mist (Ronald). Melba, s. Traviata—A me fanciulla. Lilli Lehmann, s. Il Barbiere di Siviglia—Largo al factotum. Ruffo, b. Rienzi—Gerechter Gott. Schumann-Heink, c. Hamlet—Mad Scene. Melba, s. Carmen—En vain pour éviter. Calvé, s. Iris—Un dì al tempio. Bori, s. Cavalleria Rusticana—Voi lo sapete. Eames, s. Hérodiade—Il est doux, il est bon. Garden, s. B & B 3.

These are mostly good old records, though put together they make something of a hodge-podge and there is considerable variation in the quality of the dubbings. None of them stand up too well beside the standard of RCA Victor in the Treasury series. Farrar is in good voice for her aria, though stylistically she is open to question: surely she is inordinately free with the ritards. Melba is not very well reproduced in *"White sea mist,"* and there is an intermittent hum in the background throughout the whole record. The Lehmann is mislabeled *Nozze di Figaro;* actually she sings *Traviata.* Only the first part of the scene is included, and of that not the usual first stanza, *"Ah, fors' 'e lui,"* but the second, *"A me fanciulla."* The Ruffo number comes through better than what precedes it, but still is uneven in sound. The fine Schumann-Heink is not successfully reproduced, nor is Melba's *Hamlet,* of which, again, we are given only the first half. Though labeled *"Habanera,"* the Calvé selection from *Carmen* is actually the "Card Scene." It is not one of her more forward recordings. The Bori is not very well transferred, but the Eames (her only appearance, so far, on LP) is fairly satisfactory. The Garden, always a weak recording, remains so, though there is a good deal to admire and exclaim over in the high tones it reveals.

HAGUE, CARL, tenor

SONGS OF NORWAY: Synnöve's Song; She is sweet, she is soft (Kjerulf); The herdgirl's Sunday (Bull); A vision; To Norway; And I will have a true love; Near Rondarne; I love thee; A dream (Grieg); Sing me home (Neupert); The linden; Toward evening (Backer-Gröndahl); I lay by the sea (Alnaes); Snow (Lie); Silver (Lammers); Venetian Serenade (Svendsen); Mother sings (Johansen); There cried a bird; Sylvelin; We will have our land (Sinding). Steele, pf, ML MLR 7034.

Here, obviously, is a singer of taste and a good propagandist for Norwegian music, for he has gone beyond the accepted Grieg songs and introduced us to a representative collection of music familiar in his native land. If such a song as Grieg's *"Til Norge"* still stands out as a little masterpiece, there are other things here well worth knowing. The singer is best in the more outspoken pieces, such as *"En Drøm,"* but he is never out of the picture, though the quality of his voice may be somewhat stiff. It is good to hear again *"Jeg elsker dig"* (*"I love thee"*) sung with only the one stanza of Andersen's poem, the climax made once and left to stand.

HAMLINE UNIVERSITY CHOIR *(Robert Holliday)*

Sixty-seventh Psalm (Ives); Lamentabatur Jacob (Morales); Jesu, as Thou art Savior (Britten); Christ, to Thee be glory (from St. Matthew Passion) (Schütz); Exsultate Deo (Scarlatti); Schifferliedchen; Zur Erntezeit (Křenek); Fragment of Sappho (Brunswick). 10" NR NRLP 305.

Lamentations of Jeremiah; The Seasons (Křenek); Tarye no longer (Harris); Arbolucu, te sequeste (Chávez). 10" NR NRLP 306.

This choir is at its best in modern music, the Ives and Křenek pieces coming off with special success. The Ives is in two keys, which sets a problem for the listener as well as the performers. Křenek's *Lamentations*, of which two "lessons" are given here, was presented first by the present choir in May 1952. The technique is that of Schoenberg's twelve-tone music, the thematic material based on the chant of the Church. This is not easy music, but it has a lofty expressiveness which some hearers will find growing on them. The choir performs with care and precision in matters of intonation, a little too much of these on the rhythmic side. One is conscious of the beating of time. *The Seasons* is a set of four Hölderlin settings, done here in the composer's English translations. Dating back to 1925, this music is anyone's meat. Russell Harris has caught something of the old-time flavor of the fifteenth-century Lydgate text he has set, and his piece should be a welcome addition to the choral repertoire. There is a simple dignity to the Chávez work written in memory of Kurt Schindler. The older music is less happily realized: the magnificent Morales piece is rather plowed through, as is the Scarlatti. The recording is not very strong, and at moments loses clarity.

HARRELL, MACK, baritone

RECITAL AND ENCORES: An Evening Hymn (Purcell); An die Leyer (Schubert); Mit Myrthen und Rosen (Schumann); Unüberwindlich (Brahms); Und willst du deinen Liebsten; Abschied (Wolf); Phidylé; Le Manoir de Rosamonde (Duparc); Crépuscule (Massenet); Fleur jetée (Fauré); Four Gambling Songs (Niles). Smith, pf, Rem R 199-140.

Harrell's reputation has been built on the gift of a pleasing baritone voice, impressive attainments of musicianship and style, and a diction in several languages which must be the envy of his colleagues. His opera career has been consistently successful, if unspectacular: he is known as one of the most dependable members of the Metropolitan company. Occasionally he creates a minor sensation, most recently as Nick Shadow in Stravinsky's *Rake's Progress*. His "Recital and Encores" is a miscellany designed to show the variety and extent of his song repertoire. His essentially virile style fits him especially for the more outspoken songs: in such an outpouring as *"An die Leyer"* he shows more impressively than in the superbly peaceful *"Evening Hymn"* or Massenet's super-delicate *"Crépuscule."* The novelty of the program is the set of *Gambling Songs* by John Jacob Niles, which bring down the curtain with a stopped show. Brahms' *"Unüberwindlich"* is a first and only recording.

HARVARD UNIVERSITY GLEE CLUB AND RADCLIFFE CHORAL SOCIETY (William F. Russell; G. Wallace Woodworth)

PRE-BAROQUE SACRED MUSIC: Magnificat in the Eighth Mode (Dufay); Veni sancte spiritus (Plainsong, 12th Century); Auditui meo dabis; Non avertas faciem tuam; Ipsa te cogat pietas (Lassus); Singt dem Herrn (Praetorius); O bone Jesu (Ingegneri); Non nobis, Domine (Byrd); Spiritus tuus (Lassus); Veni creator spiritus (Josquin des Pres); Magnificat in the Fourth Tone (Palestrina). Harvard Univ Ch; Radcliffe Ch Soc, Russell, 10" Fest FLP 70-202.
Supplicationes; Confitemini Domino (Palestrina); Miserere mei (Victoria); Adoremus Te (Anerio); O Maria, Diana stella (Anon.); Justorum animae (Byrd); Tibi laus, tibi gloria (Lassus). Harvard Gl Cl, Woodworth, 10" Cam CR 101.

The singing of the Radcliffe girls is first-rate in the almost unbearably lovely Dufay *Magnificat*. This is all the group does, however; from this point the Harvard boys take over, singing competently enough, but never scaling comparable heights. I find them more appealing, however, in the Palestrina *Magnificat* than the Period Choral Society (Per SPLP 513). Their singing is more solid and straightforward, lingering less along the way. One misses in the plainsong offering the aloofness the music calls for. In the second program, by the Harvard group only, several pieces are done in arrangement for male voices. The largest work in the group, the *Supplicationes*, is performed as written, except for cuts. The Byrd *Justorum animae* and the Anerio *Adoramus Te* (often attributed to Palestrina) are especially effective. The recording was made in the Busch-Reisinger Museum at Harvard, where the acoustics are very "live."

HAYES, ROLAND, tenor

Have you seen but a whyte lily grow (Old English); Come again, sweet love doth now invite (Dowland); Greensleeves (Old English); Orfeo— Vi recordo, o bosch' ombrosi (Monteverdi); Tamerlano—Figlia mia, non pianger, no (Handel); Warnung, K. 433 (Mozart); Wonne der Wehmut (Beethoven); Du bist die Ruh'; Wohin?; Nacht und Träume (Schubert); Auch kleine Dinge (Wolf); Beau Soir (Debussy); Micheu Banjo (arr. Nickerson); Poeme Persiano de "Rubaiyat" (Santoliquido); Somebody's knockin' at my door; Sometimes I feel like a motherless child; My God is so high (arr. Hayes); Five Negro Work Songs (A Cycle): Lord, how come me here?; Po' me; How long fo' de sun go down?; Day is done; Git up chillun, go 'roun' de wall (arr. Hall). Boardman, pf, A 440 12-3.

Roland Hayes, one of the truly great artists of our time, and the first Negro singer to win international reputation, has been only spasmodically represented on discs. At the age of sixty-six he has assembled a program that from another source might seem too miscellaneous, but which will bring back many memories to those who have heard him in recital. Several of the songs have been inseparably identified with the singer. Whether or not he recorded the program in its present order, he gives the impression of warming up as he proceeds, and in the course of this hour of singing we hear again the magical *mezza voce*, the beautiful diction, and the infectious rhythm so long associated with Mr. Hayes. Whether it be in Schubert, in Dowland, in Debussy, in Santoliquido, or in the songs of his own people, the tenor is a stylist of the first rank. Boardman's expert piano-playing is not so well reproduced here as the voice. A further two-disc recital, recorded by Vanguard, has just been released. In the softer numbers the voice is as lovely as it has always been; throughout the program the singer's art is of a high order (Van VRS 448/9 [2]).

HISTORY OF MUSIC IN SOUND

Vol. 2: Early Medieval Music up to 1300; Vol. 3: Ars nova and the Renaissance. V LM 6015, 6016 [2 discs each].

These are the first four discs of audible illustrations for the *New Oxford History of Music*, comprising Volumes 2 and 3, with 1 yet to come. As Volume 2 begins with Byzantine music, we may wonder how four LP sides will be filled with earlier examples. A happy marriage has been consummated in these recordings between the musicological and the listenable. Although every effort has been made to perform the music in authentic style, it is still a real pleasure to hear. In fact, the two volumes, in the order of presentation, make two thoroughly enjoyable musical programs. Beginning with the Byzantine chant and working up to the Gregorian, the ear and the perceptive faculties adjust themselves to the wonderful leisure of this music, so that it seems one could go on listening indefinitely. But presently we find ourselves concerned with medieval songs, still unaccompanied, and soon with the beginnings of polyphony. Gradually it sneaks up on us, first in two parts, then three, and so on. From *organum* to the quite elaborate *Alleluia psallat*, which brings the first period to a close, is an impressive advance. The second volume—that is, officially, the third—begins with Adam de la Halle, and carries on to Isaac, Compère, and Rubinus. The performances are in the hands of authoritative and skillful musicians: such men as Oxford's editor, Dom Anselm Hughes; Henry Washington, leader of the Brompton Oratory; the Dolmetsch family; and Safford Cape with his Pro Musica Antiqua of Brussels insure against hasty or undigested singing and playing.

HOUSTON, ELSIE, soprano

BRAZILIAN SONGS: Foi n'uma noite calmosa (Gallet); Bahia; Dansa de caboclo; Benedicto pretinho; Bia-t-tà (Tavares); Berimbaú; Tres potos de santo (Ovalle); Tayèras; Bambelè (Gallet); Canção de carreiro (Villa-Lobos). Miguel, pf, V LCT 1143 (*Villa-Lobos: Bachianas Brasileiras No. 1; Nonetto).

Victor has done a real service in restoring the Elsie Houston recital. This singer, of insinuating voice, was one of those rare artists who make every individual song sound important and still leave us with the impression of a unified, rounded program. There are, of course, several special favorites, which will stand out in the memory after a hearing of this disc: *"Bahia," "Bia-t-tà,"* and *"Bambelè,"* for examples. Though she was thought of as essentially a diseuse, Houston's voice had been carefully trained; its quality, to my ears, was outstandingly beautiful.

HUFSTADER SINGERS (Robert Hufstader)

Ce Moy de may (Jannequin); Soyons joyeux (Lassus); Rest, sweet nymphs (Pilkington); April is in my mistress' face (Morley); Sicut cervus (Palestrina); Weep you no more, sad fountains (Dowland); Three Reincarnations (Barber); Trois Beaux Oiseaux de paradis (Ravel). 10" Cook 1092.

This disc is notable for its wide range and clean, bright tone. The selections, though hardly so unusual as the liner notes would lead us to believe, represent some of the best in madrigal literature, along with some estimable modern music. The singing is direct and simple, perhaps a little confined rhythmically, but nicely balanced.

IBARRONDO, LYDIA, mezzo-soprano

SONGS OF SPAIN: Il vito (Obradors); Del cabello màs Molondròn (Obradors); Canción castellana (Guridi); Cantares (Turina); La maja dolorosa (Granados); Granadina (Nin); Songs of the Provinces—Caminto de Avilès; Charrada; En casa del Tio Vicente; Pastores de la sierra; Burlesca; Nostalgia; El pano; Vascos. Sandoval, pf, Rem R 199-139.

Ibarrondo has the dusky voice and the vivid temperament suited to these songs; she gets good variety into the first half of the program. She can produce a lovely soft tone and with it sustain a ravishing line in the quieter moods. Perhaps, with the second side, the material wears a little thin, but it is excellently presented. The reproduction has a large-empty-room effect and some echo.

THE INTERNATIONAL EISTEDDFOD

A Musical Documentary of the International Choral and Folk Dance Festival at Llangollen, North Wales, July 1952. W WAL 209 [2].

This fascinating recording was sponsored by UNESCO; it brings a fine program of international folk and art music performed by competing groups from various countries. The diverse fare includes folk dances, madrigals, a part-song by Elgar and one by Hugo Distler, as well as a motet by Victoria. Perhaps the choicest item is *"Contrappunto bestiale,"* from Banchieri's *Festino*, sung here by three strongly contrasted groups—all very different from the interpretation of the New York Pro Musica Antiqua and that of Luca Marenzio Ensemble that performs the *Festino* in the Anthologie Sonore. A running commentary by Jack Bornoff explains the program as we go along.

KLOSE, MARGARETE, contralto

In der Mondnacht (Cornelius); Herbststurm; Eros; Der Jäger; Weihnachts Wiegenlied; Unter Rosen (Grieg); Geduld (Strauss); Der Schmied; O lass dich halten, gold'ne Stunde; Über Nacht (Jensen); Im Herbst; Zum Abschied meiner Tochter; Der Einsame; Nachts (Pfitzner). Raucheisen, pf, U URLP 7053.
Nachtgesang; Der Geistertanz; Fragment aus dem Aeschylus; Iphigenie; Der König in Thule; Dem Unendlichen; Verklärung (Schubert); Arianna—Lasciatemi morire (Monteverdi); Serse—Largo (Handel); Orfeo ed Euridice—Ach, ich habe sie verloren (Gluck). Raucheisen, pf; Prussian St O, Heger, U URLP 7017.

A big, rich, dark voice like that of Margarete Klose is rare in any generation. This is a singer in the grand manner, but one who can, on occasion, modulate her tones for the projection of lieder. As a recording artist, she has put us many times in her debt by her choice of worth-while and unhackneyed music. The first recital listed above is made up mostly of "firsts." All the songs are done with such conviction that one hesitates to note even that the songs of Norway's Grieg are translated into German. Translation does damage to the second recital, however. The Monteverdi sounds incongruous in German; the famous Handel air is sung twice, the second time to a text that is new, at least, to me; the Gluck is decidedly overweight. In the feast of mostly unfamiliar Schubert, the best sung songs are those in which Klose can use her superb gift of declamation or let her rich tones pour out freely.

KOLASSI, IRMA, mezzo-soprano

Cinq Mélodies populaires grecques (Ravel); Deux Chansons populaires grecques (Anon.); Automne; Mandoline; Soir (Fauré); Le Vaincu; Le Visage penché (Aubert). Bonneau, pf, 10" L LS 568.

A RECITAL OF GERMAN LIEDER AND ARIE ANTICHE: Widmung; Die Lotosblume; In der Fremde (Schumann); Der Musensohn; Du bist die Ruh'; Der Erlkönig (Schubert); Vezzosette e care pupillette (Falconieri); Alcina—Ah, mio cor (Handel); Gli Zingari in fiera—Chi vuol la zingarella (Paisiello): Amarilli, mia bella (Caccini); La donna ancora è fedele—Se Florindo è fedele (Scarlatti); Arianna—Lasciatemi morire (Monteverdi); Orontea—Intorno all' idol mio (Cesti); L'Honestà negli Amori—Già il sole del Gange (Scarlatti). Bonneau, pf, L LL 747.

Greek by heritage and French by training, Kolassi is a distinctive as well as a musicianly artist. When I heard her voice, by way of the first disc listed above, I described it as suggesting a blend of Madeleine Grey and Ninon Vallin. She sings the Ravel songs, and the two Greek folk songs (*"La Jeune Fille d'Alatsata,"* arranged by Sapthi, and *"Dourou-dourou,"* arranged by Sfakianakis) in the original language, with special fervor. The better-known pieces on the reverse of the disc may have been done with greater distinction than she brings to them, though her Fauré *"Mandoline"* is a gem. The surprise comes with the two post-Duparcian Aubert songs, both strikingly presented, the first in a powerful way, the second quiet and atmospheric. The voice is better reproduced than the piano. After her promising debut, the second Kolassi recital is a distinct disappointment. In German and Italian she reveals her limitations. In neither language does she sound at home, and there is more shrill tone in the higher reaches than there should be. To do her justice, she captures and sustains a mood in several of the songs, for instance *"Intorno all' idol mio"* and *"In der Fremde."* But neither lieder nor classic arias can be done by intelligence alone.

KREFELD COLLEGIUM MUSICUM (Robert Haas)

MUSIC OF THE MIDDLE AGES: Mei hat wunniklich entsprossen; Der Mei hat mennik herze; So schönen wir den anger nie gesahen (Neidhart von Reuenthal); Spielmannstanz (Anon., 13th Century); Wê, ich han gedacht; Loybere risen (Witzlav von Rügen); Nu alerst lebe ich mir werde (Walther von der Vogelweide); Der May mit lieber zal (Oswald von Wolkenstein); La Quarte Estampie Royale (Anon., 13th Century); Kalenda maya (Raimbaut de Vaquieras); Lancan vei la folha (Bernart de Ventadorn); Saltarello (Anon., 14th Century); Dieus soit en cheste meson (Adam de la Halle); Lamento di Tristano (Anon., 14th Century); Chevalier mult estez quariz (Anon., 1147). Metzger-Ulrich, s; Pingel, t; Krefeld Col Mus, Haas, Vox PL 8110.

The effort here is along the lines of the Pro Musica Antiqua of Brussels, and some of the repertoire is identical. The performances are neat, always in good taste, with the excellent tenor bearing the lion's share. The music will be found to have musical interest beyond that which its historical background gives it; indeed, it should make new friends for its period and style. Fuller notes should, however, have been provided. Not only are the texts absent, but no information is forthcoming in regard to the instruments used.

LAMY ENSEMBLE (Fernand Lamy)

PARISIAN SONGS OF THE SIXTEENTH CENTURY: Las, je m'y plains; Dictes sans peur (Sermisy); Pourquoy donc ne fringuerons nous; Sur la rousée (Passereau); L'Amour, la mort et la vie; Il estoit une fillette (Jannequin); Que n'est-elle auprès de moi (Certon); Ma peine n'est pas grande (Jannequin); Plaindre l'ennui de la peine (Hesdin); O doulx regard (Gardane); Amour si haut (Sandrin); Quand je te veux raconter (Nicolas de la Grotte); Tourt ce qu'on peut en elle voir (Rore); En ce beau moys (Costeley); Amour me tue (Goudimel); Rossignol mon mignon (Le Jeune) ;Rossignol mon mignon (Boni); Mon Père et ma Mère (Bonnet); Fière cruelle (Le Jeune); Fretillarde amoureuse pucette (Anon.); Prince, la France te veut (Le Jeune). OL 50027.

These songs are all taken from a recent anthology edited by François Lesure and published by Oiseau Lyre. Though none of these particular *chansons* has been generally known before, the type is familiar. A look at the names of the composers will be enough to sell the set to anyone who knows the repertoire. The group here performing, however, is hardly the most satisfactory we have heard. In the first place, it is a little large, and consequently on the heavy side. Then, while the recording is very good of its kind, clear and full, the singers seem to be close to our ears, a fact that emphasizes a certain breathiness in their tone. Their most successful numbers are the sustained and sonorous ones, such as *"L'Amour, la mort et la vie," "O doulx regard,"* and *"Fretillarde amoureuse pucette."* The faster-moving songs are inclined to be hasty and nervous. The contrast between the two settings of the same Ronsard poem—*"Rossignol mon mignon"*— is especially interesting, with the Boni version perhaps the more effective. It is amusing, too, to recognize the text, and something very close to the music, of Tessier's *"Au joli bois"* in Bonnet's *"Mon Père et ma Mère."* Presumably one is invited to consider buying the music to go along with this recording; nevertheless, it would have been pleasant to have the texts to follow.

LASZLO, MAGDA, soprano

ITALIAN SONGS: Partenza amorosa; Arianna—Lasciatemi morire (Monteverdi); Tutto acceso a quei rai (Scarlatti); Amarilli (Caccini); Vittoria! Vittoria! (Carissimi); Quella fiamma che m' accende (Marcello); Fuor dalle placid' onde; La Serenata—Posate dormite (Bassani); Se tu m'ami (Pergolesi); Orontea—Intorno all' idol mio (Cesti); Fêtes vénitiennes—Chanson de papillon (Campra). Holetschek, pf, W WL 5119.

Magda Laszlo is primarily a stylist, though solely on the merits of her clear, bright voice she would be an exceptionally interesting singer. Most of her recording has been done with Scherchen, in his series of Bach cantatas, and in his impressive *Ninth Symphony* (W WAL 208). In her Italian songs she is not too even vocally, nor is her intonation impeccable, but the susceptible listener is not likely to be very conscious of such matters. The selection of the songs balances the deservedly famous with the little-known—with *"Amarilli,"* *"Lasciatemi morire,"* and *"Se tu m'ami"* heading the list of the former, Scarlatti's almost shockingly cruel *"Tutto acceso a quei rai"* and the two Bassani songs outstanding among the latter. Purists may object to the piano accompaniments, but the damage is by no means fatal.

LEHMANN, LILLI, soprano

Joshua—O hätt' ich Jubals Harf; Norma—Casta diva; Ah si, fa cuore (with Helbig, s); Robert le diable—Gnadenarie; Die Entführung aus dem Serail—Martern aller Arten; Ach, ich liebte; Don Giovanni—Or sai; Traviata—Sempre libera. Et ELP 0-463.
Don Giovanni—Non mi dir; Così fan tutte—Ich wähle mir (with Hel-

big, s); Nozze di Figaro—Heil'ge Quelle; Brief-Duett (with Helbig, s); Traviata—Alfredo, Alfredo; Huguenots—O glücklich' Land; Walküre— Du bist der Lenz; Mondnacht (Schumann); Freudvoll und leidvoll (Schubert). Et ELP 702.

On the evidence of her recordings, along with contemporary accounts, Lilli Lehmann may well have been the greatest singer within memory. Bear in mind that she came to the studios when she was in the neighborhood of sixty and when the techniques of reproduction were hardly beyond the primitive state. What soprano today, in her prime, would even attempt the two programs listed above? The air from Handel's *Joshua* is a matter for wonder, so even and true is the coloratura throughout. The *"Casta diva"* is a less forward recording, but it has admirable reserve in the *cantilena*, and the descending chromatic scale in the cadenza is well worth the price of the whole record. The *Entführung* arias are scarcely credible, and the *"Non mi dir"* is a model. *"Or sai"* is a little less successful, with its piano accompaniment. The long recitative catches the great singer rather frequently in the break between registers, but the aria pours out forcefully. *"Sempre libera"* can seldom have been sung with such vigor and spirit. The Wagner memento is among the less successful numbers, and the two lieder examples fail to tell the whole story of her great prowess in this field. Joining Lehmann in the duets is her niece, Hedwig Helbig, who used to travel with her, but did not have a career of her own. That she absorbed a great tradition is obvious.

LEHMANN, LOTTE, soprano

LOTTE LEHMANN'S FAREWELL RECITAL, TOWN HALL, NEW YORK, FEBRUARY 16, 1951: Widmung; O ihr Herren; Ständchen; Wer machte dich so krank?; Alte Laute (Schumann); Der Mond; Venezianisches Gondellied (Mendelssohn); Ein Ton; Wiegenlied (Cornelius); Träume (Wagner); Für Musik; Ständchen; Gute Nacht; Weisst du noch; Dies und das (Franz); Wohin?; Dankgesang an den Bach; Der Neugierige; Tränenregen; Die liebe Farbe; Des Baches Wiegenlied; An die Musik (Schubert). Ulanowsky, pf, Pem 1 [one 12" disc, one 10" disc].
A TRIBUTE TO LOTTE LEHMANN: Die Verschweigung; An Chloe (Mozart); Ungeduld; Im Abendroth; Der Wegweiser; Die Krähe; Täuschung; Mut; Die Nebensonnen; Der Lindenbaum (Schubert); Die Kartenlegerin; Alte Laute; Waldesgespräch; Du bist wie eine Blume; Früh-

lingsnacht (Schumann); Therese; Meine Liebe ist grün; Der Tod, das ist die kühle Nacht (Brahms); Für Musik; Gute Nacht (Franz). Balogh, pf; Ulanowsky, pf, V LCT 1108.

Lotte Lehmann began her career with one of the uniquely lovely voices within memory—as her very rare acoustic recordings will testify—and a personal magnetism that increased with the years, even as the voice became more limited. Always womanly and warm-hearted, her impulses sometimes routed her best-laid artistic plans, and as she grew older her never-mastered breath control became less and less reliable. None of these things mattered to her huge, loyal public, to whom she stood for everything worth while in the singer's art. Future generations may wonder at some of the vagaries preserved in her records, but they can hardly fail to be moved by the best features of her singing. Two historical mementos are available, an on-the-spot recording of her farewell New York recital, and a collection assembled from some of the Victor records she made in the 1930's. Presumably the Farewell Program is made up of her personal favorites, and it is good to note the many slightly out-of-the-way songs it contains. In her encore, *"An die Musik,"* she breaks down and in unable to finish. There is much applause, and one can feel the charged atmosphere. There is also a speech. The Victor selection duplicates some of these songs. The collection is uneven, Mozart's *"Der Verschweigung"* and Schubert's *"Im Abendroth"* showing the singer at her best, Brahms's *"Meine Liebe ist grün"* and Schumann's *"Frühlingsnacht"* failing to do so.

LEIDER, FRIDA, soprano

OPERATIC RECITAL: Ariadne auf Naxos—Es gibt ein Reich; Don Giovanni—Rache-Arie; Trovatore—Duet (with Schlusnus, b.); Tannhäuser—Dich, teure Halle; Tristan und Isolde—Liebestod; Siegfried—Final Part, Duet, Act 3 (with Soot,t.). ELP 0-477.

Frida Leider was the great Wagnerian soprano of the twenties; indeed her inability to return to the Metropolitan in 1934 led to the discovery of Flagstad. These two singers are hardly comparable, so different was their equipment. Leider, as we knew her in New York, was a very great artist past the full prime of her vocal powers, still thrilling in the vitality of her best tones, irresistible in her personal magnetism. This selection, from acoustic recordings,

shows the voice at its best, and gives some idea of the grandeur
of the style. The *Ariadne* excerpt, rare on records, is especially
valuable, though the Wagnerian scenes are most characteristic.
All of the program is sung in German.

LEMNITZ, TIANA, soprano

*Viola; Die Blumensprache; Der Blumen Schmerz (Schubert); Möchte im
Walde; Komm, wir wandeln; Hirschlein ging im Wald spazieren; Im
Lenz; Morgenwind (Cornelius); Der Knabe und das Immlein; Wiegen-
lied; Citronenfalter im April (Wolf). Raucheisen, pf, U URLP 7013.*

Tiana Lemnitz first came to the attention of record-collectors in
the early thirties; I think most of us discovered her in her superb
recording of the two *Freischütz* airs. The only criticism one could
make of the creamy-voiced singer was that she set herself a standard all but impossible to maintain, and inevitably most of her later
discs (though by no means all) were disappointing. This postwar
recital shows her voice in not quite pristine estate (the tone has
just a suggestion of the flutterings that have sometimes gotten
the best of her), but her taste is unfailing. One feels that her approach is one of quiet understanding rather than of any deep,
studied penetration. The program she has chosen is a connoisseur's dream; who would ever have expected a lieder recital made
up of Schubert, Cornelius, and Wolf in which only the Wolf songs
are familiar? The Cornelius songs may surprise some hearers into
exploring this now generally forgotten master: they are frankly romantic, melodious and appealing. The three Wolf lieder include
the little-known early *"Wiegenlied"* (not found in the Peters collected edition) offered some years ago by Grete Stückgold in a recorded Wolf recital.

LIST, EMANUEL, basso

*Rosenkavalier—Act 2 Finale (with Schürhoff); Barbiere di Siviglia—
La calunnia; La Juive—Si la rigeur; Totengräbers Heimweh (Schubert); Oh Wien, mein liebes Wien (Ziehrer); Le Caïd—Le Tambour-
Major (Thomas); Song of the Flea (Mussorgsky). ASO, Loibner; Schul-
hof, pf, Rem R 199-73.*

The big, burly Baron Ochs of the thirties here gives us his famous
waltz-finale, along with less accustomed fare. His vocal agility

in the *"Drum Major Song"* will not cause us to forget the great Plançon, nor is he able to bring to life Schubert's *"Totengräbers Heimweh."* Throughout the program, I am afraid, List remains an excellent Baron Ochs. The voice is in surprisingly good estate, and is well recorded.

LONDON, GEORGE, baritone

DRAMATIC SCENES FROM RUSSIAN AND FRENCH OPERAS: Prince Igor—Aria of Prince Igor; The Demon—Do not weep, my child; Don Quichotte—Mort de Don Quichotte; Patrie—Pauvre Martyr obscur (Paladilhe). MOO, Adler, Morel, C ML 4489.

OF GODS AND DEMONS: Das Rheingold—Abendlich strahlt der Sonne Augen; Die Walküre—Wotan's Farewell and Magic Fire Music; La Damnation de Faust—Mephistopheles' Serenade; Faust—Le Veau d'or; Mefistofele—Ecco il mondo; Song of the Flea (Mussorgsky); The Demon—Do not weep, my child. VSY, Moralt; MOO, Adler, C ML 4658.

Canadian-born and Hollywood-raised, George London came to operatic New York by way of Vienna, a ready-made sensation. His voice, characterized as a bass-baritone, encompasses the unusual combination of Boris, Figaro, and Amonasro; it has a fine virile quality and ample power, though not quite so much as his records might lead us to expect. He has a genuine flair for the theater, and one is not surprised to learn that he has been stage-struck all his life. His great model as a singer is at once apparent in his repertoire, an impression amply born out by his manner of singing it. It must have been a major thrill for him to sing Boris on the Metropolitan stage where Chaliapin had known so many triumphs, though he did not get to sing the part in Russian, as he had done elsewhere. His first recordings from abroad (discounting a couple of youthful efforts made here) showed him as soloist in choral works; as an operatic artist we have him in the Viennese casts of *Le Nozze di Figaro* (SL 114) and *Die Zauberflöte* (SL 115) and the Bayreuth *Parsifal* (L LLA 10). "Dramatic Scenes from Russian and French Operas" offers a chance for direct comparison with Chaliapin, for in the death scene from Massenet's *Don Quichotte* he copies the famous older recording to the extent of singing Sancho's part as well as that of his master. Somehow, while the great Russian could bring the show to life, London does not make us forget that the music as such is innocuous. What is missing throughout this program, I should say, is rhythmic vitality: the big aria from Paladilhe's *Patrie* can be an imposing patriotic outburst, yet here it amounts to no more than sound and fury. "Of Gods and Demons" takes us further afield, for he has plainly not yet developed into a Wotan—one wonders if he learned the finales from *Walküre* and *Rheingold* specially for the "god" side of this disc. The demons are the expected ones of Berlioz, Gounod, Boïto, and Mussorgsky, along with the title part of Rubinstein's opera, the last excerpt unfortunately repeated from ML 4489.

LUCA, GIUSEPPE DE, baritone

ITALIAN ART SONGS: Caro mio ben (Giordani); Bella fanciulla (Falconieri); La Frate 'nnamorato—D'ogni pena (Pergolesi); Dolce madonna (Anon.); Selve amiche (Caldara); Pur dicesti (Lotti); Amarilli (Caccini); Susurrate intorno a Clori (Pasquini). Cimara, pf, 10" D DL 7505.

Don Pasquale—Bella siccome un angelo; Cheti, cheti (with Corradetti, b); Hamlet—Come un romito fior; Dinorah—Sei vendicata assai; Traviata—Di Provenza; Rigoletto—Pari siamo; Occhi di fata (Denza). GAR 100.

The originals from which the GAR recital were made date from 1903 to 1911, before De Luca's coming to the Metropolitan in New York. Of special interest is the *buffo* duet from *Don Pasquale* with his colleague Corradetti. The classic Italian airs were recorded at the time of his last great comeback, after the Second World War. There was an amazing amount of voice left in his throat, old as he was, and his fine, delicate sense of style had never left him. Consequently these songs remain as a document and a lesson to the young. Though some of the presence has been lost in transfer from 78 rpm to LP, the recording sounds well in its new form.

LUCIA, FERNANDO DE, tenor

Barbiere di Siviglia—Ecco ridente; Se il mio nome; All idea; Numero quindici; Adriana Lecouvreur—L'anima ho stanca; Iris—Apri la tua finestra; Fedora—Mia madre; Mignon—Ah non credevi tu; L'Elisir d'Amore—Quanto e bella; Obbligato; Sonnambula—Son gelosa; Bohème—Che gelida manina; Don Pasquale—Cercherò lontana terra;

*Faust—Salve dimora; Manon Lescaut—Donna non vidi mai; Les Pê-
cheurs de perles—Mi par d'udir ancora; Non hai compreso; Mefistofele
—Giunto sul passo; Forma ideale; Il Guarany—Sento una forza; Rigo-
letto—Parmi veder; Carmen—Il fior; Pagliacci—Vesti la giubba; No,
Pagliaccio non son; Ernani—Come rugiada; Salve Maria (Mercadente);
Non me guardate; Oili, oila (Neapolitan Songs). CE 7002 [2].
Barbiere di Siviglia—Ecco ridente; Rigoletto—Questa o quella; Aïda
—Celeste Aïda; Les Huguenots—Love Duet, Act 4 (with de Ange-
lis,s); Werther—Ah, non mi ridestar; Amico Fritz—Oh! amore; Carmen
—Flower Song; Les Pêcheurs de perles—Della mia vita. Et ELP
0-464.*

In the generation prior to Caruso, Fernando de Lucia was a reigning tenor in Italy, and having a free and durable Italian vocal production, he still sang during the four years left in his life after
Caruso's passing. He was an amazing artist, unlike any other, for
along with a mastery of *bel canto* in the music of Bellini, Donizetti, and Rossini, he had a passionate intensity and dramatic
conviction that brought him resounding success in such then modern works as *Pagliacci, Adriana Lecouvreur, Iris,* and *Fedora.* No
one could rival his coloratura in *"Ecco ridente,"* and few have
poured out impassioned utterance as he did in such an aria as
"L'anima ho stanca." His *"Vesti la giubba"* is freely sung, but
extremely telling, and for sustained legato we may turn to his
"Mia madre." Classic Editions has made a real effort to re-record
their selections in proper pitch, but there has been little better
than the ear to guide the engineers, so erratic were both the singer
and the recording companies in this regard. If in some of the numbers the pitch is not constant, this must be laid to the imperfec-
tions of older recordings. Who the singers are who join in the
duets we have not been told, but they include Giuseppina Huguet
and Ernesto Badini. The actual reproduction of the voice is variable; some selections are well forward while others are not. Still,
the beautiful quality of the voice is impressively apparent. He
was not a musicianly singer, and he was not above making altera-
tions, as in the melody of *"Che gelida manina"* and the ending of
"Mi par d'udir ancora." For a novelty that shows his sincerity
along with the intensity of his singing at best, I refer you to *Salve
Maria.*
The Eterna set is more economical, but on the whole less satisfying. There are, to be sure, only two duplications in the two re-

citals, so fans will want both. There is some wonderful singing here, and some good forward recording. The *Werther* and *Pearl-Fishers* numbers are excellent in these respects. But the *Rigoletto* is fully a tone above the original key (surely he did not record it so!), and there are deviations in pitch in several selections. Finally, his partner in the duet is no asset.

LUDWIG, WALTHER, tenor

WALTHER LUDWIG SINGS OPERATIC ARIAS: Don Giovanni—Dalla sua pace; Il mio tesoro; Die lustigen Weiber von Windsor—Horch, die Lerche singt im Hain; Die verkaufte Braut—Es muss gelingen. WSTO, Leitner, 10" D DL 4073.

Ludwig is one of the best German lyric tenors within recent memory. Though now past the first freshness of his attractive voice, he is always a master of style and always an understanding and expressive artist. The two *Don Giovanni* arias are better done, certainly, than by any recording artist since Tauber, and they are not far behind the standard of that artist. *"Il mio tesoro"* is well phrased and nicely sustained, all but perfectly poised in rhythm. The serenade from *The Merry Wives of Windsor* is sung for the lovely piece it is, with fervor and tonal beauty; there is lots of room resonance here. No one will complain that so pleasant a moment should be extended by a repetition of part of the song. The *Bartered Bride* recitative and aria could hardly be bettered.

McCORMACK, JOHN, tenor

JOHN McCORMACK IN OPERA AND SONG: Lucia di Lammermoor—Fra poco a me ricovero; Tristan und Isolde—O König, das kann ich dir nicht sagen; Träume; The fairy tree (O'Brien); Jocelyn—Angels guard thee (with Kreisler, vln.); L'Elisir d'Amore—Una furtiva lagrima; I hear you calling me (Marshall); Adeste fideles (Hymn). V LCT 1036.

Perhaps John McCormack was the best example in history of the singer forced to lead a double life. Regarding him as their own boy who had made good, the Irish never let him leave off singing the drawing-room ballads he had popularized (one of which is included in this recital), though the artist, trained in the best Italian school, sang Donizetti as few tenors in any generation, and had grown into a passionate fondness for German lieder, for Bach, Mozart, and Handel. His popular repertoire, then, did not represent his personal taste—how sick he must have become of *"Mother Machree"* and *"I hear you calling me"*! But he was an artist, and though he gave his public what it wanted, he forced it in the same evening to hear what he wanted to sing. With this background, the program selected from his myriad recordings makes better sense than many historical "revivals." It does give us the singer at various stages of his career, singing—with one notable exception —things that were identified with him. Of course, he never sang *Tristan*, nor did he use excerpts from this work on his concert programs. The previously unreleased recording was made for his own amusement and satisfaction, perhaps to prove a point. Anyone listening to it must feel that something of the lyric quality he brings to the music would never be amiss in the most heroic of performances. Another first American edition is the little piece by the tenor's first voice teacher and onetime accompanist, Vincent O'Brien, a modern Irish song of the better type. The "Lullaby" from *Jocelyn*, recorded with his lifelong friend, Fritz Kreisler, furnishes an example of what great artists can do with too familiar music.

MADRIGALISTI MILANESI (Renato Fait)

Ecco mormorar l'onde; Lamento d'Arianna (Monteverdi); Tristis est anima mea (Palestrina); Tenebrae factae sunt (Ingegneri); Come t'aggio lasciata; L'amanza mia (Azzaiola); Folti boschetti (Falconieri); Chi la gagliarda (Donati); Ah! che debbo morire; Sonno soave; Io son farfalla; Come Fenice; D'una donna gentil (Nanino). Col CLPS 1027.

The Madrigalisti are a fifteen-voice choir, a big group for the secular numbers on this program, despite the annotator's claim to complete authenticity. The singing is of the lavish, fussy school which leaves no stones unturned in making "effects," favoring great elasticity in both rhythm and dynamics. The program, containing so much otherwise unrecorded, is therefore more valuable for its content than for its presentation. A further drawback is the reproduction, which at its very best is uneven. The Monteverdi numbers would seem to have been more recently recorded than the rest of the program, for they are reasonably clear and lifelike.

From the Palestrina on, however, it is all too frequently 'difficult to make out just what is going on. A veil seems to be drawn between us and the singers.

MARDONES, JOSÉ, basso

Les Huguenots—Piff, paff; Robert le diable—Suore, che riposate; Simon Boccanegra—Il lacerato spirito; Ernani—Infelice; La Juive— Se oppressi ognor; Salvator Rosa—Di sposa di padre (Gomez); Bohème —Vecchia zimarra; Mefistofele—Ave Signor; Son lo spirito; Ecco il mondo; Faust—Serenata; Dio dell' or; Ramenta i lieti dì; Stabat Mater —Pro peccatis (Rossini); Barbiere di Siviglia—La calunnia. Scala 810.

José Mardones, principal basso at the Metropolitan from 1917 to 1926, had a voice not matched in height and depth since his departure. His recording career began in 1910, with Columbia's Boston Opera Company series; most of the titles here revived would seem to have been made about that time. There is a surprising amount of bravado in the singing, as though the basso gloried in the very power and richness of his instrument. This spirit is not so evident in the more placid recordings he made for Victor later in his life.

MASTERPIECES OF MUSIC BEFORE 1750

Gregorian Chant to the 16th Century; The 16th Century and the 17th Century; The 17th Century and the 18th Century. Soloists & Ens, Wöldike, HS HSL-B [3].

This box of three discs is a complete recording of the music contained in *Masterpieces of Music before 1750: An Anthology of Musical Examples from Gregorian Chant to J. S. Bach*, by Carl Parrish and John F. Ohl (N.Y.: Norton, 1951). The book is valuable for several reasons, beyond the skillfully edited texts, for the most part set up in closed scores, using modern clefs and barlines, so that the pieces may be played or sung by practiced readers. Each example is prefaced by historical and analytical notes to orient the student, and full translations of the texts are given. The selection of the pieces has been careful and imaginative, in general keeping away from the expected compositions. Thus Palestrina is not represented by his *Missa Papae Marcelli*, but rather by the Mass *Veni Sponsa Christi;* Carissimi comes in with a scene from *Judicum Salomonis*, rather than *Jepthe* or *Jonas;* the English madrigal included is not by Morley, Gibbons, or Wilbye, but Bennet; and the three Handel pieces are a Concerto Grosso, an air from *Rinaldo* (not *"Lascia ch'io pianga"*), and a little-known chorus from *Solomon*. In the case of Bach, after three contrasting settings of the chorale *Christ lag in Todesbanden* have been cited, we are given the *"Golgotha"* recitative from the *Saint Matthew Passion* and the third contrapunctus from *The Art of Fugue*.

As to the recordings themselves, the fact that they have been made in Copenhagen under the direction of Mogens Wöldike, enlisting the services of such artists as Finn Viderø, Aksel Schiøtz, the Copenhagen Boys' and Mens' Choir, and the Danish State Radio Chamber Orchestra and Chorus, is in itself a high recommendation. One knows in advance that such performances will be marked by musicianship and taste; what remains to be noted is the fine clarity and the dignified expressiveness of the choral numbers and the straightforward delivery of the solos. There are, of course, some inequalities; one feels occasionally that something still lies hidden in the musical score, and in one instance a solo seems thrown off poise by shortness of breath. The recording level presents a minor problem, in that the harpsichord and clavichord pieces are louder than they should be when played with the controls set for the choral works. But these are hardly matters of first importance. In the preface to the book we are assured that "the selection of each example has been determined, first of all, by the basic requirement that it be in itself an interesting and beautiful piece of music." These recordings are the author's full justification.

MATTHEWS, INEZ, mezzo-soprano

SPIRITUALS: 'Roun about de mountain (Hayes); Hear de lambs a-cryin'?; Litl' boy (Hayes); Talk about a chile (Dawson); Lord, I didn't know (Plinton and Matthews); New-born again (Heilman); Gonna ride up in de chariot (Withers); Crucifixion (Payne); Balm in Gilead (Dett); His name so sweet; Fix me, Jesus (Johnson); I'm goin' to tell God all my troubles (Brown); Po' pilgrim; You're tired, chile; Live a humble (Hayes); Hold on; They led my Lord away; Witness (Johnson); You

*must come in by an' thro' de Lamb (Hayes); De gospel train (Burleigh);
Plenty good room (Hayes). Brice, pf, Per SPL 580.*

On the jacket a critic is quoted as comparing Inez Matthews's
voice with that of Marian Anderson, and the resemblance is striking; but the longer one listens the less alike the two singers
seem. If Matthews has actually less vocal richness, she has on
the other hand less pronounced *vibrato*. What is more important is
the warmth of the tones she produces, the simple, direct clarity of
her presentation of the songs, her wonderful ability to set and sustain a mood. Perhaps the most significant test of the success of
the program is that, long as it is, it does not tire us. One would
like the singer to go on. Outstanding, perhaps, is *"They led my
Lord away,"* an intensely moving song, though the more sustained
ones are all more or less of the same high quality.

MELCHIOR, LAURITZ, tenor

*MELCHIOR RECITAL: Tosca—Recondita armonia; E lucevan le
stelle; Pagliacci—Vesti la giubba; No, Pagliaccio non son; Emperor
Waltz (Strauss-Burke); The kiss in your eyes (Heuberger-Burke); Lenz
(Hildach); You are my heart's delight (Lehar-Graham). MGM Studio O,
Spadani, Stoll, 10" MGM E 109.*

Now that Melchior is a movie star, I suppose we must expect him
to dabble in the light classics. Probably his recording the Italian
arias is the realization of a long-held ambition. He has plenty of
power for them, but there is something open and outgoing about a
real Italian tenor which Melchior does not have. The English
songs are various degrees of awful, including the little Hildach
encore, which is translated and adapted. The accompaniments
are in the salon style.

MILANOV, ZINKA, soprano

*Forza del Destino—Madre, pietosa vergine; Il santo nome; La vergine
degli angeli (with Vichegonov, bs; Shaw C); Pace, pace; Gioconda—
Suicidio!; Aïda—Ritorna vincitor; O patria mia; Trovatore—Tacea la
notte placida; D'amor sull' ali rosee; Cavalleria Rusticana—Voi lo
sapete (with Roggero, m-s). RCAO, Cellini, V LM 1777.*

Milanov is in her finest voice throughout this set, which is to say
that here is singing of a caliber too rarely encountered these days.

Few sopranos in our time have approached her ability to float high tones, and she has temperament to give her performances conviction. These selections have all been long identified with her in the opera house; all suit her to perfection. The choral and orchestral support is superior; the assisting artists are satisfactory.

MUZIO, CLAUDIA, soprano

Otello—Già nella notte densa; Dio ti giocondi (with Merli, t); Norma —Casta diva; Sonnambula—Ah! non credea; Forza del Destino— Pace, pace; Traviata—Addio del passato; Bohème—Sì, mi chiamano Mimì; Andrea Chénier—La mamma morta; Mefistofele—L'altra notte; L'Arlesiana—Esser madre è un inferno (Cilea). O, Molajoli, C ML 4404.

O del mio amato ben (Donaudy); Se tu m'ami (Pergolesi); Umbra di nube; Ave Maria (Refice); C'est mon ami (Crist); Les Filles de Cadix (Delibes); Spirate pur, spirate (Donaudy); La Ninna Nanna della Vergine (Reger); Beau Soir (Debussy); Bonjour, Suzon (Delibes). O, Molajoli, Refice, C ML 4634.

THE DUSE OF SONG, VOL. 1: Lombardi—Se vano (Verdi); Loreley— Dove son? (Catalani); Hérodiade—Egli è bel; Vespri Siciliani—Mercè, dilette amice; Rinaldo—Lascia ch'io pianga (Handel); Eugene Onegin —Letter Scene; Africana—Figlio del sol; Carmen—Micaëla'a air. Es ES 500.

THE DUSE OF SONG, VOL. 2: Ernani—Ernani, involami; Mefistofele —L'altra notte; Mme Sans-Gène—Che me ne faccio del vostro castello? (Giordano); Pagliacci—Ballatella; Silvio! a quest' ora (with Laurenti, b); Bianca e Fernando—Sorgi, o padre (Bellini); Guglielmo Tell—Selva opaca; Madama Butterfly—Entrance of Butterfly; Trovatore—D'amor sull' ali rosee; Tosca—Vissi d'arte. Es ES 502.

THE DUSE OF SONG, VOL. 3: Trovatore—Tacea la notte placida; Adriana Lecouvreur—Io sono l'umile ancella (Cilea); La Separazione (Rossini); Contes d'Hoffmann—Elle a fui; Eternamente (Mascheroni); Se tu m'ami (Pergolesi); Andrea Chénier—La mamma morta; Forza del Destino—Pace, pace; Paride ed Elena—Spiagge amate (Gluck); Chère Nuit (Bachelet). Es ES 508.

Muzio died in mid-career in 1936, to become a legend; none of the older singers has been more honored by the "revivalists." If one were asked to define the term *lirico spinto* as applied to the soprano voice, one could scarcely do better than point to Muzio; and there is much to be learned about singing in the grand manner from listening to the many recordings she left us, primitive as most of them are. In any discussion of those now available, a line must be drawn between those dubbed from acoustic Edison and Pathé originals and Columbia's two sets dating from the last year or two of the singer's life, one devoted to opera, the other to song. Among the three Esoteric discs a choice would have to be made on personal preference in repertoire, for all have been reproduced with loving care (though it may be that here and there a recording pitch may not be accurate). The Columbia sets show the voice on the decline, but still very lovely, the artistry at its top. The song program shows a noticeable loss in vocal liveness as compared to the original 78-rpm version, but it contains some delectable legato singing, especially in the Donaudy songs, and in Bainbridge Crist's arrangement of the fine old melody supposedly by Marie Antoinette. There is a curiously unidiomatic *"Beau Soir,"* and, stranger still, Reger's *"Mariä Wiegenlied"* done into Italian.

NETHERLANDS CHAMBER CHOIR (Felix de Nobel)

Kyrie and Gloria (Okeghem); Parce, Domine (Obrecht); Ave Maria (Josquin des Pres); O Leyda gratiosa (Schuyt); Madonna, con quest' occhio (Sweelinck); Della veloce sona (Tollius); Matona, mia cara (Lassus). Ep LC 3045 (*Palestrina: Missa Papae Marcelli).

The religious pieces are very effective, especially the Okeghem. For the Italian madrigals, however, this group is surely too big. But if we accept the choral-society approach, with consequent loss of intimacy, there is little enough to criticize. Two additional Italian madrigals described in the jacket notes are not accounted for on the disc.

NEW YORK PRO MUSICA ANTIQUA (Noah Greenberg)

ANTHOLOGY OF RENAISSANCE MUSIC: Kyrie eleison (Dufay); Tu solus (Josquin des Pres); Adoramus Te (Lassus); Ave Maria (Josquin des Pres); Agnus Dei (Morley); Ave Maria (Victoria); Assumpta est (Palestrina); O Jesu Christe (Berchem); Salve Regina (Lassus); Iocundare Jerusalem (Mouton); Eheu; Domine fac mecum (Morley); O vos omnes (Victoria); Resonet in laudibus (Lassus). Per SPL 597.
ENGLISH MEDIEVAL CHRISTMAS CAROLS: Nowell sing we; Ave Maria; Gloria; Alleluia; Lullay lullow; What tidings bringest thou?; Marvel not, Joseph; Alma redemptoris mater; Make we joy now in this

*fest; Nowell, nowell, tidings true; Sancta Maria (Dunstable); Hail Mary,
full of grace; Ave rex angelorum; Tibi laus, tibi gloria; Beata pro-
genies (Power); Nova, nova. Es ES 521.*
*AN ELIZABETHAN SONGBAG FOR YOUNG PEOPLE: It was the frog
in the well; Come, let us all a-maying go; Whither runneth my sweet-
heart; The Duke of Brunswick's toye; Come, Robin, lend to me thy
bow; Messenger of the delightful spring; Shepherd's pipe; New oysters;
Now, Robin, laugh and sing; Willy, prithee go to bed; Hey boy, ho boy,
news!; Well rung, Tom boy; In Sherwood lived stout Robin Hood; Dr.
Bull's my selfe; About the maypole; Hey ho, to the greenwood; There
were three ravens; A dreame; Jack and Joan; Rest, sweet nymph. 10"
Es ESJ 6.*

It is good to have the superb music of the Renaissance program
performed by a solo group, and to note that Greenberg favors the
"detached," rather than the "expressive" treatment of the varied
selections. The singing of his ensemble is clean and reserved,
steady in pulse, but the "impersonal" never is allowed to become
callous. Such a motet as Victoria's *O vos omnes*, so often given
everything a ponderous chorus has, thus takes on new freshness
and gentle poignancy. Even more valuable as a program, because
of its unfamiliarity, is the collection of Christmas music, fostered
by the recent publication of John Stevens's *Medieval Carols.* One
wishes, however, that more time had gone into the preparation of
the recording, for the singers seem not to have quite digested the
basic style. One feels that they take great satisfaction in having
mastered the notes, and that this will have to suffice. It has been
said that proper performing style in Gregorian chant is the basis
of all good singing; one wishes for that kind of relaxed intensity
here. As it is, the interesting program is a little tiring to the listener, as he feels it must be to the singers. The *Songbag* was a
happy inspiration. Some of the music, to be sure, was not intended for the young, but it serves them well enough. Let no one
be frightened by the length of the list of titles, for the pieces are
short, and there is plenty of variety in the presentation, instrumental selections alternating with the vocal. The voice of the
counter-tenor Russell Oberlin is featured, and his fine-styled
singing will be very much enjoyed.

NIKOLAIDI, ELENA, contralto

*Don Carlo—O don fatale; Macbeth—Sleepwalking Scene; Semiramide
—Bel raggio (Rossini). COL, Cleva. Ridente la calma (in German)*

(Mozart); My mother bids me bind my hair (in German) (Haydn); Erlkönig (Schubert); Mondnacht (Schumann); Alte Liebe (Brahms). Behr, pf, 10" C ML 2165.

When Nikolaidi burst upon the New York horizon several seasons back with a Town Hall recital, she was hailed as one of the great lieder singers of her generation. She has since gone on to an established position at the Metropolitan Opera, and has been heard as soloist in oratorio. A Greek trained in the German traditions, she has extended her repertoire to the dramatic bravura of Rossini and Verdi. The operatic side of this disc affords scope to her colorful temperament, though to be honest she has not the facility to make the *Semiramide* sound easy, nor is she comfortable in the *tessitura* of the *Macbeth*. And though some may be carried by the sheer force of her *"Erlkönig,"* I doubt that anyone will derive much pleasure from her labored *"Mondnacht."*

OBERNKIRCHEN CHILDREN'S CHOIR (Edith Möller)

Der fröhliche Wanderer (Möller); Die Nordseewellen (Krannig); Löwenzahn (Knab); Landsknechtständchen (Lassus); Der Lindenbaum (Schubert); Der Wirbelwind (Möller); Es waren zwei Königskinder (arr. Möller); Unsere kleine Mandoline (Möller). 10" An 64008.

This group of young people, which has won prizes at the International Eisteddfod at Llangollen, presents its program of folk and folksy music with such purity and enthusiasm that one wishes the record lasted longer. The voices are bright and fresh, finely blended, and true in intonation; their rather clipped diction gives a special zest to their music. One could take exception to some of the interpretations—Lassus's *Matona, mia cara,* disguised as it is in the German language, is too carefully wrung dry by the conductor, and of course the true character of Schubert's *"Lindenbaum"* is lost when it is treated as a folk song. But this is healthy singing, and a record not to be missed.

PALMER, JEANNE, soprano

CONCERT PROGRAM: Paride ed Elena—O del mio dolce ardor; An die Musik; Erlkönig (Schubert); Traum durch die Dämmerung; Zueignung (Strauss); Psyché (Paladilhe); Le Moulin (Pierné); In your far country (Borodin); Forgotten so soon (Tchaikovsky); O men from the fields (Hughes); Romance (Rubinstein). Wightman, pf, Col CLPS 1001.

Jeanne Palmer (Mme Serge Soudeikin) was known around New York for her excellent singing in Russian operas long before her engagement by the Metropolitan. Hers is a big, vibrant soprano which should have won her a larger reputation. At the Metropolitan she had a few opportunities in leading Wagnerian roles, but for the most part she was among those present, a Norn or a Valkyrie. This recital gives an idea of her gifts and of her artistic scope. The Gluck is disappointing, lacking in the classic line; the Schubert is good but not extraordinary. The Russian songs are best, but the Herbert Hughes setting of Padraic Colum's touching poem is also worth having. The Rubinstein *"Romance,"* always a mistake on a serious vocal program, is no less so than usual here.

PANZÉRA, CHARLES, baritone

Cinq Mélodies populaires grecques; Quatre Chants populaires (Ravel); Priez pour paix (Poulenc); Berceuse (Milhaud); Murcie en fleurs (Honegger); Le Voyage (Trémois); Ronde (Ropartz); Enlèvement en mer (Delvincourt); Les Souliers de l'avocat (Aubert); Chanson du vieux Canada (Gallon). M. Panzéra, pf, Mer MG 10098 (*Piano Pieces).
Collectors who date back to the adventurous twenties and the halcyon thirties will always gratefully remember the services of Charles Panzéra in spreading the gospel of French song and its proper interpretation on early electrical records. The voice in its prime was a light, supple baritone, capable of a fine ringing climax, but most remarkable in mezza voce. He was long established in Paris as both opera and concert singer; among his many admirers was Debussy, who chose him as the ideal Pelléas. Fauré's *Horizon chimérique* is one of many important works dedicated to Panzéra. He was also remarkable as one of the few French singers really at home in German lieder; his prewar recording of Schumann's *Dichterliebe*, with Cortot at the piano, is now again available (V LCT 1132). It would be too much to say that nothing had been lost when Panzéra, assisted by his accomplished pianist-wife, made two discs for Mercury, the one here listed, and another considered under the works of Fauré and Debussy (MG 10097). But these recitals afford an invaluable lesson in style, as well as introducing some new and treasurable repertoire.

PENNO, GINO, tenor

Norma—Meco all' altar di Venere (with Mercuriale, t); Simon Boccanegra—Sento avvamper nell' anima; Trovatore—Di quella pira. Ch; MISO, Narducci, 10" L LD 9117.

When Penno came to the Metropolitan in 1953–4, he was immediately hailed as the loudest tenor since Lauri-Volpi. The critics acknowledged that his was a genuine voice, but they were less enthusiastic about the results he got with it. He is heard here in the complete recitative and aria from *Norma*, capably assisted by a second tenor. The effect is about what it was in the opera house: the recording certainly gives the impression of size; the quality is good, the control mostly adequate. It is pleasant to hear the unhackneyed aria from *Simon Boccanegra*, for it shows the singer at his best. His *"Di quella pira,"* however, is so fast that he finds it impossible to get in all the sixteenth-notes. And giving his all is not sufficient to get him up to the final high C.

PETERS, ROBERTA, soprano

Lucia di Lammermoor—Regnava nel silenzio; Puritani—Qui la voce; Sonnambula—Ah! non credea; Ah! non giunge; Linda di Chamounix— O luce di quest' anima. RCAO, Cellini, V LM 1786 (*Operatic Arias by Tetrazzini, Galli-Curci, Pons).

This disc was issued as a sort of "coming of age" celebration for Roberta Peters, who, since her debut in 1950, has been one of the white hopes of opera in New York. Whether or not it was wise to invite comparison so deliberately with three of her predecessors—Tetrazzini, Galli-Curci, and Pons—is an open question. In any case, it is hardly a fair test, for of the three only the last was really at her best on the example selected. But, all considerations of this kind aside, it is true that Roberta Peters displays a brilliance few of her contemporaries can equal, a vocal neatness and accuracy wholly admirable. She shows, too, in the more sustained passages, that she is a lyric singer as well as a brilliant one; one rarely hears such melting tones as hers in the *Lucia* air, or in the *andante* that introduces *"O luce di quest' anima."*

PETROFF, IVAN, baritone

Rigoletto—Cortigiani; Macbeth—Pièta, rispetto, amore; Pagliacci—

Prologo; Barbiere di Siviglia—Largo al factotum; Puritani—Ah! per sempre; Favorita—Vien Leonora. FM, Ghiglia, Rem R 199–93.

Petroff has a fine voice and authentic style: it was almost a foregone conclusion that he would perform well such a show-window program as this. The Bellini and Donizetti arias are good to hear when as well done as this, but the only really out-of-the-way item is the fine melody from *Macbeth*.

PINZA, EZIO, basso

Norma—Ite sul colle; Barbiere di Siviglia—La calunnia; Bohème—Vecchia zimarra; Simon Boccanegra—Il lacerato spirito; La Juive—Si la rigeur; Don Carlo—Ella giammai m'amò! MOC & O, Cleva, 10" C ML 2060.
ITALIAN SONGS OF THE 17TH AND 18TH CENTURIES: Arianna—Lasciatemi morire (Monteverdi); Floridante—Alma mia (Handel); L'Incoronazione di Poppea—Oblivion soave (Monteverdi); Donzelle, fugite (Cavalli); Caro mio ben (Giordani); O bellissimi capelli (Falconieri); Armida—Lungi dal caro bene (Sarti); Camilla—Pupille neri (Bononcini); To lo sai (Torelli); La Molinara—Nel cor più non mi sento (Paisiello); Eteocle—Che fiero costume (Legrenzi); Chi vuole innamorarsi (Scarlatti). Kitzinger, pf. Don Giovanni—La ci darem; Nozze di Figaro—Se a casa Madama; Non più andrai; Porgi amor; Crudel, perchè finora; Dove sono. With Rethberg, s; RCAO, Reibold, V LCT 1031.

Pinza reigned so long at the Metropolitan Opera as perhaps the world's greatest basso (Kipnis's supporters will dispute this), and has since become such a figure in the more remunerative field of musical comedy, that it may be superfluous to do more than mention his name. His recorded repertoire, could one assemble it all, embraces most of the standard and expected items, all sung with unassailable style, but with increasing evidence of waning vocal powers in recent offerings. For Pinza at his best we must haunt the shops for prewar discs and watch for the issues of Victor's "Treasury." Nevertheless, the operatic recital listed above is authoritative and vocally more rewarding than those discussed under Mozart and Verdi. Admirable concert performances (if a bit free) made in the thirties distinguish his piano-accompanied Italian airs program, but this is coupled with the unhappy duets with Rethberg. The soprano was definitely out of voice when these were made, but Pinza's one solo is good.

PLAINCHANT

Gregorian Chants, Vol.1. Trappist Monks; Benedictine Nuns, Per SPL 569.

Gregorian Chants, Vol.2. Monks of Benedictine Abbey; Boys' Choir from L'Alumnat, Per SPL 570.

Gregorian Chants, Vol.3. Benedictine Monks of St. Wandrille de Fontenelle, David, Per SPL 576.

Christmas Vespers. Benedictines of the Archabbey of Beuron, Pfaff, D DL 7546.

Gregorian chants. Mt. Angel Seminary Gregorian Ch, Nicholson, Greg Inst of Amer MA-LP 1.

Gregorian Chants. Monks of Saint-Pierre de Solesmes Abbey, Gajard, V LCT 6011 [2].

The first two volumes of the Period series were winners of the *Grand Prix du Disque* in France. The striking thing in these recordings is that there is nothing professional about them. This is chanting as it is actually done in the cloisters, as a part of daily life. Its simple sincerity is hard to resist. Vol. 3 contains some composed plainchant, the work of the conductor, Dom Lucien David, and of Dom Pothier, Abbot of St. Wandrille, the latter a leading authority on Gregorian music and the official editor of the Vatican editions. Some of this chanting is unaccompanied, some with organ. The Beuron Benedictine choir is described as "the leading organization of its kind in Germany." With this and the American recording we have an opportunity to compare style along nationalistic lines. The Gregorian Institute disc was made under the direction of Werner Janssen. These young seminarians chant more fervidly than the monks in France and Germany. There is something of an edge on the recorded sound. The Victor set will be recognized as the long standard and perhaps definitive recordings made many years ago. Whether or not they merit this this accolade, they are the official document on the subject, proceeding from the center of learning. The transfer to LP could hardly be expected to add brilliance to a somewhat time-dulled original, but it has done well enough in catching the sound and the spirit of the chants with reasonable clarity.

POLISH MUSIC

FOUR CENTURIES OF POLISH MUSIC: Deus, in nomine tuo (Mielczewski); Matthen, bs. Divertimento for String Orchestra (Janiewicz). NY

Collegium Mus, Rikko. Nova Casa, Concerto à Tre (Jarzebski); Children's Prayer—Juz siz zmierzcha (Waclaw of Szamotul); Psalm 136 (Gomólka); Sonata for Two Violins and Organ (Szarzynski). Ch; O, etc; Van VRS 6017.
MUSIC OF POLAND. VOL.1. Seven Polish Folk Songs (arr. Sygietynski); Suite of Ancient Polish Airs and Dances (arr. Panufnik). Ch; O, Van VRS 6001.
MUSIC OF POLAND, Vol.2. Seven Folk Songs; Little Suite (Lutoslawski); Six Children's Songs with Orchestra. Godlewska, m-s; Ch & O, Van VRS 6013.

> The title of the first disc may seem a little high-sounding, for of course it is possible to give only a few samples of this rich literature on one disc. Nevertheless, the recording is useful for the professor of music history, and it will prove attractive to the disinterested listener, Polish or no. The first side of the disc was made in New York, the second came from Poland. Paul Matthen sings his "concerto"—more easily recognized as a cantata—with warm expressiveness. The Polish choruses on the reverse do especially well by the beautiful Gomolka pieces. The interest of the other two discs centers around the simple folk-song arrangements, unaffectedly sung. Helpful notes are provided; with the historical disc we are given a rather elaborate booklet.

PONSELLE, ROSA, soprano

La Vestale—Tu che invoco; O nume tutelar (Spontini); Otello—Salce, salce; Ave Maria; Ave Maria (Schubert); Home, sweet home (Bishop). 10" V LCT 10.
Tosca—Vissi d'arte; Manon Lescaut—In quelle trine morbide; Sadko—Song of India; Cavalleria Rusticana—Voi lo sapete; Lohengrin—Elsas Traum; Trovatore—D'amor sull' ali rosee; Mira, d'acerbe lagrime (with Stracciari, b); Bohème—Si, mi chiamano Mimi; Maritana—Scenes that are brightest (Wallace); Madama Butterfly—Un bel dì. GA LP 1201.
Manon Lescaut—In quelle trine morbide; Tosca—Vissi d'arte; Guglielmo Tell—Selva opaca; Cavalleria Rusticana—Voi lo sapete; Madama Butterfly—Un bel dì; Norma—Casta diva; Bohème—Si, mi chiamano Mimi; Trovatore—D'amor sull' ali rosee; Maritana—Scenes that are brightest; Forza del Destino—La vergine degli angeli; Aïda—O terra, addio (with Hackett, t); Gioconda—Suicidio. Scala 803.

There is no question that Rosa Ponselle will pass into history as the possessor of one of the all-time great voices and as one of the finest operatic artists of the twentieth century. Despite the fact that her astonishing debut was made at an early age—in *Forza del Destino*, an opera never before heard at the Metropolitan, and in no less impressive company than that of Enrico Caruso himself—she was one young singer who never lost her head. Her progress was steady until her premature retirement. This progress may be studied with the aid of her recordings, the first of which were made actually before her debut, on the chance of a success. Contrast, for example, her early "*Casta diva*" with the wholly mature version recorded after she had made the role of Norma her own (V ERAT 19, 45 rpm only). Two of the above-listed discs are made up from her first (Columbia) recordings: the Golden Age is official, having been dubbed by Columbia engineers with the company's sanction. As it happens, it is also the better job of re-recording, so that the Scala has only the non-duplicated material to recommend it. But "*Selva opaca*" and "*Suicidio*," both among the best of this vintage, in themselves make the disc worth having. It is amazing to listen to "Scenes that are brightest" and realize how naturally and well this young girl supplied the embellishments on the melody. The Victor disc represents the later Ponselle, from the acoustic *Otello* sides of 1924 to the previously unpublished Schubert "*Ave Maria*" made in 1939, with Mischa Violin furnishing an obbligato and Romano Romani at the piano. As the Schubert is done to the ill-fitting Latin text, it suggests church rather than the concert hall, and certainly has little to do with Schubert's intentions. Nor do I care for this version of "*Home, sweet home*." But the *Vestale* airs, the only memento we have of one of Ponselle's great roles, have long been ackowledged a pair of masterpieces, and the *Otello* selections (from an opera she never sang) are lovely.

PRANDELLI, GIACINTO, tenor

Su, venite a consiglio (Scarlatti); Pur dicesti (Lotti); Vergin, tutto amor (Durante); Posate, dormite (Bassani); Sebben, crudele (Caldara); Orontea—Intorno all' idol mio (Cesti); Caro mio ben (Giordani); Sento nel core (Scarlatti); Paride ed Elena—O del mio dolce ardor (Gluck); A forza di pene (Gasparini); Eteocle—Che fiero costume (Legrenzi);

*Tre giorni son che Nina (att. to Pergolesi); Vittoria, mio core (Caris-
simi). Marzollo, pf, Vox PL 7930.*

Prandelli of the Metropolitan certainly deserves an A for effort
in this nicely planned program. The music is all very good, most
of it unhackneyed. Somehow, however, an Italian opera tenor is
not necessarily the artist with the right sense of style for Italian
classics, and the whole thing does not come off. The tenor is in
good voice, but his tone quality is a little soft, lacking in point,
and has a tendency to become blatty. I suspect he takes all the
old airs too seriously, though he does not emote in the accepted
Italian tenor style; certainly the sentiments expressed in songs
of this period did not strike very deep, and were not intended to
override the sheer grace of the music. I wonder what his authority
is for the unusual word grouping in the ever delightful *"Pur
dicesti."* To my mind it robs the song of its individuality. The
reproduction is exceptionally good, especially in the sound of the
piano. A side of operatic arias, from *Elisir d'Amore, Don Pasquale,
Gioconda,* and *Lucia* (L LL 534), cannot be recommended here,
as in it emotional expression is fatally overdone.

PRO MUSICA ANTIQUA (Safford Cape)

*MUSIC OF THE 12TH AND 13TH CENTURIES: In saeculum artifex
(Anon.); Deum time (Leonin); Alleluia psallet haec familia (Anon.);
Beneyto foi (Alfonso the Wise); Benedicamus Domino (Anon.); Deus
misertus (attributed to Perotin); Ave verum corpus (Anon.); A la clarté
(Anon.); Virgo (Perotin); La quinte estampie réal (Anon.); Bele doette
(Anon.); En Mai la rousée (Anon.); Mayenzeit (Neidhart von Reuenthal);
Can vei la lauzeta (Bernart de Ventadorn); Ce fut en mai (Moniot
d'Arras); In saeculum viellatoris (Anon.); Entre Copin et Bourgeois
(Anon.); Amours et ma dame aussi (Adam de la Halle); Li dous regars
(Adam de la Halle); Stantipes (Anon.). EMS 201.*
*SPANISH MUSIC FROM THE COURT OF FERDINAND AND ISA-
BELLA: (ca. 1500): Calabaza, no sé buen amor (Anon.); Pues bien
para esta (Muñoz); Ninguno cierre las puertas (Encina); Pase el agua,
mi mulieta dama (Anon.); Ay triste (Encina); Dale si le das (Anon.);
Una sanosa porfia (Encina); La cantan los gallos (Vilches); Gasa-
jemonos de hucia (Encina); Dios te salve (Anon.); De la resurrection
(Ponce); Por unos puertos (Ribera); Fata la parte (Encina); Desciende
al valle, nina (Anon.); Triste Espana (Encina); Caldero y llave,*

Madonna (Encina); A la caza (Luchas); Hermitano quiero ser: Hoy comanos y bebamos (Encina). EMS 219.

The Safford Cape *Anthology of Mediaeval and Renaissance Music* (a long-range project under way for some time) contains these miscellaneous collections, as well as several one-composer discs—the Byrd Masses, and chansons of Dufay and Josquin des Pres. The group from Brussels, with its American conductor, is unique in the variety of its programs, its mastery not only of the old styles but of intonation too, its dignified and eloquent performances. Hearing this ensemble, one realizes that such music need not sound difficult or strained, that obsolete instruments can be played for sheer musical pleasure and beauty. The Spanish record is perhaps the more surprising of these two, for it opens a whole repertoire previously known to few of us. This music is exalted and often stately, as in *Pues bien para esta* and *Ninguno cierre las puertas*, essentially homophonic works, direct in their expression. Some of the little instrumental pieces, on the other hand, are captivating in their varied rhythms and in the colors of such instruments as are used in them. Each selection on the program, whether a noble lament, a romance, a hunting song, a drinking song, or a popular song, is done in scholarly yet vital style.

PSALMODY

EARLY AMERICAN PSALMODY: Selections from The Bay Psalm Book (Cambridge, 1640). Dodd Singers; Dodd, 10" NR NRLP 2007.
MUSIC OF THE PILGRIMS: Nine Psalms from The Ainsworth Psalter; My bonnie lass she smileth; April is in my mistress' face; Fire, fire, my heart (Morley); The silver swan (Gibbons); As Vesta was from Latmos Hill descending (Weelkes); Fair Phyllis I saw (Farmer); Weep you no more, sad fountains (Dowland); Willy, prithee go to bed (Ravenscroft). Pease, b; New England Cons Alumni Ch, HS HSL 2068.

A certain amount of speculative reconstruction has gone into each of these recordings; the results are very different. The first disc takes us through multiple settings of various texts from *The Bay Psalm Book* (the first important book printed in the colonies); the music is by such distinguished composers as John Dowland, Thomas Ravenscroft, Thomas Tomkins, Giles Farnaby, John Milton, Sr., and others. After the manner of the Puritan meeting-house, the psalms are "lined out" by the precentor. That is, a solo voice introduces the melody lines to be repeated by the group. The various settings performed by the group may presumably have been done in this way among the Puritans. The Haydn Society disc goes further. After disposing of the Ainsworth Psalter, the chorus proceeds to sing madrigals that certainly existed at the time, and were very popular in England. And certainly they were never sung in this strictly choral-society manner. In the Psalms this group holds to the theory that the practice was to sing in unison; James Pease acts as precentor in some of them.

RAISA, ROSA, soprano

Mefistofele—L'altra notte; Madama Butterfly—Un bel dì; Otello— Ave Maria; Forza del Destino—Pace, pace; Cavalleria Rusticana— Voi lo sapete; Crucifix (Faure)(with Rimini, b); Aïda—La fatal pietra (with Crimi, t). Scala 808 (*Operatic Arias, Russ).

Rosa Raisa, too poorly represented on records, was one of the glories of the Chicago Opera in the great days of the twenties. Her voice, as we now hear it, has a "straightness" recalling Emma Eames, and the kind of quality that would hold the attention were the singing far less distinguished than it is. In the opera house, I can well imagine, she infused more drama into her tones than she managed to do before the acoustic recording horn; still, these not unusual arias give an idea of the ease and control of her vocal production. Only the *Otello* seems to me not to come off. We might have dispensed with Jean-Baptiste Faure's *"Crucifix"* in favor of some operatic duet with her baritone-husband Rimini (hardly an artist of comparable stature), but the *Aïda* is well sung with a satisfactory tenor partner. Raisa made a few electrical recordings when her voice was no longer so fresh as it is here: the really exciting *Andrea Chénier* aria deserves a place in Victor's "Treasury" series.

REHKEMPER, HEINRICH, baritone

Meine Rose (Schumann); Lied des Orpheus; Der Erlkönig; Frühlings- traum; Ständchen (Schubert); Prometheus (Wolf); Le Nozze di Figaro —Se vuol ballare; Non più andrai; Die Zauberflöte—Ein Mädchen oder Weibchen; Papagena; Rigoletto—Pari siamo; Ballo in Maschera —Eri tu; Trovatore—Il balen. Scala 809.

Heinrich Rehkemper, who died in 1949, was one of Germany's great baritones between the wars. As an opera artist he is remembered chiefly for his Figaro and Papageno; his reputation as a lieder singer rivaled that of the internationally known Schlusnus. Rehkemper was a less imposing figure than his colleague; he was more lithe on the stage and a more subtle actor. His style of singing, especially in lieder, was more intimate. The first side of this disc, given over to songs, consists entirely of his extremely rare acoustic recordings, which naturally lack the "presence" of his better-known electrics. But so far as I know, Rehkemper's is the only record of Schubert's *"Orpheus."* His *"Erlkönig"* certainly ranks with the best, and his *"Prometheus,"* for all the handicap of the inadequately reproduced orchestra, is worthy to stand beside Schorr's. The opera arias, all sung in German, show the singer as the incomparable Mozartean he was, and as a good Teutonic Verdian. The Mozart pieces, fortunately, are electrically recorded.

REINING, MARIA, soprano

Rosenkavalier—Marschallin's Monologue; Tannhäuser—Dich, teure Halle; Elisabeths Gebet; Meistersinger—Gut'n Abend, Meister (with Schoeffler, b). ZTO, Knappertsbusch, 10" L LPS 109.

Maria Reining, who did a stint at the New York City Center several years ago, is a well-established favorite in Vienna, one who well knows the operas and their traditions. Her voice is sweet and expressive, always used with musical feeling and taste. In this recorded recital she seems hampered by the deliberate style of the conductor. The *Meistersinger* duet with Paul Schoeffler is the best part of the program.

RIGAL, DELIA, soprano

Tosca—Vissi d'arte; Gioconda—Suicidio; Pagliacci—Ballatella; Cavalleria Rusticana—Voi lo sapete; La Wally—Romanza di Wally; Traviata—Addio del passato. O, Martini, 10" D DL 4060.

Delia Rigal is one of the potential greats among present-day sopranos. At her best on the stage she is a figure of unusual pathetic appeal, and the quality of her voice is of a piece with this. She is, however, not at all dependable; something of the reason for this is exhibited in this recording. There are phrases as lovely as one could ask, but there is also singing above the center of the pitch, some evidence of uncontrolled temperament. Strangely, through it all the quality remains healthy, and one of her virtues is a complete lack of the common curse of unsteadiness. The singing is well reproduced, although a brilliant edge on the voice must be removed with the high-control. A persistent hum underlies the recital on both sides of the disc.

ROGERS, EARL, tenor

GERMAN SONG FROM THE MINNESINGERS TO THE 17TH CENTURY: Abschied von Innsbruck (Isaac); Es flog ein kleines Vögelein (Gerle); Minnelied (Lochamer Liederbuch); Brünstiges Verlangen einer für himmlischer Liebe kranken Seel nach ihrem Jesus (Ahle); Vom Himmel hoch, o Engelein kommt (Zupfgeigenhansl); Jägers Morgenbesuch (Ott); Aderlassen der Nonnen (Anna von Cöln); Gagliarda (Hassler); Maria durch ein Dornwald ging (Jugenheimer Liederblatt); Ach Elslein, liebes Els (16th Century); Kein Feur, keine Kohle (Zupfgeigenhansl); Die Linde im Thal; Verlangen thut mich kränken (Lochamer Liederbuch); Sie gleicht wohl einem Rosenstock (Zupfgeigenhansl); Bist du des Goldschmieds Tochter? (Fabricius Liederbuch). De la Torre, guitar, All AL 90.

Earl Rogers has a light voice without a great deal of color; he sings always intelligently and with appreciation of the songs he has chosen. Nevertheless, however tempting the above list may look—and lovely things are represented on it—one tires of so much all at once. De la Torre's guitar-playing is above reproach, but again this adds up to a lot of guitar-accompanied songs.

RUSS, GIANNINA, soprano

Norma—Casta diva; Mefistofele—Spunta l'aurora; Forza del Destino —La vergine; Don Carlo—Tu che le vanità; Traviata—Addio del passato; Fedora—O grandi occhi lucenti; La morte (with Garbin, t). Scala 808 (*Operatic Arias, Raisa).

Russ was a star of Oscar Hammerstein's first Manhattan Opera season (1906-7) of whom Krehbiel wrote that her "knowledge of the conventions of the stage was complete, and expressive powers excellent, though they exerted little charm." As a recording artist she was especially successful; the *Forza del Destino* number included here (made in 1905 with chorus, but piano-accompanied) was widely heralded as a masterpiece in its day. Her solos are all well done, with a finely drawn line and neat tone. The duet with Garbin seems to me less valuable; this tenor (whom Verdi selected to create the role of Fenton in *Falstaff*) must in his time have been more of an artist and a vocalist than his recordings show.

SAN JOSÉ STATE COLLEGE A CAPPELLA CHOIR
(William J. Erlendson)

Adoramus Te, Christe (Corsi); O nata lux de lumine (Tallis); Ascendit Deus (Gallus); Ave Maria, No. 20 (Villa-Lobos). ML MLR 7007 (*Copland: In the Beginning).*

The fine material in the chorus and their excellent training, are well shown in this attractive program. The Tallis and Corsi numbers are especially admirable, and the Villa-Lobos makes a good contrast with the older styles. The last named is sung in English, not Spanish as the liner-note states.

SAYÃO, BIDÚ, soprano

Nozze di Figaro—Non so più; Voi che sapete; Sonnambula—Ah! non credea; Bohème—Addio!; Manon—Je suis encore tout étourdie; Adieu, notre petite table; Faust—Le roi de Thulé; Air des bijoux. MOO, Cleva, C ML 4056.

Nozze di Figaro—Porgi amor; Deh vieni, non tardar; Don Giovanni— Vedrai, carino; Batti, batti; Si mes vers avaient des ailes (Hahn); Chanson triste (Duparc); L'Enfant prodigue—Air de Lia (Debussy); Manon—Voyons, Manon. O, Breisach, Leinsdorf, Cimara, 10" C ML 2152.

Si tu le veux (Koechlin); Le Nélumbo (Moret); C'est mon ami (arr. Crist); Cancion gitana; El mercao de las esclaves (arr. Sandoval); Polo (Nin); The bird (Duke); Dos Cantares Populares (Obradors); Carry me back to old Virginny (Bland); Think on me (Scott). Charnley, pf, C ML 4154 (*Braga: Folk Songs of Brazil).*

The diminutive Brazilian soprano has a voice in proportion to her physical size: it is her great good fortune to have her gifts perfectly in balance, and her personal achievement to have kept well within the frame of her limitations. Small as it is, her voice is so roundly placed that it floats easily through the vast spaces of

New York's Metropolitan. In recordings it is sometimes unduly magnified, yet its quality remains always sweet and true. She distinguishes most of what she touches; one may take exception to her conception of this aria or that song, but one usually admits she carries it off in her way. The orchestration of the French songs in the second program is unfortunate, and here the recording engineers have allowed her voice to dominate too much. The "encores" that make up the third recital show the singer at her consistent best, especially those she sings in Spanish and Portuguese. John Duke's little song is lovely, despite a lack of dictional clarity. The reproduction of the piano in this recording is not good.

SCHLUSNUS, HEINRICH, baritone

Vol. 1: Ständchen; Frühlingsglaube; Der Atlas (Schubert); Denk' es, o Seele; Verborgenheit; Der Gärtner; Heimweh (Wolf); Im Frühling; Nachtstück; Die Forelle; Alinde; Die Taubenpost (Schubert). Peschko, pf; Rupp, pf, D DL 9620.

Vol. 2: Der Jüngling an der Quelle; Im Abendroth; An Schwager Kronos; Der Lindenbaum (Schubert); Verschwiegene Liebe; Abschied; Er ist's (Wolf); Heimkehr; Ich liebe dich; Ständchen (Strauss); Wie bist du, meine Königin; Botschaft (Brahms). Rupp, pf; Peschko, pf; Raucheisen, pf; Braun, pf, D DL 9621.

Vol. 3: An die Leyer; Lied eines Schiffers an die Dioskuren (Schubert); Von ewiger Liebe; Der Gang zum Liebchen; Am Sonntag Morgen (Brahms); Nachtgang; Freundliche Vision (Strauss); Der Wachtelschlag; Andenken (Beethoven); Feldeinsamkeit; Die Mainacht (Brahms); Fussreise; Auch kleine Dinge (Wolf). Peschko, pf, D DL 9622.

Vol. 4: Der Wanderer; Wohin?; Der Musensohn (Schubert); Winterliebe; Traum durch die Dämmerung; Ich trage meine Minne; Zueignung (Strauss); Wanderlied (Schumann); Aus der Jugendzeit (Radecke); Am Rhein (Humperdinck); Die Uhr; Tom der Reimer (Loewe). Peschko, pf; Braun, pf; Rupp, pf, D DL 9623.

Vol. 5: Venezianisches Gondellied; Auf Flügeln des Gesanges (Mendelssohn); O komm' im Traum (Liszt); Das Erkennen (Loewe); Talismane; Die beiden Grenadiere; Romanze (Schumann); Ständchen; Der Blumenbrief; An die Musik (Schubert). Rupp, pf; Peschko, pf; Braun, pf, D DL 9624.

In the days between the two world wars there was no more justly appreciated lieder singer than Heinrich Schlusnus. A big man with a voluminous voice that he could shade down to a

whisper or blast forth like a trumpet, he seems to have known
(and, one might almost believe, recorded) every song in the German language. There was a curious inconsistency in his singing,
for on the same disc he might perform one song like an angel and
another as though he were reading it at sight. A large portion of
his long, full list has been transferred to this LP series. The
baritone himself is said to have made the selections from what
he considered his best efforts, and his judgment was on the
whole excellent. Not everything in these programs is inspired—
witness *"Im Abendroth"* or *"Die Forelle"*—but the best is very
fine indeed, such as Wolf's *"Abschied"* or Strauss's *"Ich liebe
dich."* The transfer to LP is among the best jobs of the kind I
have heard.

SCHWARZ, JOSEPH, baritone

*Zar und Zimmermann—Einst spielt' ich mit Szepter; Guglielmo Tell
—Resta immobile; The Demon—Kind, weine nicht; Rheingold—
Abendlich strahlt; Rigoletto—Si, vendetta (with Francillo-Kaufmann,
s); O komm' im Traum (Liszt); Caro mio ben (Giordani); Die Ehre
Gottes aus der Natur (Beethoven); Kol Nidre. Et 498.*

Schwarz's voice must have been a magnificent instrument; indeed, in some of the recordings it seems almost too rich and big.
They show a tendency on the singer's part to spread things out
too much, to let the tempos drag. Not until we get to the Rigoletto
duet, in which he is joined by the famous soprano Francillo-
Kaufmann, does the singing become really interesting as such.
They sing, of course, in German, and without as much excitement
as Italians get into this scene. Still, they hold the attention. Even
better, to me, is *"O komm" im Traum"* (originally *"Oh quand je
dors"*) eloquently sung to piano accompaniment. There are some
stunning high tones in this song. *"Caro mio ben,"* with organ
and cello background, and with dragging pace, is made to sound
quite religious; *Kol Nidre* is in similar mood. The Beethoven
song, accompanied by what sounds like an old-fashioned har-
monium, displays some more fine high tones.

SCHWARZKOPF, ELISABETH, soprano

*Bist du bei mir (Bach); La Rencontre imprévue—Einen Bach der fliesst
(Un ruisselet) (Gluck); Abendempfindung; Der Zauberer (Mozart); Wonne
der Wehmut (Beethoven); Litanei; Ungeduld (Schubert); Der Nussbaum;
Aufträge (Schumann); Da unten im Tale; Och, Modr, ich well en Ding*

han!; Vergebliches Ständchen (Brahms); Wiegenlied (Im Sommer) (Wolf); Hat gesagt—bleibt's nicht dabei; Schlechtes Wetter (Strauss); Mausfallen-Sprüchlein (Wolf). Moore, pf, An 35023.

Schwarzkopf is in melting voice throughout this recital, and recorded in fine balance with the infallible Gerald Moore. I had the feeling that the first three sustained songs were extremely slow, but that the singer came to life in the arch little *"Zauberer"* of Mozart. Characteristically, the lighter songs, those which lie directly on the diction, are the most successful. There is, indeed, little to criticize in anything this singer does; yet others have breathed a warmer compassion into Schubert's *"Litanei,"* and it seemed to me the maiden in the otherwise finely realized *"Nussbaum"* settled down to her dream with a little too much sophistication. *"Aufträge,"* on the other hand, is capital. Of *"Da unten im Thale"* she makes a very sad love song, contrasting well with *"Och Modr"* and all its coyness. Wolf's *"Wiegenlied"* is sweetly crooned; his *"Mausfallen-Sprüchlein"* and the two Strauss songs are beautifully realized.

SIEPI, CESARE

I Vespri Siciliani—O tu Palermo; Don Carlo—Ella giammai m'amò; Nabucco—Tu sul labbro dei veggenti; Ernani—Infelice! a tuo credevi; Don Giovanni—Deh vieni alla finestra; La Sonnambula—Vi ravviso; L'Italiana in Algeri—Le femine d'Italia; Il Barbiere di Siviglia—La calunnia; Mefistofele—Son lo spirito che nega. Cet 50035.
Malia (Tosti); Occhi di fata (Denza); Non t'amo più; Serenata (Tosti); Mia sposa sara la mia bandiera (Rotoli); E canto il grillo (Billi); Visione veneziana (Broggi); L'ultima canzone (Tosti). Cet 50062.

Since Siepi's coming to the Metropolitan he has developed from an exceptionally promising singer with a superb bass voice into an artist of real stature. At the time these opera arias were made, his singing was on the placid side, a fact that proved fatal in the *Don Giovanni* "Serenade," but not so in most of the selections. After all, it is something to hear them proclaimed by such a voice. For the graceful Italian song-trifles his tone is heavy. So delicate a thing as Tosti's *"Serenata"* is hopelessly weighted down. And one waits in vain for the tiniest spark of humor in the program.

SINGHER, MARTIAL, baritone

TREASURY OF FRENCH SONG: Élégie (Massenet); Sérénade

(Gounod); Chant hindou (Bemberg); Les Rameaux (Faure); Ave Maria (Fauré); Viens, une flûte invisible (Caplet); Notre Père qui êtes aux cieux (Büsser); Les Vielles de chez nous (Levadé); Plaisir d'amour (Martini); Si mes vers avaient des ailes; Paysage (Hahn); Après un rêve; Nell (Fauré); L'Invitation au voyage (Duparc); Pensée d'automne (Massenet); Ballade des gros dindons; Villanelle des petits canards (Chabrier). Ulanowsky, pf; La Montaine, pf; Hubert, vlc; Norwood, fl, C ML 4258.

Three Ballades of François Villon (Debussy); Don Quichotte à Dulcinée (Ravel). CBSO, Abravanel. La Damnation de Faust— Mephistopheles's Air and Serenade; Song of the Flea; Roméo et Juliette—Ballad of Queen Mab; Hamlet—Chanson bachique; Hérodiade —Vision fugitive; Les Contes d'Hoffmann—Dapertutto's Air; Carmen —Toreador Song. MOO, Breisach, C ML 4152.

In this "Treasury of French Song" Singher has attempted to cover the field from all angles, ranging all the considerable distance from Jean-Baptiste Faure to Gabriel Fauré. Though this may be meant to show the variety of music in which Singher is at home, I suspect it is something less than canny planning; those who want to hear Fauré's *Nell*, Duparc's *Invitation au voyage*, and the two Chabrier songs are going to resent *Les Rameaux* and Massenet's *Élégie*. Somehow the singer is not at his best, and he does not succeed in compensating with artistry for the bloom the voice lacks. The recording, too, is on the dull side. The Debussy and Ravel songs are tasteful, but lack the essential spark of warm humor. The set of opera arias has been transferred from an earlier album, but with the two most interesting numbers missing: Lully's *"Bois épais"* and Grétry's *"O Richard, o mon roi."* One misses again the kind of bite Berlioz's Mephistopheles music calls for (Singher is more convincing in the more recent complete performance), and one wishes for more voice, especially in the *Hamlet* and *Hérodiade* numbers. The recording in its second incarnation is still solid and effective enough.

SLEZAK, LEO, tenor

La Juive—Aria, Act 1; Manon—Le Rêve; Ah, fuyez; La Dame blanche —Viens, gentille dame; Alessandro Stradella—Hymnus. 10" Et ELP 461. (*Flotow: Alessandro Stradella—Selections).

Das Veilchen (Mozart); Die Thräne (Rubinstein); Ständchen (Strauss);

O Komm' im Traum (Liszt); Ganz leise (Sommer); Sechse, sieben, oder acht (Brüll). 10" Et ELP 453.
Ständchen; Nacht und Träume; Im Abendroth; Trockene Blumen; An die Musik; Wohin? (Schubert); Der Nussbaum; Mondnacht (Schumann); Verschwiegene Liebe (Wolf); Ständchen (Strauss). Et 493.

Slezak used to be called the "second Tamagno" because of the size of his voice, the hugeness of his presence, and his abilities as an actor. What is most remarkable about him is his versatility, as demonstrated in the lists above. The first two discs represent the singer in the early stages of his career; on the third program most of the lieder were electrically recorded in the late twenties. All selections here are sung in German. The *Manon* pieces suffer most from translation; the forceful prayer from *La Juive* and the lovely piece from *La Dame blanche* are beautifully delivered. Perhaps the best of the opera numbers, however, is the *Stradella* hymn. For all the robustness of his operatic singing, Slezak could turn to such little pieces as the second disc contains, and do them in the most intimate manner. *"Das Veilchen"* is superbly performed, without a trace of the operatic style. The Rubinstein, Sommer, and Brüll songs are light fare, to be sure, but attractive, unhackneyed, and splendidly sung. The third recital is uneven. The Schubert *"Ständchen,"* perhaps the earliest recording, is orchestrally accompanied, and rather heavy. *"Nacht und Träume,"* from the singer's last period, is extremely curious. Tonally it is superb, done in a breathtakingly even *mezza voce* throughout, but the singer cuts all the corners rhythmically, putting the melodic line out of shape. *"Im Abendroth"* is uncomfortable and consistently sagging in pitch. *"An die Musik"* has a beautiful phrase or two, but it too is insecure. Generally, the acoustic recordings are fairer to the artist's memory.

SOUZAY, GÉRARD, baritone

CLASSIC AIRS: Berenice—Air de Demetrio; In questa tomba oscura (Beethoven); Orfeo—Elle est morte (Monteverdi); Perseus—Air des songes; Ballade de Villon, No. 2; La Grotte; Mandoline (Debussy); Don Quichotte à Dulcinée (Ravel). PCO, Lindenberg, L LLP 194.
CLASSIC AIRS, VOL. 2: La Rencontre imprévue—C'est un torrent impétueux; Un ruisselet (Gluck); Cadmus et Hermione—Belle Hermoine, hélas, hélas (Lully); Alceste—Il faut passer; Mentre ti lascio, o

figlia (Mozart); Castor et Pollux—Nature, amour (Rameau); Il Sedecia—Caldo sangue (Scarlatti). PCO, Cornman, 10" L LPS 730.

CANZONE SCORDATE (arr. Dørumsgaard); O miei giorni fugaci (Peri); Or ch'io non seguo più (Rontani); Ferma, Dorinda mia (Calestani); Apra il suo verde seno (Quagliati); Occh' immortali (Caccini); Donn' ingrata (Falconieri); Cara mia cetr' andiamo (d'India); Chi vuole innamorarsi; Cara e dolce; Bellezza, che s'ama; O dolcissima speranza; Toglietemi la vita ancor (Scarlatti); Der Herr ist mein getreuer Hirt (Helder); Kindelwiegen Lied (Anon.); Bringet meinen Herrn zur Ruh (Böhm); Liebster Gott, wann werd' ich Sterben (Vetter); Jesus in Gethsemane; Weihnachtslied; Über die Finsternis kurz vor dem Tode Jesu (C. P. E. Bach). Bonneau, pf, L LLP 731.

OLD FRENCH AIRS: Amaryllis (Louis XIII); Cette Anne si belle (Guédron); Tambourin (Anon.); Me veux-tu voir mourir?; Cachez, beaux yeux (Boesset); Ma Bergère non légère (Bataille); Noël; Brezairola; Malurous qu'o uno fenno (Anon.). Bonneau, pf, 10" L LD 9109.

One of the busiest recording artists of the postwar period is Gérard Souzay, pupil and, some would say, imitator of Pierre Bernac. Perhaps it would be fairer to put it this way: like Bernac, Souzay has a limited voice, but it is an attractive one, pre-eminently suited to recording; he sings French songs with a cultivated style and admirable diction, and he has been widely acclaimed for his interpretations of German lieder. In the first program of "Classic Airs" he ranges from Monteverdi (done in French translation, for some reason) to Beethoven; in the second he runs from Lully to Mozart. He is consistently at his best in the French repertoire: here the Lully airs and the wonderful Gluck particularly stand out. His tone is not concentrated enough for the Handel, and his voice is too light for the Mozart concert aria. His Scarlatti air is over-orchestrated by conductor Cornman, but his voice seems at home in the music. The Ravel and Debussy, which share the first record with the classics, are more characteristic of the singer. The disc of Dørumsgaard arrangements is on the whole less happy, as Souzay does not have the tonal definition needed for so much singing in Italian and German. Furthermore, the notes that introduce the set are hopelessly inadequate, however pretentious: we are not given so much as the titles of many of the pieces sung, let alone the composer's names. Dørumsgaard has elected to make the piano accompaniments "effective," without much concern for the niceties of style.

Several of the "Old French Airs" have been weighted down by the same arranger. It is good to hear the little *"Tambourin"* in the familiar and more properly simple Tiersot version, and *"Me veux-tu voir mourir?"* in the unobtrusive arrangement of Germaine Tailleferre. It is a question whether the two last songs in Canteloube's quite spicy arrangements (however effective) or the *"Noël"* with the background provided by Maurice Emmanuel really belong on what purports to be an "old-time" program.

STANFORD UNIVERSITY CHOIR (Harold G. Schmidt)

MOTETS: Sicut cervus (Palestrina); I will not leave you comfortless (Byrd); Tenebrae factae sunt (Ingegneri); Ave Maria (Victoria); Regina coeli (Aichinger); Salvation is created (Tchesnokov). 10" ML MLR 5001.

A mixed program, offering some great and unhackneyed music, sung in the best manner of a serious college choral society, cleanly and convincingly recorded. The style of performance is generally excellent, though it is inevitably affected by the fact that two of the numbers (the Byrd and the Tchesnokov) are translated from Latin and Russian. For the rest, these must rank among the best performances of this type of music available on LP.

STRIENZ, WILHELM, basso

Der Nöck (Loewe); Des Trinkes Wunsch (Nicolai); Auf das Trinkglas eines verstorbenen Freundes (Schumann); Zauberflöte—In diesen heil'gen Hallen; Bohème—Vecchia zimarra; Barbiere di Siviglia—La calunnia; Der Barbier von Bagdad—Salaam Aleikum! (Cornelius); Die lustigen Weiber von Windsor—Als Büblein klein (Nicolai); Nimm mein trauriges Herz (Roland); Zwischen Marie und Sophie (Hirgstätter). RBC & O, Steinkopf, U URLP 7026.

Strienz's magnificent big voice is better suited to opera than to songs; it is therefore probably as well that all the accompaniments here are orchestral. I prefer this faster version of *"Der Nöck"* to that in his Loewe recital (L LL 310). If the Mozart has been more nobly sung by others, and the two Italian arias lose by translation into German, the Cornelius and Nicolai opera scenes are very welcome and unhackneyed. The last two titles are songs

from films in which the singer has been successful. The recording is very broad and powerful.

SWARTHOUT, GLADYS, mezzo-soprano

*FRENCH OPERATIC ARIAS: Samson et Dalila—Printemps qui com-
mence; Amour, viens aider; Mon coeur s'ouvre à ta voix; Werther—
Letter Scene; La Périchole—Tu n'es pas beau. RCAO, Morel, V LM
1156 (*Canteloube: Chants d'Auvergne).*
*FRENCH SONGS: Roméo et Juliette—Premiers Transports que nul
n'oublie! (Berlioz); Si mes vers avaient des ailes (Hahn); Mandoline
(Debussy); Chanson triste (Duparc); Séparation (Hillemacher); Carmen
(Clergue); Hotel; Voyage à Paris; Les Chemins d'amour (Poulenc).
Trovillo, pf; Greenhouse, vlc; Agostini, hrp, V LM 1793 (*Chausson:
Poème de l'amour et de la mer).*

Swarthout is a singer who never falls below a certain standard.
Hers is a suave, smooth, insinuating voice, always beautifully
controlled, never forced to do that which lies beyond her temperament or her very adequate technique. The operatic arias show
her at her best. For sheer loveliness of tone, there has not been
a Dalila to surpass her in recent years. An interesting feature of
the song program is the selection from Berlioz's symphony, which
reminds us of her performance of this music under Toscanini
several years back. She is accompanied by harp and cello, which
is about all we need of the original orchestration. For the familiar
Hahn song, these obbligato musicians are retained, with less
happy results. The Hillemacher and Clergue songs are unfamiliar.

SZE, YI-KWEI, basso

*CHINESE SONGS: All the Red River; Separated by the Yangtze River;
Song of the Hoe; The red bean love; By the Chia-Ling River; How can
I not think of her?; Drinking Song (from The Lady of the Camellias);
Song of the Great Wall. N. L. Sze, pf, 10" CH CHC 48.*

Anyone reading the annotations on the envelope before hearing
this recording will be led to expect something more characteristically Oriental than Sze has provided. We are informed that
both folk songs and modern art songs are included in the program,
and that Chinese singing is a peculiarly nasal affair. Aside from
the haunting modality of the songs, there is little here to intimi-
date the most Western of listeners, and the voice in which they
are sung is a big, handsomely rich one. Plainly, then, this is not

a record for the anthropologist, but rather for the simple music-
lover, for whom it will open new if hardly very strange fields. The
recording is excellent, if a little over-brilliant in the voice.

TAGLIAVINI, FERRUCCIO, tenor

*L'Arlesiana—Lamento di Federico; Tosca—O dolci mani; I Quattro
Rusteghi—Luceta è un bel nome; Rigoletto—Parmi veder le lagrime;
Andrea Chénier—Come un bel dì di maggio; Barbiere di Siviglia—
Ecco ridente in cielo; Falstaff—Dal labbro il canto; L'Amico Fritz—
Ed anche Beppe amò; Sonnambula—Prendi, l'anel ti dono.   RIO,
Tansini, Rossi, Cet A 50155.*
*NEAPOLITAN FOLK SONGS: Dicitencello vuie (Falvo); Pizzichi e
vase (de Luca); Mamma mia che vo' sape (Nutile); Senza nisciuna (de
Curtis); Mattinata (Leoncavallo); Amuri, amuri (Sadero).   RCAO,
Cellini, Gallino, 10" V LM 72.*

Toward the end of the last war we began reading about Tagliavini
in the dispatches written to papers and magazines by musical
soldiers stationed in Italy.   Here was a lyric tenor of the old
school, at his best in Rossini and Donizetti, but at home too in
Puccini and Verdi.   His subsequent career in the vast auditorium
of the Metropolitan was distinguished, but not quite so imposing
as the build-up before his arrival.   The voice is light, in its best
quality reminiscent of Gigli's, but on a much smaller scale.   He
has learned to spin out a sustained tone, and he makes skillful
use of a thin and liquid head voice.   Stylistically he has the
shortcomings of so many Italians: he wants to vocalize rather
than interpret, and he is often guilty of sobbing where a properly
colored tone would convey more emotion.   One gets to know the
Tagliavini style, and then there are no surprises, no matter what
the aria in hand.   The Cetra collection takes us back, for these
recordings were sold by the importers here before the tenor
crossed the ocean.   One is grateful to him for recording at least
a few arias off the beaten track.   The set of "folk songs" should
more properly be called popular songs, the kind that has proved a
goldmine for many an Italian singer.   His way with them has its
share of charm.

TASSINARI, PIA, soprano, and FERRUCCIO TAG-
LIAVINI, tenor

OPERA DUETS: Mefistofele—Lontano, lontano; Traviata—Parigi, o cara; L'Amico Fritz—Duetto delle ciliegie; Tosca—Or lasciami al lavoro; Werther—Dividerci dobbiam. Cet A 50018.

Tagliavini is never better than when singing with his wife, who, for all that, remains the superior artist of the two. All these duets are sung with style, and all are vocally attractive. The *"Cherry Duet"* from Mascagni's comedy, of course, is quite generally identified with these singers, and *Tosca* has been long one of their best co-starring operas. The first-act duet is especially successful here. The *Werther* is effectively sung, but in Italian—so it may make an interesting comparison with the same music as done in French by the same artists in the complete recording of the opera.

TAUBER, RICHARD, tenor

Bohème—Che gelida manina; Madama Butterfly—Addio, fiorito asil; Mignon—Adieu, Mignon; Bartered bride—Es muss gelingen; Aïda— Già i sacerdoti adunansi (with Kalter, m-s); Traviata—Dei miei bollenti spiriti; Der Rosenkavalier—Di rigori armato. Et 0-466.

These acoustic recordings show Tauber in his best vocal estate. Both voice and style were distinctive, though he had not yet developed his characteristic operetta manner when these selections were made. The arias are all sung in German, which makes for some peculiar effects, especially in the *Bohème* narrative. In this number, too, the tenor slights the high tone in the climactic phrase. Sabine Kalter proves herself a more than adequate mezzo, with ringing tone and breadth of style. The duet comes off very well. But the crown of the recital is the *Rosenkavalier* aria: one stands little chance of hearing it so beautifully done in any opera performance.

TEYTE, MAGGIE, soprano

Après un rêve (Fauré); Psyché (Paladilhe); Chanson triste (Duparc); Si mes vers avaient des ailes; Offrande; L'Heure exquise (Hahn). Moore, pf, V LCT 1133 (*Debussy: Songs).

These recordings are, of course, old, but they show the singer in good form. Several of the selections, especially the Hahn songs, have long been popularly identified with Maggie Teyte. To my taste *"L'Heure exquise"* is the best, for it gives her a chance to float high tones as she loved to do, and it also shows her strong lower register. I do not care for so much freedom as she allows herself in *"Psyché."* The transfer to LP is satisfactory.

TOUREL, JENNIE, mezzo-soprano

A FRENCH SONG RECITAL: L'Adieu de l'hôtesse arabe (Bizet); Voyage à Paris (Poulenc); Romance de l'étoile (Chabrier); Poème d'un jour (Fauré); Vocalise (Ravel); Si mes vers avaient des ailes (Hahn); Air vif (Poulenc); Le Chapelier; Je te veux (Satie). Reeves, pf, C ML 4158 (*Debussy: Cinq Poèmes de Charles Baudelaire).
RUSSIAN, SPANISH AND PORTUGUESE SONGS: I still love him; My darling girls (Dargomizhsky); Lullaby; Over the steppe (Grechaninov); Hopak; On the river Don (Mussorgsky); Chacarera; Triste (Ginastera); El majo discreto (Granados); Pano murciano (Nin); Coplas de curro dulce (Obradors); Miâu (Villa-Lobos). Reeves, pf, 10 " C ML 2198.

Jennie Tourel is an international singer, at home, apparently, in any style of music, and one of the finest vocal musicians of our time. Her recorded repertoire is no more a cause for wonder and rejoicing than the standard of performance she maintains. The strongest asset of the voice itself is its appealing quality rather than size or range, though in the latter respect it is certainly adequate to the demands she puts upon it. Something of her versatility may be noted above. The French program is made up of minor works, yet for the moment they seem important. She is equally successful with the melancholy Russian melodies, though *"Over the steppe"* could do with a larger voice. The reproduction is not all first-rate.

TRAPP FAMILY CHOIR (Franz Wasner)

SACRED MUSIC AROUND THE CHURCH YEAR: Sanctus and Bene-dictus; Maria durch ein Dornwald ging (Wasner); Psallite unigenito (Praetorius); Jesu redemptor omnium (Ambrosian Chant); Resonet in laudibus (Eccard); O bone Jesu (Ingegneri); Jesu salvator mundi (Menegali); O salutaris hostia (Martini); Wer leucht' uns denn bei finstren Nacht? (Wasner); Crux fidelis (King John IV of Portugal); Tenebrae factae sunt (Eberlin); Surrexit pastor bonus (Lassus); Regina coeli, laetare (Aichinger); To Thee the Holy Ghost (Wasner); O Maria diana stella (15th Century); Salve regina (Lassus). CH CHS 1100.

The Trapp Family, making up an all-season program, offers a mixture of styles, from Ambrosian chant to compositions of their conductor. We may take it that the aim has been to reach the pious rather than the musicologically inclined, though there is valuable music here not to be found elsewhere. The voices, as everyone knows, are modest but neat; the singing is simple, pure, and pleasant.

TRAUBEL, HELEN, soprano

ITALIAN OPERATIC ARIAS: Aïda—Ritorna vincitor; Otello—Ave Maria; Don Giovanni—Or sai chi l'onore; Tosca—Vissi d'arte; La Gioconda—Suicidio!; Cavalleria Rusticana—Voi lo sapete. O, O'Connell, 10" C ML 2052.
SACRED SONGS: Elijah—O rest in the Lord; Messiah—He shall feed His flock; Komm, süsser Tod (Bach); Serse—Largo (Handel); Agnus Dei (Bizet); Messiah—I know that my Redeemer liveth; Elijah—Hear ye, Israel. O, O'Connell, C ML 4117.
FOLK SONGS AND BALLADS: Come again, sweet love doth now invite (Dowland); Lord Randal; Greensleeves (Old English); He's gone away (North Carolina); The lonesome road (Austin-Shilkret); Bygone tunes (Longone); I'm wearin' awa', John (Foote); Son tre mesi che fo il soldato (Italian Folk Song); Come to the sea (Italian Folk Song); Come back to Sorrento (de Curtis). RCAO, Armbruster, 10" V LM 7013.

Traubel's position as leading Wagnerian soprano at the Metropolitan was secure for so long that, whatever demands the night clubs may now make upon her, she will be remembered at her most majestic. Hers was one of the noblest of sopranos, and she had the good sense to work gradually into the heroic repertoire, never to push herself into a role before she was ready. Her Wagner recordings, of the early Victor, the middle Columbia, or the late Victor period, are marked by the grand manner and notable intelligence. In her set of Italian arias she shows that good clean singing is welcome in this emotional music, though one may feel that she had hardly assimilated the style. The set of sacred songs takes her into the contralto range, which she finds perfectly comfortable; that part of her voice, as a matter of fact, is gorgeous. I cannot find much to commend, however, in her fancied-up American ballads or the so-called folk songs so elaborately produced on LM 7013.

TREASURY OF IMMORTAL PERFORMANCES

Under this head a wide variety of older recordings has been re-

issued, ranging in age from vintage 1903 up to the late 1940's.
A great deal of the fine Victor heritage has been revived in this
way, though not always with proper discrimination, and not invariably in proper sequence. Thus, we often find an early acoustic
as a strange bedfellow for an electric made in the 30's and only
too frequently fine music is made to share a disc with the tawdry
and cheap. More than once, if a singer recorded the same selection several times over a period of years, the best example has
not been chosen for reissue, and, perhaps worst of all, the same
recording is likely to turn up any number of times in different
company. Still, some of the discs belong in any collection.
"Famous Duets" (LCT 1037) includes fine examples by Bori and
McCormack, and by Galli-Curci and Schipa, among others. "The
Golden Age at the Metropolitan" (LCT 1006) exploits notable
singing by Rethberg ("*O patria mia*"), Ponselle ("*Ernani, involami*"), Journet (*Berceuse* from *Louise*) and McCormack ("*Il
mio tesoro*")—though the last, a veritable masterpiece, reappears
in countless other combinations. Less fortunate is Calvé's
Habanera, a case where a better recording should have been
chosen. "Golden Age Ensembles" (LCT 1003) spans the period
from 1910 to 1932, and includes well-known moments from *Trovatore, Rigoletto, Lucia, Ballo in Maschera*, and *Samson et Dalila*,
all including Caruso; a scene from *Forza del Destino* with
Ponselle and Pinza; and the *Meistersinger* quintet by a group
including Elisabeth Schumann, Melchior, and Schorr. "Golden
Duets" (LCT 1004) is most notable for "*Mira o Norma*" by
Ponselle and Telva, the big *Otello* vengeance scene by Caruso
and Ruffo, the famous *Forza del Destino* duet, which was the
first recording made by the great Caruso-Scotti team, and the
Aïda finale by Ponselle and Martinelli. Best of "Golden Voices
Sing Light Music" (LCT 1008) is Rethberg's *Fledermaus
"Czardas,"* though the famous Chaliapin "*Volga Boat Song*" is
still worth hearing. "Sacred Songs" (LCT 1005) contains the
only LP representation of Margarete Matzenauer, in beautiful
singing of *Messiah* and *Elijah* arias, and two fine selections,
with chorus, by Chaliapin. There is also Schumann-Heink's incomparable "*Stille Nacht*." "Stars of the Golden Age" (LCT
1039) has good examples of Scotti (as Falstaff), Destinn (as
Gioconda) and Tetrazzini (in Veracini's "*Pastoral*") and the
wrong take of Melba's "*Voi che sapete*." An interesting but very

miscellaneous collection called "Critic's Choice" (LCT 1115) has been assembled by Irving Kolodin. Schipa, Schumann, Onegin, and John Charles Thomas are among those present; a late recording of *"Dove sono"* by Maria Cebotari, and only half (alas!) of Maria Ivogün's magnificent *Zerbinetta's Air* from Strauss's *Ariadne auf Naxos*.

TREVISO CATHEDRAL CHAPEL CHOIR (Giovanni d'Alessi)

MOTETS OF THE VENETIAN SCHOOL OF THE 16TH CENTURY: Cantate Domino; Bonum est confiteri Domino (A. Gabrieli); Tristis est anima mea; Ecce appropinquat hora (Nasco); Sancti et justi (Merulo); O salutaris hostia (Nasco); Adoramus Te, Domine Jesu Christe (Asola); O sacrum convivium; Missa Pater peccavi—Excerpts (A. Gabrieli); Lamentations of Jeremiah—Lesson I (Nasco); Egredimini et videte (A. Gabrieli); Sancta Maria (G. Gabrieli). Vox PL 8030.
Cantabant sancti (Asola); Benedicam Dominum (Croce); Ego dormivi (Willaert); Hoc signum crucis (Asola); Beata eritis (Croce); Virtute magna; Repleti quidem (Porta); Adoramus Te, Christe (Ruffo); Salutis humanae sator (Vecchi); Surge amica mea (Asola); Migravit Judas (Nasco); Ego sum pauper; Exaltabo Te, Domine; Cantate Domino (Croce); O Domine Jesu Christe (Ingegneri); Introduxit me rex; Omnes de Saba; Surrexit pastor bonus (Asola). Vox PL 8610.

As one listens to these Venetian pieces, sung in the pregnant style peculiar to Italian choirs, one realizes that such hearty treatment has a place. While I take exception to such an approach to Palestrina, I have to admit that it seems very right here. The voices of the boys on the first disc are earthy and indescribably appealing; the tone of the full choir is rich, almost ponderous. The sonorities of the Gabrielis are mightily impressive, and the intense, somber quality of the Nasco pieces is altogether haunting. On the other hand, the Merulo motet has spectacular brilliance. The second program is all for the lower voices; the boys have been given a holiday. Of the seventeen pieces presented, not one was familiar to me, and I found them exhilarating.

THE TRIUMPHS OF ORIANA

Madrigals by the leading English musicians, composed in honor of Queen Elizabeth I, and published under the editorship of Thomas

Morley in 1601. Randolph Singers, W WAL 212 [2]. *Madrigal Guild,
Washington, ML MLR 7000/1/2* [3].

David Randolph, in his zeal to do the job thoroughly, managed to
locate a few extra madrigals composed for *The Triumphs*, which
for one reason or another had been left out. For this reason, he
gives us thirty-two madrigals, as opposed to only twenty-five
sung by Eileen Washington's California group. That *Oriana* should
have been undertaken at all is a remarkable sign of the times:
before the days of LP such a project would have been unthinkable.
Some of the madrigals, of course, are well known and otherwise
recorded—*"As Vesta was descending," "All creatures now are
merry minded,"* and *"Hard by a crystal fountain,"* to name only a
few. But there are many others here well worth knowing. Of the
two performances, comprehensiveness aside, Randolph's group
gives the better impression of the shape and character of the
individual pieces, and its diction is clearer than that of its rivals.
Neither ensemble is perfect in intonation, but both are above
average. To clinch the matter, Randolph has put a great deal of
effort and information into the notes accompanying his set.

UNIVERSITY OF REDLANDS CHOIR *(J. William Jones)*

*HYMNS AND ANTHEMS: Jesus, meek and gentle (Monk); Breathe on
me, breath of God (Peace); Revive Thy work, O Lord (Spiess); O love
that casts out fear (Smart); We love the place, O God (Jenner); For
Thy mercy and Thy grace (Gibbons); O brightness of the Immortal
Father's face (Scholefield); O sacred head (Hassler-Bach); O darkest
woe (Bach); God omnipotent reigneth (Paques-Wood); Bow down Thine
ear (Todd); At the name of Jesus (Vaughan Williams); Father of
heaven, whose love profound (Willan); Jesu, grant me this, I pray
(Gibbons-Kitson); Magnificat in B minor (Noble); Praise to the Lord
(Whitehead). C ML 4866.*

The division between hymns and anthems is even: one side
apiece. The former, all from the Episcopal hymnal, are done in
the straightforward style favored by that church, complete with
Amens. The selection of anthems is a good representation of the
contemporary repertoire, and it shows that something of value has
been added in our time. As usual, Vaughan Williams walks off
with the honors, in his exciting setting of a fine old tune. Simi-

larly, the Whitehead piece, founded on one of the strongest of the
German chorales, makes a rousing finale to the program.

VIENNA ACADEMY CHAMBER CHOIR (Ferdinand Grossmann)

*A CONCERT OF AMERICAN MUSIC IN SCHÖNBRUNN: An Immortality
(Copland); Alleluia; Three Odes of Horace (Thompson); Let down the
bars, o death (Barber); Two Hymns from the Old South (Thomson). Vox
PL 7750 (*Piston: Concertino).*

This is a concert given in April 1952. The composers are all
contemporary: the oldest work—Copland's *Immortality*—dates
back to 1926. The choir, by this time familiar to all gramo-
philes, produces a surprise with its commendable English diction.

VIENNA CHOIR BOYS (Friedrich Brenn and Peter Lacovich)

*Rosen aus dem Süden (Strauss); Ständchen (Schubert); Bandelterzett
(Mozart); La pastorella (Schubert); Sphärenklänge (Strauss); Ascendit
Deus (Gallus); Salvator mundi (Palestrina); O bone Jesu (Ingegneri);
Tenebrae factae sunt (Victoria); Laudi alla Vergine Maria (Verdi); O
salutaris hostia (Nasco); Super Flumina (Palestrina); Exsultate Deo
(Scarlatti). C ML 4873.*

In concert it is hard to resist the Wiener Sängerknaben, no matter
what they do. In a recording it is somewhat different, for not all
that glitters musically will bear repeating. I am thinking particularly of the Strauss waltzes, which, fellow-Viennese though they
be, have something of sophistication in them and want the touch
of maturity in performance. The Mozart and Schubert are better
suited to the boys, though, going back to an earlier recording (Cap
P 8085) with a side of Schubert and one of folk-song arrangements, I somehow preferred the fresher tempos of that older, less
realistically recorded performance, and found the earlier soloist
in the delightful *"Ständchen"* definitely more appealing. The
churchly polyphonic works on side 2 of this disc include arrangements of pieces for mixed voices, but they are reverently and
proficiently performed.

VYVYAN, JENNIFER, soprano

*SONGS OF ENGLAND: Lye still my deare (Anon., arr. Dolmetsch);
Nymphs and shepherds; King Arthur—Fairest isle (Purcell); Now is*

the month of maying (Morley); I will give my love an apple (arr. Vaughan Williams); Where the bee sucks; O ravishing delight (Arne); Bobby Shaftoe (arr. Whittaker); Cherry ripe (arr. Lehmann); The sprig of thyme (arr. Grainger); Sweet Polly Oliver (arr. Britten); Foxgloves (Head); Gavotte (Howells); The new ghost (Vaughan Williams); A melancholy song (Hopkins); Love's philosophy (Quilter). Lush, pf, L LL 806.

Very, very British is the singing of Jennifer Vyvyan. In general style, she sings like a Victorian; the quality of her voice is brittle and over-refined. If one accepts these things, the program is intriguing, ranging from "*Lye still my deare*," from a 1630 manuscript, to the modern songs and folk-song arrangements.

WARFIELD, WILLIAM, baritone

ANCIENT MUSIC OF THE CHURCH: Eile mich, Gott, zu erretten (Schütz); De profundis (Hammerschmidt); Conductus: Homo vide (Perotin); Laudate Dominum (Monteverdi). Tietjen, org, C ML 4545 (*Loewe: Ballads). Deep river; Water boy; Without a song; Mah Lindy Lou; Jeanie with the light brown hair; Dusty road. O, Engel, 10" C AAL 32.

William Warfield burst upon the New York scene a few seasons ago, singing an outstanding recital in Town Hall and subsequently appearing with various choral groups. An eventual engagement in *Porgy and Bess* had to be terminated because of the demand for his recitals. His is a long-ranged, rich, and voluminous voice, beautifully controlled, at its best in music of superior quality. He has enjoyed amazing popular success with the long and difficult ballads of Loewe, a group of which he has recorded. The collection coupled with this program, rather too inclusively titled "Ancient Music of the Church," is fervently sung with an unobtrusive organ accompaniment, but it comes through less happily than the Loewe songs. Somehow a second program, called "Deep River," including spirituals and popular fare, is not presented with much conviction.

WARREN, LEONARD, baritone

SONGS OF RUDYARD KIPLING: Boots (McCall); Gunga Din (Spross); Recessional (De Koven); Danny Deever (Damrosch); Rolling down to Rio (German); Mother o' mine (Tours); Smugglers' Song (Kernochan);

On the road to Mandalay (Speaks). RCAO, Black, 10" V LM 147.
Trovatore—Il balen del suo sorriso; Per me ora fatale; Gioconda—
Barcarola; Barbiere di Siviglia—Largo al factotum; Pagliacci—
Prologo; Ballo in Maschera—Eri tu?; SEA SHANTIES: Blow the man
down; The drummer and the cook; Haul away, Joe; The drunken sailor;
A-rovin'; Low lands; Shenandoah; Rio Grande. SC; RCAO, Shaw,
V LM 1168.

Warren, chief baritone of the Metropolitan, is at his most characteristic in the operatic program, although the recordings date back
to the days before LP. It is altogether possible that an impression of rushed tempos may be owing to the need, when the recordings were made, for getting each aria into the time limit. The
sea shanties are designed obviously for a quick success on the
radio, for they are sung lustily in a cultured voice apparently out
slumming, but assisted by a virtuoso chorus and a carefully
planned orchestra. The Kipling songs are mostly popular favorites, all sung in the best he-man tradition, and all provided with
orchestrations by conductor Frank Black.

THE WELCH CHORALE (James B. Welch)

MOTETS OF THE FIFTEENTH AND SIXTEENTH CENTURIES, WITH
EASTER THEMES: Gloria (Dufay); Ave verum (Josquin des Pres); O
salutaris hostia (de la Rue); Quam pulchra es (Dunstable); Super
flumina Babylonis (Palestrina); Tantum ergo (Victoria); Tu es Petrus
(Palestrina); Confirma hoc Deus (Byrd); Beata viscera (Byrd); Ado-
ramus Te (Rosselli); Tenebrae factae sunt (Ingegneri); Vere languoris
(Victoria); Sicut cervus (Palestrina); Crucifixus (Lotti); Haec dies
(Palestrina); Haec dies (Byrd); Regina coeli (Aichinger). Ly LL 52.

This recital contains some of the best singing we have had from
the Welch Chorale. The varied program includes several rare
items by composers poorly represented on the lists, and such
famous pieces as the magnificent Lotti *Crucifixus* and the Palestrina *Sicut cervus*, which have not recently been available. The
Dufay *Gloria*, incidentally, will be recognized as the one with
trumpets included in the old "Two Thousand Years of Music."
There is a suppleness about this singing which has not always
characterized the performing group, and they prove their ability
to build up a climax from nothing. The recording is good, though
the tone is slightly veiled.

WELITCH, LJUBA, soprano

I grieve; The miller (Dargomizhski); Star, tell me (Mussorgsky); Hat dich die Liebe berührt; Valse de Chopin (Marx); Die Nacht; Cäcilie (Strauss). Ulanowsky, pf, 10" C ML 2118. (*Mozart: Don Giovanni—Arias).

Pique Dame—Es muss am Fenster lehnen; Es geht auf Mitternacht (Tchaikovsky); Die Dubarry—Ich schenk mein Herz (Millöcker-Makeben); Lied und Czardas; Die lustige Witwe—Vilialied; Der Zarewitsch—Einer wird kommen (Lehar); Un Ballo in Maschera—Ma dall' arrido stelo divulsa; Morrò, ma prima in grazia. VSO, Moralt, L LLP 69.

Salome—Final Scene; Eugene Onegin—Letter Scene; Tosca—Love Duet; Vissi d'arte (with Tucker, t); Die Fledermaus—Czardas; Der Zigeunerbaron—Habet acht. MOO, Reiner, Rudolf; PHI, Susskind, C ML 4795.

> Welitch, the sensational Salome, is, for better or for worse, an operatic personality. The voice is of peculiar quality, rather thin and acidulous, but it is expressive, and she loads it with meaning. Surprisingly enough, the little song recital is highly effective. The Russian songs, sung in the original, have a nice line, and she builds a tremendous climax in the Marx. The London recital is also very fine; the *Ballo in Maschera* arias have not been better sung in recent years; the operetta numbers reveal another facet of the singer's art. A popular-priced edition is also issued, including on a 10" disc the *Ballo in Maschera* and *Pique Dame* selections (L LD 9041). Columbia has doubled up what used to be two 10" discs, the superb *Salome* finale, the fine *Eugene Onegin*, and the rest. The two Johann Strauss bits have a spirit that is missing from the English versions we have become used to.

WILLIAMS, CAMILLA, soprano

Beau Soir (Debussy); Crepuscolo; Pioggia (Respighi); Si tu le veux (Koechlin); Se tu m'ami (Malipiero); Églogue (Delibes); Que l'heure est donc brève (Delibes); Yarmouth Fair (Warlock); When I bring to you color'd toys (Carpenter); The K'e (Dougherty). Bazala, pf, 10" MGM E 140.

SPIRITUALS: Hold on; Poor me; On ma journey; Talk about a child;

His name so sweet; When I've done; City called heaven; Oh what a beautiful city. Bazala, pf, 10" MGM E 156.

Camilla Williams has made her reputation chiefly as an exponent of *Madama Butterfly.* Her clear, and high soprano is well suited to Puccini's melodies, and she has an appealing sense of the theater. Her recital shows that she is not confined to this opera. Strangely, she is least convincing in the English songs, for her diction is not of the best. The French songs are creditable enough, but in the Italian group she achieves distinction. Her second disc is a program of spirituals, simply and beautifully sung.

YALE DIVINITY SCHOOL CHOIR (James Borden)

HYMNS OF PRAISE: Iste confessor (Plainchant); Now let every tongue adore Thee; Hosanna to the living Lord (Bach); SIXTEENTH CENTURY POLYPHONY: Call to remembrance (Farrant); Ave verum (Josquin des Pres); Repleti sunt (Gallus); Cantate Domino (Hassler); EARLY AMERICAN MUSIC: Wake every breath (Billings); O God, to rescue mee (Bay Psalm Book); Glorious things (Southern Harmony); RUSSIAN CHURCH MUSIC: Credo (Gretchaninoff); Salvation belongeth to our God (Tchesnokov); Glory be to God (Rachmaninoff); Nunc dimittis (Gretchaninoff); THREE PSALMS BY CONTEMPORARY AMERICANS: Psalm 123; Psalm 136 (Thomson); Psalm 8 (Stark). Ov LP 2.

We are told in the jacket notes that this is a strictly nonprofessional job by a group of divinity students filled with zeal to better the common choral repertoire of our churches. They sing for the most part in good, easily understandable English, and in in a remarkably relaxed and straightforward style. They are at their best in such quietly sonorous pieces as the Farrant and the Josquin, but hardly less impressive in the starker, more elemental early American numbers (these latter simply and effectively arranged by Luther Noss). The Gallus piece is more taxing, not quite so satisfactorily balanced. The Russian offerings are effective in their way, though I was conscious in listening to the *Credo* that it is all too obviously translated music. The three American psalms make an interesting contrast: Virgil Thomson's sparse settings are not without relationship to the Billings.

ZENATELLO, GIOVANNI, tenor

Otello—Esultate; Ora e per sempre addio; Si, pel ciel (with Granforte, b); Dio! mi potevi scagliar; Niùn mi tema; Vieni (Denza); Manon Lescaut—No! pazzo son! guardate; La Bohème—Act 1 Duet (with Sammarco, b); Pagliacci—Un tal gioco; Traviata—Dei miei bollenti spiriti. Et 705.

A record like this would have greater value if it contained some information as to recording dates. The first side, devoted to Zenatello's famous role of Otello, is alternately electric and acoustic recording, apparently late acoustic. In his later records, a certain vocal stiffness is characteristic, not enough to obscure the great dramatic singer's art, but distinctly noticeable. For all that, the first entrance of Otello is splendidly declaimed, though the wonderful choral build-up is somewhat muffled in reproduction. *"Ora e per sempre,"* acoustically recorded, is tremendous, and the big duet with Granforte is thrilling. Both *"Dio! mi potevi"* and the Death Scene are acoustics, and a little less wonderful than the studio recordings he made electrically for Victor. Apparently everything on the other side comes from the 1906 Fonotipia series, and here the voice is in its full glory. The Denza song is very openly sung, with no attempt at shading, but plenty of ringing tone. The *Manon Lescaut*, piano-accompanied, is superb, as is the *Pagliacci* piece.

INDEX OF PERFORMERS

(* indicates mention only in text)

INDEX OF COMPOSERS
(*indicates mention only in text)

AN ALPHABETICAL LIST OF
OPERA TITLES WITH COMPOSERS' NAMES

Lombardi alla Prima Crociata, I (Verdi)
Loreley (Catalani)
Louise (Charpentier)
Love of Three Kings, The (L'Amore dei Tre Re) (Montemezzi)
Lucia di Lammermoor (Donizetti)
Lucrezia Borgia (Donizetti)
Luisa Miller (Verdi)
Lulu (Berg)
Lustige Witwe, Die (Léhar)
Lustigen Weiber von Windsor, Die (Nicolai)

Macbeth (Verdi)
Madama Butterfly (Puccini)
Mme Sans-Gêne (Giordano)
Maestro di Capella, Il (Cimarosa)
Maestro di Musica, Il (Pergolesi)
Magic Flute, The (Die Zauberflöte) (Mozart)
Mamelles de Tirésias, Les (Poulenc)
Man in the Moon, The (Il Mondo della Luna) (Haydn)
Manon (Massenet)
Manon Lescaut (Puccini)
Mariage aux Lanternes, Le (Offenbach)
Marina (Arrieta)
Maritana (Wallace)
Marriage, The (Mussorgsky)
Marriage of Figaro, The (Le Nozze di Figaro) (Mozart)
Martha (Flotow)
Masaniello (La Muette di Portici) (Auber)
Masked Ball, A (Un Ballo in Maschera) (Verdi)
Matrimonio Segreto, Il (Cimarosa)
Mavra (Stravinsky)
May Night (Rimsky-Korsakov)
Mazeppa (Tchaikovsky)
Médée (M.A.Charpentier)
Medium, The (Menotti)
Mefistofele (Boïto)
Meistersinger von Nürnberg, Die (Wagner)
Merry England (German)
Merry Widow, The (Die lustige Witwe) (Léhar)
Merry Wives of Windsor, The (Die lustigen Weiber von Windsor) (Nicolai)
Mese Mariano (Giorano)
Mignon (Thomas)
Mikado, The (Sullivan)
Milton (Spontini)
Miserly Knight, The (Rachmaninoff)
Molinara, La (Paisiello)
Mondo della Luna, Il (Haydn)
Monsieur Beaucaire (Messager)
Mozart and Salieri (Rimsky-Korsakov)
Muette de Portici, La (Auber)

Nabucco (Nabucodonosor) (Verdi)
Nabucodonosor (Verdi)
Nacht in Venedig, Eine (J. Strauss)
Naissance de Vénus, La (Lully)
Nerone (Boïto)
Night in Venice, A (Eine Nacht in Venedig) (J. Strauss)
Niño Judio, El (Luna)
Noces, Les (Stravinsky)

Norma (Bellini)
Nozze di Figaro, Le (Mozart)

Oberon (Weber)
Oedipus Rex (Stravinsky)
Olympia (Spontini)
Olympiade, L' (Pergolesi)
Orfeo (Monteverdi)
Orfeo ed Euridice (Gluck)
Orfeo ed Euridice (Haydn)
Orontea (Cesti)
Orphée aux Enfers (Offenbach)
Orpheus in Hades (Orphée aux Enfers) (Offenbach)
Otello (Verdi)

Pagliacci, I (Leoncavallo)
Paride ed Elena (Gluck)
Paris and Helen (Paride ed Elena) (Gluck)
Parsifal (Wagner)
Pastor Fido, Il (Handel)
Patience (Sullivan)
Patrie (Paladilhe)
Pearl Fishers, The (Les Pêcheurs de perles) (Bizet)
Pêcheurs de perles, Les (Bizet)
Pélerins de la Mecque, Les (La Rencontre Imprévue) (Gluck)
Pelléas et Mélisande (Debussy)
Périchole, La (Offenbach)
Persée (Lully)
Pescatori di Perle, I (Les Pêcheurs de perles) (Bizet)
Phaëton (Lully)
Philemon und Baucis (Haydn)
Piccolo Marat, Il (Mascagni)
Pimpinone (Telemann)
Pique-Dame (Tchaikovsky)
Pirates of Penzance, The (Sullivan)
Pirro e Demetrio, Il (Scarlatti)
Platée (Rameau)
Polenblut (Nebdal)
Porgy and Bess (Gershwin)
Prince Igor (Borodin)
Princess Ida (Sullivan)
Prodana Nevesta (The Bartered Bride) (Smetana)
Prophète, Le (Meyerbeer)
Psyché (Lully)
Puritani, I (Bellini)

Quattro Rusteghi, I (Wolf-Ferrari)
Queen of Spades, The (Pique-Dame) (Tchaikovsky)

Rake's Progress, The (Stravinsky)
Re Pastore, Il (Mozart)
Renard (Stravinsky)
Rencontre Imprévue, La (Gluck)
Retablo de Maese Pedro, El (Falla)
Rheingold, Das (Wagner)
Rienzi (Wagner)
Rigoletto (Verdi)
Rinaldo (Handel)
Robert le diable (Meyerbeer)
Rodelinda (Handel)
Roi malgré lui, Le (Chabrier)
Roméo et Juliette (Gounod)
Rondine, La (Puccini)
Rosenkavalier, Der (R. Strauss)

Rusalka (Dvořák)
Russalka (Dargomyzhsky)

Sadko (Rimsky-Korsakov)
Salome (R. Strauss)
Salvator Rosa (Gomes)
Samson et Dalila (Saint-Saëns)
Scala di Seta, La (Rossini)
Schauspieldirektor, Der (Mozart)
Sedecia, Il (Scarlatti)
Semele (Handel)
Semiramide (Rossini)
Seraglio, Il (Die Entführung aus dem Serail) (Mozart)
Serenata, La (Bassui)
Serenata a tre (Vivaldi)
Serse (Cavalli)
Serse (Handel)
Serva Padrona, La (Pergolesi)
Siegfried (Wagner)
Signor Bruschino, Il (Rossini)
Sigurd (Reyer)
Simon Boccanegra (Verdi)
Snegourotchka (Rimsky-Korsakov)
Snow Maiden, The (Snegourotchka) (Rimsky-Korsakov)
Socrate (Satie)
Sonnambula, La (Bellini)
Suor Angelica (Puccini)
Sylvano (Mascagni)

Tabarro, Il (Puccini)
Taming of the Shrew, The (Der widerspenstigen Zähmung) (Goetz)
Tannhäuser (Wagner)
Tausend und eine Nacht (J. Strauss)
Telephone, The (Menotti)
Thaïs (Massenet)
Thésée (Lully)
Thomas and Sally (Arne)
Threepenny Opera, The (Die Dreigroschenoper) (Weill)
Tiefland (Albert)
Tosca (Puccini)
Tote Stadt, Die (Korngold)

Traviata, La (Verdi)
Trial by Jury (Sullivan)
Trionfo dell' Onore, Il (Scarlatti)
Tristan und Isolde (Wagner)
Trovatore, Il (Verdi)
Troyens a Carthage, Les (Berlioz)
True Blue, or The Press Gang (Carey)
Turandot (Puccini)

Venus and Adonis (Blow)
Verkaufte Braut, Die (The Bartered Bride) (Smetana)
Véronique (Messager)
Vespri Siciliani, I (Verdi)
Vestale, La (Spontini)
Vida Breve, La (Falla)
Vie Parisienne, La (Offenbach)
Vogelhändler, Der (Zeller)

Walküre, Die (Wagner)
Wally, La (Catalani)
Waltz Dream, A (Ein Walzertraum) (Straus)
Walzertraum, Ein (Straus)
Werther (Massenet)
Widerspenstigen Zähmung, Der (Goetz)
Wienerblut (J. Strauss)
William Ratcliffe (Guglielmo Ratcliffe) (Mascagni)
William Tell (Guglielmo Tell) (Rossini)
Wozzeck (Berg)

Xerxes (Serse) (Handel)

Yeomen of the Guard (Sullivan)

Zaïde (Mozart)
Zar und Zimmermann (Lortzing)
Zarewitsch, Der (Léhar)
Zauberflöte, Die (Mozart)
Zaza (Leoncavallo)
Zigeunerbaron, Der (J. Strauss)
Zigeunerliebe (Léhar)
Zingari in Fiera, Gli (Paisiello)

The text of this book was set on the Vari-Typer, in the Bodoni Book Style (by Coxhead). Composition by *The Science Press*, Lancaster, Pennsylvania. Printed by *The Murray Printing Company*, Wakefield, Massachusetts. Paper manufactured by *S. D. Warren Company*, Boston, Massachusetts. Bound by *H. Wolff*, New York. Designed by Harry Ford.